Rev. N. Calver Jan 1855

Presented by Rev. G. W. Harris.

I0754335

THE

FOUR WITNESSES:

BEING A

HARMONY OF THE GOSPELS

ON A NEW PRINCIPLE.

BY

DR. ISAAC DA COSTA,

OF AMSTERDAM.

TRANSLATED BY

DAVID DUNDAS SCOTT, ESQ.

NEW YORK:

ROBERT CARTER & BROTHERS,

285 BROADWAY.

1855.

PREFACE TO THE ENGLISH EDITION.

The work which is here presented to the English public is the result of a long and careful investigation into the structure and contents, the differences and agreements, of the four Gospels of our Lord Jesus Christ. This result had been already obtained some years before the appearance, in Germany, of Strauss's *Life of Jesus.* When that unhappy book became known in Holland, the author of these pages communicated, first in a series of lectures, afterwards by means of the press, these observations on *The Harmony of the Gospels,* in the hope of thus refuting the German Doctor in the very points which he had attacked most strongly, and apparently with the most success.

The English edition, now published under the title of *The Four Witnesses,* leaving unnoticed this immediate dispute with an infidel theology or philosophy, gives so much the more fully the observations which demonstrate the authenticity, and perfect agreement in themselves, of these important books of the Holy Scriptures. This alone is the object aimed at in the English version of the work.

May the publication be blessed to many souls in Great Britain! and may the name of Jesus Christ, to whom all Scripture beareth witness, be everywhere glorified by the truth of His Word and the power of His Spirit!

AMSTERDAM, *March* 18, 1851.

CONTENTS.

I. INTRODUCTION.

II. ST MATTHEW.

III. ST MARK.

IV. ST LUKE.

V. ST JOHN.

VI. RESULT OF THE PRECEDING OBSERVATIONS.

VII. THE NARRATIVES OF OUR LORD'S PASSION.

NOTES AND ADDITIONS.

THE

FOUR WITNESSES.

THE FOUR WITNESSES.

I. INTRODUCTION.

One has only to read with some attention the inspired quaternion of our Gospels, in order to perceive, on the one hand, their general harmony in point of facts and doctrines, but, at the same time, those numerous variations, on the other hand, by which the whole four are distinguished from each other. These variations are not confined to difference of style and language; they extend to the details themselves of the facts, doctrines, and discourses which they have recorded for us. We frequently find events, circumstances, sayings, quotations, and details of all sorts, put down in *one or more* of the Gospels, but not mentioned at all, or at least considerably abridged, or merely noticed by way of allusion, in *another*. In their relations of the same event, we find in the several Evangelists a difference, sometimes in the numbers given, sometimes in the order of time, sometimes in the connexion of facts and words. Thus, to take one example from the multitude of such variations that might be adduced, the Gospel of St Matthew speaks of the cure of *two blind men*, while those of St Mark and St Luke speak of only *one*.[1] Thus, too, St Mark, in the prediction of St Peter's denying our Lord, speaks of the cock's *crowing twice*, while the other three Evangelists make mention of this same *crowing of the cock* as foretold and heard only *once*.[2] Thus, once more, our Lord's Prayer is placed in St Luke quite in a different connexion from that in which it appears in St Matthew.[3] Thus, in like manner, the appearing of our Lord after his resurrection to the women, in St Matthew,[4] is related, in St Mark and St John,[5] as having fallen to the lot of Mary Magdalene. Where should we end were we to set about noting here the whole of these variations, some of more, others of less importance?

It was quite to be expected that unbelievers in every age should have sought to avail themselves of these discrepancies or contradictions, real or apparent, for the purpose of attacking the genuineness and authenticity of these sacred writings, and the very truth itself of the evangelical history. In our own days in particular, and chiefly in Germany, attempts have been made to deduce systematically, not only that it is impossible to believe that such contradictory narratives could have been inspired, but further, that we cannot possibly assign an historical origin to those great facts on which, as such, rests the entire truth of the New Testament revelation and of the Bible itself.

[1] Matth. xx. 30; Mark v. 46; Luke xviii. 35.
[2] Mark xiv. 30; Matth. xxvi. 34; Luke xxii. 34; John xiii. 38.
[3] Matth. xi. 9; Luke xi. 1.
[4] Matth. xxviii. 9.
[5] Mark xvi. 9; John xx. 1–17.

And as regards this last conclusion, learned and ingenious defenders of Revelation in general, and of the authenticity of the books of the New Testament in particular, have long since shewn, with great success, how, on the contrary, those differences, for the most part comparatively slight, and in the details, only make the agreement of the evangelical witnesses on the principal facts themselves all the more striking. One celebrated apologist, amongst others, of the authenticity of the New Testament, has very justly remarked, that the truth of human testimony manifests itself in most cases precisely by some variation in the statement of circumstances, provided there be agreement in the main. In proof of this, we need but go to the courts of law and justice, as is remarked by the writer just quoted.[1] Too perfect an uniformity in the declarations of different witnesses makes one rather suspect that these declarations are the result of previous arrangement among them; on the contrary, discrepancies occurring on minor points, in the mouths of witnesses, are regarded as a proof of the substantial truth of their declarations with respect to the main fact, the reality of which is sought to be ascertained.

We arrive at the same result for the defence of the historical truth of the Gospel, when we compare together those authors whose credit is best established for profane history. Shall we question their historical honesty, or the reality of the facts in general related by them, because of some discrepancy, even though a serious one, occurring here and there in matters of detail? On comparing the accounts left us by Polybius and Livy of Hannibal's passage over the Alps, a difference occurs which has given rise to eight different conjectures as to the precise track

[1] Paley.

followed by the celebrated general in that memorable expedition. But has it ever been concluded from this discrepancy, that the passage of the Alps was not a real historical fact, or that Livy, or Polybius, is not a trustworthy historian?

Certainly such a line of argument is sufficient, in general, for the defence of the truth of the evangelical history against doubts and objections deduced from discrepancies among the four witnesses. But shall we say that this reasoning is equally conclusive, when what we have to defend is the inspiration and the infallibility of those same writings? In fact, if the four Gospels do really differ on so many details, bearing upon the order, the number, the expressions of the speakers and of the Lord himself, still it would remain possible to defend the historical truth of the Gospel in general, but it would no longer be possible to defend a Divine inspiration; for that we must hold to be incompatible with palpable errors, inaccuracies, and contradictions.

It has been with the view, therefore, of shewing that in reality those alleged contradictions, errors, and inaccuracies are apparent only, that from the earliest ages of the Church attempts have been made to draw up what have been called *Harmonies of the four Gospels.* Unhappily, by far the most of these Harmonies, for want of any principle of solution drawn from the very nature and organical construction of these writings, have contributed rather to embarrass than to resolve the problem, owing to the purely mechanical and forced manner in which its solution has been attempted. Hence, when two or more Evangelists relate one and the same event in a different order as respects the connexion, it has been found most convenient to suppose that the same event had actually occurred *more than once;* or, when several of the Evangelists relate what was said by the Jews, the Apostles, and the Lord himself, with some variations in the literal expression, it has sometimes been thought that we cannot do better than accumulate *all of them together*, which ordinarily gives a meaning overcharged, heavy, one may even say *absurd*. And so in other cases. Some authors of Harmonies, learned and ingenious men, from not possessing the true key, have fallen upon this awkward and embarrassed mode of reconciling the Gospels. Nothing more common, for example, than the forced reconciliation of the narrative of St Matthew (xxvii. 44) and that of St Mark (xv. 32), on the one hand, with that of St Luke (xxiii. 39), respecting the converted thief on the cross. St Matthew and St Mark, speaking in general terms of the *kind* of persons who blasphemed the Lord Jesus on the cross, ascribe this outrage, among others, to *the thieves* (in the plural) crucified along with our Lord. St Luke, on the contrary, presenting the history in its amplest details, ascribes the blasphemy, not to both malefactors, but only to one, who was forthwith reproved by the other; and that other's prayer of faith and happy end are at the same time related to us. Now, instead of perceiving the perfect accordance which, viewed in this light, exists between the two narratives, provided we do not slavishly adhere *to the very letter* of the two first Evangelists, a most forced and unnatural construction has been put upon the matter, by supposing that at first *both thieves* had blasphemed on the cross, but that *one of the two* had repented immediately afterwards, had reprimanded his fellow-thief, and besought the Lord's forgiveness. But in making such a supposition, it has not been considered that, if the malefactor's conversion really took place in so prompt and immediate a manner, St Luke, at the least, would have noticed, in a word or two, this sudden transition, made in a moment, from the most frightful enmity to the liveliest faith! But further still, it has not been considered that if the converted malefactor had actually taken part a moment before in his companion's blasphemies, the first thing he certainly would have thought of doing would have been to abase himself on account of his last offence, not to reprimand *the other malefactor* for a sin in which he himself had just before taken part. One has but to read attentively the converted criminal's expressions, as given by St Luke (xxiii. 40, 41), to see that, while admitting himself to be a miserable sinner like his fellow, he evidently distinguishes between himself and him, in regard to the reviling of the Lord Jesus. And St Luke himself points to the same distinction when, at verse 40, he says: "But the other answering rebuked him, saying," &c. Thus, it appears that there is no way of reconciling the Evangelists, if we admit the plural of St Matthew and St Mark in its *literal* acceptation. All, on the contrary, perfectly harmonizes when, as we have just hinted, we explain that plural as a mere indication of *the species.* And this will strike us still more clearly when, by an exact analysis of the Gospel of St Matthew, we shall see that the use of the plural in cases where the other Evangelists (St Luke in particular) speak of one thing or person only, is, on the part of the first of our Evangelists, a constant mode of writing, and by no means fortuitous; the result, consequently, of his individual style and manner as an historian, not of some involuntary error or inaccuracy.

The fault almost as much of the defenders as of the impugners of the revelation and inspiration of the Gospels, lies in their not perceiving that there is in the manner in which we relate or represent things, whether with the pen or the pencil, a certain variety, nay, even a kind of apparent contradiction, necessarily resulting from the truth itself of our description, according to the particular point of view in which we contemplate an object or event, at the moment when we relate or describe it. The most ordinary language of common life presents us with such contradictions, apparent but nowise real, and the reconcilement of which is in every one's power. It is thus, that, without for a moment contradicting his science and his personal conviction with respect to the earth's revolving round the sun, an astronomer will, like every one else, speak of *the sun's rising and setting.* Or when the painter, in drawing objects seen from a certain altitude, gives to those objects on his canvass the exact height which he *sees* them have from that point, will it be said that he is in contradiction with some other painter who represents to us the same objects, seen close at hand, on level ground, and so in their natural dimensions? Both representations are true; the one, as the ancients used to say, *κατὰ τὸ φαινόμενον* (according to the impression made on the spectator), the other *κατὰ τὸ ὂν* (according to the reality of the object in itself). Our language and our thoughts are perpetually alternating betwixt these two diverse verities.

On applying this very simple principle to the investigation of the true harmony of the Gospels, we shall find the following result—a result satisfactory in every point of view: that each of the four Evangelists has described the same object, but that object seen as a model, for example, placed in the centre of four different points of view—like a building seen and drawn from four different sides. Now, no doubt, those four drawings will differ apparently; they ought to differ; there would be error or falsification if they did not differ,—and yet when combined together they would intimately coalesce; and the more they are contemplated, and the more they are compared, all apparent contradictions would vanish, and all differences and discrepancies would be accounted for.

But to justify the application of this example to the great question of the harmony of the Gospels, we must patiently analyze the leading traits in the special character of each of them in particular. We have in these pages sought to find the determining reason of this different character belonging to the four writings, each of them separately, in the individual character, the object, the plan, and the particular calling of each of the four writers themselves.

Our first endeavour, accordingly, has been to inquire into the relation that subsists between each of the four Gospels and the inspired author under whose name it has hitherto passed among us. This inquiry will at once present, of itself, a striking and decisive result in favour of the genuineness and authenticity of those writings, independently even of the external testimony of the first ages of the Church, and of the Ancient Fathers. For if, in point of fact, on scrutinizing these several writings, we find clearly demonstrated to us, in the first of the four Gospels, the distinctive marks, and seal as it were, of one of the Twelve, and specially of the one who had formerly been a publican—in the second Gospel, the unmistakeable characteristics of one who, like St Mark, was a companion and *son in the faith* of St Peter—in the third, the evident tokens of an intimate friend and faithful fellow-labourer of St Paul, as was Luke, the physician—finally, in the fourth, the no less evident marks of the *well-beloved disciple of the Lord himself*—we possess a proof of the genuineness of those four compositions, all the more strong and irrefragable when compared with the external testimony of ages, as the testing of a diamond by fire is more conclusive than the most universal external testimony to the fact that that diamond has been all along considered by its owners, and received from the hand of the jeweller, as such.

After this, when the same examination of our four Gospels shall have demonstrated to us, that the variations and the differences that they present are in exact proportion and necessary relation with the special character and particular plan of each of the respective writers, we find no difficulty in arriving at such an agreement among the four compositions as, while it preserves these differences, will be found to result in *the most perfect expression of the truth,* rendered by each from his own particular point of view, and equally just and true.

II. ST MATTHEW.

From the most remote times, and by common consent, this, the first of our Gospels, has, in conformity with its title, been attributed to the apostle whose calling from the seat of custom is related in the first three Gospels. We possess a deep-seated mark of this origin in the very manner in which the names of the apostles are noted down by the three different Evangelists. The following is the nomenclature of the twelve, as we find it in the first Gospel, and afterwards with a slight shade of difference in the second, in the third, and, last of all, in the Acts of the Apostles :—

Matth. x. 2, 3, 4

Now the names of the twelve apostles are these; *The first*, Simon, who is called Peter, and Andrew his brother; James the son of Zebedee, and John his brother; Philip, and Bartholomew; Thomas, and Matthew the publican; James the son of Alphæus, and Lebbæus, whose surname was Thaddeus; Simon the Canaanite, and Judas Iscariot, who also betrayed him.

Mark iii. 14–19.

And he ordained twelve, that they should be with him, and that he might send them forth to preach, And to have power to heal sicknesses, and to cast out devils: And Simon he surnamed Peter; and James the son of Zebedee, and John the brother of James; and he surnamed them Boanerges, which is, The sons of thunder: And Andrew, and Philip, and Bartholomew, and *Matthew*, and Thomas, and James the son of Alphæus, and Thaddeus, and Simon the Canaanite, And Judas Iscariot which also betrayed him.

LUKE vi. 13–16.

And when it was day, he called unto him his disciples: and of them he chose twelve, whom also he named apostles; Simon, (whom he also named Peter,) and Andrew his brother, James and John, Philip and Bartholomew, *Matthew* and Thomas, James the son of Alphæus, and Simon called Zelotes, and Judas the brother of James, and Judas Iscariot, which also was the traitor.

ACTS i. 13.

And when they were come in, they went up into an upper room, where abode both Peter, and James, and John, and Andrew, Philip, and Thomas, Bartholomew, and *Matthew*, James the son of Alphæus, and Simon Zelotes, and Judas the brother of James.

We see at a glance that the name of Matthew is found in all of these lists, but it is only in the first (that is, in his own) that the humbling title of *publican* is added. This could not have entered into the thoughts of any one but St Matthew himself: what fiction-writer would have dreamt of securing apostolic authority for a fabricated gospel in *such* a manner? What party, supposing that there could have been any that had an interest in the first Gospel's being ascribed to that particular Apostle, would for this purpose have thought of attaching to the name of Matthew the remembrance of his former calling, being one by no means honourable in Israel? Or rather, what other author, were he not a true disciple and imitator of Jesus Christ the Nazarene, would have *so* distinguished his name among the servants of the kingdom of God?

In yet another manner, and that quite as touching and unobtrusive, and quite as little obvious to a superficial reader, the author of the first Gospel intimates his being so in the very account he gives of his calling as a disciple and servant of the Lord. You have only to compare anew his narrative with those of St Mark and St Luke.

MATTH. ix. 9, 10.

9. And as Jesus passed forth from thence, he

MARK ii. 14, 15.

14 And as he passed by, he saw Levi the

LUKE v. 27–29.

27 And after these things he went forth,

saw *a man*, named Matthew, sitting at the receipt of custom: and he saith unto him, Follow me. And he arose and followed him.

10 And it came to pass, as Jesus sat at meat *in the* house, behold, many publicans and sinners came and sat down with him and his disciples.

son of Alphæus sitting at the receipt of custom, and he said unto him, Follow me. And he arose and followed him.

15 And it came to pass, that, as Jesus sat at meat in *his* house, many publicans and sinners sat also together with Jesus and his disciples: for there were many, and they followed him.

and saw a publican, named Levi, sitting at the receipt of custom: and he said unto him, Follow me.

28 And *he left all*, rose up, and followed him.

29 And Levi made *him a great feast in his own house:* and there was a great company of publicans and of others that sat down with them.

Speaking of himself, the first Evangelist calls the publican who was called to the apostleship, *a man* (*ἄνθρωπον*, an expression nowise honourable in this sense)—*a man named Matthew.* The second and the third Evangelists give him his own proper Jewish name; one of them adds, by way of honourable distinction, the name of his father—*Levi, the son of Alphæus.* There is, also, a particular circumstance which we find noted, not by himself, but by another Evangelist (St Luke)—that he *left all* to follow Jesus. There have been doubts, however, as to the identity of the person, on account of the names of Levi and Matthew, and particularly because, in the first of the Gospels, we are not expressly told that the feast was held in Matthew's house. But it is precisely this omission of the *feast* in the Gospel of St Matthew, and still more the omission of the name of the owner of the house in which the feast was held, that clearly shews that here he was speaking of his own proper self—a personality which the authors of these writings are accustomed to put forward as little as possible wherever any thing praiseworthy or honourable happens to have to be mentioned. Consequently it is again St Luke who, with

St Mark, supplies the void in their predecessor's narrative; and the identity of *Levi* and *Matthew* remains no less certain, on simply comparing the three Evangelists, than that of *Simon*, son of *Jonas*, and *Peter*. The mention of Matthew's *leaving all* to follow the Lord, is not to be found in his Gospel, but only in St Luke.

From these details, then, slight as they may appear, but thus only more forcible as a testimony to the plain and simple truth, it is certain that the author of the first of our Gospels is an Apostle—is the publican who was called by Jesus from the exercise of his profession. This same character of *converted publican* and *called Apostle* accompanies us throughout his whole Gospel. But before resting upon this point, let us pause again at a very simple remark suggested by the result we have obtained. It was natural in some sort that one of the Gospels, and especially the first of the four, should be written by an Apostle, and this is an idea which *might* occur to a human writer of fiction, whether in writing the book or in giving it a title. But, we venture to ask, where is the writer of a fiction—nay, where is the man—who would have charged with this honourable task a St Matthew, the seventh or eighth in rank on the list of the twelve? According to all human reasoning, would not the first that would suggest themselves for such a work be a St Peter, a St Thomas, or a St James? Divine Wisdom chose precisely the publican, who but for that would hardly have been noticed on the list; and he who had previously spent his life in noting down customs' duties and imposts, was now, after having left all for his Saviour's service, to find himself honoured by being the first to note down the wonderful doings of his saving mercy.

We have said that in the Gospel of St Matthew the

converted publican, the called Apostle, reveals himself at every turn. His whole composition is pervaded by a uniform tone of humility, of modest simplicity, of amazement at the grace that had come to *publicans* and to *sinners.* The spirit of his whole Gospel is to be found in that saying of John the Baptist to Jesus, which we find recorded only by St Matthew: *Comest* THOU *to* ME? (iii. 14). While in St Luke, as we shall yet see, the fundamental tone is *the mercy of the Lord,* so in Matthew it is *his humility and meekness.* Again, it is he alone who has preserved for us that expression of our Lord: *Learn of me, for I am meek and lowly of heart* (xi. 29).

And this fundamental feature of the holy humanity of Jesus is at once brought prominently forward by our first Gospel, in the genealogy which forms its introduction (i. 1—16). Not only are the male progenitors of our Lord, according to his human origin, enumerated there, but some of their wives are also named; and those are precisely the women over whom, in the world's apprehension, there lay a cloud of ignominy, arising either from their origin, as in the case of Ruth and Rachab, or from scandalous circumstances in their history, as in that of Thamar and of her who had been the wife of Urias, since our Lord, in his admirable humility, disdained not to reckon such personages among his ancestors. The same fundamental feature in the incarnation of Jesus is expressed in the following quotation, found only in St Matthew: *He shall be called a Nazarene* (a *Nazarene,* despised.)—Matth. ii. 23. But thus, too, no more does the disciple blush at the ignominy attached to his name, manner of life, and previous vocation. Nowhere do we see the profession of *publican* placed in a less honourable light than in the Gospel of St Matthew. We repeatedly find in the Gospel writings the names *publicans* and *sinners* conjoined, but nowhere except in Matthew (xxi. 31, 32) do we read so conjoined, the names *publicans and harlots.*—(Compare further Matth. v. 46, 47, with Luke vi. 32, 33.)

Nevertheless, with all this profound humility, with all this most modest appreciation of himself, we nowhere find that our first Evangelist dissembles his apostolic character. Not that he ever announces the proofs of it with the smallest parade, but because the apostolic character of the author reveals itself by the effect of the inherent force of truth. In St Matthew we find either more circumstantially stated, or exclusively noted here and there, what were specially the calling and the privilege of the apostles. The rules prescribed to the apostles at the time of their first mission are recorded by no other Evangelist so fully, or even with the particularity which, setting aside the commandment to the *seventy disciples* recorded by St Luke, we find in Matthew comprehended in that given to the twelve. In his pages alone we find that characteristic expression of the apostolic vocation (and of the entire doctrine of salvation): *Freely ye have received, freely give.*—(x. 8.) Further, it is he who relates the promise of the kingdom to the twelve, expressed in its richest plenitude (xix. 28): *And Jesus said unto them, Verily I say unto you, That ye which have followed me, in the regeneration when the Son of man shall sit on the throne of his glory, ye also shall sit upon twelve thrones, judging the twelve tribes of Israel.* Further, he is the only one that records the solemn institution of the apostolic teaching and baptism, after our Lord's resurrection: *Go ye therefore, and teach all nations, baptizing them in the name of the Father, and of the Son, and of the Holy Ghost: teaching them to observe all things whatsoever I have commanded you.*—(xxviii. 19, 20.)

But at the same time, this great apostolic character of the author of the first of our Gospels always goes hand in hand with his characteristic modesty. It is precisely in *this* Gospel, and in no other, that homage is paid to the personal preference of St Peter among the twelve. In the roll of the apostles quoted above, it is in St Matthew alone (x. 2) that *Simon Peter* is expressly said to be *the first.* It is only in St Matthew that we find that saying addressed to St Peter: *Blessed art thou, Simon Bar-jona: for flesh and blood hath not revealed it unto thee, but my Father which is in heaven. And I say also unto thee, That thou art Peter* (πέτρος), *and upon this rock* (πέτρα) *I will build my church; and the gates of hell shall not prevail against it.*—(xvi. 17, 18.) Peter's walking upon the waters (an effect of faith, though followed soon after by that faith failing, and by fright), as well as the miraculous fishing of the piece of money by the same apostle, St Peter, is mentioned nowhere but by his fellow apostle St Matthew.—(Matth. xxiv. 28, 31; xvii. 24, 27.)

We find an Israelite cast in close alliance with what there is of the apostolical in this character. St Matthew is emphatically an apostle for *Israel,* an evangelist who had come out from *Israel;* his point of view is exclusively that of Israel, that of the Old Testament—above all, that of the prophecies. His Gospel proclaims itself to be such from the very commencement. *The book of the generation* (let this expression be compared with the Old Testament style; for example, Gen. v. 1)—*the book of the generation of Jesus Christ, son of David, son of Abraham* (i. 1); while the genealogy which immediately follows carries back our Lord's origin, not, as in St Luke

(iii. 38), as far as Adam, but only as far as Abraham. In this and other points of a like kind, St Matthew's Gospel always connects the New Testament with the Old, forms the transition from the writings of the one economy to the other, or rather unfolds itself and comes forth, so to speak, in full life from the Israelitish oracles. The accomplishment of the promises, the proof that Jesus of Nazareth is the promised *Christ*, the great Prophet and Israel's Messiah—such is the main object of this first of the Evangelical heralds of the great king Jesus. To him more than any other of the Evangelists (though all start from the principle of the fulfilment of the prophecies in Jesus Christ), the form used in quotation is peculiarly appropriate: THAT IT MIGHT BE FULFILLED WHICH WAS SPOKEN OF THE LORD BY THE PROPHET; and, THEN WAS FULFILLED THAT WHICH WAS SPOKEN BY THE PROPHET, &c.[1] The express appeal to the prophecies occurs in St Mark and St Luke only in a few sentences;[2] while in St Matthew that appeal is the principal affair. In St John, also, we find this appeal recurring more frequently than in the two immediately preceding Gospels, but distinguished from St Matthew by a particular character (which we shall speak of afterwards) altogether his own. In the Gospel of this first Evangelist, accordingly, the preaching of Jesus Christ is found cemented, as it were, in a number of prophecies which the following Evangelists, after so positive and so powerful a testimony, needed not to repeat, such as that of EMMANUEL, *son of the Virgin*, in Isaiah;[3] that of *the great light upon Galilee of the Gentiles*,[4] in the same prophet; that of the birth of *the*

[1] Matth. i. 22; ii. 5, 15, 17, 23; xiii. 35; xxi. 4; xxvii. 9, &c.
[2] Mark i. 2; xiv. 49. Luke iv. 21; xxiv. 27.
[3] Matth. i. 22, 23. Isaiah vii. 14. [4] Matth. iv. 14–16. Isaiah ix. 1, 2.

great Governor over Israel who was to come out of Bethlehem,[1] in Micah ; that of the delivering of *the just one for thirty pieces of silver,* in Jeremiah, and several others.[2]

The same Apostle-evangelist, however, does not confine himself to the express and direct citation of the Old Testament. His whole Gospel is full of *allusions* to those passages and sayings of the Old Testament in which the Christ was *either* predicted or foreshadowed, or in any way intimated beforehand. He throws in such allusions (or rather they come of themselves) in his exhibition of the works, the sayings, and the parables of our Lord, in the way either of paraphrase, or of development, or of explanation. For it pertains to the high authority of the sacred writers not always to render *literally* their Master's words, but as it were to identify these with their own inspired conceptions and expositions of them, in such sort that often one cannot make, and that there is no need of making, a distinction. Here we may apply our Lord's saying : *He that heareth you, heareth me.* When the Apostles or Evangelists thus give our Lord's saying with their own paraphrase or explanation, let it not be forgotten that they do so *in* his Spirit and *by* his Spirit, and that thus their Scriptures have the same authority as the words of Jesus himself, and ought to be considered as his authentic interpretation. Their word is his, understood and rendered by one of their number as viewed in one aspect, by another in another aspect. The parable of the king who had prepared a marriage-feast may serve here as an example of such insertion of words, legitimately destined more fully to illustrate one of the Master's declarations, and principally

[1] Matth. ii. 5, 6; xii. 17, 20. Isaiah xlii. 1. Micah v. 2.
[2] Matth. xxvii. 9, 10. Zechar. xi. 12.

to connect them with the Scriptures of the ancient Israel. In that parable, the invitation in St Luke (xiv. 17) runs simply thus: *Come, for all things are ready.* In St Matthew much more is said (xxii. 4): *Behold, I have prepared my dinner: my oxen and my fatlings are killed, and all things are ready: come unto the marriage.* And now, what is the origin of this amplified account in St Matthew? Who can fail to recognise in this passage an allusion to the invitation of *Sovereign Wisdom* in the Book of Proverbs (ix. 1—6): *Wisdom hath builded her house, she hath hewn out her seven pillars: she hath killed her beasts; she hath mingled her wine; she hath also furnished her table. She hath sent forth her maidens: she crieth upon the highest places of the city. Whoso is simple, let him turn in hither: as for him that wanteth understanding, she saith to him, Come, eat of my bread, and drink of the wine which I have mingled. Forsake the foolish and live; and go in the way of understanding.* Is there not in this transient allusion of the Apostle to the saying of the author of Proverbs, the force of a quotation? Is there not in this equally delicate and profound conjunction, a striking call to recognise in the Sovereign Wisdom of Solomon a reference to Him to whose table the gospel of grace invites sinners?

We might go still more deeply into the nature of these apostolic allusions to the Old Testament; we may consider them in their bearing on the point of view which, generally speaking, is peculiar to the first in order of the New Testament writers. That point of view leads us not so much to a minute historical description, as to a general survey of the life and passion, of the death and resurrection, of Jesus, contemplated as the crowning of the ancient prophecies. Such was evidently that of the Apostle-evangelist. In this view, the events he sets before us are but to him *realized prophecy;* here history and prophecy meet, and become merged in each other. From this continual contemplation of history in the light of prophecy, arises that apparent (but only *apparent*) want of exactness which distinguishes St Matthew. It is by this, further, that we may explain that so frequent use of the plural in passages where his fellow-evangelists, in what they most explicitly tell us, undoubtedly employ the *singular.* The solution is not difficult. The prophets had used in their writings the *plural* employed by the apostle. The Saviour predicted by them was to open the eyes of *the blind,* to deliver *the captives,* to heal *the lame* and *the paralytic*—all these adjectives being in the plural. And did not all this actually take place in the fulfilment? Assuredly Christ's power and goodness were not contented with a single deliverance from each of these miseries. But here is the characteristic point in St Matthew, that each of these doings of his Lord calls up to his mind *the entire plenitude* of the prophecy; represents to him in one single blind person healed by Jesus all whom the prophecy had indicated. And thus there arises from this mingling of prophecy and history, of prediction and accomplishment, that *plural* which, understood literally and in appearance, is inexact, but which, when viewed in connexion with the plan and the object of the Evangelist, possesses the most essential and the most profound reality.

It is not, however, solely in this connexion with the ancient prophecies that St Matthew voluntarily makes use of the *plural.* That number is on more than one account familiar with this Evangelist. Of this we have seen a striking example in our Introduction. We shall meet again, more than once, with this same plural in the first of our Gospels.

Our attention is now called to another particularity—a particularity which we find intimately associated with the Israelitic and Apostolic character of this first Gospel. We have already pointed out the chief object for which it was written; namely, to prove that the prophecies concerning the promised Messiah were fulfilled in Jesus of Nazareth, born at Bethlehem, crucified at Jerusalem. We find in St Matthew chiefly that Messiah as *the great Prophet* predicted and prefigured by all the prophets; that Messiah who came as *King over Sion, Son of David, Prince and Saviour of Israel* and *of all nations;* while the Gospel of St Mark shews him to us more particularly in the reality of his incarnation—that of St Luke in the plenitude of his unction by the Holy Ghost—that of St John in the glory of his Divinity, as the only Son of God, as the uncreated Word of God.

Let us contemplate him, in the first place, in St Matthew, as the *great Prophet* announced for ages before. After the baptism in Jordan and the temptation in the wilderness, the Apostle at once presents him to us as such, in a passage taken from Isaiah, already adduced, on the occasion of his preaching in Galilee (Matth. iv. 16). A little after (chap. v.-vii.) we have that sublime Sermon on the Mount, which contains the foundations of the whole prophetic ministry of the Saviour, and (as we shall see hereafter) is placed by St Matthew, not in a chronological order, but in a connexion of ideas altogether peculiar, and with an object which he alone had in view. That Sermon on the Mount, as it is recorded in the first Gospel, evidently contains, not only what Jesus taught on that mountain and on that occasion, but also what he further taught of a like kind and to the same purport, in other discourses of his public life as a Teacher in Israel. In that Sermon, St Matthew places the Lord before us as a Prophet like unto Moses,[1] and yet as much greater than Moses as the *son* is greater *than the servant.*[2] In that incomparable collection of commandments for our guidance to salvation, presented to us in the Sermon on the Mount, we possess *the law of Christ* expressed, both as it harmonizes with that of Moses, and at the same time as it differs from it. As it harmonizes with that of Moses, that is to say, in that grand result of the eternal law divine, *Thou shalt love;* but also as it differs from that of Moses, as surpassing and completing the law of Sinai by a spirituality and a depth altogether new;—as, in fine, it is sealed by *benedictions,* while the law of Moses is sealed by that great *malediction,* pronounced against whosoever *should not abide in all that had been written* (Deuter. xxvii. 26).

Further, it is St Matthew who shews us the very mode of teaching which the great Prophet Messias, foretold and described in the prophecies of the Old Testament, was to employ (xii. 16-20): *And he charged them that they should not make him known: that it might be fulfilled which was spoken by Esaias* the prophet, *saying, Behold my servant, whom I have chosen: my beloved, in whom my soul is well pleased: I will put my spirit upon him, and he shall shew judgment to the Gentiles. He shall not strive, nor cry; neither shall any man hear his voice in the streets. A bruised reed shall he not break, and smoking flax shall he not quench, till he send forth judgment unto victory.*[3] And in like manner, after some examples of his teaching by similitudes (xiii. 34, 35):

[1] Deuter. xviii. 18. Acts of Ap. iii. 22. [2] Heb. iii. 3. [3] Isaiah xlii. 1–4.

All these things spake Jesus unto the multitude in parables; and without a parable spake he not unto them: That it might be fulfilled which was spoken by the prophet, saying, I will open my mouth in parables; I will utter things which have been kept secret from the beginning of the world.[1]

Finally, it is by St Matthew alone that there has been preserved to us that saying of the multitudes at the time of the solemn entry of Jesus into Jerusalem (xxi. 11): *This is Jesus, the* PROPHET *of Nazareth of Galilee.*

And now let us turn to Jesus Christ as *King*. Matthew is very full in the descriptions of our Lord with respect to this title also, not that he describes him as such exclusively, but yet in an eminent and particular manner. At the very first, the genealogy points to this title of royalty. Twice he adds to the name of David the title of *King* (i. 6): Then (i. 20) Joseph, the husband of Mary (this, again, only in St Matthew), is called by the Angel, *Son of David.* That denomination, pertaining emphatically to Jesus as Messiah, nowhere occurs with such frequent reiteration as just in the first of our Gospels. Thus, for example, at the time of his last entrance into Jerusalem, the title of *Son of David* is mentioned twice by St Matthew (xxi. 9 and 16) in the *Hosannah* of the multitude. At the coming of the wise men of the East, it is only in St Matthew that we find Jesus at the very first proclaimed *King* (ii. 2): *Where is the King of the Jews?* as afterwards, in a parable not mentioned by any other of the Evangelists, the Lord Jesus is actually represented on the great day of judgment, as a *King* sitting in judgment (xxv. 31 to the end): *And when the Son of man shall come in his glory, and all the holy angels with him,*

[1] Psalm lxxviii. 2.

then shall he sit upon the throne of his glory: And before him shall be gathered all nations; and he shall separate them one from another, as a shepherd divideth his sheep from the goats: And he shall set the sheep on his right hand, but the goats on the left. Then shall the King say unto them on his right hand, Come, ye blessed of my Father, &c. In another parable related by St Matthew (xxii. 2), *the Father* is represented as *a king* who makes a marriage feast for his son, whilst in St Luke (xiv. 16) *a man* only is spoken of. It is true that (in the parable of the talents) it is in St Luke that there is introduced mention of the *kingdom of Jesus*,[1] but at the same time it will be observed that St Luke does this of set purpose; while in St Matthew the characteristic point is just what seems not premeditated, but to drop from his pen spontaneously, in whatever reminds us in his pages of the kingship of Jesus. Even in the recital of the scoffs directed against the *royal* dignity of Jesus in Pilate's pretorium, that of Matthew we find anew most minute in its details. It is he also, in the history of the Passion (xxvii. 29), who alone speaks of *the reed put into the hand of Jesus* in mockery of a sceptre,[2] an incident, the mention of which bears at the same time an allusion, evidently prophetic, to a saying of the Psalmist (Ps. ii. 9).

Nevertheless, as we have already noticed summarily, St Matthew is far from being the only one that was commissioned to announce *Jesus* as *King*. That commission was necessarily common to all the four Evangelists. But what is special to St Matthew is the coupling of the proofs of that *kingship* with all the ancient prophecies, and indeed with the entire history of the people of Israel.

[1] Luke xix. 12, compared with Matth. xxv. 14.

[2] Matth. xxvii. 29, compared with Mark xv. 19, and Luke xxiii. 2, 3.

With the royal glory of the Saviour I find, in this same Gospel, the *worship* of that Saviour closely associated. St Matthew often speaks of this worship in a very striking manner; most frequently in such a manner, and in such a connexion, that the idea of a merely royal homage cannot be admitted; but that the kneeling to *Jesus*, in the intention of the Evangelist, indicates, in a way not to be mistaken, such a king as was at the same time *Son of God*, and according to the saying of the prophet and of the apostle—*Emmanuel*, that is to say, *God with us*, *God manifest in the flesh.*

All that has hitherto been said of the Lord's *prophetic* and *royal* ministry, as set before us by St Matthew, belongs without contradiction to the *Israelitic* character of that Gospel, as already noticed. But this attribute—(its Israelitic character)—must be understood in its true sense. St Matthew's exposition is Israelitic, not simply from its Israelite origin, still less from accommodation to the ideas of those Jews to whom, more particularly, or rather in the first instance, his Gospel was addressed; but because both the origin and the kingdom, the entire idea and the whole person of the Messiah, are and remain Israelitic; and because Christianity detached from this root would just lose its character, *both* as a Religion of all ages and for all ages, *and* as the accomplishment of all the divine promises. The Gospel of St Matthew expresses, in its historical narrative, the same truth of which St Paul, in the view of eternity, reminded his son Timothy, and through him the Churches of all ages: *Remember that Jesus Christ* OF THE SEED OF DAVID *was raised from the dead according to my gospel.*—(2 Tim. ii. 8.)

Nevertheless, that which is Israelitic in Matthew, that which with him is so strongly imbued with the national

Israelitic spirit, distinguishes itself in a very positive and glaring manner from the Jewish or rather rabbinical spirit which forms the more modern character of that same nation, down to the days of our Lord's abode on earth and since. We take as an instance of this essential difference, the hostile disposition of those Pharisee-Jews to the Gentiles, while the *Israel of God*, to whom from the very earliest times the promises were confided, rejoice (in their psalms and in their prophecies) at the prospect of *all nations* being led one day to the knowledge of the God and King of the people of Abraham. In this respect, also, our Gospel is a glorious reflection of the prophecies. Already does our Lord's genealogy in St Matthew prelude to the calling of the Gentiles in the brief mention it makes of Rachab and of Ruth among the Messiah's female ancestors; next, with no less force, the Gospel of St Matthew gives testimony to that same vocation, by quoting more than one prediction relating to it; by the account also, found only there, of the coming and of the worship of the wise men of the East (chap. ii.); and, afterwards, by the emphatic close of the quotation from Isaiah to which we have already referred: *And in his name shall the Gentiles trust* (xii. 21). Proceeding from the same point of view, our Evangelist gives a prominent place to the faith of the Gentiles; that for example of the woman of Canaan (xv. 21-23), and that of the centurion at the moment of his servant's illness (viii. 5-13). It is highly remarkable how, in the former of these examples, the principal and particular connexion of the Saviour with Israel stands fully out at the very moment of his shewing the greatest compassion to that pagan woman; in the latter, that of the centurion, the Israelite Apostle strongly forewarns the Jews against confidence in the merely carnal origin of Israel. This he does by transferring one of the Saviour's sayings, which, according to the more historical order of St Luke, is introduced by him on another occasion : *And I say unto you, That many shall come from the east and from the west, and shall sit down with Abraham, with Isaac, and with Jacob, in the kingdom of heaven. But the children of the kingdom* (Israelites by birth and not by faith) *shall be cast out into outer darkness: there shall be weeping and gnashing of teeth.*[1]

Yet this Israelite and Hebrew character of our first Gospel does not necessitate the idea entertained by many —that the original must have been written in the same language as the Old Testament. The supposition that St Matthew composed his Gospel for Israel in the ancient national tongue, the Hebrew, and that what we now possess in the New Testament collection is the translation of that Gospel of Hebrew origin, rests chiefly on the testimony of some ancient Fathers of the Church, and continues to be held down to this day by many learned men. But it is a supposition which, according to our view of the subject, has many decisive arguments against it. The question, however, becomes of much less importance the moment we adopt the view of those learned men who are of opinion that the Greek translation is from the hand of the author himself, and consequently neither more nor less than a second edition of the originally Hebrew Gospel. This is not the time to go deeply into the question that has arisen on the subject of the language in which St Matthew wrote his first or his only Gospel. Be it enough here to observe further on this point, that the freshness of style that distinguishes our Gospel of St Matthew would,

[1] Matth. viii. 11, 12, taken in connexion with verses 10 and 13, and compared with Luke xiii. 28, 29, and in connexion in that place.

of itself, exclude the idea of its being a mere translation, however exquisitely done; and that, moreover, it is a sufficiently decided point, that from the Apostles' time the Greek tongue was too generally known, not only among the Jews scattered every where, but among those even of Galilee and Judea, to make a version in Hebrew or Aramean necessary, in order to its being understood among them.

Meanwhile this Gospel, although in our opinion written in Greek, is distinguished by a still deeper tinge of that Hebrew colouring which is found engrained in all the New Testament writings, though in quite a peculiar manner in St Matthew's. The physiognomy of this first of our Gospels is eminently Oriental, as that of St Mark's Gospel is Roman, that of St Luke's Greek, that of St John heavenly. This, in St Matthew's narratives, is combined with something artless, as in the language of children, or at least *for* children, contrasting in a striking manner with the *grandiose* character of that same Gospel. It is thus, for example, that St Matthew shews a particular affection for that little word familiar to infants, *then* (τότε). We, find, also, that same perfectly simple and artless manner of relating a matter ever recurring in those frequent repetitions which St Matthew is nowise afraid of, whether for the sake of greater clearness, or in order to resume the thread of his narrative. In the issue we shall see, in this simple remark, the solution of an important passage in the history of the Passion, where St Matthew's words (xxvii. 1) will be proved to us not to contain new details, but simply the repetition or recapitulation of a fact already related (xxvi. 62-66).

This simple, artless, Oriental character is found combined with something of the poetical, nay, even of the rhythmical, in some passages of our Evangelist; among others, for example, in the concluding part of the Sermon on the Mount, which in St Luke and St Matthew is quite identical as respects the meaning, but evidently different in point of tone and rhythm, as will appear on comparing them.

MATTH. vii. 24-27.	LUKE vi. 47-49.
Therefore whosoever heareth these sayings of mine, and doeth them, I will liken him unto a wise man, which built his house upon a rock: *And* the rain descended, *and* the floods came, *and* the winds blew, *and* beat upon that house; *and* it fell not: for it was founded upon a rock. And every one that heareth these sayings of mine, and doeth them not, shall be likened unto a foolish man, which built his house upon the sand: *And* the rain descended, *and* the floods came, *and* the winds blew, *and* beat upon that house; *and* it fell: *and* great was the fall of it.	Whosoever cometh to me, and heareth my sayings, and doeth them, I will shew you to whom he is like: He is like a man which built an house, and digged deep, and laid the foundation on a rock: and when the flood arose, the stream beat vehemently upon that house, and could not shake it: for it was founded upon a rock. But he that heareth, and doeth not, is like a man that without a foundation built a house upon the earth; against which the stream did beat vehemently, and immediately it fell; and the ruin of that house was great.

Yet another particularity peculiar to St Matthew, and in some sort analogous with that of his style, but which may be most fruitfully applied to the reconciling of the Gospels, is as follows: His diction is marked throughout with a certain richness and fulness. Hence arises what may be called his *accumulation* of *homogeneous* discourses and facts. It is just this *homogeneousness* that determines the order he follows in drawing up his narrative. The chronological succession of the different events, as they actually occurred, is not with him the main point in that narrative; his rule is to be sought in the manner in which things are bound together in their nature or in their signification. Setting aside any regard to the time of their occurrence, he often associates together sayings and doings of our Lord, which naturally hang together from being all of the same kind. It is thus, as we have already remarked, that he brings together, in the Sermon on the Mount, a great many statements and lessons relating to our Lord's doctrines and commandments, although chronologically out of their proper place, and pronounced on different occasions (chap. v., vi., vii.); it is thus that, in the two chapters that immediately follow, he records a number of miracles wrought by Jesus at different times. And just as he, so to speak, here accumulates accounts of miracles, he erelong (chap. xiii.) follows that up with a series of parables. He subsequently brings together three similitudes (chap. xxv.), the connecting links of which seem again to be found (on comparing St Luke and our first Evangelist) in their *homogeneousness,* and not in the order of time. All those three similitudes (that of *the wise and the foolish virgins,* that of *the talents,* that of the *sheep and the goats*), brought together in that part of *St Matthew's* Gospel, relate to our Lord's return, of which he had fully discoursed in the part immediately preceding (chap. xxiv.); whereas in St Luke's Gospel it appears, that the parable of the talents was, in point of fact, uttered much sooner—that is to say, at the time of our Lord's last journey with his disciples to Jerusalem, as he drew nigh to that city. (Luke xix. 11—26.)

One further particularity still of St Matthew, and one that furnishes a no less important method of explaining the apparent contrarieties among the Evangelical writers, is that which we have already slightly noticed. In his narrative of all that Jesus did and taught, it is not ordinarily so much the *occurrence* itself that is mentioned, as the *personal impression* the Evangelist receives from it.

Hence, again, an apparent want of correctness in his narrative, when compared with the purely historical manner of St Luke, or with the detailed and picturesque descriptions of St Mark. But St Matthew was an eyewitness. Writing with the perfect conviction of the truth of what he saw, he troubles himself little about accessories and details. With him every thing centres in the result of the matter in hand. He states the occurrences which he saw, the words which he heard, every thing that took place in his presence as a disciple, exactly *as* he observed it, *as* he beheld it, *as* he heard it, *together with* the impression that it made upon him, the doctrines involved in it, the consequences that flowed from it. And all this he did, not in an arbitrary manner, or as acting on his own authority, but always under the promised and given guidance, teaching, and inspiration of the Holy Ghost. To this we must ascribe the *transpositions* already repeatedly mentioned. He is conscious that he knows and writes the truth where he departs, in a profoundly spiritual manner, from the *literality* of the occurrence that took place, or of the saying that was uttered. Why, then, should we allow ourselves to be astonished at finding him express in words what we have sufficient grounds, from the nature of the thing, or from a comparison with the other Evangelists, for believing to have been rather *the inward thought* of the personages he introduces, or of the Saviour himself? Here, again, we may adduce some examples by way of illustration. In the Gospel of *St Matthew* and of *St Mark*,[1] we read that Jesus warned his disciples to beware of the *leaven* of the Pharisees and of the Sadducees. The meaning of that expression was not at first apprehended by the apostles.

[1] Matth. xvi. 6–12; Mark viii. 15–21.

They thought their Master spoke of *bread for eating*, and reasoned among themselves, saying, *It is because we have taken no bread.* Jesus reminds them of *the twice-repeated multiplication of the loaves,* to make them sensible that he could not possibly have meant any allusion to *bodily* nourishment. In St Mark, *he immediately after* gives utterance to these serious and energetic words: *How is it that ye do not understand?* In St Matthew, the address is much more circumstantially related: *How is it that ye do not understand that I spake it not to you concerning bread, that ye should beware of the leaven of the Pharisees and of the Sadducees?* Who is not now sensible that St Matthew's narrative does not give us *so much* the very words of Jesus as their meaning, and an exposition or paraphrase of them, while we find visibly given in St Mark the merely literal statement of what was said? In like manner, when, at the conclusion of the parable of the lord of the vineyard and the husbandmen, Jesus asks the chief priests and scribes that striking question, "What will the lord of the vineyard do to those husbandmen?" St Matthew gives the reply made by the Pharisees to that question, while in St Mark and St Luke it is the Lord himself who draws the conclusion:

MATTH. xxi. 41.	MARK xii. 9.	LUKE xx. 16.
They say unto him, He will miserably destroy those wicked men, and will let out his vineyard unto other husbandmen, which shall render him the fruits in their seasons.	What shall therefore the lord of the vineyard do? he will come and destroy the husbandmen, and will give the vineyard unto others.	He shall come and destroy these husbandmen, and shall give the vineyard to others. *And when they heard it, they said, God forbid.*

Who sees not that, in order to explain the difference between St Mark, and still more between St Luke and

St Matthew, we must look in the two former for the manner in which the thing actually happened; while from a higher point of view St Matthew's narrative expresses that inward conviction felt by the enemies of Jesus and of his truth, which compels them involuntarily, in their own consciences, to justify the sentence he pronounces against them? The pen of St Matthew here again gives us, without prejudice to his authenticity, the *heartfelt convictions* of those men, expressed in words which, literally considered, could not have been actually heard. Yet a third such example: the prayer to obtain the first place in the kingdom of heaven for the two sons of Zebedee. According to St Matthew (xx. 20, 21), that request was preferred to our Lord by their mother. *Then came to him the mother of Zebedee's children with her sons, worshipping him, and desiring a certain thing of him. And he said unto her, What wilt thou?* &c. But St Mark does not even mention the mother. Is there a contradiction here? The matter is very simple. St Matthew and all the apostles were well aware that James and John had not ventured to make any such claim of themselves, but that they had been emboldened and encouraged to make it by their mother. And this is what our first Evangelist wishes to show. He puts into the mouth of the mother what was expressed by the mouth of her sons, but which had also been urged upon them by their mother's inconsiderate affection. And all contradiction disappears the instant we distinguish, in St Matthew, the indication of what occurred in its origin and in its principle, and, in St Mark, the simple narrative of the manner in which the thing was done and took place.

The Gospel of St Matthew is characterised by yet another quality. Placed in the collection of the Holy

Scriptures at the opening of the New Testament, this Gospel may, in some sort, be called the mother-gospel among the four. From St Matthew's Gospel, that of St Mark and that of St Luke may be said to be descended: that of St John, though differing essentially in its plan and its composition from its predecessors, essentially assumes, as we shall see *in its own place*, an acquaintance with the three first Gospels. There let us cast a glance at the grand question which in this respect divides the opinions of the learned. Some consider St Luke to have been the first author of a gospel of Jesus Christ; others admit that St Matthew is entitled to rank first in the order of time, but assign to St Mark the third, and to St Luke the second place in that respect. Another hypothesis, long maintained by the learned men of Germany, but which for some time past has greatly declined in credit, deduces all the Gospels, independently the one of the other, from a certain writing now lost, which the Apostles had originally composed as a joint work, and which afterwards had served as the basis both for oral preaching and written composition.

Without rushing into an express examination of all these conjectures and of all these assumptions, let us here only examine anew what is suggested to us by a comparison of the Gospels themselves, as we possess them in our Bibles, for the solution of the question before us. Two preliminary observations will naturally conduct us to a result.

The former of these observations impugns the incorrect opinion of those who consider the Divine inspiration of the Gospels as incompatible with their being compiled one after another, and by one being made the groundwork of another, in such sort that the second Evangelist knew the work of the first, and the third those of the first and the second, and the fourth those of the three first. The precise and simple idea of an infallible direction—of an immediate inspiration by the Holy Ghost—does not at all, or in anyhow, exclude the use of those means to which the only-wise God, in all his ways and in all his works, has at all times subordinated the execution of his divine plan and purposes. Far from this, the excellence and the peculiar fitness of the Holy Scriptures consists precisely in this, that in point of origin, and authority, and truth, they are *Divine;* but as respects the manner in which they have been composed, *human.* The Divine inspiration does *not* render superfluous the reading of books, or the examination and the use of sources of information: these it makes use of as its canals and its instruments. The prophets were not the less inspired by God because of their reading and studying the writings of Moses and their other inspired predecessors. Daniel is represented to us, shortly before receiving a revelation from heaven, as occupied in reading the writings of Jeremiah, and deducing the signs of the times from what he read.[1] And what but the fruit of his researches is it that one of the Evangelists announces at the opening of his narrative (Luke i. 1–4): *Forasmuch as many have taken in hand to set forth in order a declaration of those things which are most surely believed among us; it seemed good to me also, having had perfect understanding of all things from the very first, to write unto thee in order,* &c.? Yet that very research, as well as this writing, took place in conformity with the most express promises, under Divine guidance, and warranty from all error. Every way, then, there is far from

[1] Daniel ix. 2.

being any incompatibility between inspiration by God's Spirit, and making acquaintance with and use of the writings of predecessors.

Our second preliminary remark bears upon the hypothesis of the so-called *original Apostolical Gospel,* to which recourse is instantly had when attempts are made to account for similarity or sameness of expression in the three first Gospels especially, without admitting, however, that each successive Evangelist had had in his hands and had made use of the work of his predecessor. But setting aside the extreme weakness of the very small number of passages in the writings of the ancients, in which attempts have been made to trace the existence of such a *fifth* or *original Gospel,* the whole idea is foreign to the time to which the Scriptures must be referred. Nothing is less in the spirit of the apostolical times, or of the apostolical writings, than a conjoint work of that description, than the compilation, *in the way of common deliberation,* of any such *document,* or, if you will, *formal record,* as the groundwork of future oral discourses, or pieces of writing by each Apostle, or minister of the Gospel, in his individual capacity. Individual preaching, individual addresses *by the mouth* or *with the pen*—such, throughout, is the usual and normal New Testament practice. Thus, too, nothing more simple than the idea of the first of the Gospels having originated in the particulars of the Saviour's doings and sayings, sufferings and death, first announced by word of mouth, or understood as matters of general notoriety, being forthwith, at the fitting time and by a competent hand, reduced to writing. Nothing more natural than that such a work should be undertaken, not by the body of the Apostles in common (of which there is not the shadow of a proof), but *by one of their number,* expressly called to the task and accomplished for it. Nothing more easy to be understood than that such should have been the origin of the first of our Gospels. Nothing more simple than the composition erelong of a second, of a third, and of a fourth; in each of which severally the author may have sought to enlarge, to develop, to arrange in a more strictly historical order, or possibly to consider under a new aspect the facts originally recorded in the Gospel of their first model, St Matthew. Nor need we be surprised if any succeeding Evangelist has not repeated such or such a particular, already sufficiently noticed by his predecessor. Each of the writers wrote according to his own particular object, point of view, and vocation, as well as under God's special direction. It is just this combination of mutual *de*pendence and *in*dependence, that explains there being so many points of difference as well as of agreement among the four Evangelists. All the four, as we have already remarked, contemplate and describe the same object, but that object as viewed and observed from four different sides, and according to four several plans—each of those plans being in harmony with the character and calling of the four several sacred authors.

Let us pass from these preliminary observations to what the Scriptures themselves, when compared together, suggest to us in relation to this. And if we find that such a comparison confirms us in the sentiments we had previously entertained—if we really find St Matthew's Gospel to have been the groundwork of all the rest—then we have really fallen upon that *mother-gospel* which the learned of Germany have for some time imagined to have existed beyond the number, and independently of, the four Gospels. Let us test the matter by turning to one of those occurrences recorded by St Matthew, St Mark, and St Luke, each in his own particular manner, and yet so as evidently to harmonize with each other. We confine ourselves, with this object in view, to the first three Evangelists, because on the mutual bearings of these three being once made clear, the application of the result to St John cannot easily be gainsaid; and because, in any case, that application will be more apposite and more complete when we come to the special examination of an evangelical and prophetical Evangelist so unique and so independent of his three predecessors as St John.

The restoration of life to the daughter of Jairus, and the contemporaneous cure of the woman who had had an issue of blood for twelve years, are related in the following manner by the three first Evangelists :—

MATTH. ix. 18–26.

While he spake these things unto them, behold there came a certain ruler and worshipped him, saying, My daughter is even now dead: but come and lay thy hand upon her and she shall live. And Jesus arose and followed him, and so did his disciples. And, behold, a woman, which was diseased with an issue of blood twelve years, came behind him, and touched the hem of his garment: For she said within herself, If I may but touch his garment, I shall be whole. But Jesus turned him about; and when he saw her, he said, Daughter, be of good comfort; thy

MARK v. 22–43.

And behold there cometh one of the rulers of the synagogue, Jairus by name; and when he saw him, he fell at his feet, and besought him greatly, saying, My little daughter lieth at the point of death, I pray thee, come and lay thy hands on her that she may be healed; and she shall live. And Jesus went with him, and much people followed him, and thronged him. And a certain woman, which had an issue of blood twelve years, and had suffered many things of many physicians, and had spent all that she had, and was nothing bettered, but rather grew

LUKE viii. 41–56.

And, behold, there came a man named Jairus, and he was a ruler of the synagogue; and he fell down at Jesus' feet, and besought him that he would come into his house: for he had one only daughter, about twelve years of age, and she lay a-dying. But as he went the people thronged him. And a woman having an issue of blood twelve years, which had spent all her living upon physicians, neither could be healed of any, came behind him, and touched the border of his garment: and immediately her issue of blood stanched. And Jesus said, Who touch-

faith hath made thee whole. And the woman was made whole from that hour. And when Jesus came into the ruler's house, and saw the minstrels and the people making a noise, he said unto them, Give place; for the maid is not dead, but sleepeth. And they laughed him to scorn. But when the people were put forth, *he went in, and took her by the hand, and the maid arose. And the fame hereof went abroad into all that land.*

worse, when she had heard of Jesus, came in the press behind, and touched his garment. For she said, If I may touch but his clothes, I shall be whole; and straightway the fountain of her blood was dried up; and she felt in her body that she was healed of that plague. And Jesus, immediately knowing in himself that virtue had gone out of him, turned him about in the press, and said, Who touched my clothes? And his disciples said unto him, Thou seest the multitude thronging thee, and sayest thou, Who touched me? And he looked round about to see her that had done this thing. But the woman, fearing and trembling, knowing what was done in her, came and fell down before him, and told him all the truth. And he said unto her, Daughter, thy faith hath made thee whole; go in peace, and be whole of thy plague. While he yet spake, there came from the ruler of the synagogue's house, certain which said, Thy daughter is dead; why troublest thou the Master any further? As soon as Jesus heard

ed me? When all denied, Peter, and they that were with him, said, Master, the multitude throng thee, and press thee, and sayest thou, Who touched me? And Jesus said, Somebody hath touched me: for I perceive that virtue is gone out of me. And when the woman saw that she was not hid, she came trembling, and, falling down before him, she declared unto him before all the people for what cause she had touched him, and how she was healed immediately. And he said unto her, Daughter, be of good comfort: thy faith hath made thee whole; go in peace. While he yet spake, there cometh one from the ruler of the synagogue's house, saying to him, Thy daughter is dead; trouble not the Master. But when Jesus heard it, he answered him, saying, Fear not: believe only, and she shall be made whole. And when he came into the house, he suffered no man to go in, save Peter, and James, and John, and the father and the mother of the maiden. And all wept, and bewailed her: but he said, Weep not; she is not dead, but

the word that was spoken, he saith unto the ruler of the synagogue, Be not afraid, only believe. And he suffered no man to follow him, save Peter, and James, and John the brother of James. And he cometh to the house of the ruler of the synagogue, and seeth the tumult, and them that wept and wailed greatly. And when he was come in, he saith unto them, Why make this ado, and weep? the damsel is not dead, but sleepeth. And they laughed him to scorn. But when he had put them all out, he taketh the father and the mother of the damsel, and them that were with him, and entereth in where the damsel was lying. And he took the damsel by the hand, and said unto her, Talitha cumi; which is, being interpreted, Damsel, (I say unto thee,) arise. And straightway the damsel arose, and walked; for she was of the age of twelve years. And they were astonished with a great astonishment. And he charged them straitly that no man should know it; and commanded that something should be given her to eat.

sleepeth. And they laughed him to scorn, knowing that she was dead. And he put them all out, and took her by the hand, and called, saying, Maid, arise. And her spirit came again, and she arose straightway: and he commanded to give her meat. And her parents were astonished: but he charged them that they should tell no man what was done.

On comparing here these three accounts of this double miracle, we are struck at once with the points of coincidence as well as diversity which they present. The coincidence in the narratives of St Mark and St Luke, is such as of itself leads us to conclude that the one must have had the other in his eye, and followed him not only in the main facts, but closely too, and as it were step by step in the principal circumstances. If we proceed next to compare with both the account left us by St Matthew, we shall see how little need there is for the fountain-head being sought for in an early lost, or rather never known, mother-gospel. That fountain-head we have close at hand and in our possession. It is just St Matthew's statement, which bears every mark of a first and original, and for that very sole reason, summary and general, notice of what then took place. He nowhere deals in details. While, in Mark and Luke, the ruler of the synagogue comes only to complain to our Lord of his child's dangerous illness, and first receives the tidings of her death as he is on the way home with the Master, in Matthew we read of that decease as mentioned once for all by the mouth of her father. No less briefly does he state the fact of her restoration to life. The mention of the child's age, that of the three apostles and her parents alone being present at the miracle, the words of Jesus in performing the miracle, the order given by him at the close to give the restored daughter something to eat; of all this, so minutely detailed by Mark and Luke, Matthew has recorded absolutely nothing. He has to do only with testifying to the leading fact of the child's restoration to life, and that he mentions briefly and forcibly (ver. 25): *He went in, and took her by the hand, and the maid arose;* with the addition of a trait characteristic of himself alone (ver. 26): *And the fame hereof went abroad through all that land.* The cure of the woman who had had an issue of blood for twelve years, is in like manner related here briefly and in its grand outline (ver. 20–22); while in St Luke, and still more in St Mark, we are presented with its most striking and graphic details.

The conclusion is manifest. St Matthew wrote his Gospel *first*, and that Gospel served as the original source for his followers, especially for the two non-apostolical Evangelists. The hypothesis that St Mark or St Luke, or one of the two, had already written theirs when he took up the pen, leads us to this absurdity, that occurrences already recorded by others in their smallest details had been recorded once more in a summary, and, as in that case may be said, in an *incorrect* manner by another Evangelist, and that Evangelist an Apostle. If, on the contrary, we abide by the point of view that has been suggested, how simple and natural are all the mutual bearings of the case! The general account of the matter, the main story given off-hand as it were, appears first, and then come those minute circumstances and particulars which we owe to the research of a more elaborate writer, who has wished to complete the detail of all that occurred. The same analogy, or division of labour, if we may be allowed the expression, will be found between the first of our Evangelists and his fellow-labourers, with a like constant exactness in most, indeed in *all*, the narratives which he has in common with them. Any one may be convinced of this, by applying the example we have selected to any other such occurrence or fact, whether it be recorded in all the four Evangelists, or in the three first only, or only in St Matthew and St Mark, or only in St Matthew and St Luke—or even St Matthew and St John. Every where we shall find a confirmation of our remark, that in the Apostle, our first Evangelist, lies the *foundation* of the fourfold testimony. Turn, for example, to the account of the multiplication of the loaves of bread;[1] the healing of the man who was possessed in the country of the Gergesenes;[2] that of the great faith of the Canaanitish woman;[3] that of the cure of the centurion's servant;[4] that of our Lord's walking on the Sea of Galilee,[5] &c.

In St Mathew's Gospel, accordingly, we have the first Gospel, the mother-gospel, the true *Ur-Evangelium* of the Germans. That immediately after him, in order of time and succession, St Mark follows, and that of him again St Luke makes an ample and manifold, though always free and independent, use, will fall to be more completely demonstrated when we come to treat of those two Gospels. So far, however, as some intimation of this here comports with our avowed plan, be it enough to return for a moment to the account of the miracles wrought by our Lord in the house of Jairus and on the way to his house. A careful comparison of these two Evangelists will, in this as well as other instances, demonstrate that St Mark has borrowed nothing from St Luke, but that St Luke very certainly had the Gospel of St Mark, the friend and representative of St Peter, among the sources whence he obtained his materials, and that he drew most directly from it. In the accounts repeatedly quoted, the two Evangelists very much, *often indeed literally*, coincide. Yet there remains a notable diversity over and above that of style. Both introduce a multitude of details and minute touches no-

[1] Matt. xiv. 13–21. Mark vi. 30–44. Luke ix. 10–17. John vi. 5–13.
[2] Matt. viii. 23–34. Mark v. 1–20. Luke viii. 26, 27.
[3] Matt. xv. 21–23. Mark vii. 24–30.
[4] Matt. viii. 5–13. Luke vii. 1–10.
[5] Matt. xiv. 22–32. Mark vi. 45–51.

where to be found in St Matthew; still, there are not always the same in both. What St Mark adds to St Matthew possesses, for the most part, a peculiar force of expression, and bears most on the external aspect and import of the occurrence; while St Luke's additions, where they differ from St Mark's, go much more into its pith and marrow. Thus, for example, St Mark is very full in his description of the manner in which the cure of the issue of blood was wrought, and the felt effects of the cure (ver. 29). St Luke does not repeat these details, but, on the contrary, mentions carefully and forcibly (ver. 47), that the *woman declared unto him before all the people for what* CAUSE *she had touched him, and* HOW *she was healed* IMMEDIATELY. Afterwards, in the restoration of the damsel to life, St Mark minutely records the very words employed by our Lord when he wrought the miracle (ver. 41). St Luke, on the contrary, and he alone, gives, as a proof of the real death of the child that was restored to life, a very remarkable particular. Recording the ridicule with which the assurance of JESUS, *that the child was not dead but was asleep,* was received, he there adds at once a most important remark: *they laughed him to scorn,* KNOWING THAT SHE WAS DEAD (ver. 53). Now it may easily be seen, in matters of this sort, that a Gospel which selects and describes details rather after their external aspect, has been written in point of time *before* one which contemplates and introduces particular circumstances more according to their internal import. The greater the fulness with which the same fact is described, the more must the author who has adopted that greater fulness be supposed to have written *posterior* to one who has stated the fact in a *more* general and *less* fully developed manner. But who, after a patient examination, can fail to perceive progression and development in St Luke's manner of relating an occurrence after St Mark, just as there is in St Mark, in the details he gives, when compared with the grand outlines of which St Matthew's Gospel is composed?

And now, when we bring together, as if in one focus, all that we have observed hitherto with respect to this first book in the collection of the New Testament writings, what is the result? First of all, we find this Gospel marked as the work of the Apostle Matthew, by a stamp of authenticity which excludes all idea of human contrivance or fiction. This stamp we have found in the manner in which the author makes mention of the grace conferred on him, and of his calling to the Apostleship, without ever naming himself as such, or in any way fixing attention on his person. The Gospel of St Matthew is indeed the Gospel of the publican converted and called to the apostleship. Its character, in the second place, is truly *apostolic*, in so far as it contains the expression of the high and intimate relationship subsisting between its author and the Lord and Master of whom it testifies;—in so far as it bears the impress of a truly apostolic authority in virtue of the promise of the Holy Spirit, in such a sort that it presents events with an entire liberty, not so much according to their *historical* order or with a *literal* exactness, but according to what was required by its author's position and object, and according to a certain internal actuality in the thing recorded. In the third place, we have called St Matthew's Gospel Israelitic, in as much as it contains the special expression of the Old Testament truth with respect to the Messiatic character of Jesus, and especially of his prophetic greatness and his kingship as the Son of David. Finally, we recognised there the first and original Gospel, which lays the foundation of all the rest, and from that very circumstance furnishes matter in great abundance for new evangelical writings, as they came out one after the other, in the way of progression and development, from St Matthew to St John.

Under these four leading peculiarities we may easily range all the observations that have been suggested by our review of St Matthew's Gospel, and which will offer themselves spontaneously when, in the further prosecution of our subject, we proceed to compare the other Gospels with it and with each other.

As we do find the principal peculiarities of an Evangelist indicated by whatever has been written by himself alone, or by him in a different manner from that of the other Evangelical authors; so will these peculiarities no less significantly reveal themselves for the most part when we observe what is *not recorded* by him, what is passed over by him, with more or less evident intent. Now, this is the case very obviously with St Matthew. What he does *not* mention *at all*, or does *not* mention *with the same details* as the Evangelists who followed him, may likewise be accounted for, in a remarkable manner, by the fourfold character which we have observed in his Gospel. Thus, for example, we nowhere find there any exact indication of intervals of time, and still less of DATES, as in St Luke, and in a different way, as we shall see hereafter, in St John. Quite as little do we find in St Matthew those minute but most significant details, and those graphic touches which distinguish the Gospel of St Mark. And this we can quite understand. Nothing of all this properly belonged to the not so much historical as prophetical, not so much descriptive as summary and compendious, Gospel of the Apostle-publican—in that primary Gospel which presents the rich materials in their first freshness, and, so to speak, unmoulded amplitude.

In like manner, but owing to another peculiarity which we have remarked in St Matthew, in vain do we look in his Gospel for any mention of those Samaritans whom we repeatedly find presented to us in so interesting a light by St Luke and St John. Once only do we find that nation spoken of in St Matthew, and that on the occasion of the prohibition made by our Lord to his apostles at the time of their being first sent out (chap. x. 5). This omission belongs evidently to the Israelite character of our first Gospel, which, in conformity with the convictions of the Jews, puts the *Samaritans* and the *Gentiles* on the same level. Whatever of a peculiar and striking character that was presented, in the full daylight of the gospel, by some of that intermediate race, did not fall within the plan prescribed for St Matthew, who knew no national distinction but that betwixt Jews and Gentiles; nor, for reasons to be afterwards given, within that of St Mark. That was reserved for mention by the two last of the Evangelists.

To the apostolic character of the memorials left by St Matthew, we must further refer the omission of any notice of those seventy disciples of whom St Luke alone makes any separate mention.

In fine, to show how, by such a silence, or intentional omission, the Gospel of St Matthew proves itself to be the work of the converted publican, the striking parable of *the Pharisee and the publican* is *not* to be found in St Matthew. That parable was too honourable to the kind of men to which our first Evangelist belonged, to admit of his inserting it in his Gospel. That similitude, as well as the conversion of Zaccheus, is found only in St Luke (xviii. 9–14; xix. 1–10).

We have now to test a little more closely the application of the results we have found, and proceed, in conclusion, to place in juxtaposition a few passages, with the view of showing how the apparent discrepancy betwixt St Matthew and his fellow-evangelists is altogether removed by the mere force of the principles we have adduced.

MATTH. iv. 1–11.

Then was Jesus led up of the Spirit into the wilderness to be tempted of the devil. And when he had fasted forty days *and forty nights*, he was afterwards an hungered. And when the *tempter* came to him, he said, If thou be the Son of God, command that these *stones be made bread* (*loaves*). But he answered and said, It is written, Man shall not live by bread alone, but *by every word that proceedeth out of the mouth of God.* Then the devil taketh him up into the *holy city*, and setteth him on a pinnacle of the temple, and saith unto him, If thou be the Son of God, cast thyself down, for it is written, He shall give his angels charge concerning thee; and in their hands they shall bear thee up, lest at any time thou dash thy foot against a stone. Jesus said unto him, *It is written again*, Thou shalt not tempt the Lord thy God. Again the devil taketh him up into an exceeding high mountain, and sheweth him all the kingdoms of the world, and the glory of them; and saith unto him, All these things will I give thee, *if thou wilt fall down* and worship me. Then saith Jesus unto him, Get thee hence, Satan: for it is written, Thou shalt worship the Lord thy God, and him only shalt thou serve. Then the devil leaveth him, and,

LUKE iv. 1–13.

And Jesus, *being full of the Holy Ghost, returned from Jordan*, and was led by the Spirit into the wilderness, being forty days tempted of the devil. And in those days *he did eat nothing:* and *when they were ended*, he afterward hungered. And *the devil* said unto him, If thou be the Son of God, command this *stone* that it be made *bread.* And Jesus answered him, saying, It is written, That man shall not live by bread alone, but *by every word of God.* And the devil, taking him up into an high mountain, shewed unto him all the kingdoms of the world *in a moment of time.* And the devil said unto him, All this power will I give thee, and the glory of them: *for that is delivered unto me; and to whomsoever I will I give it.* If thou therefore wilt worship me, all shall be thine. And Jesus answered and said unto him, Get thee behind me, Satan: for it is written, Thou shalt worship the Lord thy God, and him only shalt thou serve. And he brought him to *Jerusalem*, and set him on a pinnacle of the temple, and said unto him, If thou be the Son of God, cast thyself *down from hence:* for it is written, He shall give his angels charge over thee, to keep thee: And in their hands they shall bear thee up, lest at any time thou dash thy

behold, *angels came and ministered unto him.*

foot against a stone. And Jesus answering said unto him, It is *said*, Thou shalt not tempt the Lord thy God. And when the devil had ended all the temptation, *he departed from him for a season.*

We shall not be expected to give any exposition or explanation here of this most striking and profoundly significant narrative. That, indeed, would be quite beside the purpose and plan of the views we are now elucidating. All we have to do is to compare, in their several points of agreement and difference, the accounts left us by the two Evangelists. Now, how far does the result of that comparison confirm the conclusions we have already announced?

If we read, even with the slightest attention, the two Evangelists, we shall at once perceive that the narrative of St Luke is taken from that of St Matthew—that St Luke must have had the first of our Gospels before him, and made use of it as the basis of his own account, giving at the same time more precision to that account. We see, too, that he follows a different arrangement, more in conformity with the order in which the incidents actually occurred.

Let us see first what the difference in detail is.

St Matthew, first of all, makes use here of his favourite plural (ver. 3, STONES, LOAVES) in cases where St Luke employs the singular: *Command this* STONE *that it become a* LOAF. St Matthew (verse 4), in pursuance of his Israelitic and Old Testament principle, quotes the words of Moses[1] in fuller terms than St Luke. Thus, too, in accordance with Israelitic usage, he speaks of the *holy city*,[2] called by St Luke (ver. 9) simply *Jerusalem.*

[1] Deut. viii. 3.

[2] In another place, it is called in St Matthew *the city of the great King*, v. 35; Ps. xlviii. 3.

The latter goes more into details both as respects accessory circumstances, as when (ver. 8) he says, *In a moment of time;* or in accounting for some detail or expression found in St Matthew without any such addition, as (ver. 6) where he brings out more clearly the nature of the power over this world delivered unto Satan. Whilst St Matthew (ver. 11) speaks not without allusion to one of the Psalms,[1] of the ministration of the angels offered unto Jesus; St Luke, on the contrary, concludes with the remark, that *the devil departed from him for a season* (ver. 13), having an eye to the sequel of his history, where (chap. xx. ver. 53) he relates how, in our Lord's passion, the powers of darkness were again for some hours to be let loose against their vanquisher, who had disarmed them in the wilderness.

But on comparing the two Gospels a difference occurs of more importance than the discrepancies just mentioned—a difference in *the order* in which the three temptations took place. With respect to that presented in the words, *If thou be the Son of God, command that these stones be made bread,* both Evangelists agree in its having been certainly the first that was attempted by the enemy after the forty days' fast. But the two Gospels pursue a different order in the two that follow. While in St Matthew the proposal that our Lord should cast himself down from the pinnacle of the temple *precedes,* and the offer of this world's kingdoms closes the temptations, we find this order inversed in St Luke. Some have been found who preferred the order followed by St Matthew, as supported by the nature of the thing; for, according to them, the offer of this world's kingdoms must have been most seductive, the temptations (as we

[1] Ps. xci. and others. Compare Heb. i. 6, and John i. 2.

willingly admit) naturally augmenting as they proceed. But the nature of things more deeply studied leads us to perceive this gradation precisely in the succession as found in St Luke. For, in point of fact, the temptation which seemed to propose that our Lord should give a proof of courage, of faith, and of confidence in God, in trusting implicitly to a passage taken from the Holy Scriptures, was certainly of a stronger, or, if you will, a more subtle kind than even the offer of this world's kingdoms, under the condition of worshipping the Prince of this world. Many souls that have been able to resist the temptations presented by this world's honours and splendours, or who have been insensible to them, have allowed themselves to be caught in the snares of spiritual pride, that is to say, of an imaginary confidence, wanting in the indispensable requisites of obedience to God, and dependence on God. That the Anointed One should in this, as well as other respects, remain immaculate and perfect, behoved to be shewn just in the resistance to this last temptation, so spiritual in its outward aspect. In yet another point of view, this assault is proved to have been the severest and the last. Twice had they been repelled simply by an appeal to God's word—*It is written.* The enemy himself makes the third, as if in his turn appealing to Scripture, though by an abuse of it. But this assault, as well as the two first, is repelled by our Lord's availing himself of that same weapon, even the sword of the Spirit, the Word of God—*It is written again;* or as Luke has it, not without emphasis—*It is said,* as if he would hint, that in quoting Scripture the gist and force of the matter lie, not in the bare wording of the passage, but in its purport and connexion, as being God's saying.

Thus, then, we have in St Luke evidently enough the true historical order. But how shall we account for St Matthew's having departed from that order? We have already explained how the historical succession of events is never with him the chief affair that he has to do with —never the object he has in view. What he gives is the occurrence in inseparable connexion, nay, thoroughly mingled, as it were, with the impression with which it affected his own soul. And that impression in the case of St Matthew (in whose Gospel the kingship of *Jesus Christ* occupies the first place), is produced most of all by the idea of the *kingdoms of the world* (ver. 8). Those kingdoms belonged of right to Jesus; one day they would become actually his: here they are offered to him by the tempter, *the Prince of this world.* These combined ideas give in St Matthew all the deeper significance to this *second* temptation. Hence it seems as if spontaneously to range itself under his pen in that place which, though the last, is here the highest place. And perhaps it is in this association of ideas that he immediately follows up this temptation, which he places last, with the interesting circumstances to which we have already alluded—*The devil leaveth him, and, behold, angels came and ministered to him.*

It surely follows from all this, that there is really no actual contradiction between St Matthew and St Luke. In the facts related they agree: there is a difference only in the point of view from which they are contemplated. The narrative is in each case consistent with its own object and principle—the historical with St Luke, the spiritual with St Matthew. And here the diversity as well as the agreement proves anew, in the simplest and most natural manner, the truth, the genuineness, and the authenticity of the facts related.

A second opportunity of testing the application of our principles for discovering the harmony of the Gospels, is supplied by an occurrence, which we place, as related by the Evangelist St Mark, over against the account of it left by St Matthew. We refer to the beheading of St John the Baptist.

MATTH. xiv. 1–12.	MARK vi. 14–29.
At that time Herod the tetrarch heard of the fame of Jesus, and said unto his servants, This is John the Baptist: he is arisen from the dead; and therefore mighty works do shew forth themselves in him.	And king Herod heard of him; (for his name was spread abroad;) and he said, That John the Baptist was arisen from the dead, and therefore mighty works do shew forth themselves in him. Others said, That it is Elias. And others said, That it is a prophet, or as one of the prophets. But when Herod heard thereof, he said, It is John, whom I beheaded: he is risen from the dead.
For Herod had laid hold on John, and bound him, and put him in prison for Herodias' sake, his brother Philip's wife.	For Herod himself had sent forth and laid hold upon John, and bound him in prison for Herodias' sake, his brother Philip's wife; for he had married her.
For John said unto him, It is not lawful for thee to have her.	For John had said unto Herod, It is not lawful for thee to have thy brother's wife.
And when he would have put him to death, he feared the multitude, because they counted him as a prophet.	*Therefore Herodias had a quarrel against him, and would have killed him; but she could not: for Herod feared John, knowing that he was a just man and an holy, and observed him; and when he heard him, he did many things, and heard him gladly.*
But when Herod's birthday was kept, the daughter of Herodias danced before them, and pleased Herod.	And when a convenient day was come, that Herod, on his birthday, made a supper to his lords, high captains, and chief estates of Galilee; and when the daughter of the said Herodias came in, and

	danced, and pleased Herod, and them that sat with him, the king said unto the damsel, Ask of me whatsoever thou wilt, and I will give it thee.
Whereupon he promised with an oath to give her whatsoever she would ask. And she, being before instructed of her mother, said, Give me here John Baptist's head in a charger.	And he sware unto her, Whatsoever thou shalt ask of me, I will give it thee, unto the half of my kingdom. And she went forth and said unto her mother, What shall I ask? And she said, The head of John the Baptist. And she came in straightway with haste unto the king, and asked, saying, I will that thou give me, by and by, in a charger, the head of John the Baptist.
And the king was sorry; nevertheless for the oath's sake, and them which sat with him at meat, he commanded it to be given her. And he sent and beheaded John in the prison.	And the king was exceeding sorry; yet for his oath's sake, and for their sakes which sat with him, he would not reject her. And immediately the king sent an executioner, and commanded his head to be brought: and he went and beheaded him in the prison.
And his head was brought in a charger, and given to the damsel: and she brought it to her mother.	And brought his head in a charger, and gave it to the damsel: and the damsel gave it to her mother.
And his disciples came and took up the body, and buried it, and went and told Jesus.	And when his disciples heard of it, they came and took up his corpse, and laid it in a tomb.

Here, again, a comparison of the two Evangelists produces the same result that we had before obtained. The agreement between the two accounts is manifest. Shall we regard this agreement as merely the consequence of an inspiration literally alike in both? Whence, then, the difference? Shall we ascribe it to their being both derived from one original source existing apart from the four Gospels? How much simpler what we have supposed, that the one Evangelist has drawn from the other, and thus that St Matthew, having been the first Evangelist in the order of time, St Mark afterwards repeated his predecessor's *more general narrative* in greater detail, by adding the more minute and exact circumstances of the occurrence, with an equally certain knowledge of those circumstances, and equally under the guidance of the Holy Ghost. These particular circumstances, these minute features of the case, are again found in St Mark to be many; such as, the very words addressed by the king to the daughter of Herodias (ver. 22), together with the precise terms of his oath (ver. 23); the fuller account of what passed between the mother and the daughter (ver. 24, 25); the mention of the executioner (ver. 27)—particulars all marked with a character of peculiar artlessness, such as places the authenticity of the narrative beyond all suspicion. To this we shall return in treating more specially of the Gospel of St Mark.

Some, however, see here a great discrepancy between the two Evangelists on a leading point. They will have it that the feelings of Herod towards John the Baptist are represented as essentially different by St Mark from what appears in St Matthew. While, according to the latter, Herod desired the death of John the Baptist, but could not make up his mind to slay him because he feared the multitude, by whom he was accounted a prophet (ver. 5); in St Mark it is Herodias alone that aims at having John's life, but cannot accomplish what she desires, because her husband stands in awe of him as a holy man, *hearing him even often*, and doing many things as he advised (ver. 19, 20).

This seeming contradiction finds its complete solution in the character of St Matthew's Gospel as gathered from the peculiarities that distinguish it. As that Gospel always views things in their grand general aspect, it gives prominence in the first place to the *popular opinions* entertained with respect to the Baptist, and the influence of that opinion upon Herod. But does this in the slightest degree exclude those conflicting, variable sentiments which might agitate Herod as a man, as they would reveal themselves at his court? Now, it is with regard to these last that St Mark informs us. And all perfectly tallies together. The multitude had a great veneration for John: this was what first impressed Herod, and prevented him from putting him to death. That he had the *will* to do so, is what Matthew tells us very generally, according to his usual manner. But Mark follows this up by explaining how Herod came to have that will, and how it was modified by his personal feelings. It arose from the influence exercised by Herodias over the king's mind and counsels. Thus impelled alternately by contrary impressions, Herod felt besides in his own heart, and in his own conscience, the force of the Baptist's words and authority. Can we wonder that, as he was not destitute of feeling, and even of religious feeling, he should, notwithstanding the suggestions of Herodias, find it impossible to suppress his esteem for the prophet, nay, hear him with some degree of pleasure, and even follow at times his advice? To be willing at once to gratify the resentment of a godless woman, and to spare the Baptist, from respect both to the people's conscience and his own, was just what might have been expected in that *peace-loving* prince, as he is described by Josephus. All this is so simple, so consistent with all we know of human nature, that, viewed in its true light, there remains not the shadow of a contradiction or difficulty. But betwixt St Matthew and St Mark there remains this characteristic difference:

that the former represents the king to us more in connection with the people, but also still more as, through weakness of character, the accomplice of his wife in her hatred of John; whereas the latter, on the contrary, represents him to us more as he appeared in the interior of his court, and in the difference which always really subsisted between the king's sentiments and those of Herodias.

As in the account of the beheading of the Baptist we have placed St Matthew and St Mark over against each other, and sought an explanation of their points of difference in the object and character that belonged to each of them individually; so we proceed now to observe how another kind of apparent contradiction between details given by St Matthew, St Mark, and St Luke, may be resolved by the simple application of the principles we have laid down. All three speak of the Saviour's casting out of a great many evil spirits in the country of the Gergesenes, in the following narratives :—

MATTH. viii. 28–34.	MARK v. 1–20.	LUKE viii. 26–39.
And when he was come to the other side, into the country of the Gergesenes, there met him *two possessed* with devils, coming out of the tombs, *exceeding fierce, so that no man might pass by that way.*	And they came over unto the other side of the sea, into the country of the Gadarenes. And when he was come out of the ship, immediately there met him out of the tombs *a man* with an unclean spirit, who had his dwelling among the tombs; and no man could bind *him*, no, not with chains: because that *he* had been often bound with fetters and chains, and the chains had been plucked asunder by *him*, and the fetters	And they arrived at the country of the Gadarenes, which is over against Galilee. And when he went forth to land, there met him out of the city *a certain man which had* devils long time, and ware no clothes, neither abode in any house, but in the tombs.

broken in pieces: neither could any man tame *him.* And always day and night *he* was in the mountains and in the tombs, crying and cutting *himself* with stones.

And, behold, *they cried* out, saying, What have we to do with thee, Jesus, thou Son of God? art thou come hither to torment us before the time?

But when *he* saw Jesus afar off, *he* ran and worshipped him, And cried with a loud voice, and said, What have *I* to do with thee, Jesus, *thou* Son of the most high God? I adjure thee by God, that thou torment me not. For he said unto him, Come out of the man, thou unclean spirit. And he asked him, What is thy name? And he answered, saying, My name is Legion, for we are many. And he besought him much that he would not send them away out of the country.

When *he* saw Jesus, *he* cried out, and fell down before him, and with a loud voice said, What have *I* to do with thee, Jesus, thou Son of God most high? *I* beseech thee, torment *me* not. For he had commanded the unclean spirit to come out of the man. (For oftentimes it had caught *him;* and *he* was kept bound with chains, and in fetters; and *he* brake the bands, and was driven of the devil into the wilderness.) And Jesus asked *him*, saying, What is thy name? And *he* said, Legion; because many devils were entered into him. And they besought him that he would not command them to go out into the deep.

And there was a good way off from them an herd of many swine feeding. So the devils besought him, saying, If thou cast us out, suffer us to go away into the herd of swine. And he said unto them, Go. And when they were come out, they went into the herd of

Now there was there nigh unto the mountains a great herd of swine feeding. And all the devils besought him, saying, Send us into the swine, that we may enter into them. And forthwith Jesus gave them leave. And the unclean spirits went out, and entered

And there was there an herd of many swine feeding on the mountain: and they besought him that he would suffer them to enter into them. And he suffered them. Then went the devils out of the man, and entered into the swine: and the herd ran violently

swine; and, behold, the whole herd of swine ran violently down a steep place into the sea, and perished in the waters. And they that kept them fled, and went their ways into the city, and told every thing, and what was befallen to *the possessed* (pl.) of the devils. And, behold, the whole city came out to meet Jesus; and when they saw him, they besought him that he would depart out of their coasts.

into the swine: and the herd ran violently down a steep place into the sea, (they were about two thousand,) and were choked in the sea. And they that fed the swine fled, and told it in the city, and in the country. And they went out to see what it was that was done. And they came to Jesus, and see him *that was possessed with the devil, and had the legion*, sitting, and clothed, and in *his* right mind; and they were afraid. And they that saw it told them how it befell to him that was possessed with the devil, and also concerning the swine. And they began to pray him to depart out of their coasts.

And when he was come into the ship, *he that had been possessed with the devil* prayed him that he might be with him. Howbeit Jesus suffered *him* not, but saith unto him, Go home to thy friends, and tell them how great things the Lord hath done for thee, and hath had compassion on thee. And *he* departed, and began to publish in Decapolis how great things Jesus had done for *him;* and all men did marvel.

down a steep place into the lake, and were choked. When they that fed them saw what was done, they fled, and went and told it in the city, and in the country. Then they went out to see what was done; and came to Jesus, and found the man out of whom the devils were departed, sitting at the feet of Jesus, clothed, and in his right mind; and they were afraid. They also which saw it told them by what means *he that was possessed of the devils* was healed. Then the whole multitude of the country of the Gadarenes round about besought him to depart from them; for they were taken with *great* fear.

And he went up into the ship, and returned back again. Now *the man* out of whom the devils were departed besought him that *he* might be with him; but Jesus sent *him* away, saying, Return to thine own house, and shew how great things God hath done unto *thee.* And *he* went his way, and published throughout the whole city how great things Jesus had done unto *him.*

Here again we have the same phenomena as those presented by the preceding comparison. In St Matthew we have what occurred on this occasion related summarily and briefly—in St Mark, more fully and with all the particulars—in St Luke, the same, as he follows in the footsteps of St Mark, only with the omission of all that seems too much of graphic detail for his *historical* narrative.

But here, not merely a *difference*, but a positive and manifest *contradiction* appears betwixt St Matthew and the two Evangelists that follow. According to St Matthew, there were here *two* demoniacs delivered from the evil spirit; according to St Mark and St Luke, there was only *one*. In order to remove the discrepancy, most authors of the Harmonies, and most expositors, have thought it enough to consider the *one* mentioned by the two Evangelists as the *principal*, or the most *interesting*, or the *most tormented*, who on that account alone deserved consideration and mention by those two writers. But on what external or internal basis rests this distinction, which, as the text gives no indication of it whatever, must be considered purely arbitrary?

Let us endeavour, in looking for a solution, to keep simply to the principles we have laid down. And then we have at once, in the twofold and accordant testimony of St Mark and St Luke, as it lies before us in its plain circumstantiality, the fullest guarantee that the occurrence has been recorded by them in its *full historical reality*—that, consequently, the miracle was confined to *one* possessed person only. Whence, then, comes there to be the number *two* in St Matthew? The answer is very simple. It comes from his peculiar manner of employing the plural, a peculiarity every way accordant with his relating things in a general way. But why precisely in this instance, in so particular and so extraordinary a case, have we not only the plural, but the number TWO? To explain the use made by St Matthew in this passage of the number of *two* instead of that of *one*, we should have recourse, in connexion with the whole narrative, to another peculiarity already noticed in the Evangelist. He delineates things (as we have seen above) just as they occurred in his presence, and as they caught his eye; what he puts in writing is, so to speak, his recollection, his impression. Let us, then, put ourselves only in the place from which he himself saw what passed, and from which, consequently, his account *gives* us this narrative of the demoniac who was dispossessed by Jesus. He accompanied our Lord at the time of his passing over to the country of the Gergesenes, and when, immediately thereafter (Mark v. 2), the person who was possessed met him or came within view. Now, let us merely suppose that the possessed person, when first seen by our Lord and his apostles, had attacked some passenger, and was just then struggling with him. Seen at the first glance along with the man whom he had attacked, the possessed person would seem at a distance to be not *one possessed person only*, but presented the appearance of there being *two*. Putting down this impression, this recollection, of the first glance directed to the scene from a distance, St Matthew speaks of *two* possessed persons, because he saw *two* men in the power of those unclean spirits, *one* the possessed person himself, the *other* attacked *by* the possessed person. Thus, in fact, in some sort *two* men were delivered by the powerful intervention of Jesus, and whom the general account left by St Matthew readily comprises under the same term of *possessed persons.*

We must on no account imagine that the Holy Ghost has in this manner confirmed or permitted an incorrect statement, or one that is devoid of truth. Here, as we have already said, we must not allow ourselves to think of any misrecollection or inaccuracy. There is design, consistency, and significance, in the discrepancy before us. St Matthew very well knew that his *two* were in reality only *one.* But it was fitting that *he* should present the fact to us in its external aspect, and that the two other Evangelists who follow should describe the same fact in its objective reality.

But shall we be told that all this hypothesis of the person passing being attacked by the possessed person is the mere creature of one's *arbitrary* imagination? No! St Matthew himself hints it to us by a single detail of apparently secondary, but here really of great importance in the harmonizing of the Evangelists. Let us note what he says (ver. 28), *that no man might pass that way,* because of the ferocity of the person who was possessed by the devil.

This solution of the apparent contradiction between the number of *two* in St Matthew, and the singular of the other two Evangelists that follow, receives a further confirmation from a like instance of difference, at first sight irreconcilable, but erelong finding its most simple solution in the very nature of the thing. We refer to the healing of the blind man by Jesus outside of the gates of Jericho, related by the three first Evangelists as follows:—

Matth. xx. 29–34.	Mark x. 46–52.	Luke xviii. 35–43.
And as they departed *from Jericho,* a	And they came *to Jericho:* and as he	And it came to pass, that, as he was

great multitude followed him. And, behold, *two blind men, sitting by the wayside, when they heard that Jesus passed by, cried out, saying*, Have mercy on *us*, O Lord, thou son of David. And the multitude rebuked *them*, because *they* should hold their peace: but *they* cried the more, saying, Have mercy on *us*, O Lord, thou son of David. And Jesus stood still, and called *them*, and said, What will *ye* that I shall do unto you? *They* say unto him, Lord, that *our* eyes may be opened. So Jesus had compassion on *them*, and touched *their* eyes: and immediately *their* eyes received sight, and *they* followed him.

went *out of Jericho* with his disciples, and a great number of people, *blind Bartimeus, the son of Timeus, sat by the highway-side begging. And when he heard that it was Jesus of Nazareth, he began to cry out, and say*, Jesus, thou son of David, have mercy *on me*. And many charged *him* that *he* should hold his peace: but *he* cried the more a great deal, Thou son of David, have mercy on *me*. And Jesus stood still, and commanded *him* to be called. And they call *the blind man*, saying, Be of good comfort, rise; he calleth *thee*. And *he*, casting away *his* garment, rose, and came to Jesus. And Jesus answered and said unto *him*, What wilt *thou* that I should do unto *thee? The blind man* said unto him, Lord, that *I* might receive *my* sight. And Jesus said unto *him*, Go *thy* way; *thy* faith hath made *thee* whole. And immediately *he* received *his sight*, and followed Jesus in the way.

come *nigh unto Jericho, a certain blind man sat by the wayside begging. And hearing the multitude pass by, he asked what it meant.* And they told *him* that Jesus of Nazareth passeth by. And *he* cried, saying, Jesus, thou son of David, have mercy on *me*. And they which went before rebuked *him*, that *he* should hold *his* peace: but *he* cried so much the more, Thou son of David, have mercy on *me*. And Jesus stood, and commanded *him* to be brought unto him: and when *he* was come near, he asked *him*, saying, What wilt *thou* that I shall do unto *thee?* And *he* said, Lord, that *I* may receive *my* sight. And Jesus said unto *him*, Receive *thy* sight: *thy* faith hath saved *thee*. And immediately *he* received *his* sight, and followed *him*, glorifying God: and all the people, when they saw it, gave praise unto God.

Here we have anew the same phenomena as in the account of the possessed person. In St Matthew the story is put down briefly and substantially; in St Mark, with the most minute details: for instance, we have the name of the blind man (ver. 46), and the way in which he was called to Jesus and drew near to him (ver. 49, 50). St Luke's narrative perfectly agrees with that of St Mark, only it is a little more concise, and with the addition at the close of that interesting remark, that *he that was healed followed Jesus, glorifying God: and all the people, when they saw it, gave praise unto God* (ver. 43.) And then we have the same apparent discrepancy betwixt St Matthew and his two fellow Evangelists with respect to the number: *one* blind person being spoken of by them, whereas he mentions *two*. It is clear at once, that, putting the testimonies of St Mark and St Luke together, we must conclude that there was but *one* cure and but *one* blind person in the case. Why should these two Evangelists reduce the number *two* to *one* only, if St Matthew must indeed be understood literally? We have a very good reason to account for the appearance of the number *two* in the latter. He, no doubt, identified in his description the blind man with his conductor. When, as he accompanied Jesus, the cry from the blind man reached his ears, it might naturally seem to come from *two* persons instead of *one*, and it is that impression, not the actual fact in itself, that he describes. Certainly one can no otherwise explain another couple of blind persons in St Matthew (ix. 27–31), of whom it is said that they *followed* Jesus, praying that he would heal them. If there be any truth in the saying recorded in Scripture,[1] *If the blind lead the blind, both shall fall into the ditch*;—what more unreasonable than to suppose that two blind men should have ventured out together on the highway, and should have followed Jesus *even into the house?* What more

[1] Matth. xv. 14.

simple, on the contrary, than that in the narrative of the Evangelist, both here and in that other place, *the blind and his leader* should have been *identified* from being so intimately associated together?

A second apparent contradiction in the accounts of the cure of BARTIMÆUS, near Jericho, bears upon the circumstances of time and place. St Matthew, who in this too is followed by St Mark, makes the occurrence take place at the *departure* from the city, or rather mentions it after he had spoken of the departure of Jesus and his disciples (ver. 29). St Luke, in his more exact concatenation of events, which is evident from what immediately follows (xix. 1–10), makes it happen at our Lord's approach to Jericho. The solution of the difficulty is easy. St Matthew does not ordinarily occupy himself much with any rigorous determination of time or place. His expression (ver. 29) does not bear immediately on the account of the cure of the blind which follows it, but generally to the passing of Jesus through Jericho. Then, as if from association of ideas and recollections, he, so to speak, retraces his steps, and relates an incident that had occurred *at that same time* before Jericho. St Mark, unless in the case of some circumstance having an important bearing on the course he had laid out for himself, does not ordinarily make any change in the tradition handed down by St Matthew. St Luke, in his historical exposition, relates all in its true place.

III. ST MARK.

As the first of our Gospels has been attributed by the consentient voice of antiquity to St Matthew, so has the second, in like manner, been ascribed to St Mark. This Evangelist, the *disciple*, the *servant*, and the *interpreter* of St Peter, as he is designed by certain ancient fathers of the Church, is called by that Apostle himself at the close of his first Epistle (ver. 13), in a spiritual and evangelical sense, *his son*. Indirectly, therefore, and saving always the higher guidance of the Holy Ghost, this Gospel was compiled under the manifest influence—that is, according to the oral testimony and personal communications of St Peter, and in this sense as if *under his inspection;* just as we shall hereafter see that the Gospel of St Luke was, in like manner, composed in some such, though a differently modified, connexion with St Paul. The whole of our second Gospel bears the most evident marks of this leading characteristic of its author. With St Matthew's Gospel before him, St Mark wrote his own, with the further aid of St Peter's directions and elucidations. Thus the latter is the fruit, so to speak, of two testimonies, which meet, coalesce, and mutually confirm each other—the testimony of St Peter and that of St Matthew. We shall best begin our present examination, we believe, with certain passages illustrative of the very intimate relationship that subsisted between the Gospel of St Mark and the Apostle Peter.

At the very opening of this Gospel some have thought they could trace a certain resemblance to a discourse of St Peter's, as we find it recorded in the Acts of the Apostles (x. 35, &c.) Both, at least, make the Gospel history commence with the preaching of the Baptist (Mark i. 2). A comparison of these passages comprises something more perhaps, to which we shall return again, but for the present will pursue the matter no further. The intimate relationship between our second Evangelist and St Peter at all events remains evident. We often find St Peter mentioned specially and by name, and in more than one place he is referred to as an eyewitness;—it is only in St Mark's Gospel that we find him specially named in circumstances which involved any thing that particularly interested that Apostle's heart or memory. Thus, for example, when St Mark and St Luke relate in what manner our Lord was sought by his disciples in the solitary place, when he prayed in the morning very early, the former makes express mention of *Simon*, the latter speaks of *the people* generally.

MARK i. 35, 36.

And in the morning, rising up a great while before day, he went out, and departed into a solitary place, and there prayed. And Simon, and *they that were with him*, followed after him. (In the Greek the word is still stronger: *κατεδίωξαν, hunted after him.*)

LUKE iv. 42.

And when it was day, he departed, and went into a desert place: and *the people* sought him (Gr., *ἐπεζήτουν*), and came unto him, and stayed him, that he should not depart from them.

Here it is clear that St Mark points to St Peter as an eyewitness and participant in what took place, and the original authority from whom he had learned this detail.

In the narrative of the fig-tree that was cursed, this is still more evident and striking. Among other details by which the more circumstantial account of St Mark (xi. 11–14 and 19–24) differs from that of St Matthew (xxi. 17–27), we find this: That the first disciple that perceived the drying up of the fig-tree, and made an exclamation about it to our Lord, was Peter.

MATTH. xxi. 20.	MARK xi. 21.
And when *the disciples* saw it, they marvelled, saying, How soon is the fig-tree withered away!	And *Peter*, calling to remembrance, saith unto him, Master, behold the fig-tree which thou cursedst is withered away.

Is it not also as if from the mouth of St Peter that St Mark alone gives the names of the four apostles who inquire of our Lord about the time when the temple was to be destroyed?

MATTH. xxiv. 3.	MARK xiii. 3.	LUKE xxi. 7.
And as he sat upon the mount of Olives, *the disciples* came unto him privately, saying, Tell us, when shall these things be?	And as he sat upon the mount of Olives, *over against* the temple, Peter, *and* James, *and* John, *and* Andrew, asked him privately, Tell us, when shall these things be?	*Some* asked, saying, Master, but when shall these things be?

Least of all, assuredly, can we fail to recognise St Peter's instructions and influence in the account of that Apostle's denying our Lord, which in St Mark alone is related with that strikingly significant circumstance, that the cock *crew twice* before the Apostle's conscience awoke to repentance,[1] and (not without an allusion to that dreadful moment) the expression of the angel's at the time of the resurrection, which again we find only in St Mark: AND TO PETER!

[1] Matth. xxvi. 34, 75; Luke xxii. 34, 61; John xiii. 33, xviii. 27, compared with Mark xiv. 30, and 63, 72.

MATTH. xxviii. 7.	MARK xvi. 7.
And go quickly, and tell *his disciples* that he is risen from the dead; and behold he goeth before you into Galilee.	But go your way, tell *his disciples* AND PETER that he goeth before you into Galilee.

Thus, then, the Gospel of St Mark is intimately associated with the Apostle St Peter, with respect to whom we find in it the most touching particulars that could affect his heart, so that one might suppose that he himself had written it; those only being excepted which might have seemed to raise St Peter too much above the rest. Thus, for example, St Mark does not record that St Peter, on hearing our Lord's voice, walked out upon the sea in the memorable night so circumstantially described by St Matthew.[1] It was because his doing so, although the faith and courage that led him to it were soon after alloyed with unbelief, marked him out personally too much from among his fellow-apostles.

Yet the author of our second Gospel must have been intimately associated not only with St Peter, but quite as particularly with St Paul, were it true, as is now generally understood, though without much inquiry or sufficient attention to the consequences of such an hypothesis, that our St Mark, *St Peter's son in the faith,* was the same person as the John surnamed Mark whom we meet with again and again in the Acts of the Apostles, and in St Paul's Epistles.[2] We hope, by means of a special inquiry into the authorship of this Gospel, to shew anon how directly opposed are the character and style which it exhibits, to all that is told us of *John Mark* in the Acts of the Apostles. Meanwhile we think it enough to remark as follows: *first,* how extremely improbable it is

[1] Matth. xiv. 28, 31, and Mark vi. 48, 51.

[2] Acts xii. 12, xiii. 5, 13, xv. 37, 39; Col. iv. 10; 2 Tim. iv. 11; Phil. ii. 4.

that one and the same Mark should be found either simultaneously, or (which is hardly possible) alternatively, holding the same relations with both the Apostles Peter and Paul, men so distinct and so remote from each other in their apostolical calling and operations ; *secondly*, that similarity of name does not in the slightest degree prove identity of person. Let us recollect, for example, the list of the Apostles, which, in a catalogue of twelve persons, presents no fewer than thrice, two persons bearing the same name—(two *Simons*, two *Jameses*, and two *Judases*) ; whilst, in the third place, antiquity, which ascribes our Gospel to St Mark *the son of Peter*, does not give us any reason to suppose that it ever considered him as the same Mark whom St Paul much rather distinguishes than identifies with our Evangelist, by qualifying his name with the addition, *sister's son to Barnabas.*—(Col. iv. 10).

But setting aside this question for the present, we now proceed to occupy ourselves exclusively with the examination of the particular character which is presented to us by the Gospel second in rank among the four, and by which it differs from its two fellow synoptical Gospels in a far more important and peculiar manner than has long, we suspect, been imagined. In order to have a first general idea of this essential difference, we shall again avail ourselves of the simple method of comparison among some parallel narratives, as they appear in St Mark, and the first and third Evangelist. Let us read for this purpose, and in this manner, the narrative of the transfiguration on the mount, as found in the three first Gospels, *preceded by* that of the apostolical confession respecting the Messiahship of Jesus, and *followed by* the account of the healing of the lunatic child.

MATTH. xvi. 13.	MARK viii. 27.	LUKE ix. 18.
When Jesus came into the *coasts* of Cæsarea Philippi, he asked his disciples, saying, Whom do men say that I *the Son of man* am? 14. And they said, Some say that thou art John the Baptist; some, Elias; and others, Jeremias, or one of the prophets. 15. He saith unto them, But whom say ye that I am? 16. And Simon Peter answered and said, Thou art the Christ, *the Son of the living God.* 17. And Jesus answered and said unto him, Blessed art thou, Simon Barjona; for flesh and blood hath not revealed it unto thee, but my Father which is in heaven. 18. And I say also unto thee that thou art PETRUS, and upon this petra I will build my Church; and the gates of hell shall not prevail against it. 19. And I will give unto thee the keys of the kingdom of heaven; and whatsoever thou shalt bind on earth shall be bound in heaven: and whatsoever thou shalt loose on earth shall be loosed in heaven.	And Jesus went out, and his disciples, into the *towns* of Cæsarea Philippi: and *by the way* he asked his disciples, saying unto to them, Whom do men say that I am? 28. And they answered, John the Baptist; but some say Elias; and others, one of the prophets. 29. And he saith unto them, But whom say ye that I am? And Peter answereth and saith unto him, Thou art the Christ.	And it came to pass, as he was alone *praying*, his disciples were with him: and he asked them, saying, Whom say the people that I am? 19. They answering said, John the Baptist; but some say Elias; and others say that one of the old prophets is risen again 20. He said unto them, But whom say ye that I am? Peter answering said, the Christ of God.
20. Then charged he his disciples that they should tell no man that he was Jesus the Christ	30. And he charged them *sharply*, that they should tell no man of him.	21. And he *straitly* charged them, and commanded them to tell no man that thing.

21. From that time forth began Jesus *to shew* unto his disciples, *how that he must go into Jerusalem* and suffer many things of the elders and chief priests and scribes, and be killed and be raised again the third day.

22. Then Peter took him, and began to rebuke him, *saying*, *Be it far from thee, Lord: this shall not be unto thee.* 23. But he turned and said unto Peter, Get thee behind me, Satan, *thou art an offence unto me;* for thou savourest not the things that be of God, but those that be of men.

24. Then said Jesus unto his disciples, If any man will come after me, let him deny himself, and take up his cross, and follow me.

25. For whosoever will save his life, shall lose it: and whosoever will lose his life for my sake, shall find it. 26. For what is a man profited, if he shall gain the whole world, and lose his own soul? or what shall a man give in exchange for his soul? 27. For the Son of man shall come in the glory of his Father with his angels,

31. And he began to teach them that the Son of man must suffer many things, and *be rejected* of the elders, and of the chief priests and scribes, and be killed, and after three days rise again.

32. And he spake that saying *openly.* And Peter took him, and began to rebuke him. 33. But when he had turned about, and looked *on his disciples*, *he rebuked* PETER, saying, Get thee behind me, Satan: for thou savourest not the things that be of God, but the things that be of men.

34. And *when he had called the people unto him with his disciples* also, he said unto them, Whosoever will come after me, let him deny himself, and take up his cross, and follow me.

35. For whosoever will save his life shall lose it; but whosoever shall lose his life for my sake *and the gospel's*, the same shall save it. 36. For what shall it profit a man, if he shall gain the whole world, and lose his own soul? 37. Or what shall a man give in exchange for his soul? 38. *Whosoever therefore shall be*

22. *Saying*, The Son of man must suffer many things and *be rejected* of the elders, and chief priests and scribes, and be slain and be raised the third day.

23. And he said to them *all*, If any man will come after me, let him deny himself, and take up his cross *daily*, and follow me. 24. For whosoever will save his life shall lose it: but whosoever will lose his life for my sake, the same shall save it. 25. For what is a man advantaged, if he gain the whole world, and lose himself, or be cast away? 26. For *whosoever shall be ashamed of me and of my words*, *of him shall the Son of man be ashamed*, when he shall come in his own glory, and in his Father's, and of the holy angels.

and then he shall reward every man according to his works.	*ashamed of me and of my words in this* ADULTEROUS AND SINFUL GENERATION; *of him also shall the Son of man be ashamed*, when he cometh in the glory of his Father with the holy angels.

What in this comparative view of the three narratives particularly distinguishes St Mark, seems at first sight of little importance. Here it is a single word, there a short parenthesis; sometimes a slight circumstance, or even no more than a simple accentuation, giving increased emphasis to what is said. But these diversities or additions, on being examined more narrowly, impart a striking air of life to what he says; they are of special importance or interest in their bearing on the locality or on the fact brought before us, in its most touching details; and they often strike home to the heart and the conscience.

Certainly we have a diversity of little importance in itself where St Mark (v. 27) speaks of the *towns* of Cesarea Philippi, while St Matthew has employed the more general term *coasts*. But does not this mention of *towns* at once give a more lively colour to the narrative, by placing us instantly in the midst of the busy throng? And just so also when St Mark (at the same verse) adds these words, *by the way*—does not that simple addition transport us with all the more life into the midst of all that was seen and done on that occasion?

He abridges, on the other hand, not less characteristically, where St Matthew, from his Israelitic point of view, mentions Jeremiah by name among the prophets (v. 14), because that prophet was very particularly esteemed among the Jews in the time of the Apostles. St Mark (ver. 28), with a different aim, and writing more specially for the Christians among the Gentiles, contents himself with naming Elias and the prophets in general. In this he is followed by St Luke (ver. 19). In like manner, St Mark first, and then St Luke, abridge the words of St Peter's confession as we read them in St Matthew, who gives them with greater fulness, owing to the position he held as prophetical apostle and colleague of St Peter. The whole of our Lord's address to St Peter (in St Matthew 17, 19), is not repeated in St Mark, for reasons already given. For our Lord's command (Matth. ver. 20) St Mark employs a particularly strong expression : *he straitly charged them;* in which, also, he is imitated by St Luke. In foretelling our Lord's passion, St Matthew gives most prominence to the place where Jesus was to suffer, *Jerusalem;* St Mark here, too, followed by St Luke, gives prominence to the reprobation that would signalize that passion. The rebuke addressed to St Peter is distinguished anew in St Mark by a striking feature (ver. 33): JESUS TURNED ABOUT AND LOOKED ON ALL HIS DISCIPLES when *he rebuked Peter.* The apostle that had been set before them all as an example in his confession and in his zeal, was to be all the more confounded when he allowed his precipitation or human feelings to carry him too far. Here we discover anew the close connexion subsisting between this Gospel and the Disciple whom such traits concern.

Then, where St Matthew speaks of the disciples (ver. 24), St Mark (ver. 34) adds *the people,* when those words were uttered: *If any one will come after me, let him deny himself.* St Luke (ver. 23) here inserts *all.* The word *Gospel* is not so familiar a term with any of the Evangelists as with St

Mark.[1] He uses it here, also (ver. 35), in immediate connexion with our Lord's person, *for my sake and* THE GOSPEL'S. Finally, he connects, in an impressive manner, the confessing of the Son of man at this present time with the glory of his coming.[2] St Luke (ver. 26) adopts from St Mark this supplement to St Matthew's words; but the forcible and solemn expression, *in this adulterous and sinful generation*, is found only in St Mark's Gospel.

We now continue the narrative of the synoptical Evangelists, where we find each describe in his own several style *the transfiguration on the Mount.*

MATTH. xvi. 28.

Verily I say unto you, There be some standing here, which shall not taste of death, *till they see the Son of man coming in his kingdom.* xvii. 1. And after six days Jesus taketh Peter, James, and John his brother, and bringeth them up into an high mountain apart. 2. And was transfigured before them: and *his face did shine as the sun, and his raiment was white as the light.* 3. And, behold, there appeared unto them MOSES *and* ELIAS talking with them. 4. Then answered Peter, and said unto Jesus, Lord, it is good for us to be here: if thou wilt, let us make here three tabernacles; one for thee, and one for

MARK ix. 1.

And he said unto them, Verily I say unto you, That there be some of them that stand here, which shall not taste of death, *till they have seen the kingdom of God come with power.* 2. And after six days Jesus taketh with him Peter, and James, and John, and leadeth them up into an high mountain *apart by themselves;* and he was transfigured before them. 3. *And his raiment became shining, exceeding white as snow; so as no fuller on earth can white them.* 4. And there appeared unto them ELIAS *with* MOSES: and they were talking with Jesus. 5. And Peter answered and said to Jesus, *Rabbi*, it is good for us to be here: and let

LUKE ix. 27.

But I tell you of a truth, there be some standing here which shall not taste of death, *till they see the kingdom of God.* 28. And it came to pass about an eight days after these sayings, he took Peter, and John, and James, and went up into a mountain *to pray.* 29. And as *he prayed*, the fashion *of his countenance was altered, and his raiment was white and glistering.* 30. And, behold, there talked with him two men, which were MOSES and ELIAS: 31. *Who appeared in glory, and spake of his decease which he should accomplish at Jerusalem.* 32. *But* PETER *and they that were with him were heavy with sleep;*

[1] i. 1, 14, 15, viii. 35, x. 29, xiii. 10, xvi. 15.

[2] Compare Romans ix. 9, 10.

Moses, and one for Elias.

us make three tabernacles; one for thee, and one for Moses, and one for Elias. 6. For he wist not what to say; for they *were sore afraid.*

and when they were awake they saw his glory, and the two men that stood with him. 33. *And it came to pass, as they departed from him,* Peter said unto Jesus, *Master,* it is good for us to be here: and let us make three tabernacles; one for thee, and one for Moses, and one for Elias: not knowing what he said.

5. While he yet spake, behold, a bright cloud overshadowed them: and behold a voice out of the cloud, which said, This is my beloved Son, *in whom I am well pleased;* hear ye him. 6. And when the disciples heard it, they *fell on their face, and were sore afraid.* 7. And Jesus came and touched them, and said, Arise, and be not afraid. 8. And when they had lifted up their eyes, they saw no man, save Jesus only. 9. And as they came down from the mountain, Jesus charged them, saying, Tell the vision to no man, until the Son of man be risen again from the dead.

7. And there was a cloud that overshadowed them: and a voice came out of the cloud, saying, This is my beloved Son: hear him. 8. And *suddenly when they had looked round about,* they saw no man any more, save Jesus only with themselves. 9. And as they came down from the mountain, he charged them that they should tell no man what things they had seen, till the Son of man were risen from the dead. 10. *And they kept that saying with themselves, questioning one with another what the rising from the dead should mean.*

34. While he thus spake, there came a cloud and overshadowed them: and they feared as they entered into the cloud. 35. And there came a voice out of the cloud, saying, This is my beloved Son: hear him. 36. And when the voice was past, Jesus was found alone. *And they kept it close, and told no man in those days any of those things which they had seen.*

10. And his disciples asked him, saying, Why then say the scribes that Elias must first come? 11. And Jesus answered and said unto them, Elias

11. And they asked him, saying, Why say the scribes that Elias must first come? 12. And he answered and told them, Elias verily cometh first, and

truly shall first come,
and *restore all things.*
12. But I say unto
you, That ELIAS is
come already, and they
knew him not, but
have done unto him
whatsoever they listed.
Likewise shall also the
Son of man *suffer* of
them. 13. *Then the*
disciples understood
that he spake unto them
of John the Baptist.

restoreth all things;
and how it is written
of the Son of man, that
he must *suffer* many
things, *and be set at*
nought. 13. But I say
unto you, That ELIAS
is indeed come, and
they have done unto
him whatsoever they
listed, as it is written
of him.

By merely running over this threefold narrative, we see clearly enough how each of our Evangelists relates what happened in accordance with the several points of view which we have repeatedly ascribed to them. St Matthew supplies the groundwork; St Mark and St Luke repeat so far the most necessary parts of their predecessors, so far assume these as known, and then complete them by adding details, in which their several characters unequivocally come out. For example, St Luke indicates that important particular—that the transfiguration of Jesus took place while *he prayed.* But let us confine ourselves to what is special in St Mark. Here, too, it is not so much new facts that we find, as quite a peculiar way of representing things already known. Slight insertions, and differences at first sight almost imperceptible, erelong impart, on a careful comparison, quite a different colouring from that of St Matthew. Thus (ver. 2), he adds the expression *by themselves,* which gives clearness and force to the meaning. St Matthew presents to us the transfiguration in a brilliant and poetical manner, comparing it with the *sun* and the *light* (ver. 2). St Mark, by an expression less elevated indeed, but all the more racy from its very simplicity, as taken from the language of ordinary life : *His raiment became shining, exceeding white as* snow, *so as no fuller on earth can white them* (ver. 3). St Matthew, in St Peter's address to Jesus, makes him say *Lord!* St Mark (ver. 5) has the more characteristic and correct word, *Rabbi,* translated by St Luke (ver. 33) by that of *Master.* In St Mark, the artless statement of the ignorance of the disciples is evidently taken as if from the mouth itself of an eye-witness—that is, no doubt, of St Peter *And they kept that saying with themselves, questioning one with another what the rising of the dead should mean.*—Finally, when he mentions our Lord's predicted and impending sufferings, he again expressly speaks of his being *set at naught* (ver. 12).

What immediately follows the account of our Lord's transfiguration, as given by the three synoptical Evangelists, brings out their several characteristics, that of St Mark especially, into still stronger relief.

MATTH. xvii. 14.

And when they were come to the multitude, there came to him a certain man *kneeling down to him, and saying,* 15. Lord, have mercy on my son ; for he is lunatick, and sore vexed : for ofttimes he falleth into the fire, and oft into the water. 16. And I brought him to thy disciples, and they could not cure him. 17. Then Jesus answered and said, O faithless and perverse generation, how long shall I be with you? how long

MARK ix. 14.

And when he came to his disciples, he saw *a great multitude about them, and the scribes questioning with them.* 15. *And straightway all the people, when they beheld him, were greatly amazed, and, running to him, saluted him.* 16. *And he asked the scribes, What question ye with them?* 17. *And one of the multitude* answered and said, Master, I have brought *unto thee* my son, which hath a *dumb spirit;* 18. And wheresoever he taketh

LUKE ix. 37.

And it came to pass *that on the next day,* when they were come down from the hill, *much people met him.* 38. And, *behold, a man of the company* cried out, saying, Master, I beseech thee, look upon my son : for he is *mine only child.* 39. And, lo, a spirit taketh him, and he suddenly crieth out ; and it *teareth him, that he foameth again : and, bruising him, hardly departeth from him.* 40. And I besought thy disciples

shall I suffer you?
bring him hither to me.

him, *he teareth him:*
and he foameth and
gnasheth with his teeth,
and pineth away: and
I spake to thy disciples
that they should cast
him out; and they
could not. 19. He
answereth them, and
saith, O faithless gene-
ration, how long shall
I be with you? how
long shall I suffer you?
Bring him unto me.

to cast him out; and
they could not. 41.
And JESUS answering,
said, O faithless and
perverse generation,
how long shall I be
with you, and suffer
you? Bring thy son
hither.

18. And Jesus re-
buked the devil, and
he departed out of him;
and the child was cured
from that very hour.

20. And they brought
him unto him: and
when he saw him,
straightway the spirit
tare him; and he fell
on the ground, and
wallowed, foaming.
21. *And he asked his*
father, How long is it
ago since this came unto
him? And he said,
Of a child. 22. And
ofttimes it hath cast
him into the fire, and
into the waters, *to de-*
stroy him: but if thou
canst do any thing,
have compassion on
us, and help us. 23.
Jesus said unto him,
If thou canst believe,
all things are possible
to him that believeth.
24. *And straightway*
the father of the child
cried out, and said
with tears, Lord, I be-
lieve, help thou mine
unbelief. 25. *When*
Jesus saw that the
people came running
together, he rebuked
the foul spirit, saying
unto him, Thou dumb

42. And as he
was yet a coming, the
devil threw him down,
and tare him. And
JESUS rebuked the un-
clean spirit, and healed
the child, and delivered
him again to his father.

and deaf spirit, I
charge thee, come out of
him, and enter no more
into him. 26. *And*
the spirit cried, and
rent him sore, and
came out of him: and
he was as one dead;
insomuch that many
said, He is dead. But
Jesus took him by the
hand, and lifted him
up; and he arose.

19. Then came the
disciples to Jesus apart,
and said, Why could
not we cast him out?
20. And Jesus *said*
unto them, Because of
your unbelief: for
verily I say unto you,
If ye have faith as a
grain of mustard seed,
ye shall say unto this
mountain, Remove
hence to yonder place,
and it shall remove;
and nothing shall be
impossible unto you.
21. Howbeit this kind
goeth not out but by
prayer and fasting.

28. And when he
was come into the
house, his disciples
asked him privately,
Why could not we cast
him out? 29. And
he said unto them, This
kind can come forth by
nothing but by prayer
and fasting.

43. *And they were*
all amazed at the mighty
power of God.

Here surely, if any where, the special character of St Mark's Gospel, even on a very superficial comparison with the other two, discovers itself in his talent for minute and scenic description, and in the introduction of many details which St Matthew, in accordance with the nature of his general design, omits mentioning. Thus St Mark alone, or at least first, records the contestation between the scribes and the disciples who could not cure the lunatic (ver. 14), and, in the midst of the strife thus caused among the people, *the arrival of* Jesus, to whom they run, and whom they salute, that is, welcome (ver. 15) as the well-known and mighty Deliverer; the question put by Jesus to the scribes (ver. 16), followed by the answer *of that one man of the multitude* who was chiefly interested, namely the father of the child that was possessed (ver. 17); the full, precise, and graphic description of the malady and its symptoms, both from his father's mouth (ver. 18), and by the narrator himself on the child being brought to Jesus (ver. 20). Some of these details, it is true, have been adopted by St Luke, yet with a constant adherence to his own manner, and so that the two Gospels can nowise be confounded, the moment we compare the characteristic features that distinguish them. The description, in particular, of the attacks suffered by the possessed child (ver. 18–20), is presented by our second Evangelist with a choice and force of expression that give us an insight not only into the style, but into the whole tone and bent of his mind and spirit. So vigorous a conception of the incidents he describes, gives evidence of a powerful soul, of a descriptive talent, remarkable at once for its justness and freshness, and of a mind thoroughly penetrated with every trait in an object that intensely interests it. Mark how rich in appropriate and expressive terms is the passage before us! The foul spirit *tears* (ῥήσσει) the possessed person, who thereupon *foams* (ἀφρίζει), and *gnasheth with his teeth* (τρίζει τοὺς ὀδόντας), and *pineth away* (ξηραίνεται); anon the spirit *teareth him* (σπαράσσει), and the possessed person *falls on the ground, and wallows, foaming* (κυλίεται ἀφρίζων); he afterwards reiterates this tearing of the child (ver. 26), *the spirit cried, and rent him sore* (κράξαν και σπαράξαν), *and came out of him.* St Matthew, as we have remarked, has nothing of all this, and St Luke adopts several of its traits, yet evidently in a manner suited to the peculiarly historical cast of his Gospel, and with such a modification of St Mark's fulness of expressions, as leaves the latter exclusive master of the pictorial and the scenic in describing what took place. We would further remark, that St Luke, *the physician*, speaks more of the *internal* effects of the foul spirit on the constitution of his victim (ver. 39): *bruising him* (or rather, *inwardly oppressing, excruciating him*, *συντρίβον*), *he hardly departeth from him;* while St Mark represents the phenomena purely from his *outward* and visible point of view. Then our Evangelist is absolutely the only one that reports the conversation of Jesus with the father of the possessed person—a conversation full of the most striking and instructive details; first, those touching words—*but if thou canst do any thing* (ver. 22), and the serious yet encouraging answer made by Jesus, IF THOU CANST *believe, all things are possible to him that believeth;*—then the father's exclamation (ver. 24), *And straightway the father of the child cried out, and said with tears, Lord, I believe, help thou mine unbelief!* Finally (ver. 25–27), we have the expulsion by the powerful word of Jesus; but with this interesting particular, that our Lord, when he saw *the people come running together*, now, as was his wont, avoiding all useless display, hastened to perform the cure. Last of all, the description that then follows, places in still stronger relief what gave so much impressiveness to the whole affair—the violence of the foul spirit on the one hand, and the power of the Saviour on the other: *the child became as dead, so that many said, He is dead. But Jesus took him up, and lifted him by the hand; and he arose.* The question put by the disciples, why *they* could not cast out the unclean spirit, had been already recorded by St Matthew. To that St Mark simply but significantly adds (ver. 28), that the question was put *after Jesus had come into the house.* In our Lord's answer, St Matthew (ver. 20) introduces a sentence which ought historically to be placed elsewhere. St Mark, accordingly, leaves it out here, and retains (ver. 29) those words only which St Matthew has likewise placed at the close (ver. 20). St Luke, in what we shall erelong see to be his peculiar manner, concludes his narrative at an earlier stage with *the glorification of God* (ver. 43).

Thus far, then, have we been able to obtain a general idea of the distinctive character of St Mark's Gospel. Let us now proceed to take a closer view of it, and mark what are the grand special peculiarities that characterise it, with the view of deducing from these some important consequences bearing immediately on the object of this work.

St Mark's Gospel, compared first of all with St Matthew's, is distinguished at once, on the one hand, by a very manifest curtailment; and on the other, still more remarkably, by a greater fulness in the development of what he retains. In this latter respect, much more than in the former, our Evangelist is followed by St Luke, who, generally speaking, augments St Matthew's narrations with not a few additions of various sorts.

Let us see, first, in what the *curtailments* observed in St Mark mainly consist. Many sayings, sentences, quotations, chiefly from the prophets, narrations, whole chapters, occur either in St Matthew, or in St Luke and St Matthew together, which are nowhere to be found in St Mark. Thus, for example, we find nothing in St Mark relating to our Lord's conception, birth, or infancy, the annunciation and the birth of St John the Baptist, the genealogy of Jesus Christ; in a word, of the two first chapters both of St Matthew and St Luke. Instead of entering at all into these details, St Mark commences his narrative briefly but energetically as follows: *The beginning of the Gospel of* JESUS CHRIST, *the Son of God; as it is written in the prophets, Behold, I send my messenger before thy face, which shall prepare thy way before thee. John did baptize in the wilderness*, &c. No more do we find in St Mark *the sermon on the mount* either in the full and rich form in which it appears in St Matthew, or in the more concise but historical form of St Luke. The similitudes too, although a special importance is attached by our Evangelist (iv. 33) to that mode of instruction as employed by Jesus, are given but in a small number. Of all the parables that are recorded by the other Evangelists, he gives only that of *the seed that fell into four different kinds of soil;*[1] *that of the grain of mustard seed;*[2] and, afterwards, *that of the vineyard and the husbandmen.*[3] Then, whereas St Luke as well as St Matthew have each, separately, many parables not preserved by any other Evangelist, St Mark has but one parable that does not occur elsewhere. We shall erelong return to that similitude, and to the Gospel similitudes in general. But to quote, further, a single evident example of our Evangelist's omissions, we do not find in his Gospel the twice uttered *Woe* pronounced against the scribes and Pharisees,[4] nor that against Chorazin, Capernaum, and Bethsaida,[5] nor that against Jerusalem.[6] We shall see erelong to what principle we must refer those omissions.

[1] Matth. xiii. 3–8; Luke viii. 5–8; Mark iv. 3–8.
[2] Matth. xiii. 31, 32; Luke xiii. 18, 19; Mark iv. 30–32.
[3] Matth. xxi. 33–42; Luke xx. 9–19; Mark xii. 1–11.
[4] Matth. xxiii. 14–35; Luke xi. 39-52.
[5] Matth. xi. 20–24; Luke x. 13–15.
[6] Matth. xxiii. 37–39; Luke xiii. 34, 35; xix. 41–44.

For these suppressions and curtailments we have an ample compensation in St Mark's abundant augmentations and amplifications, which are discoverable only on a careful comparison of the texts of the first two Gospels. These augmentations rarely consist of narratives altogether new; and, where they are new, they are very rarely preserved by him alone. Compared with his predecessor, he presents only the five following narratives, not previously put on record by St Matthew: 1. The cure of the possessed person in the synagogue at Capernaum.[1] 2. That of the deaf person in the coasts of Decapolis, who had an impediment in his speech.[2] 3. That of the blind at Bethsaida.[3] 4. The casting out of devils by those who were not among the immediate followers of Jesus.[4] 5. The widow's mite.[5]

Of these five narratives, only the second and the third, as appears from the passages quoted, are to be found in St Mark alone; the three remaining relate facts which have been adopted by St Luke also. But see how, in the accounts they present, however analogous, each preserves his own peculiar colouring; for instance, in the details *of the widow's mite.*

Mark xii. 41.	Luke xxi. 1.
"And Jesus *sat over against the treasury*, and beheld how *the people* cast money into the treasury: and many *that were rich* cast in *much.* 42. And there came a certain poor widow, and she threw in two mites, *which make a farthing.* 43. *And he called unto him his disciples*, and saith unto them, Verily I say unto you, That this poor widow hath cast more in, *than all they which have cast into*	"And he looked up, and saw *the rich* men casting their gifts into the treasury. 2. And he saw also a certain poor widow casting in thither two mites. 3. And he said, Of a truth I say unto you, that this poor widow hath cast in more than they all: 4. For all these have of their abundance cast in unto *the offerings of God*: but she of her penury hath cast in all the living that she had."

[1] Mark i. 23–28; Luke iv. 33–37.
[2] Mark vii. 31–37.
[3] Mark viii. 22–26.
[4] Mark ix. 38–41.
[5] Mark xii. 41–44.

the treasury: 44. For all they did cast in of their abundance; but she of her want did cast in all that she had, even all her living."

Here again St Mark gives a specimen of his characteristic fulness, force, and pictorial effect. We see Jesus *seated over against the treasury;* next we have, represented to the life, the Saviour's calling his disciples to him, to communicate what he alone had observed, and to deduce a lesson from it. As characteristic of St Mark, we find spoken of separately, first the people, and then the rich in particular; next, a short explanatory intercalation—*two mites,* WHICH MAKE A FARTHING; finally, the frequent recurrence of the leading words—*cast in.* St Luke, as an historian, has recorded the matter more concisely, rather avoiding any thing like scenic effect; but *his* narrative compensates for this by the touching expression, applied from the nature of its contents to the treasury: *the offerings of God.*

In the similitude which we had above in our eye, as to be found in St Mark alone, the same traits again occur. It is that of the kingdom of God compared to the slow, but sure and regular development of the seed when it is sown. In that concise and every way striking parable, the peculiar character and object of our second Gospel are fully brought out. We find it immediately after that other, common to all three Evangelists, of the seed sown in various kinds of ground, and to which in St Matthew (xiii. 1–23, 24–30) there is annexed the parable of the tares which the enemy sowed among the wheat; but in St Mark, who omits this last, we read the following (iv. 26): *And he said, So is the kingdom of God, as if a man should cast seed into the ground;* 27. *And should sleep, and rise night and day, and the seed should spring and grow up, he knoweth not how.* 28. *For the earth bringeth forth fruit of herself* (ἀυτομάτη); *first the blade, then the ear, after that the full corn in the ear.* 29. *But when the fruit is brought forth, immediately he putteth in the sickle, because the harvest is come.*

Here all is characteristic. In the first place, the meaning—the object of the parable; the kingdom of God viewed in its imperceptible but continual increase; in its peaceable, regular, free, powerful, surprising progress.

But how striking and pleasing are the details! The sower, as soon as his work is performed, leaves it to itself, and while he continues his ordinary course of life; meanwhile he beholds the seed shooting up, *he knows not how*;—that earth, which bringeth forth fruit *of herself*—that is, without any human, but in virtue of a divinely implanted energy (such also is the vital force of the Gospel message which from its very nature cannot remain inert);—after that, the fruit itself in its gradual and sure development; first, the *blade*; then, the *ear*; then, *the full grain* in the ear;—finally, and with St Mark's favourite word, immediately (ἐυθεως), when the fruit is fully ripe, the *sickle*, which is put in at the time of *harvest*, that is, the kingdom of God in its completion of judgment and of glory (comp. Rev. xiv. 14–20).

But, as we have said, what particularly distinguishes St Mark when compared with St Matthew, is not so much the addition of those few altogether *new* passages—it is much rather that striking exuberance of details, by means of which he expands and elucidates the narratives and memorials of his predecessor, even in their most minute and subtlest traits, and brings out their bearings with quite a new power of colouring, precision, and impressiveness. All this we see exhibited in the account of the raising again to life of the daughter of Jairus, that of the healing of the lunatic child, and of so many which we have already adduced as examples. In a word, every narrative of our second Evangelist, compared with the parallel passages, first in St Matthew and then in St Luke, superabundantly establishes the following principle: That if any one desire to know an Evangelical fact, not only in its main features and grand results, but also in its most minute, and, so to speak, its most graphic delineation, he must betake himself to St Mark.

This quite peculiar delineation, however, of facts already known, this fresh and most interesting elaboration of materials for the most part already existing in St Matthew, is not confined to that ample addition of entire sentences which we find in some of the examples quoted. St Mark presents to us an event, a parable, a circumstance, with the precision, the animation, and the scenic effect that are peculiar to him, often by the intercalation of some few words; sometimes by a *single* word intercalated, strengthened, or repeated; sometimes by the mere transposition of words in the very phrase employed already by St Matthew. Here we may illustrate the subject by some examples.

Among the first of these we may rank St Mark's usual practice of giving the *names* and *surnames*, and mentioning the *relations* and other specialties attached to persons whom St Matthew mentions more generally. For instance, St Mark alone gives the name of the blind man restored to sight by our Lord near Jericho (x. 46): *Bartimeus, the son of Timeus.*—Thus (ii. 26) he gives the name of the high priest to whom David addressed himself when he received the shew-bread as food, in the time *of Abiathar the high priest.*—Thus we find recorded in our

St Mark, for the first time, the Jewish name of the publican-apostle and that of his father (ii. 14) *Levi, the son of Alpheus.*—Thus also, but for St Mark we should not have known the very significant surname of the sons of Zebedee (iii. 17), *and he surnamed them* BOANERGES, *which is, The sons of thunder.*[1]—Thus St Mark alone informs us that Simon of Cyrene, who bore the cross after Jesus, *was the father of* ALEXANDER *and of* RUFUS (xv. 21), well-known persons in the circle of the Roman Christians, for whom St Mark wrote in the first instance, as, with respect to Rufus at least, seems evident from one of the greetings addressed by St Paul to the Romans (Rom. xvi. 13).

Still more important are the very slight additions thrown in by St Mark, in which he has preserved for us some of the identical words uttered by Jesus in the Aramæan tongue, employed by our Lord. Thus, in the account of the young woman's restoration to life, in St Mark alone we find the words (v. 41) TALITHA CUMI, *which is, being interpreted, Damsel, I say unto thee, arise:* while St Matthew mentions the bare fact of her being raised again, and St Luke adds only the words in Greek. On another occasion he likewise gives the proper Aramæan word used by Jesus, when he healed a blind person in the coasts of Decapolis (vii. 34): *Ephphatha, that is to say, Be opened.* Thus, in Gethsemané (xiv. 36), he puts the Syriac *Abba!* first, where the other Evangelists give simply, Father: *Abba, Father, all things are possible unto thee.* St Mark has further inserted, though in ordinary language, a most important word of command in the account of the storm at sea. St Matthew and St Luke merely relate how Jesus, with a word, *rebuked the winds*

[1] It is remarkable how our Evangelist does not directly reckon St Peter in the list of the Twelve, but simply says of him that Jesus surnamed him Peter.

and the waves; St Mark (iv. 39) gives the two brief words of command themselves: *Peace, be still!*

The details, however, which St Mark has contrived to throw in by means of such parentheses or short amplifications, whether it be to elucidate words or things, or to make them stand out more forcibly to the mind and eye, or to make them more deeply and widely felt, are too various and too numerous to admit of our presenting them here under any special rubrics. We have only to glance here and there over the book of our interesting Evangelist, and we shall readily perceive them, together with the remarkable instructions they involve.

I. 13. The account of our Saviour's temptation in the desert is given very briefly in St Mark. Yet even here there is a distinctive trait, and that, too, strikingly significant: *and Jesus was with the wild beasts.* We feel at once the impression this slight addition must produce. Does it not recall to our minds the first man in Paradise, who, by his disobedience, lost his dominion over the animal tribes,—and, contrasted with that, the second Adam (a greater than Daniel!) among the wild beasts of the wilderness, reconquering that dominion by obedience and the Word of God? Here let us think too of Isaiah xi.

I. 20. Jesus, when walking by the sea of Galilee, called fishers to the apostleship; first Simon and Andrew, immediately after that, James and John, the sons of Zebedee. These also leave their nets at the call of Jesus; and the two last mentioned leave their father likewise. This both St Mark and St Matthew intimate, but St Mark makes a short further addition—they left their father Zebedee in the ship *with the hired servants.* These four little words involve two particulars, or, say rather, elucidations. First, they prove that the father of the two who were called, was not left alone by his sons at his advanced age; in the second place, they throw some light on the social position of the apostles. They had hired servants in their employment, and belonged to what is called the middle class in society.

III. 5. The adversaries watch Jesus to see if he will heal the man with the withered hand on the Sabbath-day. Jesus bids him stand forth, and asks him if it be lawful to do good on the Sabbath-day, or to do evil? Whereupon he heals the man's hand, according to St Luke and St Mark, *after that he had looked round about upon them*—but our second Evangelist delineates with greater depth and fulness the outward expression and inward feelings of Jesus: *And* WHEN HE HAD LOOKED ROUND UPON THEM WITH ANGER, *being* GRIEVED *for the hardness of their hearts.* Here we have what St John calls, *the wrath of the Lamb* (Rev. vi. 16).

III. 20. The unremitting activity of our Lord himself, and of his apostles, is intimated to us in the following manner, immediately after the giving of their names, by St Mark, and by him alone, *so that they could not so much as eat bread.* And still later (vi. 31), *they had no leisure so much as to eat.* And in the same verse Jesus addresses those amiable words, recorded nowhere else, but which transport us so completely into the daily and intimate circle of our Lord and his disciples: *Come ye yourselves apart into a desert place, and rest awhile* (ἀναπαύεσθε ὀλίγον).

VI. 4. We have it recorded (Matth. xiii. 57) that Jesus said: *A prophet is not without honour, save in his own country, and in his own house.* St Mark gives it more fully; but who feels not that in his short extension there is something particularly striking? *A prophet is not without honour but in his own country,* AND AMONG HIS OWN KIN, *and in his own house.*

VI. 47, 48. After the multiplication of the loaves and the fishes, the disciples went into the ship; Jesus remained some time alone to pray. St Matthew (xiv. 24–32) and St Mark record this almost in the same terms. But note how lively and how graphic the detail found only in St Mark: *And he saw them toiling in rowing.*

VI. 52. And when, about the fourth watch of the night, they saw Jesus walking upon the waters towards the ship, and come into it, and the contrary wind cease, the disciples were sore amazed and worshipped; but St Mark connects this amazement with what touches the heart more deeply: *They considered not the miracle of the loaves, for their heart was hardened.*

VII. 1. The expression, *defiled hands,* which was perfectly intelligible among the Jews, St Mark here elucidates with a short parenthesis, *that is to say, with unwashen hands.* In like manner, afterwards (ver. 11), he alone gives the term peculiar to the Jews, but explains it for his Gentile readers: *It is* CORBAN, *that is to say, a gift.*

VII. 27. The Canaanitish woman, when our Lord wished to try her faith, receives the following reply from him: *It is not meet to take the children's bread, and to cast it unto the dogs.* Thus we read in St Matthew (xv. 26), and in St Mark at the verse above cited. But the latter first intercalates another saying of our Lord: *Let the children first* (πρῶτον) *be filled.* Who perceives not what secret encouragement there was in the expression *first* for the woman, who was a Greek by birth? Have we not here in history what St Paul in his Epistle (Rom. i. 16) expresses in these words: *To the Jew* FIRST, *and* ALSO *to the Greek?*

X. 17–30. The discourse with the rich young man, and what follows in immediate connexion with it, are mentioned by the three first Evangelists—in St Mark anew, with some few characteristic intercalations. The touching incident, that Jesus, before pronouncing the decisive words *One thing thou lackest,* looked upon him *and loved him,* without anywise softening the severity of his declaration on account of this natural amiability, is recorded only by our Evangelist. He immediately afterwards adds (ver. 22) to the *follow me,* which we find both in St Matthew and St Luke, the important words, TAKING UP THE CROSS (ἄρας τὸν σταυρὸν). But when, further on, those terrible words of the Saviour are heard: *How hardly shall they that have riches enter into the kingdom of God!*—still it is St Mark alone who follows this up with the astonishment of his disciples, and the Master's *repeated* yet *explanatory* saying: *And the disciples were astonished at his words. But Jesus answereth again, and saith unto them, Children, how hard is it* FOR THEM THAT TRUST IN RICHES *to enter into the kingdom of God!* And when our Lord then goes on to say, that *it is easier for a camel to go through the eye of a needle, than for a rich man to enter into the kingdom of God,* and the disciples thereupon, in still greater astonishment, *say* AMONG THEMSELVES (this too only in St Mark), *Who then can be saved?* it is St Mark anew who records, in the most forcible yet simple manner, that saying so full of comfort to the heart truly in search of salvation, in *repeating* the expression of God's almighty power in man's salvation, *for with God* ALL THINGS ARE

POSSIBLE. When, shortly afterwards, he promises to the disciples, that whatever any one shall have left on earth for his sake he shall have restored to him an hundred-fold, and that he shall receive eternal life in the world to come, our faithful and conscientious companion of St Peter, adds farther what might have been but too easily forgotten, that this recompense, in so far as this life is concerned, shall be coupled *with persecutions* (μετὰ διωγμῶν).

X. 32. Jesus goes up to Jerusalem with his disciples for the last time. To the simple statement of this by St Matthew (xx. 17), St Mark further adds the following picture, both of the feelings of the Apostles, and of the pastoral character of the Master by whom they were led: *And Jesus went before them* (ἦν προάγων ἀυτοὺς): *and they were amazed; and as they followed, they were afraid.* Thereupon he declared to them anew his approaching sufferings, and rising again on the third day.

XII. 29. When Jesus reminded the scribes of the greatest of the commandments, the quotation from Deuteronomy is preceded in St Mark alone by, *Hear, O Israel; the Lord our God is one Lord.* In a Gospel mainly designed for being read among the Gentiles, it was fitting that the doctrine of the unity of the Godhead, that grand foundation of all commandments as well as of all truths, should retain its place of pre-eminence.

XV. 42. We have a *slight* augmentation here, yet involving an elucidation which is found nowhere else in the Gospels: *it was the preparation*, THAT IS, THE DAY BEFORE THE SABBATH (παρασκευὴ, ὅ ἐστι προσάββατον.)

XVI. 3, 4. St Luke and St John, as well as St Mark, speak of the gravestone which the women found already rolled away; but St Mark alone records the question that disquieted the women: *Who shall roll us away the stone?* Immediately after, we have the artless and truth-breathing remark of the narrator; *for it was very great.*

It is not, however, by such parentheses only, be they long or short, that St Mark, in the way we have indicated, has contrived to give quite a fresh colouring, and quite a new interest to his predecessor's narrative; for he often produces the same effect by the intercalation of a single word—often of a simple but very significant participle. Of this take the following examples:—

I. 7. The baptism of St John, the forerunner. He points to the *mightier one* who was to come after him. In St Matthew, he himself confesses *that he is not worthy to bear his shoes;* in St Luke, that *he was not worthy to unloose the latchet of his shoes.* In St Mark we have a single participle more, *not worthy,* STOOPING DOWN (or rather BOWING DOWN, *κύψας*), *to unloose the latchet of his shoes.* One can better feel than describe the feeling of respect and adoration involved in this single added word!

I. 9. Soon after this, Jesus appears among the crowd in order to be baptized by John. *Then cometh Jesus from Galilee,* we read in St Matthew; in St Mark, *Jesus from* NAZARETH *of Galilee.* Our Evangelist would put a double emphasis on the contempt cast in Israel on the place from which our Lord came, and where he had been brought up. He clings to this expression to the very close of his Gospel. In St Matthew, we read simply in the address of the angels to the women in the sepulchre: *Ye seek* JESUS, *who was crucified;* in St Mark, *Ye seek* JESUS OF NAZARETH, *who was crucified* (xvi. 6).

I. 41. A leper comes to our Lord desiring to be healed. In St Matthew and St Luke we read, *Jesus put forth his hand and touched him, saying, I will, be thou clean.* St

Mark adds a *single* word (σπλαγνισθεὶς), MOVED WITH COMPASSION.

IV. 3. Our Lord teaches by parables. He begins with that of the *sower*. But in St Mark he uses the impressive preliminary word, HEARKEN. It is the word of authority. In the whole New Testament we find it used only by Him of whom the Father said, *Hear ye him* (Matt. xvii 5).

VI. 53. After the calming of the contrary wind in the night when Jesus walked on the sea, St Matthew writes (xiv. 34), *And when they were gone over, they came to the land of Gennesaret.* Graphically, and in proper sea phrase, St Mark adds, AND DREW TO THE SHORE (προσωρμίσθησαν).

VII. 21. Impurity lies not in the *food* that enters into the mouth, but in the *heart*, whence proceed evil thoughts and all sins. After St Matthew, St Mark gives some further extension to this saying of our Lord; but still more, he by a single word brings more fully out the force of the antithesis—FROM WITHIN (ἔσωθεν) *the heart of man proceed evil thoughts.* And this expression, *from within*, we find in him alone (ver. 23), by way of antithesis to that of FROM WITHOUT (ἔξωθεν), ver. 15, 18.

X. 13. The disciples rebuke those who bring little children to Jesus. In St Matthew, Jesus says, *Suffer little children to come unto me.* This we find preceded in St Mark by, *he was much displeased* (in the Greek in one word, ἠγανάκτησε).

XII. 36. In quoting the 110th Psalm, we read in St Matthew (xxii. 43), *David* (speaking) *in spirit:* St Mark fixes the force of the term more fully, *David* (*speaking*) *by the Holy Ghost.*

XV. 43. Joseph of Arimathea goes to Pilate to crave the body of Jesus. By the intercalation of a single participle, St Mark here gives quite a new colour to the deed of this noble Pharisee: HAVING EMBOLDENED HIMSELF (τολμήσας), we read in our Evangelist, *Joseph went to Pilate to crave the body of Jesus.* This simple word discovers to us one of the first and most striking effects of our Saviour's death. Joseph of Arimathea, until that time a secret disciple of Jesus, acquires sufficient boldness to declare himself such in the most open manner—at the moment of his death, and when concerned about his crucified body.

XV. 29. We shall conclude with one further example of the impression produced in St Mark by the insertion of a single little word. Jesus, when nailed to the cross, is railed at and outraged by four sorts of people—the populace, the chief priests and the scribes, the malefactors, and the soldiers. The grossest and most revolting insults are addressed to him by the populace; they apostrophise him directly: *they reviled him, wagging their heads, and saying, Thou that destroyest the temple and buildest it in three days, save thyself,* &c. Here St Mark closely follows St Matthew, adding nothing but a little word—an interjection: AH! (Οὐὰ) *thou that destroyest the temple,* &c. In this short exclamation we have the whole fury of a rabid mob brought before us. And does not this word at the same time recall to our recollection that Psalm where David expresses, by the same sound, the insulting exclamations of his enemies? (Ps. xxxv. 25.)

By merely transposing the phrase, our second Evangelist, in the same manner, gives at times a peculiar freshness and significance to what he says. Thus, for example, in the preaching of St John the Baptist, which St Luke (iii. 16) and St Matthew (iii. 11) render in the same order: *I indeed baptize you with water unto repentance: but he that cometh after me is mightier than I, whose shoes I am not worthy to bear: he shall baptize you with the Holy Ghost,*—we read more characteristically and energetically in St Mark: *There cometh one mightier than I after me. I, indeed, have baptized you with water; but he shall baptize you with the Holy Ghost.*

After yet another manner, but by no means fortuitously, we have the transposition at the end of the parable of the sower. In St Matthew (xiii. 23) it runs: *But he that received seed into the good ground is he that heareth the word, and understandeth it; which also beareth fruit, and bringeth forth, some an hundred-fold, some sixty, some thirty.* St Mark (iv. 20) reverses this order, so as to make a CLIMAX: *some thirty-fold, some sixty, and some an hundred.* The purpose cannot be mistaken; it is to make us feel, together with the general doctrine to be found already in St Matthew, this further particular, elsewhere expressed by our Lord in St John's Gospel: *In this is my Father glorified, that ye bear* MUCH *fruit* (John xv. 8).

A transposition, coupled with a short periphrasis, makes a striking impression in the similitude of the husbandmen, as recorded by St Mark. *But last of all he sent unto them his son,* we read in St Matthew (xxi. 37); and in St Luke (xx. 13)—*What shall I do? I will send my beloved son.* But in St Mark (xii. 6)—*Having yet therefore* ONE SON, HIS WELL BELOVED, *he sent him also last unto them*—a most touching expression, particularly in the original: *Ἔτι οὖν ἕνα υἱὸν ἔχων ἀγαπητὸν αὐτοῦ, ἀπέστειλε καὶ αὐτόν.*

We have yet another transposition of this kind in the history of our Lord's passion, hardly perceptible indeed, and yet important. When the multitude, led by Judas, drew near to the garden of Gethsemané, Jesus said, as recorded by St Matthew (xxvi. 46), *Behold, he is at hand that doth betray me;* according to St Mark (xiv. 42), with a turn given to the words that evidently strengthens the impression to the hearing: *Lo! he that betrayeth me is at hand.*

Finally, turn we once more to the account of the resurrection. The Angel announces the grand news in these words, rendered thus by St Matthew and St Luke: *He is not here; for he is risen.* St Mark (xvi. 6), with more animation, without the FOR, and in the inverse order, has: *He is risen; he is not here.*

Numerous, also, are the passages in St Mark, where, with the same tendency to increased energy and emphasis, the less precise or more general word that had been employed by St Matthew is superseded, not without a striking effect, by another more characteristic, more distinctive, and more graphic. Thus we read in St Matthew (iii. 16), as well as St Luke (iii. 21), that at the baptism of Jesus in the river Jordan, *the heavens were* OPENED *unto him* (ἀνεῴχθησαν); in St Mark (i. 10), *he saw* the heavens RENT OPEN (σχιζομένους). Thus afterwards in St Mark (ver. 12), *the Spirit* DRIVETH HIM (ἐκβάλλει) *into the wilderness,* for St Matthew's expression (iv. 1), *he* WAS LED UP, and St Luke's (iv. 1), *he* WAS LED. So likewise, in our Evangelist (i. 30), the proper expression for a sick person, *lay sick of a fever* (κατέκειτο[1] πυρέσσουσα), for what we find in St Matthew, *lay and was sick of a fever* (viii. 14). In like manner (ii. 12) *they were all amazed* (ἐξίστασθαι, *to be beside one's self*), for the less forcible expression in St Matthew (ix. 8), *they marvelled* (ἐθαύμασαν). And in the account of the para-

[1] In Latin: *decumbebat.*

lytic, who was let down through the roof to the feet of Jesus, we have anew in St Mark (ii. 4) the same selection of precise and forcible expressions: that *they could not come nigh unto Jesus,* AND UNCOVERED *the roof* (ἀπεστέγασαν τὴν στέγην); *they* LET DOWN (χαλῶσι) *the bed.* And then (ii. 7), *who can forgive sins but the* ONE *God?* (εἷς ὁ Θεός), where St Luke (v. 21) has *but God* ALONE (μόνος ὁ Θεός.) And in the description of the storm at sea, where St Matthew (viii. 24) says, *the ship was* COVERED *with the waves* (ὥστε—καλύπτεσθαι); St Mark says (iv. 37), *the ship was* FULL (γεμίζεσθαι). And when our Lord sent away the multitudes whom he had fed, St Matthew (xiv. 23) uses the ordinary expression *having sent* the multitudes *away* (ἀπολύσας); Mark (vi. 46) has a more military word: ἀποταξάμενος—when he *had disbanded* the multitudes. And at another place, speaking to the Pharisees, in St Matthew (xv. 3) we find: ye TRANSGRESS (παραβαίνετε) *the commandment of God by your tradition;* in St Mark (vii. 9), ye MAKE VOID[1] (ἀθετεῖτε) *the commandment of God.* In the account of the believing Canaanitish woman, the sole change of a preposition doubles the impression: *The dogs eat of the crumbs which fall* FROM *their master's table,* is what we read in St Matthew (xv. 27); but St Mark (vii. 28), with a more decided shade of humility, has, *the dogs* UNDER *the table.* In the parable of the vineyard and the husbandmen, St Mark gives us another example (xii. 1) of his greater correctness in naming an object: an *under place for the wine-fat* (ὑπολήνιον), instead of the ordinary but less appropriate word ληνὸν (*wine-press*), in St Matthew (xxi. 33). In the history of our Lord's passion also, examples not unfrequently occur of such words

[1] In the text of the English Bible, *reject;* on the margin, *frustrate.*

substituted for others, less strictly correct or less forcible, in St Matthew. Thus, where the latter (xxvi. 37) says, that in the garden of Gethsemané our Lord *began to be sorrowful* (λυπεῖσθαι), St Mark (xiv. 33) employs a stronger expression: *to be sore amazed* (ἐκθαμβεῖσθαι). Thus, in fine, for examples might be greatly multiplied, St Mark mentions under its correct and proper name of *wine mingled with myrrh,* the stupifying drink, which on account of its bitter taste, and with an allusion to the prophecy,[1] is called by St Matthew (xxvii. 34), *vinegar mingled with gall.*

This emphatic manner of expressing himself further appears in St Mark's repetitions, either of a phrase or of the leading word *in* the phrase. Thus it is not without emphasis that he repeats the words: *kingdom of God,* and *gospel* (i. 14, 15)—*Jesus came into Galilee preaching* THE GOSPEL OF THE KINGDOM OF GOD, and saying, *The time is fulfilled, and* THE KINGDOM OF GOD *is at hand; repent ye and believe* THE GOSPEL.—Likewise (ii. 16), *And when the Scribes and Pharisees saw him* EAT *with* PUBLICANS AND SINNERS, *they said unto his disciples, How is it that* HE EATETH *and drinketh* WITH PUBLICANS AND SINNERS? And after that (ver. 19), *Can the children of the bride-chamber fast* WHILE THE BRIDEGROOM IS WITH THEM? *As long as* THE BRIDEGROOM IS WITH THEM *they cannot fast.* And in the account of our Lord's teaching upon the shore, the triple repetition of the word SEA (iv. 1): *And he began again to teach by the* SEA*-side: and there was gathered unto him a great multitude, so that he entered into a ship and sat in the* SEA; *and the whole multitude was by the* SEA, *on the land.* And when his future

[1] Ps. lxix. 22.

sufferings were foretold: *They shall* KILL *him, and after that he is* KILLED, *he shall rise the third day.* And (xi. 28), *They say unto him, By* WHAT AUTHORITY *doest thou these things? and who gave thee* THIS AUTHORITY *to do these things?* In like manner, in the reply to the captious question of the Sadducees with respect to the resurrection of the woman who had had seven brothers for husbands, the reiteration of the words *left no seed* (xii. 20—22). Still more do we find a peculiar impressiveness in the repetition of the great command of love, in that striking passage where Jesus replies to the question of the Scribes (xii. 29—31): *The first of all the commandments is; Hear, O Israel! the Lord our God is one Lord; and thou shalt love the Lord thy God with all thy heart, and with all thy soul, and with all thy mind, and with all thy strength: this is the first commandment. And the second is like unto it, namely this, Thou shalt love thy neighbour as thyself. There is none other commandment greater than these.* Upon which the Scribe (in St Mark) gives his assent to this reply by repeating the same sublime words (ver. 32, 33): *Well, Master, thou hast said the truth: for there is one God, and none other but he: and to love him with all the heart and with all the understanding, and with all the soul and with all the strength, and to love his neighbour as himself, is more than all whole burnt-offerings and sacrifices.* Does not our Evangelist shew in all these repetitions a sort of exactness, and at the same time fervour of mind, which reminds us of the Apostle's words: *To write the same things to you, to me is not grievous, and for you it is safe* (Philip. iii. 1)?

Analogous to these repetitions are such phrases as the following, which again are peculiar to St Mark: BLAS-

PHEMIES *wherewith soever they shall* BLASPHEME (iii. 28); *your* TRADITION *which ye have* DELIVERED (παραδόσει ᾗ παρεδώκατε)—(vii. 13); *from the beginning of the* CREATION *which God* CREATED (xiii. 19); *and they* FEARED *with a great* FEAR (iv. 41); and *they were* ASTONISHED *with a great* ASTONISHMENT (v. 42). This last kind of repetition will remind any one who knows the genius of the Latin tongue of a very similar phraseology in it.[1]

Assuredly, if it may be said any where that *the style is the man*,[2] it is in the sacred Scriptures. But in the style of the Gospel of St Mark, in so far as we have been able to follow it into its minutest details, we have found something so characteristic, so original, so distinctive, that that saying is peculiarly applicable to him.

That style, that whole manner of seeing and observing facts, that peculiar mode of reducing them to writing, followed out in the case of St Mark with unvarying consistency, easily supplies us with a clear and distinct idea of the person and of the individuality of the author himself. They betoken, in point of gifts and endowments, extraordinary clearness, depth, and power, in his view and conception of whatever he undertakes to describe;—in point of character, what we would call strong individuality;—and in point of personal and practical excellence as a Christian, a mind of lofty aim and great sincerity, a steadfast disposition and fervid spirit, equally penetrated with the importance of all that he relates, and the value of the souls in whose behalf he gives his testimony. Who but such an one could have produced a Gospel history so carefully elaborated in its details, and at the same time, sentence after sentence so nervous in

[1] The well-known one of *vivere vitam, ludere ludum*, &c.

[2] *Le style c'est l'homme.*

its instructions, and so directly and earnestly addressed to the conscience? But there is something more; it is perhaps not the character only, but also the profession, and to a certain degree the history, of the author of this Gospel, which we see decidedly indicated in the observations we have thus far collected and combined. In order to find these results, let us advert for some moments further to our second Evangelist, as he falls under our contemplation when compared with his predecessor St Matthew. The latter presents to us the language and the tone of an apostle who contemplates and relates things as seen from the point of view suggested by the ancient prophets; St Mark, his fellow-worker, occupying a lower point of view, but not less assured of his holy vocation and his competency, seizes and delineates things *in the most visible and palpable* (I had almost said *prosaic* and *matter-of-fact*) reality of their accomplishment. St Matthew supplies an ample treasure, an abundant overflow of doings and sayings; St Mark, a wise conciseness, and, as it were, economy of expressions, conjoined with a successful elaboration of each detail, *so that nothing may be lost.* In St Matthew we have the freedom and copiousness of expression to be expected from an eyewitness, who has *the full consciousness* that he saw and was himself present, and never dreams of any distrust among his readers; in St Mark we have the scrupulous exactness of a more subaltern witness, whose office it is to fill up, to point off, and to finish the work of the eyewitness and apostle, with the aid of another apostle, who was likewise an eyewitness. In the Gospel of St Matthew we have, so to speak, the flowing costume of the stately East, which sweeps the ground with its folds; in that of St Mark, the close-girt dress of the man who runs for a prize, or of the soldier on duty. Every where in St Matthew we have the Eastern and Israelite life, element, and principle; in St Mark, the Western and Roman life, element, and principle.

This Roman and non-Israelite character has been recognised and remarked by many in the plan and style of St Mark's Gospel. In our opinion, however, they have taken quite a wrong view of it, as resulting from the object for which the author wrote, or from his particular vocation, as called, in the first instance, to instruct and edify Gentiles or Romans. But no. This Roman, this non-Israelite character which distinguishes St Mark, is not sufficiently explained by alleging that he wrote originally *for* readers born in heathendom, or *for* Roman Christians. Why not prefer this simple explanation, that he, the son of St Peter in the faith, was in point of fact born himself among the heathen—nay, was himself a Roman? No doubt, we must dismiss any such idea if we are to assume his being the JOHN MARK, son of Mary, and nephew of Barnabas the Levite, whom the book of *Acts* brings us acquainted with. But we have already shewn how little real ground there is for this supposition, however generally it may be entertained. And why should not the friend and fellow-labourer of St Peter have been a Gentile by birth, as well as St Luke, the friend and companion of St Paul? Yes, how striking, if the fact be once admitted, that our four Gospels should thus have had for authors, not only two apostles of Israel, but two evangelists also, one Greek and one Roman, from the nations that were admitted to the fellowship of the Gospel! How striking that thus, from the very first among the historical witnesses of the Gospel of Jesus Christ, *the middle wall of partition is seen to be taken away!* But before entering more fully into this hypothesis, or rather, the better to follow out our inquiry into the person of our second Evangelist, this seems to be the fitting place for a review, in some particulars, of this Roman, and, to speak more generally, Christian-Gentile character of St Mark, which we have stated our reasons for conjecturing that he possessed.

With respect to what is characteristically Roman in St Mark, we have already fixed our regards on certain modes of constructing sentences that are peculiar to him, and that are conceived in the spirit of the language of the Romans. But, over and above this, he employs certain Latin words in a Greek form, which occur in the New Testament nowhere else. Thus (vi. 27), the word σπεκουλάτωρ (the purely Latin word *speculator*), which the translations render less correctly *executioner*. We shall recur to this expression hereafter. So, likewise, the *centurion* is not called by him as by St Matthew and St Luke, in pure Greek, ἑκατοντάρχης, but in Latin-Greek, κεντυρίων (*centurio*).—xv. 39—44. The same Evangelist, and only he, explains the *two mites* of the widow by the Latin-Greek word χοδρὰντης (*quadrans*), being the fourth part of the well-known Roman *as*.

The Roman point of view in St Mark further comes out in the division, found only in his Gospel, of the *night* into *four watches*, with which, according to his usual practice, he partly abridges, partly extends, the parallel passage in St Matthew. This occurs in the everywise important parable which we read in the three first Gospels with the following differences:—

MATTH. xxiv. 42.	MARK xiii. 33.	LUKE xii. 35.
Watch therefore: for ye know not what hour your Lord doth come.	Take ye heed, *watch and pray:* for ye know not when the time is.	Let your loins be girded about, and your lights burning; 36.

43. But know this, that if the good man of the house had known IN WHAT WATCH the thief would come, he would have watched, and would not have suffered his house to be broken up. 44. Therefore *be ye also ready:* for in such an hour as ye think not the Son of man cometh. 45. Who then is a faithful and wise servant, whom his lord hath made ruler over his household, to give them meat in due season? 46. Blessed is that servant, whom his lord when he cometh shall find so doing.

34. For the Son of man is as a man taking a far journey, who left his house, and gave authority to his servants, and to every man his work, and commanded the porter *to watch.* 35. *Watch ye therefore:* for ye know not when the master of the house cometh, at EVEN, or at MIDNIGHT, or at the COCK-CROWING, or IN THE MORNING: 36. Lest, coming suddenly, he find you sleeping. 37. And what I say unto you, I say unto all, WATCH.

And ye yourselves like unto men that wait for their lord, when he will return from the wedding; that when he cometh and knocketh, they may open unto him immediately. 37. Blessed are those servants, whom the lord when he cometh shall find watching: verily I say unto you, that he shall gird himself, and make them to sit down to meat, and will come forth and serve them. 38. And if he shall come in the SECOND WATCH, or *come in the* THIRD WATCH, and find them so, blessed are those servants. 39. And this know, that if the good man of the house had known *what hour* the thief would come, he would have watched, &c.

This division of the night into *four* night watches is of Roman origin; the Jews reckoned properly but *three,* and it was not until a subsequent period that they adopted the Roman *fourth.* Hence we find in St Matthew (xiv. 25) this *fourth* watch of the night, although it is remarkable that in St Luke, at the passage quoted, mention is made only of the *second* and *third* watch of the night. But the Roman characteristic remains, at all events, in St Mark, in the full and detailed designation of the four watches of the night, each with its special name, *evening, midnight, cock-crowing* (gallicinium), and *morning.*

A principal and decisive passage, serving to elucidate not only the peculiar position of St Mark, but also his national descent, is presented to us anew in an important extension with which he enlarges a passage in his predecessor.

Matth. xv. 1.	Mark vii. 1.
Then came to Jesus scribes and Pharisees, which were of Jerusalem, saying, 2. Why do thy disciples transgress the tradition of the elders? for they wash not their hands when they eat bread, &c.	Then came together unto him the Pharisees, and certain of the scribes, which came from Jerusalem. 2. *And when they saw some of his disciples eat bread with* DEFILED (*that is to say, with unwashen*) *hands, they found fault.* 3. *For the Pharisees, and* ALL THE JEWS, *except they wash their hands oft, eat not, holding the tradition of the elders.* 4. *And when they come from the market, except they wash, they eat not. And many other thiugs there be which they have received to hold, as the washing of cups, and pots, brazen vessels, and of tables.* 5. Then the Pharisees and scribes asked him, Why walk not thy disciples according to the tradition of the elders?

Here we find in St Mark an extension, a development, an elucidation of St Matthew's text, through the addition of details that are evidently given for the benefit of a circle of non-Israelite readers. The explanations relate to matters perfectly well known in Israel, and which, as such, did not require to be mentioned by St Matthew at all. Such an elucidation, however, was required for Gentile readers, whether they were already converted, or had still to be converted. Yet this explanatory statement, if I mistake not, is not given by our author as one of Jewish birth would have given it to a foreigner, but manifestly in the tone and with the words to be expected from a well-informed narrator, who nevertheless was just as much a foreigner and a Gentile as those whom he addressed. The more we reflect on the expression *all the Jews,* the more we feel convinced that he who wrote thus was not himself a *Jew by birth;* and consequently, that whatever in this Gospel is written from a non-Israelite point of view, must be explained not only by the position of those to whom this Gospel was addressed, but also by the national origin and national peculiarities of the person by whom it was written.

And now, having once adopted this principle, how much more natural and more simple becomes the explanation of what we have observed to be left out in this second Gospel, specially, for example, the mention of Samaritans, the exclamation of *Woe* upon the Pharisees and the Scribes, and over the three cities of Galilee, and over Jerusalem. Nothing of this fell within the scope of St Mark and his Gospel. Writing as a Roman, and for readers who did not belong to Palestine, the Samaritan part of the population of the Holy Land seemed of less consequence from the point of view he occupied, and his eye was naturally fixed more steadily on the *grand* division of the world *into Jews and Gentiles.* And as for the Woes pronounced upon the Pharisees, he was no doubt called upon as a faithful Evangelist to mention, in general, the testimony of our Lord against the errors and the traditions of the Pharisees, who made the law of no effect; but a feeling of delicacy made it most natural, that in doing so, he, an Evangelist from among the Gentiles, and writing for the Gentiles, should not give any special emphasis to judgments pronounced on Jewish descriptions of men alone. And how much more still may this be said with respect to Jerusalem? He could not, he might not, allow to pass unnoticed the minute prediction by our Lord of the destruction of that city (chap. xiii.); but to have inserted here still further particulars respecting that denunciation of the Holy City of the Jews, might, from the pen of a converted Roman, have looked like a shout of triumph, incompatible with the delicacy of feeling becoming a true convert to the Christ of Israel. Desirous to avoid the very appearance of any thing of this sort, his pen, in its rapid course, touches not those details which St Luke, on the contrary, though no less a Gentile by birth, was called upon to adopt in *his* Gospel, for a reason and in a manner which we shall see afterwards.

We have now advanced some steps further in an acquaintance with the person of the author of our second Gospel. St Mark wrote not only for the Gentiles by birth, but as a man who was himself a converted Gentile —a Roman who had become a Christian. His Gospel, so characteristic in all respects in point of style, enables us perhaps to discover something more with regard to him, on our scrutinizing it still more deeply. What if St Mark, our second Evangelist, may be proved to have been not only a Roman by birth, but a Roman soldier also by profession?

It strikes me that we may discover in the style, in the disposition, and the whole spirit of our second Gospel, a *military* character, which reveals itself more and more the more we study it in a sufficient number of details. And, first of all, methinks I see this character in the union of two qualities which in several parts of St Mark strike one at a glance; the *rapidity* with which he carries you along in his narrative, and, at the same time, the *exactness* and *precision* with which he states his details. The better to understand this, let us take up, for the purpose of comparison, some military report or narrative of ancient or modern times, drawn up in the spirit of that profession, and by a more or less practised hand, and we shall invariably find these two qualities combined —economy, so to speak, of words — compression and terseness of style, on the one hand; and copiousness of details, on the other hand, on local, and indeed all sorts of circumstances. It has been chiefly upon a deliberate comparison of the style of Cæsar's *Commentaries* with that of our second Gospel, that I have found a striking resemblance between them in the qualities just mentioned. In both we have the same emphatic repetition of the same leading words and things, combined with the same rapidity of movement in the narrative. The same animation and celerity, combined with an equal copiousness of scenic description, distinguish both authors. The very word *straightway* (εὐθέως), which is such a favourite with St Mark, and is employed in his Gospel about forty times, appears in the writings of the great Roman captain in his ever-recurring *celeriter*.

But, besides this, the soldier betrays himself at every turn in our Evangelist St Mark, by many expressions which must have become familiar to him in the course of his professional life, and which, so to speak, seem to escape unwittingly from his pen. Thus, for example, in the above-quoted mention of the man who beheaded John the Baptist, and whom he calls by the Latin-Greek name *speculator*. This *speculator* was by no means, as we have remarked, an executioner, but *a soldier*, such as among the Romans, and, in this case, in conformity with Roman customs, was employed by Herod to carry into effect a sentence of death.[1] Still more evidently does the soldier shew himself in that other strong expression which St Mark employs (xiv. 44) in place of that used by St Matthew (xxvi. 48) as the sign used by the traitor Judas to point out which of the party was his Master to the armed multitude. This word sign (σημεῖον) becomes under the pen of St Mark a sort of *token, a preconcerted sign*, a word employed by ancient authors to express a military sign—a *watchword* (σύσσημον).[2]

But while thus led on by the observations and examples that have occurred to us, to enter more deeply into an examination of St Mark's Gospel, we find ourselves every where forcibly reminded of military customs in that curtness of speech, that tone of command, which characterise his narrations every time we compare him with the other Evangelists. Have we not, for example, a soldier's mode of thinking and expressing himself in the three simple words with which St Mark (iii. 13) makes us feel the elective power of Jesus in the calling of the Apostles: *And he goeth up into a mountain, and calleth unto him* WHOM HE WOULD (οὓς ἤθελεν αὐτός)? Or when our Lord, in a passage already quoted, introduces the similitude of the sower with that short but terse and authoritative call to attention—HEARKEN (iv. 3)? Or when afterwards he closes another parable of our Lord's, which has also been quoted, that of the householder who gives directions to

[1] SENECA *de Ira*, l. i. c. 16: *Centurio supplicio præpositus condere gladium speculatorem jubet.* Here Lipsius remarks: *Speculatorem genus militum. Milites rem pœnalem fere administrabant; i. e.*, the *speculator* was a kind of soldier, soldiers generally executing penal sentences.

[2] Many places confirming this meaning of the word may be seen in Wetstein, in the Annotations of his edition of the New Testament (A? 1751) on Mark at the above passage. Σύσσημον, λόγος ἐν πολέμῳ ἐπὶ γνωρίσμῳ τῶν οἰκείων δεδομενος—*a watchword used to distinguish friends from enemies* IN WAR.

his servants on leaving them, with these words to be found in his Gospel only (xiii. 27): *What I say unto you, I say unto all,* WATCH! Or when, prior to that, he alone records the two words of authority and power, *Peace, Be still!*—with which Jesus appeased the stormy sea and the unbridled winds—do we not recognise in the tone of these two words the idea that would impress itself on a soldier, familiar with the giving of the word of command, and with the idea of discipline?

But when we speak of the tone and manner of a soldier in the style of St Mark, we trust that no one will attach to that expression a meaning unworthy of the subject in hand. What we contemplate is the manly, the decided, the grave, the steadfast—whatever, in short, marks the genuine soldier in the ordinary course of life, and in the gospel gives such a charm to a faith like that of the centurion, so strikingly represented to us in Matthew (viii. 5-13), and in St Luke (vii. 1-10.) It is with the force and firmness of such a faith that St Mark expresses himself. In such a spirit, resolute, clear, dutiful, earnest in regard to the most urgent of all affairs, does he, at the close of his Gospel, give, as it were, the essence of the whole in these words of our Lord: *He that believeth and is baptized shall be saved; but he that believeth not shall be damned* (xvi. 16). Compare this short terse passage of the soldier-Evangelist with the closing announcement recorded by the apostle-Evangelist: *Go ye therefore and teach all nations, baptizing them in the name of the Father, and of the Son, and of the Holy Ghost, teaching them to observe all things whatsoever I have commanded you* (Matth. xxviii. 19).

We may now, perhaps, advance one step further in our investigation with respect to the person of so important an author as that of the second Gospel. Are we sure that something more may not possibly be found recorded in the New Testament, besides the *name* of our St Mark, and the *ties* by which he was associated *with St Peter?* That in natural character, in social relations, in national descent, he was quite a different person from the JOHN MARK who accompanied Paul and Barnabas in their ministrations, and who was the Israelite son of a mother who belonged to Jerusalem,[1] seems now, after all that we have said, to be placed beyond a doubt. But who then is OUR ST MARK, the son of St Peter in the faith? He is nowhere mentioned *by name* except in the well-known passage of the Epistle (1 Pet. v. 23). But what should we light upon him in another passage of the New Testament, *though his name be not given?* What if somewhere we meet with *a devout soldier*, at a highly important crisis, standing in so interesting a relationship with St Peter, that he might by pre-eminence be called *his son in the faith?* Be it observed that, in the gospel, every one is not understood to be such a son, whom any leading gospel minister may have by his preaching won to Christ; but only such exclusively as by means of that preaching has been brought into a peculiarly tender relationship with the preacher himself. Thus, for example, every one that was converted to the Lord through the instrumentality of St Paul, was not called by him *his son;* but such only as Timothy, for instance, was, who at a highly critical moment of the Apostle's life, became intimately associated with him, by and for the gospel.[2] Now, does not the New Testament history point out to us such a moment, as connecting St Peter with a

[1] Acts xii. 12; xiii. 5, 13.
[2] Acts xvi. 1–3. 2 Tim. iii. 10, 11. Compare Acts xiv. 19.

soldier, like the one we think we have seen in St Mark? We believe that it does so. Let us open the book of the Acts. There we find (ch. x. and xi.) the Gospel preached by St Peter for the first time to the Gentiles. This preaching is preceded and accompanied with some remarkable circumstances. Cornelius, the Roman centurion at Cesarea, is commanded in a vision to send to Joppa for the apostle, St Peter. He sends, accordingly (x. 7), two of his household servants, and, as the principal person naturally when such was the errand, *a devout soldier of them that waited on him continually*—a soldier, consequently, who must have been a fellow-proselyte in serving the God of Israel, and living in fellowship of prayer and good deeds with his pious superior officer. The Apostle Peter, on his side, had seen a vision, signifying and announcing to him, on the part of God, the approaching full communion that was to unite Jews and Gentiles in the worship of the one true God. Anon the arrival of the deputed triumvirate was announced, and the devout soldier becomes one of the first Gentiles whose faces met St Peter after his receiving that new revelation from God. With him, and the other messengers and witnesses, St Peter sets off to the centurion's house. This is followed by his preaching there, by the outpouring of the Holy Ghost, and the baptism of Cornelius and all his house. Well may that hour have fixed itself on the apostle's memory; and well may that have proved, not only an indissoluble, but the closest possible bond which united the apostle to the house, the person, and every individual member of the family of the privileged centurion. From this bond the *devout soldier* could not have been excluded; on the contrary, he was just the person with whom the apostle must have contracted a particular intimacy, in the course of his preaching, and in the bonds of the faith. What a moment was that in the life of these two men, and in the whole history of the gospel! But now, what more natural also, than that this subaltern from so highly privileged a house, should have been considered by the apostle afterwards as specially *his son* in the Gospel, and should have been associated as a companion and servant in the Gospel with St Peter; that thus the author of the first Gospel that was addressed to the Gentiles should have been himself one of the first among the Gentiles to receive the Holy Ghost; in other words, that our first Evangelist, St Mark the Roman, the thoughtful and devout soldier, was no other than that same *devout soldier* of whom the book of Acts makes mention at the passage to which we refer?

This idea, however, I propose here only as a conjecture, although convinced that it will seem more and more probable the more we scrutinize and ponder our second Gospel. One word more let me add, as it will serve to strengthen this idea by a sort of proof, if not strictly mathematical, at least in harmony with the nature of the thing. Let any one, after all that has been observed, compare the preaching of St Peter to the Gentiles by birth,[1] with this Gospel of the soldier converted to Christ. What will he find? Why, first of all, the opening in both cases is the same: *The Gospel of Jesus Christ, beginning with the baptism of John.* But now for the conclusion also; in Mark (xvi. 19, 20): *So then, after the Lord had spoken to them, he was received up into heaven, and sat on the right hand of God. And they went forth and preached every where, the Lord working with them, and* CONFIRMING THE WORD WITH SIGNS FOLLOWING.

[1] Acts x. 36, 37, and following verses.

In the account also given in the Acts (x. 44), the preaching of St Peter is instantly CONFIRMED by the descent of the Holy Ghost on all that heard the word. Here at least there is harmony. But this harmony may be traced to an effect of Mark's memory, if we have only any good ground for concluding that our Evangelist, as a fellow-believer in the house of Cornelius, had been an eye-witness of St Peter's first preaching to the Gentiles, and of the signs that immediately followed; and in that case, the impression made, and the gift received on that day, were more than probably the originating causes to which we may trace his whole Gospel—that Gospel which some Church fathers have not inappropriately called a *Gospel preaching of St Peter.*[1]

Thus, then, by the many distinguishing traits which our second Gospel presents, have we been able, perhaps, to penetrate to a knowledge, not only of the internal tissue and grand leading principle of that important Biblical composition, but also of the person of its author. In the peculiarities of his Gospel we seem to have discovered his character, his profession, his country, nay, the very history of his conversion. But our examination of the internal structure of the four Gospels has an incomparably higher object in view. In connexion with the observations we have made, we would seek out the characteristic points that distinguish the portraiture of the person of our Lord Jesus Christ, as presented by each of our four sacred authors. What, then, is it in St Mark that peculiarly characterises this to us the dearest and most important of all delineations—the portraiture of our Lord?

And here we would again recall, with the view of

[1] Κήρυξις Πέτρου.

giving it a closer and more definite application, the general remark with which we started respecting the agreement and the diversity of the Gospels. It is the individual characters, the special gifts, the several distinct relationships, objects, vocations, and plans, of the four different Evangelists, to which we must look for an explanation at once of the intimate and perfect unity, and of the fourfold diversity of their writings. Let us now try the application of this principle to the diversity and to the agreement in the manner with which the Person itself of the Saviour is portrayed to us in the four different Gospels. And how possibly could there fail to be diversities in their manner of accomplishing this, the highest object of their writing? In Jesus Christ there is a fulness of which no one disciple or apostle could have given any adequate idea. Here was a subject which it is self-evident never could have been exhausted by any number of authors, whoever they might be.[1] Thus to picture Christ to the eye in equal *fulness*, that is, as an actual *whole*, and that in all his aspects, one witness was very far from being sufficient; but Divine Wisdom could here accomplish its object by means of a *fourfold* testimony and a *four-sided* delineation. In order to this, each of the four Evangelists behoved to represent to us not only the doings and the sayings, but the very person of the Saviour, from his own individual point of view, and in harmony both with his own personal character and disposition, and with the special gifts bestowed on him by the Holy Ghost, under whose immediate inspiration he wrote. Through that promised Spirit they beheld and they described the Lord Jesus, from a special, distinct, and always very definite position—all, however, as he really

[1] John xxi. 25.

and truly was and shewed himself to be—and so that, as a final result, all these separate aspects meet together and harmonize in the most perfect and glorious ONE. But in order to this very result, it was necessary that these several views taken of that one grand object, besides being all equally true, should be each characteristically different, and consequently distinguishable. Hence we meet in one Gospel, as we have already said, Jesus Christ specially as *the promised Messiah;* in another, as *really come into the world;* in a third, as *conceived and anointed by the Holy Ghost;* in a fourth, as the *gift of the Father;*—in one, as *king* and *prophet;* in another, as *shepherd and ruler;* in a third, as *high priest;* in a fourth, as the *only begotten Son;*—in one, as EMMANUEL, *God with us;* in another, as *the man Christ Jesus;* in the third, as the *great physician both of body and soul;* in the fourth, as *the true God and life eternal;* and so on, in many different ways. Not so, however, as if these various modes of contemplating and delineating our Lord mutually excluded each other in any measure: far from this; in *all* four Gospels, *all* these different qualities or manifestations of the Lord Jesus are assumed to be equally essential; only, in *one* of them, one of the above qualities—in *another*, another such quality—stands out more prominently, occupies more of the foreground, or, finally, forms the groundwork or kernel of the evangelical narrative. Now, the particular point of view from which each of the Evangelists contemplates and portrays the Saviour, stands in the closest connexion with his own proper personality, including in this term his personal disposition, his intellectual and spiritual wants, and his intellectual and spiritual gifts;—for even in this sense it may be said with truth, *Out of his fulness have we all received*;—and, under the directing guidance of the Holy Ghost, each gives back what he has received, and what has been confided to him.

Now, then, let us proceed to observe this special feature in the Gospel of St Mark. Here, too, we shall find our views elucidated by a comparison with that of St Matthew. If, in the Gospel of that apostle, we had Jesus Christ exhibited to us as the promised EMMANUEL, *God with us*, in St Mark's he stands more distinctly before us as having become really and truly *man*—*man* in all points like as we are, except sin—*man* as respects soul and body—*man* among men and before God.

To exhibit this humanity—this true and real humanity—in all our Lord's doings and sayings, yea, in all the emotions of his soul and all the movements of his body—such is the vocation of this Evangelist, with whose special talent and bent of mind we have now familiarized ourselves in so many ways, as one pre-eminently skilful in painting things to the life, and conceiving all things in their most visible reality. Hence St Mark's Gospel, placed side by side with that of St Matthew's, is that of *the Son of man* placed side by side with that of the *Messias, the Son of God.* Nevertheless, that it may be seen how, among the sacred authors, the most decided diversity in their points of view may be coupled with the most perfect unity in all truth, it so happens that this very Gospel, which exhibits to us the Christ in his entire humanity, is that which bears this superscription (i. 1), *The beginning of the Gospel of* JESUS CHRIST, THE SON OF GOD; while St Matthew calls his (i. 1), *The book of the generation of* JESUS CHRIST, THE SON OF DAVID, THE SON OF ABRAHAM.

What, then, are the respects, and of what sort are the

particulars, by which this second Gospel may be recognised as the Gospel of our Lord's *humanity?* These are many and various. Nowhere, in the first place, do we see the human emotions of the sinless Saviour so minutely detailed and exhibited to us in appropriate expressions as in St Mark. Thus, in the cure of the deaf and dumb man in Decapolis, we here read of Jesus (vii. 34), *that, looking up to heaven, he* SIGHED (ἐστέναξε, a word nowhere else employed in speaking of our Lord). With a similar word, *he* SIGHED DEEPLY (ἀναστενάξας, an expression occurring here alone in the New Testament), the Saviour's anguish of soul at the malice of the Pharisees in tempting him is signified to us (viii. 12). Thus we have seen already the striking exhibition of our Saviour's mingled emotions with respect to the enmity felt towards him by the Scribes and Pharisees, recorded by St Mark (iii. 5): *And when he had looked round about on them with anger,* BEING GRIEVED *for the hardness of their hearts.* In like manner, it is St Mark who records *how much displeased* Jesus was (ἠγανάκτησε) at the disciples for preventing children being brought to him (x. 14); and how, on the other hand, he *loved* (x. 21) with a kindly feeling, more of a human nature, the rich young man on account of his natural amiability.

The four Evangelists have repeatedly given us an idea of the *look*, or of *the act of lifting the eyes upwards,* in the blessed Saviour. Turning to St Luke (xxii. 61), let us but think of that look which went through the heart of St Peter when he had denied his Master, and which brought him to repentance; or in St John (vi. 5) and St Luke (vi. 20), of that *lifting up of the eyes of* JESUS on the multitude when an hungered, or on the disciples as they longed to be taught by him, or, finally, in St John (xi. 41; xvii. 1), of his *lifting up his eyes* in prayer. St Mark notes for us one further movement still, and a no less expressive movement of the eyes of our Lord in a word which seems to transport us into the circle immediately around him, and to place us, as it were, in his very presence, as he moved about among friends and foes. It is the Saviour's look as expressed by the Greek word περιβλέπεσθαι, *to look round on all sides*—a word which, with the single exception of a passage in St Luke (and that, too, adopted from St Mark), occurs only in our second Evangelist; as, 1st, In the passage more than once referred to (iii. 5): where *Jesus* LOOKED ROUND ABOUT *on the Pharisees with anger and grief.*[1] 2nd, Where he replies to the message brought to him from his mother and his brethren (iii. 34): BY LOOKING ROUND[2] ABOUT ON *them which sat about him*, he declares that he looked upon them *as his mother and his brethren.* 3d, Where, upon being touched in the crowd by the woman who had an issue of blood, HE LOOKED ROUND ABOUT *to see her who had done it* (ver. 32). 4th, Where, previous to his declaration with respect to the difficulty of a rich man's entering into the kingdom, he, as it were, first prepares his disciples for so solemn a declaration, by LOOKING ROUND ABOUT. Finally, 5th, Where, on entering the temple at Jerusalem, *he* LOOKED ROUND ABOUT *upon all things* (xi. 11), and when the evening was come, went out unto Bethany with the twelve, as preparatory to his purifying the temple on the following day, a circumstance, with respect to the purification of the temple, equally

[1] St Luke (vi. 10), has so far adopted this phrase thus: *And* LOOKING ROUND ABOUT *upon them all.*

[2] Properly, *to look all round as in a circle* (περιβλεψάμενος κύκλῳ.)

minute and important, and found in St Mark alone (xi. 11-15).

We are conducted by St Mark still further into the minute details of our Lord's life as man, and of his relations with men on this earth, when he informs us with respect to his descent and parentage, always in his own peculiar manner, by means of a slight discrepancy between him and St Matthew and St Luke, forcibly and significantly detailed and extended. At Nazareth, the town in which he was brought up, his doctrine and his miracles had given rise to much amazement and scandal. *Whence hath this man this wisdom, and these mighty works? Is not this the* CARPENTER'S *son? Is not his mother's name Mary?* Thus do we read in St Matthew (xiii. 54, 55); but in Mark (vi. 3), *Is not this the* CARPENTER, *the son of Mary?* This discrepancy between our two Gospels, apparently so unimportant, clearly reveals to us two striking circumstances in the private life of Jesus; *first*, that he himself, along with his father, and apparently until his baptism in Jordan, followed at Nazareth the trade of a carpenter; *secondly*, that in those days Joseph, the husband of Mary, must have long been dead. And thus it is that the Lord from heaven, he by whom the heaven and the earth were created, is found in his human nature exercising a trade on this earth, and by that trade, that labour of his own hands, provided, as a son and support, for Joseph's widow, the daughter of David, whose eldest son he was according to the flesh.

Further, it is only in St Mark that we read the following detail, which throws a great deal of light on the manner in which the relations of Jesus at first contemplated his public teaching and actions (iii. 20, 21): *And they went into an house. And the multitude cometh together again, so that they could not so much as eat bread. And when his friends heard of it, they went out to lay hold on him; for they said, He is beside himself.* By *the friends of* JESUS, or rather *those of his house* (οἱ παρ' αὐτοῦ), we must understand *his mother and his brethren*, as appears from that passage in Matthew (xii. 46), and Luke (viii. 19), compared with Mark iii. 31, where the expression, THERE CAME THEN, evidently connects the narrative with the detail recorded by St Mark alone (ver. 21). Verse 21st must not be understood as if the *kinsmen* of Jesus said, that *he is beside himself.* By the word ἔλεγον, THEY *said* (*people said*), it is clear that we must understand the circulators of this opprobrious report. It was a report, however, which had sufficient influence on the mother and brethren of Jesus, particularly the latter, to make them think it proper for them to endeavour to restrain him, and to moderate those indefatigable labours which were causing so much talk among the multitude.

Some other details of great importance, which yet have met with little attention, are given by St Mark, bearing upon our Lord's daily intercourse with his disciples, and his conduct in public. No one speaks so much as St Mark does of *the house*, and of *Jesus being in the house;* for example, *how at Capernaum he was in the* HOUSE, *and straightway many were gathered together, insomuch that there was no room to receive them,* NO NOT SO MUCH AS ABOUT THE DOOR (ii. 1, 2). In like manner, shortly before (i. 32, 33), *And at even, when the sun was set, they brought unto him all that were diseased, and them that were possessed with devils.* AND ALL THE CITY WAS GATHERED TOGETHER AT THE DOOR. We have elsewhere seen already how he notes, by an expressive repetition, the custom of Jesus to assemble the multitude, and to teach them *by the seaside.*[1] A detail extremely simple, but one that transports us into the whole truth and reality of the scene, is recorded by him in the following extension of the extremely short notice given by St Matthew :—

MATTH. xii. 15.

But when Jesus knew it, he withdrew himself from thence: and great multitudes followed him, and he healed them all.

MARK iii. 7.

But Jesus withdrew himself with his disciples to the sea: and a great multitude *from Galilee* followed him, and from Judæa, and from Jerusalem, and from Idumæa, and from beyond Jordan; and they about Tyre and Sidon, *a great multitude, when they had heard what great things he did, came unto him.* AND HE SPAKE TO HIS DISCIPLES, THAT A SMALL SHIP[1] SHOULD WAIT ON HIM, BECAUSE OF THE MULTITUDE, LEST THEY SHOULD THRONG HIM. For he had healed many.

At yet another place St Mark has recorded one more highly characteristic detail with respect to our Lord's daily life, in an expression no less natural and affecting than it is short. It occurs at the commencement of the account of the storm on the sea of Galilee (iv. 36): *The disciples took him,* EVEN AS HE WAS, *into the ship,* that is to say, without any preparation for the *comfort* of the voyage.[3] Thus, perhaps, does St Mark give us in two words what we read in St Matthew, in a passage presenting the same idea (viii. 20): *The foxes have holes,*

[1] Page 101.

[2] *πλοιάριον.* St Mark frequently makes use of diminutives, and in that too shews the spirit of the Latin tongue: *θυγάτριον,* little daughter; *κοράσιον,* little maid; *ἰχθύδιον,* little fish, &c.

[3] For thus, unquestionably, must we translate the Greek sentence, *παραλαμβάνουσιν αὐτὸν* ΩΣ ΗΝ' *εν τῷ πλοίῳ,* and not, as many translations have it, *They took him, as he was in the ship.* Here, too, we have the Latin *ut erat.*

and the birds of the air have nests; but the Son of man hath not where to lay his head.

This detail is followed immediately after by another, intimately associated with what we have just noticed. While the storm is sweeping over the waters, Jesus lies asleep in the small ship. Thus we read in the three Gospels (Matt. viii. 24, Mark iv. 38, Luke viii. 24). But St Mark adds a circumstance equally picturesque and significant: *And he was* IN THE HINDER PART OF THE SHIP *asleep* UPON THE BENCH (τὸ προσκεφάλαιον). By this word we are to understand the bench covered with leather, on which the rowers sat, and consequently by no means, as the translations most improperly render it, *a pillow.*[1] No conveniency brought on board for that purpose, but only what the place itself offered, served for some moments as a couch to him who otherwise, on his own earth, had not where to lay his head.

Peculiar to St Mark, also, are the different modes of representing our Saviour as *walking in the temple,*[2] as *seated over against the treasury in the temple,* and as *seated on the Mount of Olives over against the temple* (xi. 27, xii. 41, xiii. 3).

But, above all, do we find something particularly striking in the following minute circumstances bearing on our Lord's daily intercourse with his disciples, and recorded by St Mark alone. Like a tender and faithful shepherd, ever watching over his sheep, or like the general of an

[1] HEYSCH. Τὸ δερματινὸν ὑπηρέσιον ἐφ' ᾧ καθίζονται οἱ ἐρέσσοντες; See several passages quoted in WETSTEIN on this verse. BENGEL is somewhat stronger also on this verse of St Mark: 'It was a part of the ship, as must be assumed from the article τὸ, and a wooden part too, as THEOPHYLACT remarks.'

[2] St John is the only other that represents our Lord as on one occasion making this movement (x. 23): *And Jesus walked in the templein Solomon's porch.*

army seeing to the comfort of his wearied troops, and taking a kindly interest in their welfare—such do we see the blessed Saviour as represented by St Mark: *Come ye yourselves apart into a desert place*, he says to his disciples (vi. 31), *and rest awhile; for there were many coming and going, and they had no leisure so much as to eat.* And in another place (x. 32), *And they were in the way going up to Jerusalem; and Jesus* WENT BEFORE THEM, *and they were amazed, and as they followed they were afraid.*

In yet another manner St Mark places in strong relief the human relations and the real humanity of Jesus. While St Matthew every where thinks of the worship addressed *to* Jesus, St Mark and St Luke bring chiefly before us the prayers offered *by* Jesus; each, however, in his own peculiar manner, and in connexion with his own particular point of view—Luke, to wit, in connexion with the mighty results or events that followed on the Saviour's prayer[1]—Mark, on the contrary, with his characteristic force of expression and repetition, and with important details with respect to time and place (i. 35): *And in the morning, rising up* A GREAT WHILE BEFORE DAY, *he went out, and departed* INTO A SOLITARY PLACE, *and there prayed.*

The means, or rather in general the interventions, in our Lord's miracles of healing, are nowhere placed in such strong relief as in St Mark. He shews us, first of all, how, in the objects of the Saviour's healing virtue, there was required faith, or at least the absence of all positively resisting unbelief. St Matthew (xiii. 58) notes

[1] Luke iii. 21, 22; ix. 29, &c.

this also: *He did not many mighty works there because of their unbelief;* but how much more forcible and expressive is St Mark in the parallel passage (vi. 5): *And he could there do no mighty work, save that he laid his hands upon a few sick folk and healed them. And* HE MARVELLED BECAUSE OF THEIR UNBELIEF. Such are the clearness and the force with which our second Evangelist exhibits to us our Lord's humanity in his actions and in his movements. And yet he does not leave out of sight the divinity of the incomparable Saviour. For example, he energetically gives prominence to his Divine essence, by the mere connecting of these two phrases in the history of the cure of the possessed person who had the legion (v. 19): *Go home to thy friends, and tell them how great things the* LORD *hath done for thee, and hath had compassion on thee. And he departed,* the narrator immediately proceeds to say (v. 20), *and began to publish in Decapolis how great things* JESUS *had done for him.* St Luke has evidently borrowed from St Mark in the parallel passage (viii. 39) this striking interchange of expressions: *Return to thine own house, and shew how great things* GOD *hath done unto thee. And he went his way, and published throughout the whole city how great things* JESUS *had done unto him.*

But besides this *faith* on man's part, in which lies the capacity for receiving every benefit from the Lord, who restores and heals, Jesus always accompanied his healing and saving power with the *intermediate instrumentality* of prayer, or thanksgiving, or of a word of authority, or of the uplifting or some other motion of the hands, or of some other bodily movement. The apostles, when performing cures in his name, in like manner accompanied what they did, or, if you will, operated intermediately, with the intervention of some object or other, such as the handkerchiefs mentioned in the Acts (xix. 12). In particular, they made use of *oil*, a circumstance which we find recorded by St Mark alone (vi. 3), and to which, most probably, allusion is made in the oft-abused passage in St James (v. 14, 15). We never read that Jesus himself made this use of oil, though certainly of his own spittle, of which we have a remarkable example in the Gospel of the apostle St John, on the occasion of the cure of the man who was born blind (chap. ix.) But beyond this *single* passage in St John, the author of our second Gospel is the *only one* (and *this*, again, with the exuberance of details which is peculiar to him) that has fixed our attention on the cures wrought by our Saviour with *spittle*, by *touching with his hands*, or by the *impression of his fingers*. And this it is that brings us back here to two narratives of St Mark's, which have nowhere else (as we have said above) been recorded in the four Gospels. Let us read both at full length, placed in juxtaposition, in order to see more clearly their points of agreement.

MARK vii. 32.

And they bring unto him one that was deaf, and had an impediment in his speech; and they beseech him to put his hand (τὴν χεῖρα) upon him. And he took him aside from the multitude, and put his fingers into his ears, and he spit, and touched his tongue; and looking up to heaven, he sighed, and saith unto him, *Ephphatha*, that is, *Be opened*. And straightway his ears were opened, and the string of his tongue was loosed, and he spake plain. And he charged them that they should

MARK viii. 22.

And he cometh to Bethsaida; and they bring a blind man unto him, and besought him to touch him. And he took the blind man by the hand, and led him out of the town; and when he had spit on his eyes, and put his hands upon him, he asked him if he saw aught. And he looked up, and said, I see men as trees, walking. After that he put his hands again upon his eyes, and made him look up: and he was restored, and saw every man clearly (ἐνέβλεψε τηλαυγῶς). And he sent him away to tell no man: but the more he charged them, so much the more a great deal they published it; and were beyond measure astonished, saying, He hath done all things well: he maketh both the deaf to hear, and the dumb to speak.

his house, saying, Neither go into the town, nor tell it to any in the town.

In these two narratives we still meet with that minute exactness of detail which is every where so peculiar to St Mark—the separation of the suffering person from the midst of the multitude, or the taking him out of the town; the prohibition of any reporting of the matter abroad; then, in the *one* narrative, the *looking up* and *sighing* of Jesus, the proper Syrian word pronounced by him at the moment of his operating the cure, and, finally, the astonishment and exclamations of the multitude, *He hath done all things well,* &c.; in the *other* narrative, the repeated touching of the blind man's eyes, in consequence of which he first sees things dimly and indistinctly, and afterwards clearly and correctly. What is common to both is the use of the *spittle,* and the touching with the *hands,* but in the case of the deaf and dumb, specially with the *fingers.* From these examples we learn, in a very definite manner, and as if by ocular demonstration, how the power of God which was in Jesus, and which gloriously displayed itself in the sight of men, pierced continually through the covering of his proper humanity. Here all took place supernaturally, and yet at the same time by the intervention of means, of operations, of methods. Here all is *Divine*—but all, too, is likewise *human;* and so we find the Divine and the human united, that is to say, indivisibly *one,* in the God-man JESUS CHRIST. Here St Mark gives palpable evidence of the truth of St Peter's preaching in the house of Cornelius : JESUS OF NAZARETH, *whom God anointed with the Holy Ghost and with power:* WHO WENT ABOUT DOING GOOD, AND HEALING ALL THAT WERE OPPRESSED OF THE DEVIL ;[1] *for God was with him* (Acts x. 38). The part which the Holy Ghost had in all this is distinctly explained to us by St Luke, as we shall see afterwards.

Having in this manner made ourselves acquainted with the Gospel of St Mark, we can no longer be surprised to find in it precisely that intercalation which is so much spoken of, and which, on a superficial view, seems to indicate a positive inferiority on the part of *the Son of God* to the *Father*. Speaking of the great day of the consummation of all things, the Saviour, according to St Matthew, had said (xxiv. 36), *But of that day and hour knoweth no man, no, not the angels of heaven, but my Father only.* In St Mark we read (xiii. 32), *But of that day and that hour knoweth no man, no, not the angels which are in heaven,* NEITHER THE SON, *but the Father.* Here it is evident that what is meant is only the *human knowledge* of Jesus. Had he not said shortly before, that *heaven and earth should pass away, but* MY *words shall not pass away* (xiii. 31) ? How, then, could He, who was *one* with the Father, and to whom the Father had so positively given the power of exercising judgment (John v. 27), *according to his Divine nature,* and as having an existence identical with that of the Father, have been *ignorant* of any thing ? Accordingly, what is meant here can only have been that human

[1] It is remarkable, again, in connexion with this place and the relation between St Mark and St Peter, the frequent mention in our Evangelist of *wicked*, in his Gospel generally called *unclean*, *spirits* (*πνεύματα ἀκάθαρτα*).

nature which was adopted by the Son of God, who, having in his infancy been capable of growth and progress, could likewise, at the moment here referred to, look forward to an increase of knowledge, and in a relative sense know *neither the day nor the hour*. In what manner this *knowing* and *not knowing* could be alike real and true in the person of *Jesus Christ,* remains ever a mystery, just as the nature of the most high God in all things necessarily is. Further, that it should be St Mark who so expressly testifies here to the *human not-knowing* of the Lord Jesus, is quite in harmony with what we have hitherto remarked with respect to the special relation between this Gospel and the description of the human nature of our Saviour. And if the question be put, why our Lord's humanity comes to be indicated here by a name which ordinarily, in the Evangelical writings, designates his *divinity* (*the* SON), this difficulty may be solved by the simple remark, that the sacred writers are always accustomed to couple with the mention of the Saviour's *divinity* or glory, some name pertaining to his humanity or his state of humiliation; and so in like manner, *vice versâ,* to attach to something that characterises his *humanity,* a name or title pertaining to his *divinity.* Of this there are numerous examples: *Worthy is the* LAMB THAT WAS SLAIN *to receive* POWER, AND RICHES, AND WISDOM, AND STRENGTH, AND HONOUR, AND GLORY, AND BLESSING (Rev. v. 12); CRUCIFIED THE LORD OF GLORY (1 Cor. ii. 8); KILLED THE PRINCE OF LIFE (Acts iii. 15); and hence also, and in conformity with the same rule: *the* SON *of that day and hour knoweth* NOT, that is, He who as respects his Godhead is the Son, in his state of human humiliation, of himself *knew of the day and hour nothing.*

It is time now that we should sum up and review the remarks we have had occasion to make on St Mark and his Gospel. First, then, we saw that this Gospel bears the indications of a close relationship betwixt its author and the apostle St Peter, and that, in virtue of this relationship, it comprises within itself a *double* apostolic testimony, in conformity with the two different sources whence our Evangelist drew his information—the WRITTEN testimony of St Matthew, which he knew, which he had before him, and which supplied him with the first materials for his sublime subject; and the ORAL testimony of St Peter, to whom he was in a great measure indebted for that multiplicity of details by which his Gospel is so eminently distinguished. Next, we found those details incorporated by our Evangelist in the form of a multitude of amplifications of the work of St Matthew—phrases intercalated, remarks thrown in, short parentheses, sometimes a single word inserted, altered, or rendered more emphatic, sometimes mere *transpositions*, or mere *repetitions* of a single word, and the whole equally terse and nervous. On the other hand, much that in St Matthew may be traced to the apostolic, Israelitic, prophetic—in a word, to the personal view he took of the matters which he relates, is either omitted altogether, or visibly compressed and abridged by St Mark. The spirit and tendency of those augmentations, as well as of these abridgements, are always referable to the special character of that Gospel; to wit, a determination, by a careful and minute expiscating of particulars, to delineate with more precision what St Matthew had sketched rather than described—to compress it powerfully, and work out and picture it to the mind in all its finest strokes and richest colouring. Then we found St Mark's whole style in perfect harmony with this his special gift and calling. That style betokens an author of an ardent temper, a powerful character, a firm and thoughtful spirit—a mind penetrated, above all things, with the truth, the reality, and the practical importance of the things which he describes, and to which he gives his testimony. In his general method of composition and description, as well as in many of the peculiarities exclusively pertaining to our second Evangelist, we could trace at once his national descent, his social profession, and, if we are not mistaken in following out the same course of conjecture, the very story of his conversion, and some of the details connected with that event. We recognised in him the *Gentile* by birth, the *Roman* by nation, the *soldier* by his calling—personally, no other than the *soldier who formed part of the household of Cornelius,* and who, as well as his commanding officer, was a godly proselyte to Judaism, and in his name carried a message to St Peter, inviting him to come to Cæsarea, and to commence the preaching of the gospel to the Gentiles. Thus it is that his title, and the relationship it implies, *son of St Peter,* first becomes clear and important. Finally, as the grand characteristic of the Gospel of St Mark is, in general, the lively and graphic representation of the matters which it puts on record; so, in point of result, we saw the person itself of our Lord Jesus Christ portrayed in the most minute truth of that humanity which he assumed, which he presented in this world as an object for men's eyes to behold and their hands to touch, and which he exhibited in all the various intercourse of everyday life. The EMMANUEL, announced to us by St Matthew as come forth, as it were, from the higher regions of the prophecies, the promises, and the counsels of the God of Israel, we behold, in St Mark, come down into the realities of human nature and human life, always excepting sin. In this Gospel we saw the Christ *very man*, exhibited to us in all the details of his daily life and daily conversation, without its author having a thought of investing his subject with any adventitious ornaments—placed before us, in imposing simplicity, by the able pen of the frank and unsophisticated soldier. The Gospel of St Mark, commencing with the baptism of Jesus in the Jordan, and closing with his being seated at the right hand of God, became to us, when viewed in this light, the brief and terse narrative of that three years' *campaign*, so to speak, of the *supreme Captain of our Salvation*—whose name from of old was *Warrior* as well as *Prince of Peace*—carried on and completed, for the deliverance of our souls, the bruising of Satan, the glorifying of the Father, in his labours, his sufferings, his death, his resurrection and final triumphs.

And now let the reader peruse for himself this Gospel, and in this perusal let him test the applicability of the remarks and views we have presented. But let it be read as a whole, and only *as a whole*. Both in the daily reading and in the scientific study of the Bible, people are too little accustomed to read it in this manner. They read and they study single passages and paragraphs; they read it chapter by chapter. Now, no doubt, in the reading of God's Word, there are various methods and different plans with respect to the order to be pursued. But if one would obtain a complete idea of the whole, and pierce into the essential character of any apostolical or evangelical writing, let him read at one sitting an epistle, or a gospel, as a whole, and each by itself, as one would read a letter addressed and sent to us at the present day from far or near; or as one reads in a history some account of any particular period or series of events, where all hangs together, from beginning to end, from introduction to conclusion. In this manner let any one take up for once St Mark also, and view his production as, what it really is, one consistent *whole*. Then it is that a sound and simple mind will be convinced of the impossibility of any fictitious writing or embellishment, *premeditated* or *unpremeditated*, in that remarkable production, and of the impossibility of there having been any other object contemplated in its composition than the truth, the pure truth, the truth of God.

Let us now conclude with an application of these remarks on the harmony of our Gospels. The agreement with St Matthew on the one hand, and with St Luke on the other, presents in the principal points few, or rather no difficulties. In so far, in particular, as the difference between St Matthew and St Mark consists in this, that the former relates matters in a summary and general manner, the latter more at length and in detail, one may say that there is not even the semblance of contradiction. Betwixt St Mark and St Luke the case is still more evident. Even in matters of detail these two (each, however, always in his own style and peculiar colouring) are so accordant with each other, that the third Gospel has evidently taken these from the second. True, each has its characteristic amplifications, as we had occasion at first to remark; but these again are so *meted out* between the two Evangelists, that they nowise come into collision with each other, or even in outward appearance contradict each other.

With respect to the numerical statements of St Matthew and St Mark, we have seen that they occasionally differ. But St Mark has this difference in common with St Luke; and it has already been shewn in what manner the combined testimony of the second and third Evangelist,—as, for example, in the mentioning of *one* blind and of *one* possessed person, instead of the *two* spoken of by St Matthew, decides the matter in favour of the *singular* number; whilst in the Gospel of this last we found the reasons which explain the ordinary employment by him of the *plural* or *dual* in such passages.

Nevertheless, St Mark has not always changed this somewhat vague *plural* of St Matthew into a positive *singular*. Thus, for example, he speaks of the *thieves* who reviled Jesus—in this exactly following St Matthew. And, in like manner, he does not always differ with St Matthew in the order of his narratives, but, at the same time, he is not always at one with him. Whence this apparent inconsistency with himself? It is because St Mark does not apply himself *of set purpose* to give a more correct and definite chronological arrangement, or to state numbers precisely, where he found looseness and indefiniteness in his predecessor, but *then* only does this when the special object and character of his narrative seem likely to be served by it. Wherever this is not the case, he simply adopts the account given by that predecessor. St Luke, on the contrary, writes his Gospel with the *set purpose* of reviewing and arranging the whole *in order* from the commencement (Luke i. 1–4), and St Mark smooths the way for this, without, however, himself following any fixed chronological order, or observing any rigorous accuracy of *this* kind in his narratives.

We have in this, again, a clear proof that St Mark did

not compose his Gospel *after* and *according to* that of St Luke. Had he had that of St Luke before him, there could have been no reason whatever for his departing, from time to time, from the evident order observed in that Gospel, to return to that of the first Gospel, which we have observed to be vague and general. Here, on the contrary, by keeping to the common order of succession, first St Matthew, next St Mark, after him St Luke, we have a regular gradation, a progression which we can perceive, a decided organical development. The Gospel in St Matthew (as if the glorious *child* hardly born of the fulfilled prophecies of the Old Testament) develops itself into *adolescence* in St Mark, attains its *full manhood* in St Luke, and becomes at last, in the hands of the nonagenarian St John, the living expression of the *hoary saint,* who, still full of life, and looking back on the glorious things which he had witnessed, and in which he had taken part in his youth, puts them now, at the close, in connexion with the future which he sees approaching, and with the eternal life upon which he is just about to enter.

And now one question further with respect to the words of Jesus, as recorded in manifestly different ways by the different evangelical authors. Shall we pronounce this difference the consequence of caprice and inaccuracy on the part of the writers, or shall we consider it as casual and a matter of indifference? But here anew all is involved in the difference in the points of view, in the personality, in the calling of the authors, and in the special but equally real direction, operation, and influence put forth by the Holy Ghost upon each. As from the very first there was in the person of our Saviour a richness and fulness which were capable of being drawn upon, and behoved to be drawn upon, in various ways, so was it with the words which he uttered. None of the Evangelists presents these words with a complete *literal* fidelity, except only when, for example, our very St Mark, as we have seen, gives us an idea of the *actual* language in which Jesus spoke, by rendering a few of his words in the Aramæan, which was his national and everyday dialect. But all had the liberty, the right, the vocation, to render the same words of our Lord, one in this, another in that other particular connexion and order; one in a more, another in a less fully developed manner; one with a copiousness of explanation, another with more terseness and compression. But more than this: the Evangelists, writing in the meaning and in the spirit of their Lord, had the liberty, the right, the vocation, to render by words, and to translate, so to speak, in their narrative, not only the words pronounced, but also the ideas not pronounced—the meaning conveyed by a gesture, a movement of the countenance, a look. Hence many a difference, and hence the solution of those differences. Thus, for example, the peremptory and respect-commanding word, HEARKEN! which in the Gospel of St Mark alone precedes the similitude of the sower, may very well have been in his Gospel the expression in words of a simple look of authority on the part of our Lord in the actual circumstances of the case—of that authority with which Jesus always taught, and which is spoken of on a former occasion.

Does any one still ask what certainty we can have of the correctness of such personal apprehensions and interpretations of our Lord's meaning by the Evangelists, he may just as well ask what certainty we can have of the correctness of any other detail, of any other testimony recorded by each of them from his own separate point of view.

Let it not, however, be forgotten, that we know Jesus historically, whether in his words or deeds, no otherwise than through his Apostles and Evangelists. But faith, the nature of the case, the word itself, and its truth, direct us, for all this, to the explicit promise made to the witnesses whom the Lord had called: *He that heareth you, heareth me.*

IV. ST LUKE.

IN St Paul's Epistles we find mention made, again and again, and in a very marked manner, of the name of the person to whom, by common consent, from the very beginning, our third Gospel has been attributed. In several of those greetings which often throw so much light at once on the history and on the truths of Christianity, we find LUKE, *the physician*, named with affectionate commendation, among the most faithful fellow-labourers and most intimate friends of the much-tried Apostle. Writing during his first captivity at Rome to the Church of the Colossians, the Apostle speaks of him in these terms (iv. 14), *Luke, the beloved physician, and Demas, greet you.* In the epistle written at that period likewise to Philemon, he writes of him, among his fellow-labourers and fellow-prisoners, as follows (v. 23 and 24): *There salute thee Epaphras, my fellow-prisoner in Christ Jesus; Marcus, Aristarchus, Demas, Lucas, my fellow-labourers.* In the last of his epistles (the second to Timothy), we find that, in the critical moments of the Apostle's final struggle for the faith, amid the many sufferings, privations, and trials of that period, Luke, and Luke alone, stands by him: *At my first answer no man stood with me, but all men forsook me* (iv. 16). *Demas hath forsaken me, having loved this present world, and is departed unto Thessalonica; Crescens to Galatia, Titus unto Dalmatia* (ver. 10). To his Timothy he writes (ver. 9): *Do thy diligence to come shortly unto me;* but soon after he says, *Only Luke is with me.* There is yet another circumstance which we may infer concerning this faithful brother, from the above salutation at the close of the Epistle to the Colossians. In the nomenclature that appears there (iv. 10-16) of the several fellow-labourers by whom he was then surrounded at Rome, the Apostle assigns distinct places to the brethren *who are of the circumcision,* and to those who by their national origin did *not* belong to ancient Israel. Among the latter we find Luke, who consequently appears, from this passage, to have been a Christian converted *from among the Gentiles,* and in all probability a *proselyte,* before his conversion to Christ. The whole passage runs thus: *Aristarchus my fellow-prisoner saluteth you, and Marcus, sister's son to Barnabas (touching whom ye received commandments: if he come unto you, receive him); and Jesus, which is called Justus, who are* OF THE CIRCUMCISION. *These only are my fellow-workers unto the kingdom of God, which have been a comfort unto me. Epaphras, who is one of you, a servant of Christ,* &c. *Luke, the beloved physician, and Demas, greet you,* &c.

Here, then, we have three particulars with respect to St Luke, and these present him to us in a characteristic and interesting manner; to wit, that in point of national origin he was a Gentile, that by profession he was a physician, and that, moreover, he was a beloved and faithful fellow-labourer of St Paul's in the ministry of the Gospel. Now, it is precisely these three characteristic marks that we find in the author of our third Gospel—that Gospel of which the Book of the Acts of the Apostles is *universally* admitted to be an immediate sequel, written by the same hand throughout, in conformity with the dedication of that second book to the same Theophilus to whom the Gospel had been inscribed (Acts i. 1, compared with St Luke's Gospel, i. 1-4, and xxiv. 51). *The* FORMER *treatise have I made, O Theophilus, of all that Jesus began both to do and to teach, until the day in which he was taken up*, &c.

Now, in the Book of the Acts, in the first place, the author makes himself known most unequivocally, though in the most unsought, the most unintentional, and withal, the humblest manner, as a servant of the Gospel in the strictest connexion with St Paul. It is true he nowhere introduces the name LUKE; nowhere records a single word spoken, or action done, by himself individually; but concealing himself, as it were, under the plural pronoun *we*, he sufficiently reveals himself to us as an eyewitness and participant in a considerable number of the matters recorded in that second book. As a fellow-traveller of St Paul's we first meet with him, shortly after the second sending out of that Apostle, in company with Silas, from the mother Church at Antioch (Acts xv. 40, 41, xvi. 1, and following verses). Having always spoken before this of St Paul and his fellow-labourers in the *third* person, he now begins at once, at an important moment, to include himself as one of that wayfaring and God-conducted mission (ver. 9, 10): "*And a vision appeared to Paul in the night; There stood a man of Macedonia, and prayed him, saying, Come over into Macedonia, and help us. And after he had seen the vision, immediately* WE *endeavoured to go into Macedonia, assuredly gathering that the Lord had called* US *for to preach the gospel unto them.* From this time forward we can clearly distinguish, according as he makes use of the first or the third person of the pronoun (*we* or *they*), the times at which St Luke accompanied St Paul, from those at which he was separated from him for a season, to rejoin him afterwards. Following this infallible rule, we see him first accompanying the Apostle to Philippi in Macedonia (xvi. 12-17), after which, it would seem, from his disusing the pronoun *we*, employed till then, that he was left in that city to continue the instruction of the hardly constituted Church. Then, some years afterwards, on the occasion of St Paul's passing through that same Philippi on his journey to Asia (xx. 1-4), we again find him evidently one of the Apostle's immediate circle (ver. 5, 6) : *These going before tarried for* US *at Troas. And* WE *sailed away from Philippi after the days of unleavened bread, and* WE *came unto them in Troas.* From this period forward (guided always by this artless but significant *we*), we find him accompanying the Apostle on the most perilous of the missions that the book records—first to Assos, Mitylene, Samos, Trogyllium, and Miletus (xx. 13–38, xxi. 1) ; after that, to Coos, Rhodes, Patara, on to Cyprus, from thence to Syria and Tyre, to Ptolemais, and finally to Cæsarea (xxi. 1-8), where St Paul received an intimation from the Holy Ghost that bonds and persecutions awaited him (verses 8–11). St Luke, although he never introduces himself by name, had a part, beyond all doubt, in the affecting struggle of faith and charity that arose betwixt St Paul and his fellow-travellers (verses 12–14). *And when* WE *heard these things, both* WE, *and they of that place, besought him not to go up to Jerusalem. Then Paul answered, What mean ye to weep and to break mine heart? for I am ready not to be bound only, but also to die at Jerusalem for the name of the Lord Jesus. And when he would not be persuaded,* WE *ceased, saying, The will of the Lord be done.* Our historian then accompanies the heroic apostle to Jerusalem (v. 17 and 18): *And when* WE *were come to Jerusalem, the brethren received* US *gladly. And the day following Paul went in with* US *unto James; and all the elders were present.* It is true that the persecution which shortly after overtook the apostle, being of a purely personal nature, did not immediately affect our author; but from what he straightway records with respect to St Paul's detention at Cæsarea (xxiv. 23), we may assuredly conclude that St Luke was one of those who availed themselves most of the perfect liberty granted by Felix to the apostle, to forbid none of his acquaintance to minister or come unto him. When afterwards, in consequence of his appealing unto Cæsar, the apostle embarked as a prisoner for Italy, the author of the Acts very expressly includes himself in the number of those who accompanied him (xxvii. 1), *And when it was determined that* WE *should sail into Italy, they delivered Paul and certain other prisoners unto one named Julius, a centurion of Augustus' band.* Thus, after all the hardships described in chapters xxi. to xxvii., they arrived together at Rome. This second book of our evangelist concludes with the apostle's two years' imprisonment there; and we then find him, as we have seen, mentioned by his name Luke, in the epistles written by St Paul during his first residence at Rome. Here accordingly, we have anew, in conformity with the ancient and universal traditions to that effect, but at the same time quite independent of these traditions, clear proof that the author of our third Gospel, and of the book of Acts, was a well-beloved fellow-labourer of the apostle St Paul, a faithful brother in his bonds and persecutions, one who remained to the last at his side. The influence of so close a tie on St Luke's writings in general, but especially on his Gospel, will appear hereafter in our examination of their details. But let us first contemplate St Luke in another relation mentioned by the Apostle, and occurring in the writings of the Evangelist.

LUKE *the physician saluteth you.* So runs the salutation mentioned in the Epistle to the Colossians. Now, the *physician* plainly enough reappears in both of the writings that have been transmitted to us from the Evangelist. Thus in our third Gospel, the maladies that are mentioned in it are partly described with more detail, partly indicated by their proper technical terms. For example, the fever of which St Peter's wife's mother was cured by the Saviour, is spoken of only by St Luke as a strong, a great fever (*πυρετὸς μέγας*), in conformity with a scientific distinction still found in Galen.[1] By a like technical term he describes the loss, or, properly speaking, the obscuration of the vision, in the sorcerer Elymas (Acts xiii. 11).[2] Besides the healing of the blind, the paralytic, and the possessed, which he records in common with his two predecessors, we read exclusively in his Gospel of the woman who was bowed together (Luke xiii. 11), of the man afflicted with dropsy (xiv. 2), &c. He describes very exactly the illness of which St Paul cured Publius at Malta (xxviii. 8), as *fever* and *dysentery* (*πυρετοὶ καὶ δυσεντερίαι*).[3] The disease of which

[1] GALENUS de Diff. Feb. i., *σύνηθες ἤδη τοῖς ἰατροῖς ὀνομάζειν—τὸν μέγαν τε καὶ μικρὸν πυρετόν.*

[2] GALENUS ii. in Protr. ii., *ἀχλὺς, ὀφθαλμοῦ πάθος—διά τινος ἀχλύος οἴονται βλέπειν.*

[3] WETSTEIN ad Act., xxviii. 8. AUL. GELLIUS, viii. 10. "*Ibi alvo mihi citâ accedente febre rabidâ decubueram.* Lucas medicus morbos accuratius describere solet."

Herod Agrippa died, mentioned in more general terms by Josephus, is more exactly known to us from St Luke's account (Acts xii. 23), as *an eating by worms* (*σκωληκόβρωτος, ἐξέψυξεν*). It likewise deserves notice, that the Evangelist *physician* alone, in the history of the passion, mentions the healing by the hand of our Lord of the ear of Malchus, when it had been cut off by the disciple (Luke xxii. 51). It is he likewise who speaks of the sleep of the disciples, during the anguish endured by their Master in the garden of Gethsemané, as arising from depression of mind (xxii. 45). He alone mentions the sleep of those same disciples on the occasion of that awful scene, the transfiguration on the Mount (ix. 32). The commission given to the twelve on their being sent forth, recorded so much more fully by St Matthew (x. 7, 8), is summed up by St Luke in these few words, *to preach the kingdom of God, and* TO HEAL THE SICK (ix. 2). The sending forth of the seventy disciples, recorded by St Luke alone, comprises in like manner all the miraculous gifts in that same command (x. 9), HEAL THE SICK, *and say unto them, The kingdom of God is come nigh unto you.* Whereupon soon after (v. 17), the disciples that had been sent forth, *returned again with joy, saying, Lord, even the devils are subject unto us through thy name.* And how much more deeply still, than can be made to appear from these detached passages, is the stamp of the physician imprinted on St Luke's Gospel! How in his, more than in any other Gospel, does the glorious union come out, in the works of Jesus (according to the words of the Psalmist), between *the forgiving of our iniquities and the healing of our diseases!* How distinctly is our Saviour exhibited to us by him as *the great Physician of Israel!* All this will be more clearly perceived on our scrutinizing St Luke's Gospel more minutely. Occupying ourselves for the present, so to speak, with the surface only, we would simply remark further, that it is St Luke alone who has preserved for us the proverb that fell from our Lord's lips, *Physician, heal thyself* (iv. 23). And is it not the physician that speaks to us anew in the attitude in which he describes our Lord by the side of the sick-bed of Simon's mother-in-law ?

MATTH. viii. 15.	MARK i. 31.	LUKE iv. 39.
And he touched her hand, and the fever left her.	And he came and took her by the hand, and lifted her up: and immediately the fever left her.	And he stood over her, and rebuked the fever (Gr. ἐπάνω αὐτῆς); and it left her.

St Luke's following the profession of a physician is so far connected with his national descent. We have seen that he was designated by St Paul as *not of the circumcision*, consequently as a Gentile by birth. The art of medicine was at that time very much in the hands of the Greeks, and particularly of slaves and freedmen, a sort of people among the Romans of that era that were often found, as is well known, highly gifted and civilized. Syria in particular was, in those days, highly reputed for the practice of medicine. Now, there is an ancient tradition preserved by some of the Fathers of the Church, that St Luke was a native of Antioch in Syria, at least that he had his usual residence there, and had there been gained to Christ, while the termination of his name (in ᾶς) was, at all events, common to him with many of the slaves and freedmen of that time. However that may be, no less manifestly than the *Roman proselyte* reveals himself in St Mark's Gospel, do we recognise the *Greek proselyte* in that of St Luke. Both his language and his style as an historian perpetually remind us of his Greek origin and education—a point on which all who are versed in philology and archæology agree. The style of the ancient classical historians meets us at once in the introduction and dedication of his Gospel (i. 1–4): *Forasmuch as many have taken in hand to set forth in order a declaration of those things which are most surely believed among us, even as they delivered them unto us, which from the beginning were eyewitnesses, and ministers of the word; it seemed good to me also, having had perfect understanding of all things from the very first, to write thee in order, most excellent Theophilus, that thou mightest know the certainty of those things wherein thou hast been instructed.*

By this preface, so full of instruction to us in several respects, first of all it most clearly appears that he himself had in no way been an eyewitness of the doings of the Lord Jesus, and therefore could not, as some would have it, have been of the number of the seventy disciples sent out by him. It will be seen that he distinctly disconnects himself from those who, *from the beginning, were* EYEWITNESSES *and ministers of the word;* but, nevertheless, it is an ancient tradition that St Luke, already for some time a proselyte to Judaism, and familiar with the whole religion and nation of Israel, had through that medium, probably at Antioch, been brought into the Church of Christ, which tradition we shall see fully confirmed by the nature and contents of his Gospel.

But setting aside for a few moments the consideration of the three chief characteristics which meet us at once in St Luke's writings, we proceed to contemplate his Gospel as viewed from another side. We would direct the reader's attention to the peculiar structure of this, the third of our Gospels, as respects the course it pursues—

its method and plan, in so far as these *distinguish it from* the Gospels of St Matthew and St Mark, and make it *harmonize with* the Acts of the Apostles.

If the Gospel of St Matthew suggests to us the idea of a perpetual comparing of the person of Jesus Christ with the predictions of the prophets ; if we found in Mark the mighty deeds of the Lord related in the form of a compressed but consistent and lively report—we recognise in St Luke that one among the four Evangelists who was more peculiarly *the historian.* His Gospel announces itself as such from its very introduction. What he proposes is, first, to set forth in order a declaration (ver. 1), (ἀνατάξασθαι διήγησιν). In order to this (ver 3), he had examined all things *from the very first* (ἄνωθεν). *That* he is to write to Theophilus *in order* (καθέξῆς), *so that he might know the certainty* (ἀσφάλειαν, *the infallible certainty*) *of those things wherein he had been* previously *instructed.* Here we find at once two of the main objects of a true historian :—1st, To draw up a continuous narrative, derived from a careful examination of the testimonies of eyewitnesses and ministers of the word (v. 2) ; 2nd, To commit it to writing in chronological order.

The historical narrative itself answers to these two objects for which it was written. Our third Gospel does not, like that of St Matthew, content itself with a short notice of our Lord's conception and birth. It carries events further back in their sublime continuity ; it leads us to the first beginnings, and, as it were, to the very dawn of our Lord's coming in the flesh ; it commences with various details relating to the annunciation, the conception, and the birth, not only of our Lord himself, but also of his forerunner, the Baptist,—(Chap. i.) It opens with an expression (i. 5) which subsequently occurs above sixty times in the two compositions of St Luke. *There was*, or *it happened that* (Gr. ἐγένετο).

And in like manner, as St Luke carries his narrative much further back than the two evangelists who preceded him, so also neither does he conclude it, as they do, with the resurrection and ascension of our Lord; but adds a second historical book, relating what was done by our Lord after he had seated himself at God's right hand in the heavens, the fulfilment of the promise of the Spirit, the preaching, and the works and signs done by the apostles in the name and power of their glorified Master.

A due attention to dates is peculiarly requisite in a professed historian. We find accordingly in St Luke, from the very commencement, the dates of the great things related in his gospel carefully determined (i. 5): IN THE DAYS OF HEROD, KING OF JUDEA, *a certain priest named Zacharias*, &c., anon more fully, on the appearance of the Baptist in his public ministry (iii. 1, 2): *Now in* THE FIFTEENTH YEAR OF THE REIGN OF TIBERIUS CÆSAR, Pontius Pilate *being governor of Judea, and* Herod *being tetrarch of Galilee, and his brother* Philip *tetrarch of Ituræa and of the region of Trachonitis, and* Lysanias *the tetrarch of Abilene*, Annas *and* Caiaphas *being the high priests, the word of God came unto* John *the son of* Zacharias *in the wilderness.*

But he is no less accurate in giving epochs, days, and years when he has occasion to speak of private persons. In the case of Anna, the prophetess in the temple (ii. 36, 37), he not only mentions her being about *fourscore and four* years old, but the *seven* years also during which she had lived with her husband in her youth. He repeatedly gives the duration also of the diseases, the cures of which were wrought by our Lord or his apostles: the sufferings endured for *eighteen years* by the woman who was bent double, in the Gospel (xiii. 11); the palsy of which Æneas had been ill for *eight years*, in the Acts (ix. 33); the *forty* years' lameness of the man who was cured at the gate of the temple by Peter and John (iii. 1, iv. 22). In the same book of the Acts he carefully puts down the years, months, and days that the Apostle St Paul had spent at Corinth, at Ephesus, at Cæsarea, at Rome, and elsewhere (xviii. 2; xx. 31; xxi. 4; xxiv. 1; xxviii. 30). With respect to our Lord himself, it is St Luke alone who speaks of his being circumcised *on the eighth day* (ii. 21); of his being brought into the temple *after the days of the purification* were fulfilled (ii. 22, and following verses); of Jesus, at the age of *twelve years*, sitting in the midst of the doctors in the temple (ii. 42, &c.) He is the only evangelist also that informs us of Jesus being of the age of *thirty years* when he received the rite of baptism at the hands of John, and from the Holy Spirit from heaven (iii. 23). It is from St Luke alone that we also learn that *forty days* elapsed between the resurrection and the ascension of our Lord (Acts i. 3).

None of the evangelists, again, enters so deeply into the Jewish history of those times as St Luke does. He alone, for example, records our Lord's allusion to the massacre of a number of the Galileans by the governor, Pontius Pilate, on the occasion of a festival (xiii. 1–3); likewise (v. 4) the fall of the tower of Siloam, which caused the death of eighteen persons. And in the Acts (v. 36, 37) he makes mention of the two insurrections in those stormy days in Israel—the one that of Theudas, and the other that of Judas the Galilean.

Notices of the family of the Herods occur more frequently in St Luke's than in any other of the New Testament writings. Thus we find him mention not only, as St Matthew and St Mark do, the elder Herod, surnamed *the great*, and his son Herod Antipas, *the Tetrarch*, as also his brother Philip, the husband of Herodias: but likewise in the book of the Acts, Herod Agrippa (grandson of Herod *the great* by Aristobulus), better known from the writings of Josephus; and finally, his son and daughter, Agrippa and Bernice, persons well known otherwise, and chiefly from the figure they make during the closing period of the national existence of Judea (Acts xii., xxv.) St Luke, too, over and above what the other Evangelists say of Herod Antipas in connexion with John the Baptist, gives us some details in connexion with Jesus himself. He alone records (xiii. 31, 32) that there came certain of the Pharisees, saying unto him, *Get thee out, and depart hence: for Herod will kill thee;* and the answer given by our Lord: *Go ye, and tell that fox, Behold I cast out devils, and I do cures to-day and to-morrow, and the third day I shall be perfected.* In the history of the passion none but St Luke mentions our Lord's being sent to that same Herod, and how the murderer of John the Baptist became the reviler of the Saviour, although at the same time one of the witnesses of his innocence (xxiii. 5–12; Acts iv. 27). Further, from quite another side, St Luke makes us acquainted with the history of the Herod family, by informing us in his Gospel (viii. 3), that among the godly women from Galilee who ministered unto Jesus of their substance, *there was Joanna, the wife of Chusa, Herod's steward;* and afterwards, in the Acts (xiii. 1), he speaks of Manaen, one of the prophets and teachers of the church at Antioch, as having been *brought up with Herod the Tetrarch.*

In this and many other ways, while perusing the writings of St Luke, we find ourselves transported into the domain of *general history.* Not that the three other Gospels (far from it) are not equally pure, genuine, authentic histories, but that their narratives are more circumscribed within the limits of the Jewish territory and nation, of Jewish affairs and Jewish persons; whereas St Luke continually, and in various ways, leads us into the history of antiquity, as known to us from other quarters, and from profane sources, whether heathen or Jewish, such as Josephus and others. This applies particularly to the Book of Acts, a book so pre-eminently remarkable for the light it derives from history and antiquities. There, in a most especial manner, and from most manifest causes, there is such a complex and varied intermingling with the whole, of Jewish, Greek, and Roman antiquity; there, the whole civilized world of the Europe and Asia of those days is so often touched upon, that, thanks to the accumulated treasures of philological, antiquarian, and historical learning which we possess in our time, the slightest error, the smallest inaccuracy, nay, the most trifling mistake, must necessarily be brought to light on being subjected to scrutiny. Now, what has been the result of the most searching scrutiny of the two writings left us by St Luke, sifted fact by fact, detail by detail, expression by expression, in the light of all that the most civilized and the most enlightened antiquity directly witnesses or incidentally suggests to our researches? Why, nothing but an acknowledgment of the most satisfactory correctness in every thing that bears upon philology, history, geography, and antiquities, that ever was found in the most authentic contemporary historian. Whithersoever the author of the book of Acts conducts us, whether in Judea, to Jerusalem, or into Galilee; upon the territory, or into the details of the lives of the Herods and Agrippas; under the governorship of Pilate, of Felix, or of Festus; under the pontificate of Caiaphas, or Annas, or Ananias; into the towns of Samaria, or amid the hostile feelings that subsisted betwixt the inhabitants of that country and the Jewish nation; or to Cesarea, the seat of the court, at one time of a Herod, at another time of a Roman governor; to Damascus, under the governor appointed by King Aretas; to Tarsus in Cilicia, to Antioch in Syria, to Antioch in Pisidia, to Iconium, to Lystra, to Derbe in Lycaonia, into Pamphylia, into Attalia, into Mysia, into Bithynia, to Troas, to Ephesus in Asia Minor; or from thence into Europe, to Philippi, the first Roman colonial city in Macedonia, to Athens, and before the Areopagus; or into that Corinth which was once so famous throughout the world, and into its maritime port, Cenchrea; or, afterwards, over the waters of the Mediterranean; or under the large and famous island of Crete; or under the small islet of Clauda; to the Syrtis, to the island of Malta, to Syracuse, or finally, over the territory of Italy, to Rhegium and Puteoli, thereafter to Appii Forum, and to the Three Taverns on the road to Rome, and to Rome itself: whether he transports us into all these different places, and takes us before kings, governors, and chiefs; into the temple, into the synagogues, into the houses of the great or the small, of Jews or of Gentiles; amid the sanctuaries and idolatries of different nations; into the society of military officers and soldiers, ship-captains and sailors; into the market-place, the tribunals, or the prisons;

whether to the coasts of a semi-barbarous people, or on board the ship whose sign was *Castor and Pollux;* whether he commits to writing, for our perusal, the discourses of St Peter or St Paul, of St Stephen the deacon, or of St Philip the evangelist, or the speech of the advocate Tertullus, or a letter from the chief captain, Claudius Lysias; whether he brings us into contact with Jewish, Greek, Roman, or barbarian manners, with the legislation and judicial forms, the military or civil institutions of different countries;—we every where find the utmost simplicity of style and exposition, conjoined with the utmost truthfulness of colouring, and the language that is appropriate to the subject purely and naturally employed—every where we find the strictest accuracy in all the circumstances, even the most minute and hardly noticeable, confirmed and verified by all the light that in our days has been poured upon us from the most authentic sources of antiquarian lore, with respect to the times, the princes, the governments, the nations, the men, in one word, with respect to the very things mentioned or described in the two books of our Evangelist historian, St Luke.

Paley, in his excellent work *On the Evidences of Christianity,* has given abundant examples of the manner, often quite unexpected and surprising, in which the testimony of profane historians brings out the truth and correctness of the Evangelical writings. But particularly as respects St Luke's Gospel, one could here considerably enlarge the number by the examples we might adduce of discoveries made since Paley's time, after further study and comparison of ancient writings and monuments bearing on this same accuracy in the most minute and least obvious details. We shall confine ourselves to a single example. We read in the book of the Acts (xix. 28

and 34), that the multitude having risen against St Paul, gave vent to their zeal for the worship which was threatened by his preaching, in the cry: *Great is Diana of the Ephesians!* Such exclamations in honour of the pagan divinities are well known in profane antiquity. Still, nowhere had learned men met with a passage in any part of the writings of antiquity, proving that this title of *great goddess* had been specially given among the Greeks to *Diana.* Now a Greek manuscript of Xenophon the Ephesian, discovered about the middle of the last century, gives us the utmost possible certainty of it by a passage where a virgin of Ephesus swears, in so many words, by the goddess of her native town, *the great Diana of the Ephesians.*[1]

Such a harmony even in the most minute details of language, of institutions, and of customs, could not by any imaginable possibility have been an effect of any human invention, myth, or embellishment whatever. The designedly or undesignedly embellishing or idealizing it, from the very nature of the thing, will be found carefully to avoid all such explicitness of statement and allusion, with respect to individual things and persons, which it might safely have omitted to mention at all, or have done so much more indefinitely. No one but the historian, the faithful and conscientious historian, living himself in the midst of the times and scenes he describes, could preserve such a perfect fidelity to the truth, the condition, the colouring, and all the characteristic peculiarities of those times; whilst, moreover, the style and whole cast of the book every where clearly testify, that this accuracy has not been the result of effort and studied design. It would have been all the more difficult for any but a con-

[1] VALCKENAER, Schol. in Act. Apost., xix. 28.

temporary to attain it, in proportion as the period of which it treats was fertile in great events, in changes in the governments, and in the boundaries and names of countries and peoples, in such sort that many particulars, true at one time, if transposed to a period a few years either sooner or later, would be found to be incorrect. But from this side, too, our sacred writings, and particularly those of St Luke, are all the more strongly proof against all attack, or even doubt. Of all the apparent contradictions, and of all the difficulties that have been proposed against some places of his two books, the often cited parenthesis respecting the government of Cyrenius, in his Gospel (ii. 2), with two or three further difficulties of less consequence in the Acts, are the only points which, down to the present day, have not yet been *perfectly* cleared up. And for those places, perhaps, the solution is more simple than many think.

Thus, then, in St Luke, we have in a peculiar manner the Evangelist historian. But this being the case, it is then in his Gospel that we must, from the very commencement, look for a true solution and correct arrangement, on every occasion of discrepancy among the Gospels, with respect to the *order* of the matters that they relate. At the very opening of his book he has announced it to be his object to set forth *in order;* what he undertook was to write *in order* (Gr. καθεξῆς). Already, in our examination of St Matthew's Gospel, we have seen that it was not in the first of our Gospels, which arranges facts rather according to the *homogeneity* of the subjects, but that it was in St Luke's that we might expect to find the true order in which events took place. Here seems the fittest opportunity for placing in a still clearer light, by adducing some more detailed examples, this characteristic specialty of our third Gospel.

For the purposes of a comparison in this important respect between St Matthew and St Luke, the sermon on the Mount, which occupies a prominent place in both, presents several particulars to our notice. First of all, let us mark the place which that discourse occupies in the series of our Lord's sayings and doings. St Matthew places it (v. vi. vii.) immediately *after* the calling of St Peter, St Andrew, St James, and St John, and *after* a very short mention of the miracles and of the preaching of our Lord in the synagogues of Galilee (iv. 13–25), but long *before* the naming of the twelve (x. 1–4). In St Luke, the sermon on the Mount is placed (vi. 20–40) immediately *after* the calling and naming of the twelve, (vi. 13–40)—a difference in each case perfectly in accordance with the very different construction of their whole narratives. St Matthew, whose grand aim it is to give a representation of the great Prophet like unto Moses, naturally places on the foreground of his Gospel the proclamation by his Master's mouth of the doctrines and commandments of the kingdom of heaven. Jesus, according to St Matthew, opens upon a mountain the preaching of the Gospel, as Moses received the law upon the Mount. But, historically, the place is of necessity that assigned to it by St Luke, in whose Gospel the solemn discourse on the mountain was, as the very nature of the case intimates, delivered in presence of the *already constituted* number of twelve Apostles.

The sermon on the Mount, in St Matthew's Gospel, as we have already said, comprehends not only what was actually spoken by the Saviour at that hour and on that place, but (in virtue of his apostolic authority and of the wider scope assigned to him by the Holy Ghost in the special purpose his Gospel was designed to subserve), much more besides, in the way of sayings and similitudes, really and expressly uttered by Jesus, but on other occasions or in a different connexion. Thus, among other instructions of the sermon on the Mount, St Matthew inserts the Lord's Prayer: *Our Father which art in heaven*, &c. In quite a different connexion, yet one that clearly shews itself to have been the true historical connexion, we read this model prayer in St Luke. Let the passages themselves be compared, as follows :—

Luke xi. 1, 2.	Matth. vi. 7, 9.
And it came to pass, that, as he was praying in a certain place, when he ceased, one of his disciples said unto him, Lord, teach us to pray, as John also taught his disciples. And he said unto them, When ye pray, say, Our Father which art in heaven, Hallowed be thy name. Thy kingdom come. Thy will be done, as in heaven, so in earth, &c.	But when ye pray, use not vain repetitions, as the heathen do: for they think that they shall be heard for their much speaking. Be not ye therefore like unto them: for your Father knoweth what things ye have need of, before ye ask him. After this manner therefore pray ye: Our Father which art in heaven, Hallowed be thy name, &c.

Immediately after the Lord's prayer in St Luke (xi. 5–9) there follows a similitude—that of the friend who comes at midnight asking for the loan of three loaves—which is nowhere to be found in St Matthew. Of another similitude, introduced by St Luke immediately after, we find a portion in another part of the sermon on the Mount in St Matthew, but not connected with the Lord's prayer.

Luke xi. 10–13.	Matthew, vii. 6–11.
For every one that asketh receiveth; and he that seeketh findeth; and to him that knocketh it shall be opened. If a son shall ask bread of any of you that is a father, will he give him a stone?	Give not that which is holy unto the dogs, neither cast ye your pearls before swine, lest they trample them under their feet, and turn again and rend you. Ask, and it shall be given you, &c. For

or if he ask a fish, will he for a fish give him a serpent? Or if he shall ask an egg, will he offer him a scorpion? If ye then, being evil, know how to give good gifts unto your children: how much more shall your heavenly Father give the Holy Spirit to them that ask him?

every one that asketh receiveth, &c. Or what man is there of you, whom if his son ask bread, will he give him a stone? Or if he ask a fish, &c. If ye then, being evil, know how to give good gifts unto your children, how much more, &c.

In the same sermon on the Mount, we read in St Matthew (vi. 25-34), the exhortations against *being careful* about the things of this life, immediately after the warning (24) against *serving God and mammon.* In St Luke we find the same exhortation delivered almost in the same terms, but in quite a different connexion and at quite another time. The connexion in which St Luke places them (xii. 13-31), is too natural to permit of a doubt as to its being the true historical one. The circumstances speak for themselves. One of the company had come to Jesus, asking him that he would speak to his brother that he would divide an inheritance with him. Jesus declines any pretension of the kind: *Man! who made me a judge or a divider over you?* He follows this up immediately with an exhortation against avarice (ver. 15), which is afterwards enforced by the powerful similitude of the rich man, of whom his soul was required in the midst of his projects of aggrandizement and enjoyment (ver. 16–21). Whereupon the Saviour turns *to his disciples and saith unto them, Therefore I say unto you, Take no thought for your life, what ye shall eat; neither for the body, what ye shall put on,* and what further follows in both Evangelists.

The same thing holds with respect to our Lord's invitation to *enter in at the strait gate.* This we find taken by St Matthew, without any definite connexion, into the series of the lessons comprised in the sermon on the Mount; it occurs elsewhere in St Luke, but this both for reasons supplied by the most striking historical connexion, and elucidated by that connexion.

MATTH. vii. 12, 13.	LUKE xiii. 23, 24.
Therefore all things whatsoever ye would that men should do to you, do ye even so to them: for this is the law and the prophets. Enter ye in at the strait gate: for wide is the gate, and broad is the way, that leadeth to destruction, and many there be which go in thereat.	*Then said one unto him, Lord, are there few that be saved? And he said unto them,* Strive to enter in at the strait gate: for many, I say unto you, will seek to enter in, and shall not be able.

In like manner, as we saw the commandments and exhortations, so did we find the similitudes also collected together by St Matthew in several places in the way of *accumulation.*[1]

The similitude of *the talents,* which St Matthew (xxv. 14-30) places immediately after, and makes, as it were, of a piece with that of *the wise and foolish virgins,* and which he connects with our Lord's appearance on the great day of judgment as king and judge, the history of the passion commencing immediately after—that very similitude we find referred in St Luke to a much earlier period. On the last journey of Jesus with his disciples to Jerusalem, shortly before the solemn procession from Bethphage and Bethany, we read it in the following evidently historical connexion (xix. 11–29): *And as they heard these things, he added and spake a parable,* BECAUSE HE WAS NIGH TO JERUSALEM, AND BECAUSE THEY THOUGHT THAT THE KINGDOM OF GOD SHOULD IMMEDIATELY APPEAR. *He said therefore, A certain nobleman went into a far country to receive for himself a kingdom, and to return. And he called his ten servants, and delivered them ten pounds, and said unto them, Occupy*

[1] Page 29.

till I come, &c. &c. *And when he had thus spoken, he went before, ascending up to Jerusalem. And it came to pass, when he was come nigh to Bethphage and Bethany,* &c.

It is the same with regard to the similitude of the invitation to the marriage feast, which, placed in a more indefinite connexion by St Matthew, we find recurring in St Luke at a much later period, but evidently in its really historical connexion, in the following manner :—

MATTH. xxii. 1–4.	LUKE xiv. 1–17.
And Jesus answered and spake unto them again by parables, and said, The kingdom of heaven is like unto a certain king, which made a marriage for his son. And sent forth his servants to call them that were bidden to the wedding: and they would not come. Again, he sent forth other servants, saying, Tell them which are bidden, Behold, I have prepared my dinner: come unto the marriage.	*And it came to pass, as he went into the house of one of the chief Pharisees, to eat bread on the Sabbath-day, that they watched him,* &c. *And when one of them* THAT SAT AT MEAT WITH HIM heard these things, he said unto him, Blessed is he that shall eat bread in the kingdom of God. *But he said to them,* A certain man made a great supper, and bade many: and sent his servant at supper time to say to them that were bidden, Come ; for all things are now ready.

The similitude of *the grain of mustard-seed* and that of *the leaven that was hid in three measures of meal,* are, in like manner, again included by St Matthew in the general series (chap. xiii.) ; while in St Luke we find them in a more definite and every way characteristic connexion. When the Pharisees were indignant, and the multitudes rejoiced at the cure of the woman who was bowed together, *and for all the glorious things that were done by him* (xiii. 10–17), he lays hold of the fact of that resistance on the part of the great, and that affection on the part of the small, as an opportunity for introducing the similitude (verses 18–21): *Then said he, Unto what is the kingdom of God like? and whereunto shall*

I resemble it? It is like a grain of mustard-seed, &c. *It is like leaven,* &c.

We might here adduce many more examples of the doings and sayings of Jesus, recorded by St Matthew in the connexion suggested by their *homogeneity,* and which is peculiar to him, but which are, on the contrary, transposed and re-arranged by St Luke according to the requisitions of the *historical* connexion. We shall adduce only two additional instances. The *woes* which our Saviour is recorded to have pronounced upon the Pharisees and Scribes, and on their manifold acts of wickedness (xxiii. 13–30), are conjoined in St Matthew with a warning addressed to the multitude and his disciples against the Scribes and Pharisees that sat in Moses' seat (xxiii. 1–12). St Luke, at the same stage in his gospel (xx. 45–47), gives the *warning* indeed, but not the *woes.* The reason is that he had previously recorded these, and again, evidently in the true historical connexion, on a very marked and peculiar occasion (xi. 37–53). Having been invited by a certain Pharisee to dine with him, he had seated himself at the table, when the Pharisee *marvelled that he had not first washed before dinner.* This very remark gave our Lord an opportunity of correcting the hypocrisy of those doctors (ver. 39–41). This he follows up with the fearful denunciations uttered against the Scribes and Pharisees (ver. 42–44), which he afterwards extends to the lawyers (*νομικοὶ*) (ver. 46), in reply to the observation made by one of them (ver. 45): *Master, thus saying, thou reproachest us also.*

The signs that were to accompany the last times are enumerated in a discourse of Jesus, very fully recorded by the three first Evangelists, in connexion with the foretelling of the approaching destruction of Jerusalem. But we find several details brought together by St Matthew, which St Mark passes over in silence, and which St Luke mentions at a much earlier period, and upon quite a different occasion. Compare Matthew xxiv. 26–28, and 37–51, with Luke xvii. 20–37. Here again the key is to be found in the historical order preferred by St Luke, while St Matthew arranges his materials chiefly by the rule of homogeneity. Accordingly we read in St Luke, in express terms, the circumstances that led to that part of the predictions concerning the kingdom of God and our Lord's second advent (ver. 20-23). *And when he was demanded of the Pharisees, when the kingdom of God should come, he answered them and said, The kingdom of God cometh not with observation: Neither shall they say, Lo here! or, Lo there! for, behold, the kingdom of God is within you. And he said unto the disciples, The days will come when ye shall desire to see one of the days of the Son of man, and ye shall not see it. And they shall say to you, See here; or, See there: go not after them, nor follow them.*

Exceptions to the rule of St Luke's always giving the preference to the historical order, there may sometimes appear to be, and even in some cases there actually are, when a special reason for it occurs. We shall, erelong, meet with an example of this last being the case. When, however, he mentions for instance, in his Gospel (iii. 18-21), the imprisonment of St John the Baptist, between his preaching and the baptism of our Lord in the Jordan, this anticipation of a subsequent part of the history may *appear* to be a departure from the rule of strictly following the order of time; but if we reflect a little, we shall readily perceive the reason for this apparent exception. Even those historians that are most exact in point of chronology, occasionally *anticipate* the events they have to relate, on account of some intimate connexion between two incidents or facts, the date of which otherwise sufficiently explains itself. Such manifestly is the case with respect to the facts recorded at verses 18 and 19 of the passage referred to.

But enough has been said here about the *historical* character of St Luke and his writings. We now return to those distinguishing features of his Gospel with which our review of it commenced, and which we now proceed to trace out more minutely in details of a less obvious description. Already have we found in our third Gospel the most convincing indications of the author's having been a *bosom friend of St Paul's*, a *believer of Gentile origin*, and a *physician*. We shall now see the marks of these three different attributes, every where interwoven, so to speak, with all that he writes, and his whole Gospel moulded in composition, tendency, spirit, and materials, by this threefold relationship discovered at first in its author.

Behold then, in St Luke, the *bosom friend, the fellow labourer, and the travelling companion of St Paul!* It is impossible but that this should have had a marked influence on the whole of the preparation and moulding of his character, as the author of one of the Gospels—an influence more or less of the same sort with that of St Peter on the work of Mark, yet with some not quite unimportant difference nevertheless. St Mark received his information in a great measure from the personal communications of a principal eyewitness, the first among the twelve original Apostles. St Luke was the fellow-labourer of an apostle, but one who was called at a subsequent period to exercise that high function, and who was just as little as St Luke himself an eyewitness from the beginning of all that Jesus *began to do and to teach.* Therefore it is, that in the very opening of his work he speaks of *more than one* source of information (i. 1, 2): *Even as they delivered them unto us, which* FROM THE BEGINNING WERE EYEWITNESSES, AND MINISTERS OF THE WORD.

It may well be conjectured, *a priori,* that the influence of an apostle like St Paul, though nowise exclusive, must have been very considerable, on the work of his faithful fellow-labourer, St Luke; and, in particular, we may naturally look for a *kindred* spirit and tendency in their writings. This we find to be actually the case. The Epistles of St Paul, and the two books left to us by St Luke, when placed together, are often found the readiest helps for mutually explaining, elucidating, and confirming each other. We meet with, or recognise in both, the same fundamental ideas, the same points of view, the same representations of the highest doctrines of the Gospel. And so much is this the case, that from the most remote times the Gospel of St Luke has been thought a Pauline Gospel; and that, following out this idea, the Marcionites (the adherents of a false doctrine, who owned no authority except that of St Paul, understood in their own way) admitted none of the Gospels but that of St Luke exclusively.

We have a striking view of the close relationship between these two sacred writers, in the manner, for instance, in which the institution of the Lord's Supper is recorded by St Paul in the First Epistle to the Corinthians, and by St Luke in his Gospel. Let us compare both these places with what St Matthew and St Mark have left us on the same subject.

MATTH. xxvi. 26–28.

And as they were eating, Jesus took bread, and blessed it, and brake it, and gave it to the disciples, and said, Take, eat; this is my body. And he took the cup, and gave thanks, and gave it to them, saying, Drink ye all of it; for THIS IS MY BLOOD OF THE NEW TESTAMENT, which is shed for many for the remission of sins.

MARK xiv. 22–24.

And as they did eat, Jesus took bread, and blessed, and brake it, and gave to them, and said, Take, eat: this is my body. And he took the cup, and when he had given thanks, he gave it to them: and they all drank of it. And he said unto them, This is MY BLOOD OF THE NEW TESTAMENT, which is shed for many.

LUKE xxii. 19, 20.

And he took bread, and gave thanks, and brake it, and gave unto them, saying, This is my body, which is given for you: THIS DO IN REMEMBRANCE OF ME, (Gr. *ἀνάμνησιν, to make be thought of.*) Likewise also the cup AFTER SUPPER, saying, THIS CUP is THE NEW TESTAMENT IN MY BLOOD, which is shed for you.

1 COR. xi. 23–25.

For I have received of the Lord that which also I delivered unto you, That the Lord Jesus the same night in which he was betrayed took bread: And when he had given thanks, he brake it, and said, Take, eat: this is my body, which is broken for you: this do in remembrance of me. After the same manner also he took the cup, WHEN HE HAD SUPPED, SAYING, THIS CUP IS THE NEW TESTAMENT IN MY BLOOD: this do ye, as oft as ye drink it, in remembrance of me.

What we have remarked will here be seen at a glance. St Paul and St Luke, while they differ from St Matthew, whom St Mark almost follows to the letter, record the institution of the Supper in almost literally the same terms. It is by them only that the object for which the Holy Supper was destined, is expressed in this commandment, *Do this in remembrance of me*—words whose meaning is elucidated by St Paul in the verse that follows (ver. 26). In both alike we find the circumstance which bears so much on the history of the institution, that the cup was blessed and drunk *after supper*. In both alike the words of St Matthew and St Mark, *This is my blood*, receive that most important explanation, *This cup* IS THE NEW TESTAMENT IN *my blood*.

It is further remarkable, for elucidating the close connexion between the Epistles of St Paul and the Gospel of St Luke, that the appearance of our Saviour after his resurrection, to which St Paul appeals in the same Epistle to the Corinthians, we again find recorded by St Luke, and St Luke alone.

1 COR. xv. 5.	LUKE xxiv. 34.
And that he was seen of CEPHAS, then of the twelve.	Saying, The Lord is risen indeed, and hath appeared to SIMON.

But not only does this close relationship appear from single instances of actions being recorded, or persons mentioned by both, it still more clearly appears from a principle pervading both, from a tendency common to both. Thus, if what we are chiefly taught in St Paul's Epistles be *the forgiveness of sins*, that grand foundation of the whole Gospel in its most profound acceptation, *as righteousness by faith before God;* the same idea, the same doctrine, so that in its amplest development and fullest expression it may emphatically be called *the Gospel of* PAUL,[1] we find recalled to our notice in more than one similitude or narrative in St Luke. It is clear that the gist of the parable of the *Prodigal Son*, which we find in St Luke's Gospel alone (xv. 11–32), lies in its opposing (precisely as in St Paul's Epistles) man's *own* righteousness to the righteousness *bestowed*, which is the forgiveness of sin and the adoption by grace—the self-righteousness of the Pharisees being represented by the elder son, the poor sinner by the prodigal child.

[1] Rom. ii. 16, xvi. 25; 2 Tim. ii. 8.

The same antithesis we again meet with in a similitude or narrative of our Lord's, recorded by St Luke alone—that of *the Pharisee* and *the publican* (xviii. 9-14): *And he spake this parable unto certain* WHICH TRUSTED IN THEMSELVES THAT THEY WERE RIGHTEOUS, AND DESPISED OTHERS: *Two men went up into the temple to pray; the one a Pharisee, and the other a publican. The Pharisee stood and prayed thus with himself: God, I thank thee, that I am not as other men are, extortioners, unjust, adulterers, or even as this publican. I fast twice in the week, I give tithes of all that I possess. And the publican, standing afar off, would not lift up so much as his eyes unto heaven, but smote upon his breast, saying, God be merciful to me a sinner. I tell you, this man went down to his house justified rather than the other: for every one that exalteth himself shall be abased: and he that humbleth himself shall be exalted.*

Finally, under this head we may rank that most affecting of incidents, recorded by St Luke *alone*, of the woman that was a sinner, at the feet of Jesus in the house of the Pharisee. In order to give stronger relief to the doctrine involved in this narrative, let us put it in juxtaposition with a similitude which St Matthew, in his turn, *alone* records. The fundamental idea in both is the *gratuitous forgiveness of sins;* but the characteristic difference in what further is intended to be taught deserves to be noticed.

MATTH. xviii. 23–35.	LUKE vii. 36–50.
Jesus saith, Therefore is the kingdom of heaven likened unto a certain king, which would take account of his servants. And when he had begun to reckon, one was brought unto him, which owed him *ten thousand talents.* But foras-	And one of the Pharisees desired him that he would eat with him. And he went into the Pharisee's house, and sat down to meat. And, behold, a woman in the city, which was a sinner, when she knew that Jesus sat at meat

much as he had not to pay, his lord commanded him to be sold, and his wife, and children, and all that he had, and payment to be made. The servant therefore fell down, and worshipped him, saying, Lord, have patience with me, and I will pay thee all. Then the lord of that servant was moved with compassion, and loosed him, and forgave him the debt. But the same servant went out, and found one of his fellow-servants, which owed him *an hundred pence:* and he laid hands on him, and took him by the throat, saying, Pay me that thou owest. And his fellow-servant fell down at his feet, and besought him, saying, Have patience with me, and I will pay thee all. And he would not: but went and cast him into prison, till he should pay the debt. So when his fellow-servants saw what was done, they were very sorry, and came and told unto their lord all that was done. Then his lord, after that he had called him, said unto him, O thou wicked servant, I forgave thee all that debt, because thou desiredst me: Shouldest not thou also have had compassion on thy fellow-servant, even as I had pity on thee? And his lord was wroth, and delivered him to the tormentors, till he should pay all that was due unto him. So likewise shall my heavenly Father do also unto you, if ye from your hearts forgive not every one his brother their trespasses.

in the Pharisee's house, brought an alabaster box of ointment, and stood at his feet behind him weeping, and began to wash his feet with tears, and did wipe them with the hairs of her head, and kissed his feet, and anointed them with the ointment. Now when the Pharisee which had bidden him saw it, he spake within himself, saying, This man, if he were a prophet, would have known who and what manner of woman this is that toucheth him: for she is a sinner. And Jesus answering said unto him, Simon, I have somewhat to say unto thee. And he saith, Master, say on. There was a certain creditor which had two debtors: the one owed *five hundred pence*, and the other *fifty*. And when they had nothing to pay, he frankly forgave them both. Tell me therefore, which of them will love him most? Simon answered and said, I suppose that he, to whom he forgave most. And he said unto him, Thou hast rightly judged. And he turned to the woman, and said unto Simon, Seest thou this woman? I entered into thine house, thou gavest me no water for my feet: but she hath washed my feet with tears, and wiped them with the hairs of her head. Thou gavest me no kiss: but this woman, since the time I came in, hath not ceased to kiss my feet. My head with oil thou didst not anoint: but this woman hath anointed my feet with ointment. Wherefore I say unto thee, Her sins, which are many, are forgiven; for she loved much: but to whom little is forgiven, the same loveth little. And he said unto her, Thy sins are forgiven. And they that sat at meat with him began to say within themselves: who is this that forgiveth sins also? And he said to the woman, Thy faith hath saved thee; go in peace.

The reader will here see what it is that, in general, these two narratives have in common with each other—the capital point of *the forgiveness of sins.* Yet the several doctrines which are further connected with that capital point in these two different Evangelists, unequivocably harmonize with all that characteristically distinguishes them otherwise. The similitude in St Matthew exalts our Lord as king and judge: the narrative in St Luke as the searcher of men's hearts. The similitude in St Matthew points to the amount of the debt remitted, together with the immensity of the sum which rendered payment impossible (*ten thousand talents*), contrasted with the very small amount of the debt which the servant himself had to remit to his fellow-servant; the narrative in St Luke points to the readiness of the creditor to acquit both debts, the greater and the less, the *five hundred* and the *fifty pence.* In the similitude related by St Matthew, the two servants are placed over and against each other without any decided characteristic difference betwixt them; in St Luke, on the contrary, we again find a sinner contrasted with a Pharisee. The similitude in St Matthew represents to us a practical example of the Christian's prayer, *Forgive us our trespasses, as we forgive them that trespass against us;* the narrative in St Luke might, so to speak, have for its title that saying of St Paul, that *in Jesus Christ nothing is of any avail, but faith which worketh by love* (Gal. v. 6).

It is, further, one of the peculiar characteristics of St

Paul, that the development of evangelical truth ever and anon resolves itself—ever and anon, so to speak, refreshes itself *in the ascription of glory and honour to God.* Thus not only does the conclusion of the Epistle to the Romans run into an ascription of praise (xvi. 27), *To God only wise, be glory through Jesus Christ for ever, Amen;* but different divisions or paragraphs of that same Epistle are wound up with thanksgivings to God, or with the giving of glory to God, as (vii. 25), *I thank God through Jesus Christ our Lord,* and (xi. 36), *For of him, and through him, and to him, are all things.* Nay, in the very midst of a line of argument, according as the nature of his subject or the occasion may suggest, we often meet with such ascriptions of praise, as (i. 25), *who worshipped and served the creature more than the* CREATOR, WHO IS BLESSED FOR EVER. AMEN; and (ix. 5), *of whom as concerning the flesh Christ came, who is over all* GOD BLESSED FOR EVER, AMEN. In St Paul's doctrine and Epistles, the end and the crown of all throughout is the glorifying of God. *For all the promises of God in him are yea, and in him Amen,* UNTO THE GLORY OF GOD BY US, (2 Cor. i. 20), and (iv. 15). *For all things are for your sakes, that the abundant grace might through the thanksgiving of many redound* TO THE GLORY OF GOD; and (viii. 19), *this grace, which is administered by us* TO THE GLORY OF THE SAME LORD, &c.; as in Gal. i. 5. 24, Eph. i. 21, 1 Tim. i. 17, 2 Tim. iv. 18, Heb. xiii. 21. Now, in casting our eyes over the four Gospels, we find that this meets us again in a strikingly characteristic manner, particularly, in that of St Luke. His two predecessors speak in passing of the glorification of God by the multitude when they saw the works of JESUS (Matth. ix. 18, xv. 31; Mark ii. 12); but it is only St Luke who super-abounds in the express mention of that glorification. Thus not only in relating the birth of Jesus (ii. 20), *the shepherds returned,* GLORIFYING AND PRAISING GOD *for all the things that they had heard and seen;* and in the account of the cure of the paralytic, who was let down from the roof (v. 25, 26), *And immediately he rose up before them, and took up that whereon he lay, and departed to his own house,* GLORIFYING GOD. *And they were all amazed, and they* GLORIFIED GOD, *and were filled with fear, saying, We have seen strange things to-day;* but also on the occasion of the resurrection of the young man of Nain (vii. 16), *There came a fear on all: and they* GLORIFIED GOD, *saying, That a great prophet has risen up among us; and, That God hath visited his people;* and on the occasion of the cure of the woman who was bowed together (xiii. 13), *And he laid his hands on her: and immediately she was made straight, and* GLORIFIED GOD. Afterwards at the healing of the two lepers (xvii. 15), *And one of them, when he saw that he was healed, turned back, and with a loud voice* GLORIFIED GOD; and when the eyes of the blind man at Jericho were opened (xviii. 43), *And immediately he received his sight, and followed him,* GLORIFYING GOD; *and all the people, when they saw it,* GAVE PRAISE UNTO GOD; and finally, when Jesus, on the cross, cried with a loud voice, and gave up the ghost (xxiii. 47), *And when the centurion saw what was done,* HE GLORIFIED GOD, *saying, Certainly this was a righteous man.*

A like harmony between St Paul and our Evangelist discovers itself in the point also of the *rejoicing* of faith. We find the Apostle ever and anon repeating the exhortation: REJOICE *in the Lord alway; and again I say unto you,* REJOICE (Phil. iv. 4), and afterwards throughout the whole of this Epistle, and several times elsewhere. The words *joy, rejoice, be glad*, are in none of the Gospels found so frequently employed as by St Luke, both in his Gospel and in the book of the Acts. The birth of St John the Baptist was *to give joy and gladness* to his father and to many (i. 14). The babe, St John, *leapt for joy* in his mother's womb (ver. 41, 44). Mary's spirit *rejoiced in God her Saviour* (ver. 47). *Good tidings of great joy* were brought by the angel to the shepherds of Bethlehem (ii. 10). *There shall be joy in heaven over one sinner that repenteth* (xv. 7). *For joy* (xxiv. 41), *the disciples believed not their own eyes* when Jesus appeared in the midst of them after his resurrection; and after his ascension (xxiv. 52), they *returned to Jerusalem with great joy.* The book of Acts likewise makes mention of this joy among the disciples and believers in different circumstances, whether of prosperity or of persecution.[1] We are far from finding so frequent a recurrence of the word in St Matthew, and in St Mark it hardly occurs at all. With the latter every thing of the kind is comprised in his favourite expression of *the good news.*[2]

The intimate tie between the Apostle and his faithful companion, unequivocally shews itself even in the peculiarities of style and language. A remarkable effect of this resemblance is found in the conjecture of Grotius, who attributes to St Luke the Epistle of Paul to the Hebrews. But this only by the way.

One more highly characteristic peculiarity, however, of the Apostle St Paul's, and not without its echo in St Luke, remains yet to be mentioned, and demands a

[1] ii. 26, 45, v. 41, viii. 8, 39, xii. 14, xiii. 52, xv. 3, xvi. 34, xx. 4, &c.
[2] P. 74.

moment's observation—a peculiarity all the more important, as it is deeply seated in the soul as well as in the doctrine of the two sacred writers. We refer to St Paul's well-known predilection for the number *three*, which repeatedly bears even upon the construction of his sentences, and forces itself on our notice in his constantly tracing back all doctrine to the most Holy Trinity of *God, Jesus Christ, and the Holy Ghost*;[1] and in the practice of the Christian life, to the trinity of faith, hope, and charity.[2] St Luke, too, has a liking for this number. If he any where deviates from the strict historical sequence of events, it is perhaps because here and there he would give a *triplet* of examples of some one or other important action or cherished doctrine. Thus, for instance, in the similitudes intended to animate to believing prayer, he adds a third to the two adduced by St Matthew:—

MATTH. vii. 9, 10.	LUKE xi. 11, 12.
Or what man is there of you, whom if his son ask bread, will he give him a stone? Or if he ask a fish, will he give him a serpent?	If a son shall ask bread of any of you that is a father, will he give him a stone? or if he ask a fish, will he for a fish give him a serpent? *or if he shall ask an egg, will he offer him a scorpion?*

After the similitude of the lost sheep, to which, in St Matthew (xviii. 12-14), the wandering sinner restored to favour is compared, we read in St Luke (xv.) two others to the like effect, though with striking additional embellishments,—the *lost piece of silver*, and *the prodigal son*.

To the two examples recorded by St Matthew, of what is required in order to our following Jesus every where and unconditionally, St Luke adds a third:—

[1] Rom. i. 1-4, v. 1-5, viii. 9, 15, xvi. 30; 1 Cor. ii. 10-16, xii. 3-6; 2 Cor. xiii. 13; Eph. iv. 4-6, &c.

[2] 1 Cor. xiii. 13; Rom. v. 2-5; 1 Thess. i. 3; Heb. vi. 10-12, &c.

MATTH. viii. 19–22.	LUKE ix. 57–62.
And a certain scribe came, and said unto him, Master, I will follow thee whithersoever thou goest. And Jesus saith unto him, The foxes have holes, and the birds of the air have nests; but the Son of man hath not where to lay his head. And another of his disciples said unto him, Lord, suffer me first to go and bury my father. But Jesus said unto him, Follow me; and let the dead bury their dead.	And it came to pass, that, as they went in the way, a certain man said unto him, Lord, I will follow thee whithersoever thou goest. And Jesus said unto him, Foxes have holes, and birds of the air have nests; but the Son of man hath not where to lay his head. And he said unto another, Follow me. But he said, Lord, suffer me first to go and bury my father. Jesus said unto him, Let the dead bury their dead: but go thou and preach the kingdom of God. *And another also said, Lord, I will follow thee; but let me first go bid them farewell, which are at home at my house. And Jesus said unto him, No man, having put his hand to the plough, and looking back, is fit for the kingdom of God.*

In like manner, at the place where, in St Matthew, the Lord gives *two* examples of the difference that the great day of his coming would make in the condition of persons most resembling each other externally, St Luke anew adds a *third*.

MATTH. xxiv. 40, 41.	LUKE xvii. 34–36.
Then shall two be in the field; the one shall be taken, and the other left. Two women shall be grinding at the mill; the one shall be taken, and the other left.	*I tell you, in that night there shall be two men in one bed; the one shall be taken, and the other shall be left.* Two women shall be grinding together; the one shall be taken, and the other left. Two men shall be in the field; the one shall be taken, and the other left.

The kindred feelings that united the souls of St Paul and his beloved *companion in labour*, are thus made clear to us from more than one leading feature—more than one deep-seated harmony subsisting between their writings. But it is not only with respect to St Paul, but with respect also to the brethren of the Church of Christ in general, that the pleasing title of *beloved* may be applied to St Luke with special propriety. It is long since the Fathers of the Church and expositors have been of opinion, that that faithful friend, that dutiful servant of the Gospel and physician, St Luke, was the very person sent by St Paul, along with Titus, to superintend the collection for the poor, with this remarkable recommendation (2 Cor. viii. 18), *the brother whose praise is in the gospel throughout all the churches.* Is it a far-sought idea, if with this characteristic warmth of heart, and amiability, and high estimation in all places, we connect the observation, that nowhere in the Gospels does the word friend (φίλος) occur so frequently as in that of St Luke?[1] It happens more than once among those writers, that a single often-repeated or favourite word from their pen, betrays as it were the deepest thoughts and affections of their hearts. Be that as it may, the whole tenor of his two compositions makes us acquainted with St Luke as a man who must necessarily have maintained intercourse, and lived on terms of friendly intimacy, with a great many believers of all ages and conditions. This was just what enabled him to collect such a number of details as are contained in his Gospel, respecting what happened, previous to and at the time of the Lord's nativity, at Nazareth, at Bethlehem, at Jerusalem, as harbingers of and preparations for the grand advent of salvation in Israel. *They were* (he says in his introduction) *delivered unto him, by those which from the beginning were eyewitnesses, and ministers of the word.*

St Luke, we have already remarked in general terms,

[1] Luke vii. 6, xi. 5–8, xiv. 10, 12, xv. 6, 9, 29, xvi. 9, xxi. 16, xxiii. 12, &c.

was a Gentile by birth. It is, however, more than probable, that he did not pass immediately from paganism to the Christian faith, but that, as most commentators for a long time have thought, he had been *for some time before* a Jewish proselyte, and in this way came afterwards to the knowledge of the Lord Jesus Christ. His Gospel accordingly bears internal marks of this peculiarity. He shews a familiar acquaintance with the country, the manners, the law, and the institutions of Israel; but this is combined with such an affection for the people of Israel, as is strikingly brought before us in the words of St Paul, where he reminds the Gentile converts (Rom. ix. 4, 5), that to the Israelites *pertain the adoption, and the glory, and the covenants, and the giving of the law, and the service of God, and the promises, and the fathers;* and when even with respect to their state of unbelief and obstinacy for a time, he thus exhorts the Gentiles who had believed: *Boast not against the branches. But if thou boast, thou bearest not the root, but the root thee. As concerning the gospel, they are enemies for your sakes: but as touching the election, they are beloved for the fathers' sakes* (Rom. xi. 18, 28). He loves the Lord's ancient people with the love of the centurion in his own Gospel (vii. 5), a love flowing not from oneness of origin according to the flesh, but from a sentiment of gratitude towards Israel, because of his being grafted by grace into *their* olive-tree. His Gospel bears the marks of this feeling throughout. If on any occasion Jesus gave the name of *a son* or *daughter of Abraham* to a believing man or woman whom he had benefited, from the stock of Israel, we find that St Luke, and he alone, has recorded it. Thus we read in him only of the conversion of Zaccheus, intimated by the Saviour in these words (xix. 9), *This day is salvation come to this house, forsomuch as he also is* A SON OF ABRAHAM; and of the cure of the woman who was bowed together, who was defended against the hypocritical ruler of the synagogue by these words addressed to him by our Lord (xiii. 16), *Ought not this woman,* BEING A DAUGHTER OF ABRAHAM, *whom Satan hath bound, lo, these eighteen years, be loosed from this bond on the sabbath-day?*

It has been remarked, that it is with an ardently heartfelt interest that St Luke runs into that multiplicity of details with respect to the law of Moses and the national constitution of Israel in general, in which, from the nature of his plan, the commencement of his Gospel particularly abounds. He willingly admits into his share of the compilation of the Gospels, the news announced by the angel with respect to the Baptist (i. 16), *And many of the children of Israel shall he turn to the Lord their God;* as well as the exclamation afterwards of Zacharias (v. 68), *Blessed be the Lord* GOD OF ISRAEL; the annunciation to Mary of the kingdom of Jesus (v. 32, 33), *The Lord God shall give unto him* THE THRONE OF HIS FATHER DAVID: *and he shall reign* OVER THE HOUSE OF JACOB *for ever.* It is with an expression of respect full of unction, that he places before us the exercise of the priest's office in the temple, and the prayers of the whole multitude of people during the time of incense (v. 8–10). Further, it is his pen alone that records for us how, on the eighth day, the law of circumcision, and after the days of purification were over, that of the presentation in the Temple, were fulfilled with regard to the infant Jesus, and that too by an exact repetition of the very words of that institution by Moses (ii. 22–24), *And when the days of her purification according to the law of Moses were accomplished, they brought him to Jerusalem, to present him to the Lord; (as it is written in the law of the Lord, Every male that openeth the womb shall be called holy to the Lord); and to offer a sacrifice, according to that which is said in the law of the Lord, A pair of turtle-doves, or two young pigeons.*

None of the other Evangelists conducts us, as St Luke (that proselyte from among the Gentiles) does, as if into the midst of the ancient and truly Israelitish hopes which in those days were still kept alive in the heart of a Simeon, of an Anna, and others (ii. 25, 28). In fine, none presents to us Jerusalem as the centre, from which the word of salvation went forth for all nations, so often as *he* does in his Gospel (xxiv. 47), and afterwards in the Book of Acts, in several instances.

But if St Luke, in harmony with the Apostle Paul (Rom. iii. 1, 2, and elsewhere), recognises the prior claims of the Jews, all the more because he himself does not belong by birth to the elect people, his Gospel nevertheless nowise spares on that account either their prejudices or their sins, their *self-righteousness* or their *national pride.* The woes (Gr. ὀυαὶ) pronounced in St Matthew on the perverseness of the Pharisees, and which are not to be found in St Mark,[1] re-occur in St Luke, as we have said already, in all their details.[2] His Gospel, quite as much as St Matthew's,[3] testifies against the utter vanity of trusting to *mere descent from Abraham according to the flesh.* He prefers, however (with the delicacy becoming a Christian of Greek or Syrian descent), confounding the infidelity and obstinacy of Israel by the example of one or other Samaritan, rather than by that of a Roman,

[1] P. 84. [2] P. 164.

[3] Matth. iii. 9; Luke iii. 8; Matth. viii. 10; Luke vii. 9.

or especially a Greek. We find, also, the Samaritans presented to us under a rather favourable aspect by St Luke, as we shall see hereafter.

With respect to Jerusalem, how deeply soever the ancient mother city lay at his heart, least of all does he forget to record the judgment pronounced upon her. We find it, on the contrary, repeatedly occurring; yet nowhere in so touching a tone of sadness and tenderness as with him. *O Jerusalem, Jerusalem! how often would I have gathered thy children,* &c., we read in St Luke just as we do in St Matthew;[1] yet in the former alone we have also another very striking saying of the Saviour to the guilty city, which yet was too much loved to be disowned for ever. It was uttered on his entering it on the ass's colt; the Pharisees being sore displeased. In St Matthew we are reminded of those words of Scripture: *Out of the mouths of babes and sucklings thou hast ordained praise* (xxi. 15, 16). But St Luke preserves for us what follows (xix. 40–44): *And he answered and said unto them, I tell you that, if these should hold their peace, the very stones would cry out. And when he was come near, he beheld the city, and wept over it, saying, If thou hadst known, even thou, in this thy day, the things that belong to thy peace! but now they are hid from thine eyes. For the days will come upon thee, that thine enemies shall cast a trench about thee, and compass thee round, and keep thee in on every side, and shall lay thee*

[1] With each of them, however, as before, in a different place and connexion. In St Matthew, to wit, at the close of the woes pronounced upon the Pharisees (xxiii.); in St Luke, evidently according to the chronological order, as suggested by the message sent to Herod (xiii. 33), *it cannot be that a prophet perish out of Jerusalem.* On this there immediately follows (v. 34, 35), the exclamation, *O Jerusalem, Jerusalem,* THOU THAT KILLEST THE PROPHETS, AND STONEST THEM THAT ARE SENT UNTO THEE; *how often would I have gathered thy children together!* &c.

even with the ground, and thy children within thee; and they shall not leave on thee one stone upon another; because thou knewest not the time of thy visitation. There is yet a third lamentation over the city of the sanctuary, which occurs in St Luke alone. On his way to Golgotha, Jesus bears his cross. *And,* as we read in our Evangelist (xxiii. 27–31), *there followed him a great company of people, and of women, which also bewailed and lamented him. But Jesus turning unto them said, Daughters of Jerusalem, weep not for me, but weep for yourselves, and for your children. For, behold, the days are coming, in the which they shall say, Blessed are the barren, and the wombs that never bare, and the paps which never gave suck. Then shall they begin to say to the mountains, Fall on us; and to the hills, Cover us. For if they do these things in a green tree, what shall be done in the dry?* Finally, it is St Luke who, in addition to the detailed prophecy of the destruction of Jerusalem, given by all the three synoptical Evangelists,[1] records the hint that was given of the restoration that she might one day expect. In his Gospel alone, we read in the prediction uttered by Jesus on the mount of Olives, these significant words (xxi. 24), *And they shall fall by the edge of the sword, and shall be led away captive into all nations: and Jerusalem shall be trodden down of the Gentiles,* UNTIL THE TIMES OF THE GENTILES BE FULFILLED.

Thus, even in recording the judgments impending over Judea and its capital, the author of this Gospel invariably shews himself the friend of Judah and Jerusalem, a true servant and worshipper of Israel's God. Yet no more does he forget the blessings in reserve for the Gentiles. *Is God the God of the Jews only? Is he not also*

[1] Matth. xxiv., Mark xiii., Luke xxi.

of the Gentiles? Yes, of the Gentiles also! thus writes the apostle to the Gentiles (Rom. iii. 28). Such, too, is the spirit, and such is the leaning shewn by St Luke in writing his Gospel. There we find Simeon's outburst of praise recorded with peculiar fitness (ii. 32), *A* LIGHT *to lighten the Gentiles, and* THE GLORY *of thy people Israel!* And that not to Israel alone, but to all who are come of Adam, the Son of God became kin, in taking man's nature upon him, is signified at once in his genealogy, as it runs in St Luke (iii. 23–28), not, as according to his predecessor (Matth. i. 1), up to David and Abraham, but up to Adam himself. Again, we find that St Luke alone records the powerful discourse in which our Saviour, by adducing two striking examples from the Scriptures of the Old Testament, places on the foreground the grace shewn to the Gentiles, yea, even to the passing over of Israel, (iv. 25–27): *But I tell you of a truth, many widows were in Israel in the days of Elias, when the heaven was shut up three years and six months, when great famine was throughout all the land; but unto none of them was Elias sent, save unto Sarepta, a city of Sidon, unto a woman that was a widow. And many lepers were in Israel in the time of Eliseus the prophet; and none of them was cleansed, saving Naaman the Syrian.* Moreover, is not almost the whole book of the Acts a glorification of the grace made known, not only to Israel, but also to all nations far and wide? presenting anew an historical exposition of that passage in St Paul (Rom. xv. 8–10), where he says, *Now I say that Jesus Christ was a minister of the* CIRCUMCISION *for* THE TRUTH *of God, to confirm the promises made unto the fathers: and that the* GENTILES *might glorify God for* HIS MERCY.

Such is the fundamental idea that runs through all

the writings of our Evangelist. In St Matthew we are told of the Saviour witnessing of himself (xx. 28), *that the Son of man came not to be ministered unto, but to* MINISTER.[1] In St Luke, the work, nay, the whole soul of Jesus, reveals itself in that one expression of the discourse in the house of the centurion (Acts x. 38), *who went about* DOING GOOD. The Epistle to the Hebrews represents him to us as the merciful and compassionate high priest (iv. 15), *We have not an high priest which cannot be touched with the feeling of our infirmities; but was in all points tempted like as we are, yet without sin.* Such precisely is the priestly compassion which every where meets us in the Gospel of St Luke.

But to *do mercy*, to *exercise compassion*, to *bring healing*, are there any ideas more akin than these to the title of Physician of Israel?[2] Most characteristically, therefore, have we the Saviour presented to us as such in the Gospel of the beloved *physician.* No doubt, in the other Gospels also, we have persons afflicted with maladies of soul and body, the needy, the feeble, the poor, the wretched, going to Jesus, and whom He seeks, whom He calls to him, whom He draws to him. But nowhere else do we find so *rich a diversity*, such *an abundant fulness* of cures administered to the needy, as here. Let us look into the cases of these objects of the deepest compassion of Jesus, as they are brought before us in St Luke, in some of their details.

We have already seen sufficiently, in how particular a manner the sick, and their maladies and cures, are introduced in this Gospel.[3] Turning our view, then, from the ailments of the body, to sin, that great malady of the soul, we find recovery from that malady also glorified in

[1] Comp. p. 14, 15. [2] Exod. xv. 26. [3] Page 146.

St Luke, in his record of the most striking examples. None of the other Gospels has pictured to us the work of repentance and forgiveness with an equal degree of depth and fulness. In his we have the affecting picture, already referred to, of the penitent woman in the house of the Pharisee, as, with the love and gratitude arising from faith in his grace, she not only anointed the feet of Jesus with costly perfume, but bathed them with her tears, and dried them with the hairs of her head. There, and only there, do we find the saying of the distinguished Apostle recorded, on the occasion of the miraculous draught of fishes (v. 8), *Depart from me; for I am a sinful man, O Lord.* In his Gospel *alone* we read the confession and the prayer of the malefactor on the cross (xxiii. 39–42), *Lord, remember me when thou comest into thy kingdom;* and the compassionate Saviour's reply, *To-day shalt thou be with me in paradise.* There we have the first beginnings of remorse, and of sorrowing unto repentance in the multitudes, who, after having been present at the crucifixion (xxiii. 48), *smote their breasts* as they returned from Golgotha. In connexion with this striking detail, we find recorded in the Book of the Acts, the serious question put by those who were pricked in their hearts on the day of Pentecost (ii. 37), *Men and brethren, what shall we do?* and the answer given to it by God's ambassadors: *Repent, and be baptized every one of you in the name of Jesus Christ for the remission of sins.* In that second book of our Evangelist there may further be classed in the same category, the conversion *of a great company* of once bitterly hostile priests (vi. 7), the conversion of the persecuting Saul (ix. i. 19), and the conversion of the jailer when at the point of committing self-murder (xvi. 25–33).

With *sinners, publicans* also are associated in the Gospels. We have seen how St Matthew makes *himself* known to us, as an example of the grace of God accorded to a publican. But in St Luke examples of this are multiplied. In him, besides the Apostle who received his call while at the receipt of custom at Capernaum, we have the chief among the publicans of Jericho, Zaccheus (xix. 1–10). In his Gospel, likewise, we read expressly and exclusively (iii. 12), how the publicans came to John the Baptist, saying: *Master, what shall we do?* In his Gospel, finally, we have the parable of the publican and his affecting prayer, *God be merciful to me a sinner.*

The Samaritan too, so despised in Israel, finds in St Luke's Gospel more than one occasion of being introduced in a heart-touching manner. Here alone we find recorded (xvii. 12, 18), the healing of the ten lepers, *of whom one alone turned back, and with a loud voice glorified God, and fell down on his face at the feet of Jesus, giving him thanks; and he was a* SAMARITAN. Here alone, likewise, is there preserved for us (x. 30–37) the parable of the *Samaritan* who shewed the deepest compassion towards his Israelite neighbour, bound up his wounds, poured wine and oil upon them, and provided for their complete cure. In the Acts, also, we meet with *Samaria* placed by St Luke next to *Judea,* in the command given to the disciples that they should preach the Gospel to the uttermost parts of the earth (i. 8). Soon after we find there (viii. 5–25), the preaching of Christ and the gift of the Holy Ghost extended to *Samaria* and many of its villages, notwithstanding their exclusion at an earlier period, as recorded by St Matthew.[1]

[1] P. 47.

But there is yet another sort of men, not like the Samaritans, despised by a single nation only, but little respected by the world in general, whom nevertheless the Saviour treated with special regard. The first benediction in his sermon on the Mount, was pronounced on these: *Blessed are the* POOR. Now there is abundant mention of the *poor* in St Luke, and his mention of them is deeply significant. He it is who has preserved for us in his Gospel that Lazarus, in whom we behold the image of the most deplorable, and yet also of the most blessed poverty, as contrasted with the miserable *rich man* (xvi. 19–31).—Nowhere do we read so often of almsgiving to the poor as in St Luke, particularly in the Acts.[1]—In the parable of those who were invited to the marriage-feast of the king's son, which St Matthew also has recorded (xxii. 2–14), St Luke alone gives this detail, forming a leading feature in the picture (xiv. 21), *Go out quickly into the streets and lanes of the city, and bring in hither* THE POOR, AND THE MAIMED, AND THE HALT, AND THE BLIND; this, too, in connexion with the immediately preceding warning given by Jesus at the chief Pharisee's table (v. 12–14), *Then said he also to him that bade him, When thou makest a dinner or supper, call not thy friends, nor thy brethren, neither thy kinsmen, nor thy rich neighbours; lest they also bid thee again, and a recompense be made thee. But when thou makest a feast, call* THE POOR, THE MAIMED, THE LAME, THE BLIND: *and thou shalt be blessed; for they cannot recompense thee: for thou shalt be recompensed at the resurrection of the just.* But also it is St Luke who, with respect to poverty, at least *in the things of this life,* beyond all others gives prominence in characteristic

[1] Acts iii. 1; ix. 36; x. 2, 4, 31; xxiv. 17.

details to the manner in which he who exhorted to these things, even the Lord Jesus Christ, though he were rich, *yet for our sakes became poor.*[1] To him we are chiefly, though not altogether indebted, for what we know of the lowly condition of Joseph and Mary, which, if not poor, at least bordered on poverty. Among the circumstances attending the birth of our Lord at Bethlehem, recorded in detail by St Luke alone, we find this (ii. 7): that Mary *brought forth her first-born son, and wrapt him in swaddling clothes, and laid him in a manger; because there was no room for them in the inn.* From St Matthew, as well as St Luke, we learn, that the Son of man *had not where to lay his head;* yet there is a characteristic difference between these two Evangelists when they come to speak of the manner in which our Lord's necessities on this earth were provided for. St Matthew sets him before us, denuded indeed of this world's wealth, but rich in power, and receiving the tribute-money from the fish, which appeared with it at his command (xvii. 27): St Luke represents to us the human consequences of this poverty, when the Lord condescended to be ministered unto of their substance by certain godly and grateful women who followed him (viii. 3).

Women, the weaker sex, whose part and influence in religion were destined first to be rightly seen under the New Testament economy—women have their diligence and God-glorifying love recorded and particularized more by St Luke than by any other of the sacred writers. At the first opening of his Gospel, we find, next to *the* SON *of Aaron,* the DAUGHTER *of Aaron,* his wife, mentioned with commendation (i. 5); nay, soon after, we

[1] 2 Cor. viii. 9.

find Elizabeth *speaking* from the impulse of her faith, while Zacharias was still *dumb* in consequence of his unbelief (v. 20 and 41). The mother herself of our Lord we never should have known in the days of her miraculous conception, and of the birth and infancy of her divine Son (i. ii.), from any other Gospel, in such amplitude of detail, as from St Luke's. He alone brings her before us, after our Lord's resurrection and ascension (Acts i. 14): *These all continued with one accord in prayer and supplication, with the women, and Mary the mother of Jesus, and with his brethren.* St Luke makes us acquainted with the women who followed our Lord under the cross and to the tomb, long before that time, by name, and with many interesting circumstances. He places them, as if they were a sort of female apostles, next to the chosen disciples (viii. 1, 2, 3): *And the twelve were with him, and certain women, which had been healed of evil spirits and infirmities, Mary called Magdalene, out of whom went seven devils, and Joanna the wife of Chuza, Herod's steward, and Susanna, and many others, which ministered unto him of their substance.* To St Luke we owe our acquaintance with Martha and Mary, the one in the zeal of her *much service,* the other *at the feet of Jesus* (x. 38–42); just such as we afterwards find them again with their brother Lazarus, at Bethany, in the Gospel of St John (xi). Among all the sinners who find mercy and salvation in Jesus, where is there an example to be compared with the *woman that was a sinner,* as we have already contemplated her under more than one point of view in St Luke? The *daughters of Zion,* who bewailed our Lord on the way to Golgotha, are mentioned only by St Luke (xxiii. 27, 29). In the Acts, it is not the least part, in point of multiplicity and importance, that is given to what he has to say of *women.* As the objects of the persecuting zeal of Saul, he distinguishes *men and* WOMEN (ix. 2) ; as *believers* baptized by Philip *the Evangelist* at Samaria, he mentions WOMEN *as well as men* (viii. 12) ; as he proceeds with his narrative, he mentions by name *Tabitha of Joppa, full of good works and alms deeds,* and her being raised from the dead by St Peter (ix. 36–42) ; afterwards at Jerusalem (xii. 12–15), Mary, the sister of Barnabas, and mother of John Mark, in whose house the Church met for mutual prayer, at the time of the persecution directed against James and Peter ; and the damsel named Rhoda, who with such a natural feeling of gladness ran in to announce the delivered apostle, before she had opened the door ; afterwards the mother of Timothy at Derbe (xvi. 1) ; then as the first convert made in Europe, *Lydia, the seller of purple, whose heart the Lord opened, that she attended unto the things which were spoken by* Paul (xvi. 14) ; later still, among the small number of those who were led to the faith at Athens, *a woman of the name of Damaris* (xvii. 34) ; then the excellent Priscilla, wife of Aquila, to whom Apollos, who was mighty in the Scriptures, was indebted for a more perfect knowledge of the way of God in the Gospel (xviii. 2, 26), and whom St Paul had to thank for the services of the most faithful friendship, given even at the risk of his life (Rom. xvi. 3, 4) ; finally, at Cesarea, the four daughters of Philip, who prophesied (xxi. 8).

Among the women whom St Luke so particularly mentions, the *widows* occupy the foremost place. *Widows* are most particularly presented to us in the pages of this Evangelist in an affecting connexion with the service of God and of the Church of Christ. Do we not find the image traced by St Paul of a widow *who is a widow indeed,* one, to wit, *that trusteth in God, and continueth in supplications and prayers night and day* (1 Tim. v. 5), in ANNA, *the daughter of Phanuel, who being a widow of about fourscore and four years, which departed not from the temple, but served God with fastings and prayers night and day*—she also being mentioned by St Luke alone. In St Luke (iv. 25, 26) our Lord reminds the people of Nazareth, that *many widows were in Israel in the days of Elias, when the heaven was shut up three years and six months, when great famine was throughout all the land;* and how that *unto none of them was Elias sent, save unto Sarepta, a city of Sidon, unto a woman* THAT WAS A WIDOW. A *widow* in the parable of *the unjust judge,* a parable recorded by St Luke alone (xviii. 1-8), is proposed as an example of that continual prayer in which God's elect ought to be ever occupied while waiting for the great day of their Lord. The young man who was restored to life by Jesus near Nain, was the son of a *widow* (vii. 11–16).

The good deed done to this last-mentioned widow, whose tears were dried by a single word from our Lord, when he delivered her son to her (v. 15), suggests to us another class of persons, to whom, as by predilection, his mercies were displayed with peculiar lustre, namely, *only children.* In what is related of the restoration to life of the daughter of Jairus, we have it remarked in St Luke, and in St Luke alone, that she was an *only daughter* (viii. 42). In like manner, in the account of the cure of the lunatic child, we read only in St Luke how feelingly the father, in his prayer to Jesus, emphatically pleads this circumstance (ix. 38): *Master, I beseech thee, look upon my son, for he is* MINE ONLY CHILD.

To the class of the helpless belong also *children.* Children to our Lord were welcome and precious. We know what he said of them, as recorded by all the three synoptical Evangelists: *Suffer little children to come unto me;*[1] and at another place: *Except ye be converted, and become as little children, ye shall not enter into the kingdom of heaven.*[2] St Luke, however, has recorded some still more touching particulars with respect to childhood. In his Gospel we have, first of all, John the Baptist, who, while still in his mother's womb, *leapt for joy* at the approach of his Lord (i. 44); and with regard to whom, soon after the singular circumstances attending his circumcision, many were led to say, *What manner of child shall this be?* (i. 66). But he exhibits the Lord Jesus himself when a child, as no other Evangelist has done. He alone brings us acquainted with Jesus when he was twelve years old, sitting in the midst of the doctors in the temple, making them astonished at his wisdom, and anon returning to be subject to his parents at Nazareth (ii. 40–52). There is something remarkable in the whole human growth and development of the *holy child,* as indicated by our eminently *historical* Evangelist. We have represented here in regular succession: *the fruit of Mary's womb* highly blessed (i. 42)—a *babe* (Gr. *βρέφος*) *lying in a manger* (ii. 12, 26)—circumcised anon on *the eighth day* (v. 21)—thereafter as a *child* (Gr. *παίδιον*) brought into the temple, and taken up by Simeon in his arms (v. 27)—later still (v. 40, 43, 52), increased *in wisdom and stature, and in favour with God and man,* as a youth (Gr. *παῖς*); and, finally, at

[1] Matth. xix. 14, Mark x. 13, Luke xviii. 15.
[2] Matth. xviii. 3, Mark x. 15, Luke xviii. 17.

the age of thirty years (iii. 23), as full-grown man (Gr. ἀνὴρ) (Acts. ii. 22, xvii. 21).

Thus, then, have we presented to us, in this our third Gospel, in a way altogether peculiar to it, the helpless, the poor, the despised, the weak, the wretched, and sinners, gathered round Jesus, the compassionate Saviour, received by him, called to him; nay, we see himself repeatedly, according to the depths of the riches and the strength of his divine love, identified, as it were, with all that is weak, and poor, and despised.[1] Is there not an admirable fitness and consistency in the Gospel of *tender-heartedness* and *compassion*, being also emphatically the Gospel of *prayer?* Mercy and prayer, supplication and compassion, are kindred and mutually corresponding ideas. And so, in point of fact, it is in our Evangelist Luke. As the Epistles of Paul abound in urgent calls to perseverance in supplication and prayer; so, too, are the writings of the Evangelist, who was his companion in labour, in the impressive examples he records. His Gospel opens at once with an instance of answered prayer, (i. 13), *Fear not, Zacharias; for thy prayer is heard.* Anon we have the aged prophetess brought before us, serving God in the temple *with prayers night and day* (ii. 37). Just before, we have Simeon's prayer (ii. 29), *Lord, now lettest thou thy servant depart in peace!* As for the *similitudes* recorded in this Gospel, to prompt to believing, importunate prayer, we have already had before us that of the son, to whom his father would not assuredly give a stone, a serpent, or a scorpion, on his

[1] Here we would again refer to 2 Cor. viii. 9; to which may be added 2 Cor. xiii. 4, Phil. ii. 5–8.

asking for bread, or a fish, or an egg. In the other similitude employed for the same purpose, that of the friend awakening his friend at midnight to ask for bread, there is one further trait which well deserves being noticed; it is, that he does not ask for the loaves merely for *himself*, but for the benefit of *a third party*, to whom he was called upon to exercise hospitality (xi. 5, 6)—a particular which seems to hint, that in prayer to God we should be mindful of the communion of the saints. In another similitude, the necessity and the advantage of an unbounded and importunate *perseverance* in prayer are inculcated (xviii. i. 8). In Gethsemané, the exhortation *to pray that we enter not into temptation*, occurs twice in St Luke, and in St Luke alone (xxii. 40–46). Afterwards at Golgotha, we have the prayer of the thief on the cross, brief and expressive, like that of the publican in the parable. But it is chiefly in the Book of the Acts that we find numerous recorded instances of *supplication and prayer*, by persons very different from each other, and placed in very different circumstances; the prayers of the Apostles at their meetings, between the day of the ascension and that of Pentecost (i. 14, 24, 25); the prayers in common of the first believers in Jerusalem (ii. 42); a prayer heard and answered immediately, amid the oppressions endured by the Apostles in the Gospel testimony (iv. 24–31); the prayer of Stephen at the time of his martyrdom, for his own soul and for the conversion of his murderers (vii. 59, 60); and when prayer was answered in the conversion of Paul—conversion intimated by our Lord himself to a disciple at Damascus, by that one most comprehensive expression: *Behold! he prayeth* (ix. 11);—then Tabitha restored to life on Peter kneeling down and praying at her side (ix.

11); the assiduous prayers of Cornelius the *centurion*, heard in so glorious a manner (x. 2, 4); the prayers offered up for St Peter while he lay in prison, looking for death, and answered while he was asleep (xii. 5–11); the prayers of the Church met at Antioch, soon followed by an explicit command from the Holy Ghost (xiii. 1–4); St Paul's prayers on his taking leave of his friends at Miletus (xx. 36)—at Tyre (xxi. 5), with men, women, and children, made on their knees, and in common, &c.

But it is not only the disciples, it is also their Lord and Master himself, whom St Luke in his Gospel sets before us, in striking circumstances, and with glorious results, *as praying.* This we no doubt find in St Mark and St Matthew also, though in the latter we have more of prayer addressed *to* Jesus than of the prayers *of* Jesus brought before us; but in Luke the instances are more frequent, and are found in a connexion, and followed by effects altogether of a peculiar kind. Thus when Jesus was baptized, when the heaven was opened and the Holy Ghost descended, St Luke alone (iii. 21) records that this took place *while Jesus* PRAYED. Before relating the cures performed on many that were sick, St Luke in a few short words notes, that Jesus *withdrew himself into the wilderness,* AND PRAYED (v. 15–17). Before the solemn calling of the Apostles, according to the same Evangelist (vi. 13), our Lord went into a mountain to pray, *and continued all night in* PRAYER TO GOD (v. 12). That most weighty question put by Jesus to his disciples, *Whom say the people that I am?* and again, *But whom say ye that I am?* and St Peter's answer, The *Christ of God,* are in the Gospel before us shortly preceded with *prayer* (ix. 18, 19). Peculiar emphasis is laid on the *praying* of the Lord Jesus, in the account of his transfiguration on the mount, ever again in St Luke (ix. 28, 29): *And it came to pass about an eight days after these sayings, he took Peter and John and James, and went up into a mountain* TO PRAY. *And* AS HE PRAYED, *the fashion of his countenance was altered, and his raiment was white and glistering.* But what gives us yet a deeper insight into the nature of our Lord's praying, is the following passage in St Luke (xxii. 31, 32): *Simon, Simon,* said our Lord to Peter at the Paschal supper on the night preceding his passion, *behold, Satan hath desired to have you, that he may sift you as wheat;* BUT I HAVE PRAYED FOR THEE, THAT THY FAITH FAIL NOT. This was the intercessory prayer of the compassionate High Priest, of whom it stands written, that *he ever liveth to make intercession for his people* (Heb. vii. 25, Rom. viii. 34). The prayer of our Saviour in Gethsemané, when *exceeding sorrowful even unto death,* is recorded by all the three synoptical Evangelists; but St Luke alone adds the details of his *agony,* his *praying yet more earnestly,* and his *bloody sweat* (xxii. 43, 44). St Luke has preserved three of our Lord's seven sayings on the cross, and two of these are prayers to God: *Father, forgive them; for they know not what they do* (xxiii. 34): and (46), *Father, into thy hands I commend my Spirit.*

Now, when we would comprise in one idea all these leading features of our third Gospel—all these several elements that go to compose it—what do we find? Is it true that the distinctive character of the facts and doctrines collected by St Luke is, that they, in the most marked and profoundly interesting manner, place over against the depths of man's sinfulness, wretchedness, weakness, and poverty, in strong relief, mercy, compassion, charity, salvation, prayer, and answers to prayer, faith, grace, and joy?—then know we no word that is better fitted to convey an impression of all this, than *unction.* The Gospel of the beloved physician and Evangelist, the fellow-labourer of St Paul, is emphatically a Gospel full of *unction.* But that very word involves a new suggestion with respect to the harmonies to be found among these writings. *Unction,* according to the writers of the Old Testament, but still more according to those of the New, proceeds from the *Holy Ghost.*[1] Now, one of the grand characteristic features of St Luke's evangelical history, appears precisely in his mentioning, more or less directly, in a variety of ways, and in an almost unbroken sequence, the Holy Ghost and his gifts, operations, and divine personality. The very first scene opened to us in his Gospel, points us to the *Holy Spirit.* The promise made to Zacharias and to Elizabeth is accompanied with this glorious specialty (i. 15), *He shall be great in the sight of the Lord, and shall drink neither wine nor strong drink; and he shall be* FILLED WITH THE HOLY GHOST, *even from his mother's womb.*[2] We find immediately after, in the Gospel of St Luke, the literal accomplishment of this prediction in the imposing yet very simple circumstance (i. 41–44), that the babe John leapt for joy under his mother's heart at the approach of her who was already the mother of the Lord (v. 43). To the latter—to her who was blessed among women—the sublime mystery of the Saviour's conception had already been announced, then, with a fulness which was not re-

[1] Isa. lxi. 1, John ii. 20, 27, and elsewhere.
[2] Compare Ephes. v. 18.

quired in the message of the angel to Joseph, as recorded by St Matthew (i. 20, 21), in St Luke (i. 35), *The Holy Ghost shall come upon thee, and the power of the Highest shall overshadow thee: therefore also that holy thing that shall be born of thee shall be called the Son of God.* Thereafter Elizabeth, Mary, and Zacharias, being *filled with the Holy Ghost,* spoke and sang as inspired by Him (41, 46, 67). Later still, we find mention there made of the aged Simeon (ii. 25, 26), that *the Holy Ghost* was upon him, and how it was revealed to him by *the Holy Ghost,* that he should not see death before he had seen the Lord's Christ, and how also he came *by the Spirit* (v. 27) into the Temple, just as the parents of the child Jesus had brought him there to do unto him after the custom of the law. On the occasion of our Lord's being baptized in the Jordan, as well as upon that of his retiring immediately after into the wilderness, again it is St Luke who lays an emphasis on that name of *the Holy Ghost,* and who explains more fully his descent *as a dove* (Matth. iii. 16, Mark i. 10), by adding, *in a bodily shape* (iii. 22, and iv. 1). What, in the encouragement to prayer, is called in St Matthew (vii. 11) *good gifts,* is in St Luke (xi. 13) specifically defined as *the Holy Ghost.* But it is chiefly in the Book of the Acts that we find reference made and glory ascribed to the Holy Ghost, in such a multiplicity of circumstances of all sorts, that it is not without reason that some have called it *the Gospel of the Holy Ghost.* In fact, the Spirit is spoken of at its very commencement as the living medium, too, of communion between our Lord and his disciples (i. 2): *He through the Holy Ghost had given commandments unto the apostles whom he had chosen.* Forthwith we find in that highly important Book *the outpouring of the Holy*

Ghost, first at Jerusalem, and among the first disciples (chap. ii.); after that at Samaria, by the imposition of the hands of the Apostles (viii. 15, 16); then at Cesarea, in a Gentile family, and on Gentiles (x. xi.) In more than one passage of that same book, *the Spirit* is represented to us in his divine *personality*. It is *the Spirit* who commanded Philip to go near and join himself to the chariot of the Ethiopian while reading the prophet Esaias (viii. 29), and who again caught him away (v. 39). It was the same *Spirit* who in a like personal manner intimated to St Peter, that he must follow to the house of Cornelius the messengers who had been sent from it (x. 19, 20), *The Spirit said unto him, Behold, three men seek thee. Arise, therefore, and get thee down, and go with them, doubting nothing:* FOR I HAVE SENT THEM. And subsequently to that, at Antioch, where the Church, with its prophets and teachers, prayed and fasted (xiii. 1, 2), *we hear the Holy Ghost* SAYING, *Separate* ME *Barnabas and Saul for the work whereunto* I *have called them.* The Old Testament writings, in fine, are several times quoted there as the SAYINGS *of* THE HOLY GHOST (i. 16): *This scripture must needs have been fulfilled, which the* HOLY GHOST BY *the mouth of David* SPAKE *before*, &c.; and (xxviii. 25), *Well* SPAKE THE HOLY GHOST *by* ESAIAS *the prophet unto our fathers.* Compare also the Epistle to the Hebrews (iii. 7, x. 15, ix. 8).

Connected also with this frequent mention of the Holy Ghost, is the representing of Jesus definitely as the *Anointed* (*Messias, Christ*), which again is characteristic of both these books. Thus, for example, in the annunciation made by the angels at Bethlehem (ii. 11), *Unto you is born a Saviour, which is* CHRIST *the Lord;* and anon, when the promise to Simeon is spoken of (ii. 26), that *he should not see death, before he had seen the Lord's* CHRIST; and in the discourse to the family of Cornelius (Acts x. 38): *Ye know, how God* ANOINTED *Jesus of Nazareth* WITH THE HOLY GHOST *and with power.* Nay, it may be said that the whole essence of our third Gospel will be found concentrated in that passage of Isaiah (lxi. 1, 2), which portrays the mission of the Anointed One in some most striking particulars. We find this passage quoted by St Luke alone, as it was read in the book of that prophet by Jesus, in the synagogue at Nazareth, and applied to himself (iv. 16–21): *And he came to Nazareth, where he had been brought up: and, as his custom was, he went into the synagogue on the sabbath-day, and stood up for to read. And there was delivered unto him the book of the prophet* ESAIAS. *And when he had opened the book, he found the place where it was written, The Spirit of the Lord is upon me, because he hath anointed me to preach the gospel to the poor; he hath sent me to heal the broken-hearted, to preach deliverance to the captives, and recovering of sight to the blind, to set at liberty them that are bruised, to preach the acceptable year of the Lord. And he closed the book, and he gave it again to the minister, and sat down. And the eyes of all them that were in the synagogue were fastened on him. And he began to say unto them, This day is this scripture fulfilled in your ears.*

Here we have alike in the prophecy and in the Gospel, the Saviour set before us in the riches of his *mercy.* A prophecy of the same prophet Isaiah has been recorded by St Matthew, who places it where he relates the coming of Jesus to Capernaum, situate by the seaside, on the confines of Zebulon and Naphtali (iv. 14, 16):

That it might be fulfilled which was spoken by Esaias, the prophet, saying, The land of Zabulon, and the land of Nephthalim, by the way of the sea, beyond Jordan, Galilee of the Gentiles; the people which sat in darkness saw great light; and to them which sat in the region and shadow of death light is sprung up.

One sees at a glance the characteristic difference between the two Gospels and the two prophecies, which seem respectively to symbolize them. In St Matthew it is the prophecy of the *great light*, in St Luke that of the *unction by the Holy Ghost.*

Thus, then, with regard to the manner in which our Saviour's person is represented to us, we find in the three Gospels that we have hitherto examined, Jesus invariably the same as Israel's Messiah, the Son of God made man, the Saviour of sinners; but in St Matthew we behold him more on the side of his prophetic-royal *grandeur*—in St Luke more on that of his *unction* as high priest—while in St Mark, the reality of his *human nature* stands most prominently forward.

We shall now close our observations on St Luke with a succinct notice of the relation in which his Gospel stands to its two predecessors, and especially to that of St Matthew. In order to this, we shall *first* glance at certain particulars exclusively belonging to one of the two; *next*, at the facts equally recorded by both, sometimes *with the same details*, sometimes *with a difference in the details*, but this difference in perfect harmony with the several individual characteristics to which we have already directed the reader's attention in our analysis, as far as we have carried it, of the three first Gospels.

As to the facts that are recorded by one and omitted by the other, we find, for example, the adoration of the wise men of the East related by St Matthew (ii.), but not repeated by St Luke. It is because St Matthew, in proving the fulfilment of the prophecies, necessarily behoved to mention that homage (foretold by the prophets) as offered to the king of Israel by the Gentiles (Ps. lxxii). To compensate for this, St Luke gives us all those incidents in the history of the childhood of Jesus which occurred in the interior of the Temple, and of the families of Joseph and Mary, and of Zacharias and Elizabeth. St Matthew (xiv. 22, 23) relates our Lord's walking upon the sea, an incident omitted by St Luke, who records, on the other hand, the miraculous draught of fishes by the ship of St Peter (v. 1–11). This, because it is St Matthew's grand object to exhibit the *greatness* of Him who makes a path for his feet in the great waters; whereas St Luke's grand object was to exhibit the *mercy*, and the riches of *the goodness* of the same Saviour-God, who puts forth his power in doing good, and conferring benefits on his people. Such is the key which every where accounts for the differences between St Matthew and St Luke, in so far as the one omits what the other mentions.

But in the greater number of cases they both record the same facts *in their grand features;* and then they *often* so agree in the details to the very letter, that one clearly perceives that St Luke has simply followed St Matthew's Gospel as it lay before him. *Sometimes,* on the other hand, the details are very differently given by the two Evangelists; that is to say, the one *mentions* particularly a detail altogether *omitted* by the other. And in this last case the mention and the omission alike are still found in the most perfect harmony with the plan and the character of the two Evangelists, as we have observed these in the preceding pages.

Let us take a few examples of a perfect, or almost perfect, literal harmony between these two Gospels :—

MATTH. iii. 7–10.

But when he saw *many of the Pharisees and Sadducees* come to his baptism, he said unto them, O generation of vipers, who hath warned you to flee from the wrath to come? Bring forth therefore fruits meet for repentance: and think not to say within yourselves, We have ABRAHAM to our father: for I say unto you, that God is able of these stones to raise up children unto ABRAHAM. And now also the axe is laid unto the root of the tree: therefore every tree which bringeth not forth good fruit, is hewn down, and cast into the fire.

LUKE iii. 7–9.

Then said he to the *multitude* that came forth to be baptized of him, O generation of vipers, who hath warned you to flee from the wrath to come? Bring forth therefore fruits worthy of repentance, and begin not to say within yourselves, We have ABRAHAM to our father: for I say unto you, That God is able of these stones to raise up children unto ABRAHAM. And now also the axe is laid unto the root of the trees: every tree therefore which bringeth not forth good fruit is hewn down, and cast into the fire.

And at another place :

MATTH. xi. 21–23.

Woe unto thee, Chorazin! woe unto thee, Bethsaida! for if the mighty works, which were done in you, had been done in Tyre and Sidon, they would have repented long ago in sackcloth and ashes. But I say unto you, It shall be more tolerable for Tyre and Sidon at the day of judgment, than for you. And thou, Capernaum, which art exalted unto heaven, shalt be brought down to hell.

LUKE x. 13–15.

Woe unto thee, Chorazin! woe unto thee, Bethsaida! for if the mighty works had been done in Tyre and Sidon, which have been done in you, they had a great while ago repented, *sitting* in sackcloth and ashes. But it shall be more tolerable for Tyre and Sidon at the judgment, than for you. And thou, Capernaum, which art exalted to heaven, shalt be thrust down to hell.

And yet at another place :

MATTH. xii. 39–45.

But he answered and said unto them, An evil and adulterous generation seeketh after a sign; and there shall no sign be given to it, but the sign of the prophet Jonas: *for as Jonas was three days and three nights in the whale's belly; so*

LUKE xi. 29–32, and 24–26.

And *when the people were gathered thick together*, he began to say, This is an evil generation: they seek a sign; and there shall no sign be given it, but the sign of Jonas the prophet. *For as Jonas was a sign unto the Ninevites, so shall the Son of man be three days and three nights in the heart of the earth.* The men of Nineveh shall rise in judgment with this generation, and shall condemn it: because they repented at the preaching of Jonas; and, behold, a greater than Jonas is here. The queen of the south shall rise up in the judgment with this generation, and shall condemn it: for she came from the uttermost parts of the earth to hear the wisdom of Solomon; and, behold, a greater than Solomon is here. When the unclean spirit is gone out of a man, he walketh through dry places, seeking rest, and findeth none. Then he saith, I will return into my house from whence I came out; and when he is come, he findeth it empty, swept, and garnished. Then goeth he, and taketh with himself seven other spirits more wicked than himself, and they enter in and dwell there: and the last state of that man is worse than the first. *Even so shall it be also unto this wicked generation.*

shall also the Son of man be to this generation. The queen of the south shall rise up in the judgment with the men of this generation, and condemn them: for she came from the utmost parts of the earth to hear the wisdom of Solomon; and, behold, a greater than Solomon is here. The men of Nineve shall rise up in the judgment with this generation, and shall condemn it: for they repented at the preaching of Jonas; and, behold, a greater than Jonas is here. 24. When the unclean spirit is gone out of a man, he walketh through dry places, seeking rest; and finding none, he saith, I will return unto my house whence I came out. And when he cometh, he findeth it swept and garnished. Then goeth he, and taketh to him seven other spirits more wicked than himself; and they enter in, and dwell there: and the last state of that man is worse than the first.

Let us next take an instance of one and the same fact related both by St Matthew and St Luke; but by the former in a general way and in its main features, by the latter with characteristic details.

MATTH. viii. 5.

And when Jesus was entered into Capernaum, there came unto him a centurion, beseeching him. 6. And saying, Lord, my servant lieth at home *sick of the palsy*, grievously tormented.

LUKE vii. 1.

Now when he had ended all his sayings in the audience of the people, he entered into Capernaum. 2. And a certain centurion's servant, *who was dear unto him*, was sick, and *ready to die*. 3. And when he heard of JESUS, he sent unto him the elders of the Jews, beseeching him that he would come and heal his servant. 4. And when they came to JESUS, they be-

	sought him instantly, saying, That he was *worthy* for whom he should do this. 5. *For he loveth our nation, and he hath built us a synagogue.*
7. And Jesus saith unto him, I will come and heal him. 8. The centurion answered and said unto him, Lord, I am not worthy that thou shouldest come under my roof:	6. Then JESUS *went with them. And when he was now not far from the house, the centurion sent friends to him*, saying unto him: *Lord, trouble not thyself; for* I am not worthy that thou shouldest enter under my roof: 7. Wherefore *neither thought I myself worthy* to
but speak the word only, and my servant shall be healed.	come unto thee: but say in a word, and my servant shall be healed.
9. For I am a man under authority, having soldiers under me: and I say to this man, Go, and he goeth; and to another, Come, and he cometh; and to my servant, Do this, and he doeth it.	8. For I also am a man set under authority, having under me soldiers, and I say unto one, Go, and he goeth; and to another, Come, and he cometh; and to my servant, Do this, and he doeth it.
10. When Jesus heard it, he marvelled, and said to them that followed, Verily I say unto you, I have not found so great faith, no, not in Israel. 11. And I say unto you, that many shall come from the east and west, and shall sit down with Abraham, and Isaac, and Jacob, in the kingdom of heaven. 12. But the children of the kingdom shall be cast out into outer darkness: there shall be weeping and gnashing of teeth.	9. When Jesus heard these things, he marvelled at him, and turned him *about*, and said unto the people that followed him, I have not found so great faith, no, not in Israel.
13. And Jesus said unto the centurion, Go thy way; and as thou hast believed, so be it done unto thee. And his servant was healed in the selfsame hour.	10. *And they that were sent, returning to the house, found the servant whole that had been sick.*

The respective characters of these two narratives are evident. We have the incident related in its grand fundamental traits in St Matthew, and these St Luke literally adopts: the great faith of the centurion, and the characteristic illustration from military life, in which he expresses that faith (Matth. v. 9, Luke v. 8); after that the amazement of Jesus at finding such faith in a Gentile, and the comparison with Israel (Matth. x., Luke ix). But now come the striking particulars by which the more fully wrought out narrative of St Luke is distinguished. With respect to the sickness of the servant; he assumes to be known what St Matthew says of it, that he *was sick of the palsy*, adding the important circumstance, that he was *ready to die* (v. 2). He alone brings out the fact of the godly centurion, in his undissembled humility, accounting himself unworthy either to receive the Saviour into his house, or to come to him in person. First (v. 3 and 4), he sends, as intercessors to present his urgent prayer in behalf of his faithful servant, some Elders of the Jews; next, when Jesus was already on his way to visit him, he sends *some friends* to meet him, with the expressions of humility which St Matthew also records (v. 8), attributing, however, immediately to the centurion what the latter, properly speaking, did through a double intervention of other persons, according to a common though less accurate mode of statement (v. 8 and 13). Then we have in St Luke a striking antithesis in the sense of *unworthiness*, expressed by himself, and the character for *worthiness* given to him by the elders on account of his liberality and love to their nation (v. 4 and 5). What we read in St Matthew as having been declared by our Lord with respect to the calling of the Gentiles, and the reprobation of unbelieving Israel (v. 11 and 12), is suppressed here in our third Gospel, because uttered by our Lord in point of fact on another occasion; but thus the conclusion is put in stronger relief, that *they that were sent, returning to the house, found the servant whole that had been sick* (v. 10).

while St Matthew, suppressing anew all mention of the intermediate persons, simply states the result.

The respective characters of the two Gospels come out in another way; to wit, in their modes of relating the *words* or *declarations* of our Lord. In this we again recognise in St Luke *the historian*, who states what was said more according to the letter, in Matthew *the apostle* rather, who in virtue of his high commission, and of his more immediate relationship to the Saviour, was empowered to explain and paraphrase his words according to their essential object, in full accordance with the meaning and spirit of the speaker. Thus, for example, St Matthew and St Luke give the opening of the sermon on the Mount, with some differences, as follows :—

MATTH. v. 3–6.	LUKE vi. 20, 21.
Blessed are the *poor in spirit:* for theirs is the kingdom of heaven. Blessed are they that *mourn: for they shall be comforted.* Blessed are the meek: for they shall inherit the earth. Blessed *are they* which do hunger and thirst *after righteousness;* for they shall be filled.	Blessed *be ye* poor: for *yours* is the kingdom of God. Blessed *are ye* that hunger now: for *ye shall* be filled. Blessed *are ye* that *weep* now: for *ye shall laugh.*

The minute yet nowise meaningless differences in this twofold record, as well as the essential sameness of the matters recorded, are perceived at a glance. In St Matthew the third person plural is employed: *Blessed* ARE THEY. In Luke these sayings are directly addressed to the men themselves, in the second person: *Blessed* ARE YE. There can be no doubt that our Saviour used the latter form of expression, from what we are told immediately before in St Luke, that *he lifted up his eyes on his disciples, and said,* &c. St Matthew (v. 2) speaks generally of *teaching.* St Luke, who here evidently gives our Lord's words most literally, speaks of *the poor ;* St Matthew explains the deeper meaning of the word, by saying—*poor in spirit.* We again meet with St Luke's version in another apostle, St James, who in his Epistle (ii. 5, 6) speaks of *the poor of this world* as *rich in faith.* In like manner, in his fourth beatitude, St Matthew has apostolically elucidated and paraphrased what in St Luke is expressed more briefly and generally : BLESSED ARE *they that hunger and thirst after righteousness.* In like manner, too, those very artless expressions in St Luke (v. 21) : *weep* and *laugh,* bear evidently enough the stamp of the words originally uttered ; while those employed by St Matthew, *mourn* and *be comforted,* may be regarded as an exposition of them. (Verse 5th, in St Matthew, is evidently taken from Psalm xxxvii. 11).

The relation of St Luke's Gospel to St Mark's, as well as of St Mark's to St Matthew's, wherever two only of the three synoptical writers have recorded any thing that was done, seems to us sufficiently established by our preceding review of these two last Gospels.[1] In like manner, we have seen the peculiar characteristics of each stand out in the case of all three relating one and the same occurrence. In the case of the already analysed narratives of *the restoration to life of the daughter of Jairus*—of *the cure of the possessed person in the country of the Gadarenes*—of *that of the blind at Jericho*—of *the confession of the Messiahship of Jesus*—of *the transfiguration on the Mount*—and of *the cure of the young lunatic,* each of our readers, after the closer acquaintanceship we have made with St Luke, may be convinced, after a repeated perusal, how—*first,* from the narrative of St

[1] P. 53.

Matthew—who has given us a summary account of occurrences in their grand features—*secondly*, the representation of them by St Mark begins immediately, by a process of elaborating particular circumstances into his narrative; and how, *thirdly*, St Luke, availing himself of both these preceding works as the source whence he drew the materials of his own history, adopts from St Mark whatever might serve to elucidate a leading fact, or to give greater precision to the more general outline of St Matthew; while, besides, St Mark's more scenic delineation of details is followed up in St Luke by deeper, more tender, and more connected communication of motives and feelings.

We find the mutual bearings we have indicated as existing among the first three evangelical writers, in point of character and the order of time in which they wrote, reappear in a remarkable manner in the incorporation into their Gospels of that most important part of our Lord's instructions—the *parables.*

The *parables* have been preserved for us on the pages of the three synoptical Evangelists alone. They are not to be found in St John, at least in their ordinary historical form. But at the same time they are divided among the former after this fashion, that some of the parables have been recorded by all three Evangelists, others by only two, others by only one of them.

There is something characteristic, in the first place, in the distribution of those *parables* which occur only *once* in those writings. Of these parables, we have in St Matthew alone, that of *the tares among the wheat* (xiii. 24–30); that of *the treasure hid in the field* (v. 44); that of *the pearl of great price* (v. 45, 46); that of *the net of the fishermen* (v. 47–50); that of *the householder's treasure* (v. 52); that of *the king who forgave his ungrateful servant ten thousand talents* (xviii. 21–34); that of *the labourers in the vineyard* (xx. 1–16); that of *the two sons who spoke otherwise than they did* (xxi. 28–32); that of *the five wise* and *the five foolish virgins* (xxv. 1–13). The parable of *the seed that grew up without the sower knowing how,* is found only in St Mark. One sees at once the analogy of that similitude with the whole plan and character of his Gospel.[1] It is only in St Luke, and always with a clear indication of the precise time, and in the most significant connexion, that we find the parable of the *two debtors, of whom the one was forgiven much, and the other little,* on the occasion of the forgiveness of the woman who was a sinner (vii. 41–43); that of *the charitable Samaritan,* in answer to the lawyer's question, *Who is my neighbour?* (x. 30–36); that of *the friend who came to his friend at midnight wanting bread,* in connexion with the model prayer, *Our Father which art in heaven* (xi. 5–8); that of *the rich man whose soul was required of him in the midst of his worldly plans,* on the occasion of our Lord's giving a warning against avarice (xii. 15); that of the *barren fig-tree,* in connexion with the judgment pronounced on all the unconverted (xiii. 6–9); that of *the invited to the marriage-feast,* when our Lord had occasion to reprimand those who chose out the chief rooms (xiv. 7–11); that of the man *who wished to build a tower,* and that of the king *who went out to battle,* meant as an explanation of the saying, *Whosoever doth not bear his cross, and come after me, cannot be my disciple* (xiv. 28–33); the parable of *the lost piece of money,* and of *the prodigal*

[1] P. 87.

son (with that of *the lost sheep,* recorded by St Matthew also), directed against the Pharisees and the scribes (xv); that of *the unjust steward,* on the same occasion, directed against the avarice of the Pharisees (xvi. 1–14); that again of *the rich man and Lazarus,* on the same occasion (xvi. 19–31), and shortly after the declaration, that *that which is highly esteemed among men is abomination in the sight of God* (v. 15); that of *the servant returning from the field,* in our Lord's discourse on faith and forgiveness (xvii. 7–10); that of *the widow and the unjust judge,* in direct connexion with the announcement of the last days, and the exhortation to persevering prayer (xvii. 20–37, xviii. 1–8).

Besides this obvious characteristic of attention to chronological order which distinguishes the arrangement of the parables that are found only in St Luke, some further distinctive marks deserve being noted here. The similitudes introduced by St Matthew are, on the whole, taken rather from public and professional, those in St Luke rather from domestic, life. Those in St Matthew present our Lord to us rather as *King*—his kingdom more in connexion with this world and this world's destiny; those of St Luke more in connexion with the life of the soul. Those in St Matthew are more of an oriental and poetical cast, those of Luke have a nearer resemblance to real events; so much so, that the parables of the good Samaritan and of the rich man and Lazarus, may be taken for narratives of actual occurrences almost as much as parables.

Let us next take the parables that St Matthew and St Luke have *in common.* Here we find the double records differ, sometimes more, sometimes less, either in the nature or in the fulness of the details that are peculiar to each. In some cases they are perfectly identical.

Such perfect identity we find between the two Evangelists in the similitude of *the leaven*.

MATTH. xiii. 33.	LUKE xiii. 20, 21.
Another parable spake he unto them; The kingdom of heaven is like unto leaven, which a woman took and hid in three measures of meal, till the whole was leavened.	And again he said, Whereunto shall I liken the kingdom of God? It is like leaven, which a woman took and hid in three measures of meal, till the whole was leavened.

Here we see that St Luke has made use of St Matthew's Gospel, in the way of simple transcription, We find, on the contrary, a not insignificant difference between the first and third Gospel, in the similitude of *the lost sheep*.

MATTH. xviii. 12, 13.	LUKE xv. 4–7.
How think ye? If a man have an hundred sheep, and one of them *be gone astray*, doth he not leave the ninety and nine, and goeth into the mountains, and seeketh that which is gone astray? And if so be that he find it, verily I say unto you, he rejoiceth more of that sheep, than *of the ninety and nine which went not astray*.	What man of you, having an hundred sheep, *if he lose* one of them, doth not leave the ninety and nine *in the wilderness*, and go after *that which is lost*, until he find it? And when he hath found it, *he layeth it on his shoulders* rejoicing. *And when he cometh home, he calleth together his friends and ne'ghbours, saying unto them, Rejoice with me; for I have found my sheep which was lost.* I say unto you, *that likewise joy shall be in heaven over one sinner that repenteth, more than over ninety and nine just persons, that need no repentance.*

Here we see in St Luke the similitude brought more fully out, and a milder spirit is shewn both in the details that are added, and the expressions that are employed. What St Matthew speaks of as *gone astray*, St Luke calls *lost*. The sheep that is found again is *laid on the shoulders of the shepherd; his neighbours and friends are called together to participate in his joy;*[1] finally, the reproof is administered to persons possessed with an opinion of their own righteousness, as thinking that *they need no repentance.*

Still greater is the difference, though without prejudice to the identity of the parables in the main, in that of *the guests at the marriage feast,* and that of *the talents.*

MATTH. xxii. 2–14.

The kingdom of heaven is like unto *a certain king, which made a marriage for his son,* and sent forth his servants to call them that were bidden *to the wedding:* and they would not come. Again he sent forth other servants, saying, Tell them which are bidden, Behold, I have prepared my dinner: my oxen and my fatlings are killed, and all things are ready: come unto the marriage. But they made light of it, and went their ways, one to his farm, another to his merchandise: *and the remnant took his servants, and entreated them spitefully, and slew them. But when the king heard thereof, he was wroth: and he sent forth his armies, and destroyed those murderers, and burned up their city.* Then saith he to his servants, The wedding is ready, but they which were bidden were not worthy. Go ye therefore into the highways, and as many as ye shall find, bid to the marriage. So those servants went out into the highways, and gathered together all as many as they found, *both bad and good:* and the

LUKE xiv. 16–24.

A certain man made a great supper, and bade many: and sent *his servant at supper-time* to say to them that were bidden, Come; for all things are now ready. And they all with one consent began to make excuse. The first said unto him, I have bought a piece of ground, and I must needs go and see it: I pray thee have me excused. And another said, I have bought five yoke of oxen, and I go to prove them: I pray thee have me excused. And another said, I have married a wife, and therefore I cannot come. So that servant came, and shewed his lord these things. Then the master of the house being angry said to his servant, Go out quickly into the streets and lanes of the city, and bring in hither the poor, and the maimed, and the halt, and the blind. And the servant said, Lord, it is done as thou hast commanded, and yet there is room. And the lord said unto the servant, Go out into the highways and hedges, and compel them to come in, that my house may be filled. *For I say*

[1] In the two parables that follow in St Luke, we find the same demonstrations of joy: verses 9 and 10, and verses 23, 25, and 32.

wedding was furnished with guests. And when the king came in to see the guests, he saw there a man which had not on a wedding-garment: and he saith unto him, Friend, how camest thou in hither not having a wedding-garment? And he was speechless. Then said the king to the servants, Bind him hand and foot, and take him away, and cast him into outer darkness; there shall be weeping and gnashing of teeth. For many are called, but few are chosen.

unto you, that none of those men which were bidden shall taste of my supper.

It will at once be seen that the parable here related is in both Gospels fundamentally the same. In both it points plainly and decidedly to the preaching of the Gospel; in other words, to the call to enter the kingdom of God. That kingdom is likened here, as elsewhere in Scripture, to a supper to which many guests are invited, who on various pretexts decline the invitation. First of all it is the Jews that are invited, but will not come; and in their place others of the motley multitude of mankind, and from the streets and the highways, are sent for, and with these the house of the host who has provided the supper is filled. This groundwork is then filled up by the insertion of various particulars in harmony with the characteristic tendencies of the two Gospels. In St Luke the host is called simply *a certain man;* in St Matthew it is *a king*, and a king, too, who *makes a marriage feast for his son.* In St Luke it is *his servant* that is sent to invite the guests; in St Matthew we have the plural, *his servants.* In St Luke the excuses are fully detailed (verses 18 and 20); St Matthew, on the contrary, gives the words of invitation in fuller terms, and in Old Testament style.[1] In St Matthew, after the refusal of the

[1] See pages 16–18.

invited, all sorts of people, good and bad (the respected and the despised of this world), are brought in; in St Luke it is only the poor and the wretched of all sorts. In St Luke the refusal is punished with the recall of the intended honour (verse 24); in St Matthew the refusal is associated with the spiteful and outrageous treatment of the messengers (verse 6), and (not without a prophetical allusion to the destruction of Jerusalem) the judgment executed on the authors of that treatment (verse 7). The parable in St Luke closes here. What St Matthew alone further relates, the discovery and the expulsion of *the guest without the marriage garment,* is evidently quite a new parable, brought into connexion, in that Evangelist's peculiar manner, with that of the invitation to the royal marriage feast.

And now as to the parable of *the talents.* This, too, in its grand outlines, is the same in both Gospels; yet the filling up, as well as the place it occupies, of which we have spoken already,[1] is different.

MATTH. xxv. 14–30.	LUKE xix. 12–28.
For the kingdom of heaven is as *a man* travelling into a far country, who called his own servants, and delivered unto them his goods. And unto one he gave *five talents*, to another *two*, and to another *one;* to every man according to his several ability; and straightway took his journey. Then he that had received the five talents went and traded with the same, and made them other five talents. And likewise he that had received two, he also gained other two. But he that had received one went and digged in the earth, and hid his lord's money.	A certain *nobleman* went into a far country to receive for himself a kingdom, and to return. And he called his ten servants, and delivered them *ten pounds*, and said unto them, Occupy till I come. But his citizens hated him, and sent a message after him, saying, We will not have this man to reign over us.

[1] See page 162.

After a long time the lord of those servants cometh, and reckoneth with them. And so he that had received five talents came and brought other five talents, saying, Lord, thou deliveredst unto me *five talents:* behold, I have gained besides them *five talents* more. His lord said unto him, Well done, thou good and faithful servant: thou hast been faithful over a few things, I will make thee ruler over many things: *enter thou into the joy of thy lord.* He also that had received two talents came and said, Lord, thou deliveredst unto me *two talents:* behold, I have gained *two other talents* besides them. His lord said unto him, Well done, good and faithful servant; thou hast been faithful over a few things, I will make thee ruler over many things: enter thou into the joy of thy lord. Then he which had received the one talent came and said, Lord, I knew thee that thou art an hard man, reaping where thou hast not sown, and gathering where thou hast not strawed: And I was afraid, and went and hid thy talent in the earth: lo, there thou hast that is thine. His lord answered and said unto him, Thou wicked and slothful servant, thou knewest that I reap where I sowed not, and gather where I have not strawed: Thou oughtest therefore to have put my money to the exchangers, and then at my coming I should have received mine own with usury. Take therefore the talent from him, and give it unto him which hath ten talents. For unto every one that hath shall be given, and he shall have abundance: but from him that hath not shall be taken away even that which he hath. *And cast ye the unprofitable servant into outer darkness: there shall be weeping and gnashing of teeth.*

15. And it came to pass, that when he was returned, having received the kingdom, then he commanded these servants to be called unto him, to whom he had given the money, that he might know how much every man had gained by trading. Then came the first, saying, Lord, *thy pound hath gained ten pounds.* And he said unto him, Well, thou good servant: because thou hast been faithful in a very little, *have thou authority over ten cities.* And the second came, saying, Lord, *thy pound hath gained five pounds.* And he said likewise to him, Be thou also over *five cities.* And another came, saying, Lord, behold, here is *thy pound*, which I have kept laid up *in a napkin:* for I feared thee, because thou art an austere man: thou takest up that thou layedst not down, and reapest that thou didst not sow. And he saith unto him, *Out of thine own mouth will I judge thee*, thou wicked servant. Thou knewest that I was an austere man, taking up that I laid not down, and reaping that I did not sow: wherefore then gavest not thou my money into the bank, that at my coming I might have required mine own with usury? And he said unto them that stood by, Take from him the pound, and give it to him that hath ten pounds. (*And they said unto him, Lord, he hath ten pounds.*) For I say unto you, That unto every one which hath shall be given; and from him that hath not, even that he hath shall be taken away from him. *But those mine enemies, which would not that I should reign over them, bring hither, and slay them before me.*

The main design of the parable, as appears evidently enough, is the same in both Gospels. In the details, however, it is St Luke who on this occasion introduces the subject of our Lord's *kingship*. Very naturally, inasmuch as the similitude according to him (xix. 11) was delivered *when Jesus was nigh to Jerusalem, and when they thought that the* KINGDOM *of God should* IMMEDIATELY *appear*. On this account our Saviour first desired to make people aware that He (the *nobleman* of the parable) behoved first to return to heaven (the *far country*), there to receive his kingdom, and then first to be revealed as king in glory. With this introduction to the parable as found in St Luke, we find the conclusion connected (verse 27), where we have represented to us the doom pronounced on his citizens or fellow-countrymen (the Jews), who hated him, and *would not have him to rule over them* (verse 14). St Matthew says nothing here of a kingdom, probably because that very idea had been *already* introduced in the parable of the *guests invited to the marriage feast*, which he had previously recorded. Further differences occur in minute, but not unimportant details. St Matthew, with the copiousness peculiar to him, speaks of *talents*, instead of the humbler term *pounds* used by St Luke. There is a difference likewise in the proportion of profit gained. In St Matthew the two diligent servants doubled the number they had received, whereas in St Luke one had increased what he had received *tenfold*, the other *fivefold*. In St Luke also, in conformity with the point from which he starts (verse 12), the recompense of the faithful servants extends to *ten* and *five* cities (verses 17, 19). In St Matthew there is an antithesis betwixt *entering into the joy of their Lord* (verses 21–23), and (verse 30) the adjudging to outer darkness, *where there shall be weeping and gnashing of teeth*.

The similitudes common to all *three* synoptical Evangelists are only three in number,—that of *the sower on different sorts of ground*, that of the *grain of mustard-seed*, and that of the *wicked husbandmen*. Here the discrepancy between the three Gospels is really very slight, yet it is enough to enable us to recognise in it the peculiar object and tendency of each of them. First, let us take up that of the sower:—

MATTH. xiii. 3–8.

Behold, a sower went forth to sow; and when he sowed, some seeds fell by the way-side, and the fowls came and devoured them up: some fell upon stony places, where they had not much earth: and forthwith they sprung up, because they had no deepness of earth: and when the sun was up, they were scorched; and, because they had no root, they withered away. And some fell among thorns; and the thorns sprung up, and choked them: but other fell into good ground, and brought forth fruit, some an *hundred-fold*, some *sixty-fold*, some *thirty-fold*.

MARK iv. 3–8.

Hearken; Behold, there went out a sower to sow: and it came to pass, as he sowed, some fell by the way-side, and the fowls *of the air* came and devoured it up. And some fell on stony ground, where it had not mnch earth; and immediately it sprang up, because it had no depth of earth: but when the sun was up, it was scorched; and, because it had no root, it withered away. And some fell among thorns, and the thorns grew up, and choked it, and *it yielded no fruit*. And other fell on good ground, and did yield fruit that *sprang up and increased;* and brought forth, some *thirty*, and some *sixty*, and some an *hundred*.

LUKE viii. 5–8.

A sower went out to sow his seed: and as he sowed, some fell by the way-side; and it was *trodden down*, and the fowls *of the air* devoured it. And some fell upon a rock; and as soon as it was sprung up, it withered away, because it lacked moisture. And some fell among thorns; and the thorns sprang up *with it*, and choked it. And other fell on good ground, and sprang up, and bare fruit *an hundred-fold*.

It will be seen that there is very little difference among the three versions of the parable. St Mark, for the most part, follows his predecessor. St Luke follows both, but with a notable shortening of the narrative, by leaving out more than one detail. Yet even here the one does not merely adopt what has been recorded by the other. St Mark, as well as St Luke, throw in here and there an expression full of meaning and emphasis. Thus, according to the latter, the seed was not only devoured by the fowls, but also trodden down of men. Thus, St Mark observes that the *choked seed yielded no fruit,* and that what fell on good ground regularly *sprang up and increased.* Thus St Luke shews us the good seed and the thorns springing up *together.* We have already observed how St Mark, in speaking of the quantity of the fruit produced, not unimpressively reverses the order in St Matthew;[1] while St Luke, with historical compression, mentions *a hundred-fold only.* In the explanation of the parable[2] the three Evangelists are, for the most part, almost literally alike.

The similitude of the mustard-seed runs thus in the three Gospels :—

MATTH. xiii. 31, 32.	MARK iv. 31, 32.	LUKE xiii. 19.
The kingdom of heaven is like to a grain of mustard-seed, which a man took, and *sowed in his field*: which indeed is the least of all seeds: but when it is grown, it is the greatest among herbs, and *becometh a tree*, so that the birds of the air come and lodge in *the branches thereof.*	The kingdom of God is like a grain of mustard-seed, which, when it *is sown in the earth*, is less than all the seeds that be in the earth : but when it is sown, it groweth up, and becometh greater than all herbs, and *shooteth out great branches;* so that the fowls of the air may lodge *under the shadow of it.*	The kingdom of God is like a grain of mustard-seed, which a man took, *and cast into his garden ;* and it grew, and waxed a great tree; and the fowls of the air lodged in the branches of it.

[1] Pp. 98.
[2] Matth. xiii. 18-22; Mark iv. 13-20; Luke viii. 11-15.

Here there is almost a literal agreement, and yet neither the graphic style of St Mark nor the historic style of St Luke belie themselves. In the description given by the former, the tree is represented as shooting out great branches, and the birds as lodging under its shadow. In that given by the latter, the whole similitude is thrown into the form of something that once actually happened, rather than of a thing of daily occurrence. The seed WAS cast, the birds MADE their nests in the branches (in the past tense[1]), while the two other Evangelists use the present.

In the similitude of the wicked husbandmen we find more difference in the details.

MATTH. xxi. 33.	MARK xii. 1.	LUKE xx. 9.
There was a certain householder, which planted a vineyard, *and hedged it round about, and digged a winepress in it, and built a tower*, and let it out to husbandmen, and went into a far country:	A certain man planted a vineyard, *and set an hedge about it, and digged a place for the wine-fat, and built a tower*, and let it out to husbandmen, and went into a far country.	A certain man planted a vineyard, and let it forth to husbandmen, and went into a far country *for a long time*.
34. And when the time of the fruit drew near, he sent his servants to the husbandmen, that they might receive the fruits of it.	2. And at the season he sent to the husbandmen a servant, that he might receive from the husbandmen of the fruit of the vineyard.	10. And at the season he sent *a servant* to the husbandmen, that they should give him of the fruit of the vineyard: but the husbandmen *beat him*, and sent him away *empty*.
35. And the husbandmen took *his servants, and beat one, and killed another, and stoned another*.	3. And they caught him, and beat him, and sent him away empty.	11. And AGAIN he sent *another* servant: and they beat him also, and entreated him shamefully, and sent him away empty.
36. AGAIN, he sent other servants *more*	4. And AGAIN he sent unto them *another* ser-	12. And AGAIN he sent a THIRD: and they

[1] The Greek aorist.

than the first: and they did unto them likewise.	vant; and at him *they cast stones, and wounded him in the head, and sent him away shamefully handled.* 5. And AGAIN *he sent another; and him they killed, and many others; beating some, and killing some.*	wounded him also, and cast him out.
37. But last of all he sent unto them *his son*, saying, They will reverence my son.	6. Having yet therefore *one son, his well-beloved*, he sent him also *last* unto them, saying, They will reverence my son.	13. Then said the lord of the vineyard, what shall I do? I will send *my beloved son:* it may be they will reverence him when they see him.
38. But when the husbandmen saw the son, they said among themselves, This is the heir; come, let us kill him, and let us seize on his inheritance.	7. But those husbandmen said among themselves, This is the heir; come, let us kill him, and the inheritance shall be ours.	14. But when the husbandmen saw him, they reasoned among themselves, saying, This is the heir: come, let us kill him, that the inheritance may be ours.
39. And they caught him, and cast him out of the vineyard, and slew him. When the lord therefore of the vineyard cometh, what will he do unto those husbandmen? *They say unto him, He will miserably destroy those wicked men*, and will let out his vineyard unto other husbandmen, which shall render him the fruits in their seasons.	8. And they took him, and killed him, and cast him out of the vineyard. What shall therefore the lord of the vineyard do? he will come and destroy the husbandmen, and will give the vineyard unto others.	15. So they cast him out of the vineyard, and killed him. What therefore shall the lord of the vineyard do unto them? he shall come and destroy these husbandmen, and shall give the vineyard to others. *And when they heard it, they said, God forbid.*

Each of the three Evangelists, it will be seen, in the differences among them, again maintains his consistency in regard to style and tendency. Thus St Luke at once (v. 9) leaves out the description of the vineyard, given minutely by St Matthew and St Mark, contenting himself with the grand outline of the parabolic narrative. Thus St Matthew again (v. 34 and 36) adopts the plural number, and speaks twice of *servants;* while St Mark and St Luke mention only one, but, on the other hand, state that the sending was repeated *thrice.* We have already remarked[1] what is fitted to affect the reader in St Mark when he speaks of the sending of the son (v. 37); St Luke gives, *My beloved son.* In relating the repulse and ill treatment of the servants that were sent, St Mark runs most into details: it is only in his Gospel that we read (v. 4) of one of the servants being *wounded in the head;* and both St Matthew and he speak of the *stoning,* not perhaps without prophetical allusion to the lot that awaited the witnesses of Jesus Christ himself. St Luke (v. 12) bears principally on *the rejection. The expulsion of the* SON *from the vineyard* is given in details by all the three. St Matthew (v. 41) puts the condemnation of the enemies in the mouth of the Pharisees; while St Luke, on the contrary, gives the very exclamation they uttered, *God forbid!*'[2]

Let us now glance over the results of our now concluded review of St Luke's Gospel, and we are confident that the following leading points will be brought home to the conviction of our readers.

The person who penned the third of our Gospels, can be no other than he whom all Christian antiquity from the very first, without a single dissentient voice, has pronounced him to be: Luke, a physician of Gentile descent and Greek education, a proselyte to Judaism, and afterwards, as a Christian disciple, the beloved

[1] Page 98.

[2] Page 32.

companion and fellow-labourer of Paul, the apostle to the Gentiles.

From his fellow Evangelists he is distinguished by the eminently historical character, as well of the plan and contents as of the whole style and manner of his two writings—the Acts of the Apostles being to be regarded as forming one continuous whole with his Gospel.

It is true that nowhere does he introduce himself personally as physician, proselyte, and Christian from among the Gentiles, whether by name, or by mentioning his own labours; yet by this self-concealment, this individual personality is all the more powerfully brought out in all that stands recorded by him. Thus we have found St Paul's doctrine and preaching reappear, as it were, in a historical form, in St Luke. Thus we recognise the proselyte from the heathen brought over to Christ, both in the delicacy and kindly feelings with which he touches every thing Israelitish, and in the manner in which he sets forth the calling of the Gentiles to the communion of Israel's God and Messiah. The physician reveals himself not only in some traits that betoken a man familiar with diseases and their cures, but also, in his entire conception of the good news of salvation and grace, in his whole view of the person of the Lord Jesus. This same Jesus, the ever to be praised Lord and Saviour, we have seen, in this third Gospel, set before us very distinctly as the Almighty Physician of soul and body; in close connexion, moreover, with that Israelitish title given to the God-man, as the merciful, compassionate High Priest, anointed with the Holy Ghost, and going about every where *doing good*. Here we have seen him, in an ampler diversity of instances than any where else in the Gospels, surrounded with all manner of suffering and necessitous persons—

the wretched, the despised, and the weak. These characteristic marks in St Luke's Gospel we find recurring, ever and anon, even in the details of numerous *parables* as they have been recorded by him. Finally, we have seen in St Luke, the historian not only of Jesus Christ in the flesh, but also of the Holy Ghost, by whom He, the blessed seed of the woman, was conceived, and whom He, after his own return to heaven, sent forth from the Father as the Comforter whom He had promised.

Here we close our review of the third of our Gospels. The fourth and last now demands our attention: it is the testimony of the bosom friend, no longer of Peter or of Paul, but of—the Lord.

V. ST JOHN.

WHEN, passing from the Gospel of St Matthew, one takes up and finishes a review of the much more elaborated writings of St Mark and St Luke, it might *seem* as if the works of the two Apostolical disciples more or less eclipse that of the Apostle, and as if the Gospels of the two heathen converts, in point of fulness and interest at least, surpass that of the witness out of Israel. No doubt such an idea has but a *show* of truth: it can have no solid ground to rest upon. Each of the Gospels has its own proper value; each of the Evangelists his own special gift and peculiar excellence. The Gospel of St Matthew, such as we have described it, the *mother Gospel*, the Gospel that breathes the spirit of the prophets, will ever retain its high importance among the sacred four; the writer's Apostolic character, even after a comparison with his two successors, remains a special guarantee of the truth of the testimony. And yet one cannot but feel that, even with the apostolic testimony of St Matthew, a second testimony from one of the twelve is desirable; and that the harmony will be more complete and delightful, if, instead of being closed with the composition of a companion of St Peter or of St Paul, it should be crowned, as it were, with the testimony of an immediate disciple—a highly privileged apostle of Jesus Christ. In the writer of the fourth of the Gospels, then, we again meet with an Apostle, one of the three specially selected from the chosen twelve; and again, that very one of the three who was the specially beloved and chosen bosom disciple. It is John, whom we have seen in the days of our Lord's sojourn upon this earth, admitted and called, along with his brother James, and with Peter, to behold the restoration to life of the daughter of Jairus, to witness the transfiguration of their Master on the Mount, and afterwards, to be present at the scene of our Lord's agony in Gethsemané. It is John, who, while he sat at supper, leant with affectionate confidence on the bosom of his Lord; to whom, as he stood by the cross, his Lord's mother was confided, to be regarded thenceforward as his own. It is John, whom first, after the descent of the Holy Ghost, we find, along with St Peter, exercising his apostolical functions in signs, and wonders, and the laying on of hands in the name of the Lord; who along with St Peter, and St James, the Lord's brother, is called by St Paul a pillar of the Church at Jerusalem. Yet not a single word remains to us of his preaching during all those days subsequent to the return of Jesus to heaven. It was a long while after that, that the Churches first received from him his Epistles, his Gospel, and one other most sublime writing from his pen. More than half a century had elapsed since John, the son of Zebedee, was directed by another John, the son of Zacharias, *to the Lamb that taketh away the sin of the world,* and followed him. The Benjamin among the twelve Apostles was now a patriarch far advanced in life. His fellow-disciples and contemporaries were no more. James his brother had fallen a victim, long before, to the violence of Herod; Peter had died upon the cross; Paul had been slain by the sword; and the other apostles, each at his post, in various parts of the world. Then came the destruction of Jerusalem. The sacrifices had ceased to be offered; Israel had become a people *without a king, without priests, without sacrifices, without ephod* and *teraphim*, without a country. The line of demarcation between Christians converted from Judaism, and Christians converted from heathenism, was effaced. Jerusalem, utterly destroyed, was no longer the city either of the Temple and Synagogue, or of the first Apostolic Church. The great cities of heathendom had now become the mother-churches of Christendom; Ephesus, among others, where the beloved disciple, as elder of the Church, closed his long protracted life. Either while still residing in the midst of that Church, or during his banishment to the island of Patmos, he took up the pen for the last time. He lays his testimony before the Churches to the remotest ages, under the guidance of that Holy Spirit who had been promised to him as well as to the rest, *to lead him into all truth, to bring all things to his remembrance,* and also *to shew him the things that were to come.*[1] His first writing is *historical;* with it he winds up and completes the Gospel testimony of the life, sufferings, death, and resurrection of our Lord. His last writing is *prophetical;* and in it he connects the last things with the first—the prophecies of the Old Testament with the language of the New, for the revelation of the final object of all—*our Lord's second coming,* and *the establishment of his glorious kingdom, as in heaven so likewise on earth.*

As the author was a special object of his Master's

[1] John xiv. xv. xvi.

choice, so is his Gospel a select and exquisite production. It is not like any of the three that preceded it, and, nevertheless, it is one and the same testimony with them to Jesus Christ, the Son of God, come into the world, crucified for sin, and gone back to glory. It is the same testimony; but, like the sun seen in the sky of Italy or Greece, brighter and more glorious than as it appears in any of his fellow-witnesses. It is a voice from heaven; it is the language of a seer. It is a Gospel from the *height*, and likewise from the *depth*.

From the *height!* It does not start, like that of St Mark, from the baptism in Jordan, nor like St Matthew's, from our Lord's descent from Abraham and David, nor like St Luke's, from the first promises regarding our Lord and his forerunner; no, but from a period *before the world was.* Thus does he characterise his testimony in the Epistle (1 John, i. 1, 2): *That which was from the beginning, which we have heard, which we have seen with our eyes, which we have looked upon, and our hands have handled, of the Word of Life* (Gr. τὸν λόγον τῆς ζώης, the living Word); *for the Life was manifested, and we have seen it, and bear witness, and shew unto you that eternal Life, which was with the Father, and was manifested unto us.*

Thus does he characterise that testimony in the Gospel itself, in its opening words: IN THE BEGINNING WAS THE WORD (ch. i. 1). And that Word the Gospel of John defines for us as it was before all things in His uncreated divine nature: *it was in the beginning* WITH GOD, *and it was* GOD (i. 1). Following out the golden thread of that supreme glory from this point through the whole of his Apostolical writings, he has preserved for us the testimonies uttered by the mouth of Jesus himself respecting his eternal Godhead: *Before Abraham was,* I AM (viii.

58); *I and the Father are* ONE (x. 30); *he that hath seen* ME *hath seen* THE FATHER (xiv. 9); in perfect harmony with which stand the words addressed to Jesus by St Thomas in that same Gospel (xx. 28), *My Lord and my God!* and again, in the book of the Revelation, the testimony of our glorious Redeemer respecting himself (i. 17): *I am the First and the Last.*

And in like manner as this Gospel of the son of Zebedee observes and describes all things from the highest point of view, so also does he contemplate them in their *depth,* and present them to us again in all the *fulness* of their truth and reality in ordinary life. No one has testified to the reality of our Lord's becoming man with an expression at once of such depth of meaning, and of such simplicity: *The Word was made* FLESH. No one shews this Word to us, when come into this world, when manifested in human flesh, so fully, and in such a multiplicity of aspects, as St John, in contact and controversy with men, arguing with sinful men, enduring the contumelies of sinful men (called *a Samaritan,* and *one that hath a devil,* viii. 48); the hand of men incessantly lifted up against him, to seize him—to stone him.

And yet even here we find an indescribable glory encircling Jesus in all that he suffers as well as all that he says. It is as if the exceeding brightness, of which St John was a witness on the Mount of Transfiguration, threw life and lustre into all his delineations of the Redeemer. On every subject that he touches, his expressions are characterised by a festive sublimity, a tone of celestial elevation. What is called *conversion* by his predecessors, is with him the *new birth,* the *being born of God;* the *crucifixion* is the *lifting up* as of a sacrifice; the *Crucified* is called the *Lamb.* Under that last name especially, the book of *Revelation* worships and glorifies the Son of God, who was slain for the sins of the world.

The *Gospel* and the *Revelation* of John! the *first things* and the *last.* The *first* coming of Jesus Christ in the flesh, witnessed and described by the disciple who, at the table of the last feast, lay as a youthful follower on his breast; the *second* coming of Jesus, seen in visions, and described in prophetical scenes, by the same disciple in his extreme old age. In both he glorifies, both in heaven and on earth, Him who is the *First and the Last, the Beginning and the End, the Alpha and the Omega.*

The *Gospel* and the *Revelation!*—a harmonious and glorious testimony to Him who was already beheld in his eternal kingdom with the marks on his body of the wounds by which he accomplished the atonement, in like manner as he bore, during his humiliation on earth, the glory of the Godhead in his essential being, and manifested it in words and works. What pen could bestow both these writings upon us but that of him who, when an old man in Patmos, recognised that Master whom he had once seen with his own eyes suffering death on the cross,—in the King of kings, seated far above all heavens, and who, though thus changed from what he once had been, could not separate a single trace of his completed sufferings on this earth from those splendours of the Godhead which irradiate that Lord of lords in heaven? The *Gospel* of the Word made flesh!—the *Revelation* of the glory, and of the kingdom, and of the coming of the Lamb that was slain! This the disciple *whom Jesus loved* was honoured to write before entering into the rest of his Lord.

Such, at the very threshold of our fourth Gospel-survey, are a few of the traits that naturally suggest themselves as indicative of the peculiar character of a writer who, in all that he has recorded, makes himself known to us as an eyewitness, as a trusted bosom friend, as a most enlightened minister and seer, as one before whose eyes, while he stood on the brink of eternity, the great spectacle of salvation appeared in all the glory of its truth. The reader may possibly fear that, in this short review, we are about to give him rather a poetical representation than a satisfactory demonstration of the truth which we would here establish in the face of the infidelity of the age in which we live. If so, let him follow, with an attention all the more severe, the very simple and prosaic analysis which we have undertaken, and from which both the genuineness and the divine inspiration of *this*, as well as of the other Gospels, will appear. Here, too, the method of observation and comparison will, we are confident, prove the most likely to conduct us to our point, and the most convincing in its all-important results.

We may assume the fourth of our Evangelical writings to be fresh in the recollection of all our readers.

On comparing this recollection with the impression left on us by the three synoptical Gospels, we must at once be sensible that our fourth Gospel has something in it powerfully distinctive, something profoundly illustrative, something that takes a strong hold on our minds. There are here, as in the other Gospel writings, historical incidents taken from the life, and sufferings, and resurrection of Jesus Christ. But no sooner do we enter upon it, than we find something more than the artless and childlike simplicity of St Matthew's narrative ; more than the rapidity and terseness of St Mark's record ; more than the calm and flowing historical style of St Luke. With that artlessness, and that terseness, and that calmness, there is here mingled a higher and more elevated tone—a tone derived from the monuments of the remotest sacred antiquity, as well as from the hidden depths of the most profound theology; a tone, reminding us sometimes of the Mosaic account of the creation, sometimes of the wise sayings of Solomon, sometimes akin even to the later theology of Jewish-Alexandrine philosophers. Let us but read and compare. Moses had said: IN THE BEGINNING *God created the heaven and the earth;* and John says, IN THE BEGINNING *was* (ἦν) *the Word. By him were all things made* (ἐγένετο); *and without him was not any thing made that was made* (ἐγένετο οὐδὲν ὅ γέγονε). The Supreme Wisdom had said in Solomon (Prov. viii. 22), *Jehovah possessed me in the beginning of his way, before his works of old. I have been set up (anointed) from everlasting, from the beginning, or ever the earth was. When there were no depths, I was brought forth; before the mountains were settled, before the hills was I brought forth. Then I was with him as a nursling, and I was daily his delight, rejoicing always before him.* And of the Word, says St John, that *it was in the beginning with God, that the world was made by it;* and that *the only begotten Son, who is in the bosom of the Father, hath revealed the Father unto us.* The philosophy of Philo placed a *Logos* (Word), a second god (δεύτερος Θεὸς), beside the eternal God. St John, sifting the fundamental truth from human error, acknowledges and teaches the existence of that *Word with God,* but not as a *second* or fellow-*god;* no, but as *very God,* and anon (verse 14) as manifested in the *flesh.* Thus the opening statements, and the prevailing tone of our fourth Gospel, indicate quite a new element in the Evangelical records; they indicate a Gospel, not merely of a narrative character, but doctrinal also, and full of divine philosophy. Here we have not only a historical testimony, but also, for the first time in the Gospels, an Apostolical *theology*.

And this peculiar tone and stamp are intimately connected with the whole object of this Gospel. While the synoptic Gospels only link narratives together, without remark, elucidation, or parenthesis, our fourth Evangelist pauses, as it were, at every turn, at one time to give a reason, at another time to fix the attention, to deduce consequences, or make applications, or to give utterance to the language of praise. Thus, when (ii. 19) he records the saying of Jesus: *Destroy this temple, and in three days I will raise it up again,* he follows it up with the explanation (verse 21): *But he spake of the temple of his body,* and connects it (verse 22) with another striking circumstance, namely, that the disciples first bethought themselves of this saying of their Master's after he was risen from the dead. Thus, after having stated at the same place (verse 23) that many at Jerusalem believed in the name of Jesus, he goes on to remark that *Jesus did not commit himself unto them* (verse 24), and this (verse 25) *because he knew all men, and needed not that any should testify of man: for he himself knew what was in man.* Thus, after having (iii. 14, 15) related the words of Jesus to Nicodemus, that *as Moses lifted up the serpent in the wilderness, even so must the Son of man be lifted up: that whosoever believeth on him should not perish, but have eternal life,* he immediately, and with hardly any perceptible transition, follows it up with those striking evangelical declarations, possessing the character partly of powerful preaching, partly of a beautiful burst of praise:

For God so loved the world, that he gave his only begotten Son, that whosoever believeth on him should not perish, but have everlasting life. For God sent not his Son into the world to condemn the world; but that the world through him might be saved. He that believeth in him is not condemned: but he that believeth not is condemned already, because he hath not believed in the name of the only begotten Son of God. And this is the condemnation, &c. Anon (verses 22, 23), he interjects an explanatory statement that Jesus and John were both baptizing at that time; *for*, says he (verse 24), John *was not yet cast into prison.* Subsequently, in a parenthesis of the same sort, he explains how he means the baptizing by Jesus to be understood (iv. 1, 2): *When therefore the Lord knew how the Pharisees had heard that Jesus made and baptized more disciples than John (though Jesus himself baptized not, but his disciples), he left Judæa, and departed again into Galilee.* When Jesus met with the Samaritan woman, our Evangelist again explains how Jesus could go to her for a drink of water (iv. 8): *For his disciples were gone away unto the city to buy meat.* When, subsequently, the Lord returned to Cana in Galilee, it recurs to the Evangelist's recollection that this was the place where, shortly before, the water had been changed into wine (verse 45). On another occasion he by a short parenthesis notices the progress made by Nicodemus in the faith, when that leader in Israel publicly reprimanded his colleagues on account of their opposition to Jesus (vii. 50). *Nicodemus* (HE THAT CAME TO JESUS BY NIGHT, BEING ONE OF THEM) *saith unto them, Doth our law judge any man before it hear him, and know what he doeth?* In like manner, differing in this entirely from his three predecessors, he steps aside for the purpose of explaining who the Mary of Bethany was, in the parenthesis (xi. 2): *It was that Mary which anointed the Lord with ointment, and wiped his feet with her hair.* After mentioning the remarkable saying of Caiaphas, *That one man must die for the people, that the whole nation perish not,* he emphatically calls attention to the peculiar connexion between that saying and the high office of the person who uttered it: *And this spake he, not of himself, but being high priest that year, he prophesied that Jesus should die for that nation;* and then he adds, of himself, the following explanation and extension of what was said: *And not for that nation only, but that also he should gather together in one the children of God that were scattered abroad* (xi. 49–52). He afterwards, in the way likewise of parenthesis and explanation, recurs to this Balaamite prophecy. When he represents our Lord in the history of his passion (xviii. 13) as brought first before Annas, and after that before Caiaphas, *the high priest for that year,* he goes on to say (verse 14), *Now Caiaphas was he which gave counsel to the Jews, that it was expedient that one man should die for the people.* Our fourth Gospel is rich above all in expositions (always in the way of parenthesis and remark) of the words spoken by Jesus himself. Thus (vii. 37–39), when its author records our Saviour's exclamation in the temple, on the last day of the feast of tabernacles, *If any man thirst, let him come unto me, and drink,* he immediately follows it up with the remark, *But this spake he of the Spirit, which they that believe on him should receive.* In like manner (xi. 11–13), where we are told that Jesus had said of Lazarus, when dead, that he *slept,* and the disciples had remarked upon that, *Lord, if he sleep he shall do well,* there immediately follows the Evangelist's elucidation, *Howbeit Jesus spake of his death:*

but they thought that he had spoken of taking of rest in sleep. And at the close of this Gospel (xxi. 18, 19), after communicating the words of our Lord to St Peter, *When thou wast young, thou girdedst thyself, and walkedst whither thou wouldest: but when thou shalt be old, thou shalt stretch forth thy hands, and another shall gird thee, and carry thee whither thou wouldest not,* he at once solves the enigma involved in the prediction by saying (verse 19), *This spake he, signifying by what death he should glorify God.* The words of Jesus *to the disciple whom he loved* are given in like manner in that same chapter (verses 20–23) with an explanation of them, and correction of a mistake that had prevailed among the brethren with respect to the future lot of that disciple.

These, out of many examples, may suffice to shew *this* peculiarity of our fourth Gospel, that it proceeds upon the principle of not merely presenting a narrative of occurrences, but also of giving explanations, remarks, elucidations, and arguments. Hence that multitude of parentheses, indicated by the words *now* (δὲ), and *then* (οὖν) or *therefore* (διὰ τοῦτο), which we find in this Gospel, and which, of themselves, give it quite a peculiar colour when compared with the synoptical. The reader may further compare ch. i. v. 18; vi. 22–24; ix. 22; xi. 5, 18, 30; xii. 37–43; xviii. 2, 3–24, 28; xix. 35; xx. 30, 31; xxi. 12, 24, 25.

Intimately connected with the above peculiarity of plan, there is yet another by which this is distinguished from the other Gospels. As we have already remarked, it gives us no connected narrative of our Lord's doings and sayings, but rather a choice selection of the most remarkable tokens of his divine majesty, followed up very fully by the reflections and doctrines suggested by those wonderful occurrences. We find only six of our Lord's miracles recorded in this Gospel; but these are all of the most remarkable kind, and surpass the rest in depth, specialty of application, and fulness of meaning. Of these six there is only one that we find in the other three Gospels—that of the multiplication of the loaves. That miracle, chiefly, it would seem, on account of the important instructions of which it furnished the occasion (chap. vi.), is here recorded anew.

The five other tokens of divine power to which we allude, are distinguished from among the many that are known to us from being recorded in the three other Gospels, by their furnishing a still higher display of power and command over the ordinary laws and course of nature. Thus we find recorded here the first of all the miracles that Jesus wrought: the changing of water into wine at the marriage-feast—that of the son of the nobleman of Capernaum (iv. 48–54), cured by our Lord *at a distance* from Cana, at Capernaum; afterwards, of the numerous cures of the lame and the paralytic by the word of Jesus, only one: that of the man who had suffered from an infirmity *thirty and eight years* (chap. v.) Anon, out of the many cures performed on the blind, we have only one instance, but that is the case of a person *who had been born blind* (chap. ix.) In fine, we have the restoration of Lazarus to life, not from a death-bed, like the daughter of Jairus; not from a bier for the dead, like the young man of Nain, but *from the grave*, when, having lain buried there for four days, he had already begun to sink into corruption (chap. xi.) Lastly, from among the signs and wonders which Jesus did while still upon the earth after his resurrection, and which are nowhere else recorded by the Evangelists, we have one example in the miraculous draught of fishes on the sea of Tiberias (xxi.), when the disciples, at the command of their risen Lord, had threwn out the net on the right side of the ship, and Simon Peter *went up, and drew the net to land full of great fishes, an hundred and fifty and three: and for all there were so many, yet was not the net broken.*

Yet, as we have remarked, all these signs in our fourth Gospel furnish occasion chiefly for communicating the reasonings, discourses, and conversations of Jesus, alike with friends and foes, with his disciples and with the multitude. The miracle at the marriage-feast of Cana is recorded not for its own sake alone, but also for the sake of the weighty words that passed between Jesus and his mother, and between them and the servants at the feast, before his manifesting his glory at that place. The cure of the invalid at Bethesda having been performed on the Sabbath-day, leads, in like manner, not (as repeatedly happens in the case of the other Evangelists) to a single saying, but to a whole series of statements and instructions from the Saviour, respecting himself and his relation to the Father (ch. v.) To the account of the multiplication of the loaves, there is here annexed the sublime doctrine taught by Jesus at Capernaum, by which, leading off men's thoughts from the earthly and the visible, he bids the multitudes which were following him only for the sake of the meat that perisheth: *labour for that meat which endureth unto everlasting life,* and declares of himself: *I am the bread of life.* The opening of the eyes of the man that had been blind from his birth, is still less confined to a simple statement of the miracle, and mentioned for its own sake; but appears with all the more important circumstances attending it, and especially with all the animated dialogues that took place between Jesus and the man whom he had cured—between the latter and the Pharisees—between the Jews and the man's parents on that occasion. The restoration of Lazarus to life, in like manner, presents a copious and ample narrative, not only of the miracle itself, but also of all that passed on the occasion between Jesus and his disciples—between Jesus and the two sisters of the deceased—between these again and the Jews who came to comfort them—then between the Pharisees, the chief priests, and finally Caiaphas; while a little after (xii. 17) our last Evangelist connects that miraculous event with the supper at Bethany, and our Lord's entrance into Jerusalem from Bethphage.

Thus, then, every where throughout this Gospel the Lord *speaks;* a remarkably appropriate distinction in a Gospel which may be said to bear on its very title—*The Word.* With a fulness which we find in no other Evangelist, the Evangelist Apostle St John has preserved for us consecutive sayings and lengthened conversations of Jesus with his disciples, with the multitudes, with his adversaries, and with interesting individual souls. We have already called attention to those which were exchanged on each occasion of a miracle being wrought, and which threw the clearest light on the object for which it was designed, and the depth of meaning it bore. Not less copious and full of sublime truth, is our Lord's discourse with Nicodemus on the *new birth,* and the *lifting up on the cross;* as also that with the Samaritan woman, who, by means of seven questions and answers, became captive to the faith in that *Saviour* not of the Jews only but also *of the world* (ch. iv.): that with the Jews, on the occasion of the last day of the feast of tabernacles (ch. vii. viii.) The last instructions, promises, and predictions to the disciples, on the night in which the Saviour was betrayed, are recorded here with a fulness (ch. xiii. xiv. xv. xvi.) to which there is nothing to be compared in the other three Gospels. Finally, whereas in those Gospels we find but here and there a single exclamation addressed by Jesus to God his Father, we have in the Gospel of St John that solemn and richly developed prayer at the commencement of the great night and day of his passion, and which, known by the name of our Lord's intercessory prayer, comprehends at once an address to the Father, and a declaration of the sublimest truths and the most precious promises to believers of all ages.

In that prayer, in all the discourses held with his disciples and people of every condition, we find opened for us in this Gospel a treasury of sublime truths respecting the very person of our Lord—his oneness with the Father—his mission from the Father—his love to men, to his own—the intimate fellowship and spiritual unity that sinful men shall enjoy with him through faith, under the revelation and mighty energies of the Holy Ghost, whom he was to send in his stead—and so forth. In no other Gospel does the Son testify more directly, or repeatedly, concerning himself. In no other Gospel, when God is spoken of, does the name of *Father, the Father, my Father*, recur so very often, in its special and exclusive relation to Jesus, as he himself here distinguishes that transcendent, and to himself peculiar relationship, from that which, by Him, and in Him the Mediator, God desires to sustain with the children of men. *I ascend unto* MY *Father, and* YOUR *Father* (xx. 17). The nature of that relationship of the Father to the Son, and of the Son to the Father, he explains in this Gospel as he does nowhere else. His *equality* with the Father (v. 17), *My Father worketh hitherto, and I work;* which the Jews at that instant understood so well, that their animosity was all the more inflamed on that account (v. 18): *Therefore the Jews sought the more to kill him, because he not only had broken the sabbath, but said also that God was* HIS FATHER, *making himself equal with God* (ἴσον ἑαυτὸν ποιῶν τῷ Θεῷ); whereupon our Saviour proceeds to testify of himself so much the more strongly: *Verily, verily, I say unto you, The Son can do nothing of himself, but what he seeth the Father do: for what things soever he doeth, these also doeth the Son likewise. For the Father loveth the Son, and sheweth him all things that himself doeth: and he shall shew him greater works than these, that ye may marvel. For as the Father raiseth up the dead, and quickeneth them; even so the Son quickeneth whom he will. For the Father judgeth no man, but hath committed all judgment unto the Son: that all men should honour the Son, even as they honour the Father: He that honoureth not the Son honoureth not the Father which hath sent him.*—His *oneness* with the Father (x. 28–30), *And I give them* (my sheep) *eternal life; and they shall never perish, neither shall any pluck them out of* MY HAND. *My Father, which gave them me, is greater than all; and none is able to pluck them* OUT OF MY FATHER'S HAND. *I and my Father are* ONE; which again was clearly understood by the Jews to be a declaration of his proper Godhead: *Then the Jews took up stones again to stone him, saying, For a good work we stone thee not, but for blasphemy; and because that thou, being a man, makest thyself God.*—His *dwelling in* the Father, and the Father in him (xiv. 11): *Believe me that I am* IN *the Father, and the*

Father IN *me:* and (xvii. 21): *That they all may be one; as* THOU, *Father, art* IN ME—*I in them, and thou in me;* but we have also his no less real oneness, as *the Son of man* with men, than as *Son of God* with God. Therefore (and here there is a depth in the expression which we do not remark in any of the other Gospels) he employs equally with *men,* as with God his Father, that word which implies essential likeness and oneness of being: WE, US;—in speaking to men, OUR *friend Lazarus sleepeth* (xi. 11);—to God (xvii. 22), WE *are one;* and elsewhere (xiv. 23), *If a man love me, he will keep my words: and my Father will love him, and* WE *will come unto him, and make* OUR *abode with him.* But the spiritual oneness that subsists through faith, between Jesus and his own true disciples of all ages, as between the head and members of the selfsame body, he expresses in this very Gospel, in a manner no less special and profoundly impressive (xv. 1, 4, 5), *I am the true vine,—Abide in me, and I in you. As the branch cannot bear fruit of itself, except it abide in the vine; no more can ye, except ye abide in me. I am the vine, ye are the branches: he that abideth in me, and I in him, the same bringeth forth much fruit; for without me ye can do nothing.* And elsewhere (vi. 48–57), *I am that bread of life. He that eateth me, even he shall live by me.* And of the Holy Ghost, he testifies in discourses of a like deeply impressive character, under the title of *Comforter,* a term which nowhere else occurs in the New Testament (xiv. 16, 26): *And I will pray the Father, and he shall give you another Comforter, that he may abide with you for ever;—the Comforter, which is the Holy Ghost, whom the Father will send in my name, he shall teach you all things, and bring all things to your remembrance, what-*

soever I have said unto you; and elsewhere, under an image, and that image borrowed from the Old Testament prophecies, and which we find occurring again at the close of the Book of the Revelation (vii. 37, 39): *If any man thirst, let him come unto me and drink. He that believeth in me, out of his belly shall flow rivers of living water.* (*But this spake he of the Spirit,* &c.) And (iv. 14), *But whosoever drinketh of the water that I shall give him, shall never thirst; but the water that I shall give him, shall be in him a well of water springing up into everlasting life.* Compare Isaiah lv. 1, xii. 3, and Rev. xxi. 17.

And in like manner, as our Lord in this Gospel reveals his manifold majesty, and the depths of his love and grace, very much in discourses and reasonings, so do mere men also make themselves known to us here chiefly by their *words.* By means of some few of the sayings recorded of them in this Gospel, we have many persons of all sorts brought, as it were, immediately before us in all the individuality of their characters, natural endowments, rank, and condition in life. Thus, for example, the vocation, the sentiments, and whole personal bearing of the Baptist in relation to Jesus (i. 20–36): *And he confessed, and denied not; but confessed, I am not the Christ. I baptize with water: but there standeth one among you, whom ye know not: He it is, who, coming after me, is preferred before me, whose shoe's latchet I am not worthy to unloose. Behold the Lamb of God, which taketh away the sin of the world! This is he of whom I said, After me cometh a man which is preferred before me: for he was before me. And I knew him not: but that he should be made manifest to Israel, therefore am I come baptizing with water. I saw the Spirit descending from heaven like a dove, and it abode upon him. And I knew him not: but he that sent me to baptize with water, the same said unto me, Upon whom thou shalt see the Spirit descending, and remaining on him, the same is he which baptizeth with the Holy Ghost And I saw, and bare record that this is the Son of God;* and afterwards (iii. 27, 31): *A man can receive nothing, except it be given him from heaven. Ye yourselves bear me witness, that I said, I am not the Christ, but that I am sent before him. He that hath the bride is the bridegroom: but the friend of the bridegroom, which standeth and heareth him, rejoiceth greatly because of the bridegroom's voice: this my joy therefore is fulfilled. He must increase, but I must decrease. He that cometh from above is above all: he that is of the earth is earthly, and speaketh of the earth: he that cometh from heaven is above all.* Thus, in a couple of exclamations, we have expressed to us the entire change of mind and heart in the upright Nathanael, effected by a single sentence from the lips of Jesus (i. 46, 49): *And Nathanael said unto him, Can any good thing come out of Nazareth? Philip saith unto him, Come and see. Jesus saw Nathanael coming to him, and saith of him, Behold an Israelite indeed, in whom is no guile! Nathanael saith unto him, Whence knowest thou me? Jesus answered and said unto him, Before that Philip called thee, when thou wast under the fig-tree, I saw thee. Nathanael answered and saith unto him, Rabbi, thou art the Son of God; thou art the King of Israel.* Thus have we the mingled state of doubt, longing after truth, and spiritual ignorance in Nicodemus, in that simply natural reply to our Lord's announcement of the necessity of the new birth (iii. 4): *How can a man be born when he is old? Can he enter the second time into his mother's womb, and be born?* Thus, at another place, the malignant sneer of the Jews of Capernaum on Jesus declaring that he was to give his own flesh for the life of the world (vi. 52): *How can this man give us his flesh to eat?* Thus, the slow transition from a purely carnal conception of the Saviour's words to confidence and faith in his person, in the woman of Samaria, when the Lord speaks to her of *the fountain of living waters* (iv. 15): *Sir, give me this water, that I thirst not, neither come hither to draw.* Thus, the impression made by the person and the words of Jesus on the officers that were sent out against him (vii. 46): *Never man spake like this man.* Thus the scowling enmity of the multitudes on the rebuke administered by Jesus (vii. 19, 20): *Did not Moses give you the law, and yet none of you keepeth the law? Why go ye about to kill me? The people answered and said, Thou hast a devil: who goeth about to kill thee?* And shortly before, the divided sentiments of the multitude on the subject of Jesus and his doctrine (vii. 12): *And there was much murmuring among the people concerning him: for some said, He is a good man: others said, Nay; but he deceiveth the people.* At a later period, we have the tact shewn by the parents of the man who was born blind, when the Pharisees inquired of them about their son who had been cured (ix. 20–22): *His parents answered them and said, We know that this is our son, and that he was born blind: but by what means he now seeth, we know not; or who hath opened his eyes, we know not: he is of age, ask him: he shall speak for himself. These words spake his parents, because they feared the Jews.* Then, the consentaneous faith of the two sisters of Lazarus, in the strikingly consonant exclamation, first of Martha, afterwards of Mary (xi. 21, 32): *Lord, if thou hadst been here, my brother had not died.* Thus we have presented to us all that was desponding, hard to be convinced, and yet reflective and resolute, in the character of the Apostle St Thomas, when Jesus announced to his disciples the journey to Bethany, notwithstanding the hostile projects of the Jews (xi. 16): *Let us also go, that we may die with him;* and at the last supper, on Jesus saying (xiv. 14): *And whither I go ye know, and the way ye know* (verse 5), *Thomas saith unto him, Lord, we know not whither thou goest; and how can we know the way?* and in that most important appearance of the risen Saviour, first to the Apostles without Thomas, afterwards to the eleven, including him (xx. 24–28): *But Thomas, one of the twelve, called Didymus, was not with them when Jesus came. The other disciples therefore said unto him, We have seen the Lord. But he said unto them, Except I shall see in his hands the print of the nails, and put my finger into the print of the nails, and thrust my hand into his side, I will not believe. And after eight days again his disciples were within, and Thomas with them: then came Jesus, the doors being shut, and stood in the midst, and said, Peace be unto you. Then saith he to Thomas, Reach hither thy finger, and behold my hands; and reach hither thy hand, and behold my side: and be not faithless, but believing. And Thomas answered and said unto him, My Lord and my God!* Thus, among many other examples, we have the simplicity of Mary Magdalen's zeal and affection, when, though really addressing her risen Master, yet, thinking she was speaking to the gardener, she exclaimed (xx. 15), *Sir, if thou have borne him hence, tell me where thou hast laid him, and I will take him away.*

It could not fail that a Gospel which delineates persons and things principally by means of the very words spoken, and conversations held by those persons, must have quite a peculiar aspect, and must make quite a distinct impression, when compared with its three predecessors. This peculiar character, however, manifests itself still more strongly when we proceed to scrutinize and dissect those many exquisite beauties of expression and phraseology which, like gems, adorn this whole Gospel, and by which it comes to be distinguished in its details, not less than in its general plan and arrangement. We shall now give some illustrations of this in the case of words that occur in this Gospel either exclusively, or oftener than usual, or in a very special and eminently significant sense.

Let us begin with that sublime word with which this Gospel opens: the WORD (Gr. ὁ Λόγος). This word we find not only in no other Gospel, but in no other writings whatever of the whole New Testament, except those of St John.[1] In his Gospel it occurs thrice, even within the narrow compass of his first sentence; *In the beginning was the Word, and the Word was with God, and the Word was God;* and shortly after (v. 14) the incarnation of the Saviour is expressed thus: *And the Word was made flesh,* (Gr. καὶ ὁ Λόγος σαρξ ἐγένετο). From that time forward it recurs no more throughout the whole Gospel. *The Word made flesh,* being no other than the *only begotten Son of God* who came into the world, thenceforward is made known to us either by his human name of Jesus, or by that of *the* SON. The appellation of THE WORD, so fitting and so impressive at the first introduction of Christ

[1] Yet most improperly has the expression *the Word*, in Luke (i. 2), and in the Epistle to the Hebrews (iv. 12), been sometimes applied to our Lord's *Person.* The context shews in both places, that nothing more than the *common* meaning of the expression is to be thought of.

in his eternal pre-existence with the Father, with like perfect propriety and fitness disappears altogether when the Gospel assumes a narrative character, and becomes properly historical. Yet we read anew at the beginning of the Epistle (1 John i. 1, 2): *That which was from the beginning—the* WORD OF LIFE. And once more, thereafter, in one of those dread prophetical scenes in which the book of the Revelation announces the advent, the final triumph, and the kingdom of Jesus Christ (xix. verses 11–13), the same expression recurs: *And I saw heaven opened, and behold, a white horse; and he that sat upon him was called Faithful and True, and in righteousness he doth judge and make war. His eyes were as a flame of fire, and on his head were many crowns; and he had a name written, that no man knew but he himself. And he was clothed with a vesture dipped in blood: and his name is called the* WORD OF GOD. The source whence is derived this appellation of the Son from the glory which he had with the Father from eternity, we clearly discover, both from the above cited passage,[1] from the Proverbs of Solomon (viii. 22–36), and from its connexion with the whole of the ancient Jewish theology, in which *the Word* often occurs as that living organ, that second *I* of the great I AM (Jehovah), by whom he created the world, and reveals himself to men.[2]

Closely allied to the sublime signification of *Logos*, when employed to express the Christ in his divine pre-existence, we further find in this Gospel other appellations applied to Him, such as the *Light*, the *Truth*, the *Life*,

[1] See p. 233.

[2] We often read in the Jewish Targums (expository commentaries on the Old Testament), of the מֵימְרָא דַי יְהֹוָה (the *Word of Jehovah*) for Jehovah, and more particularly for the revelation of God in all the fulness of his life and working, which is likewise expressed to us in the Jewish Theology by the SHECHINA.

&c. Such appellations, used in a sense altogether unique, and applied *absolutely* and *exclusively* to a divine person, properly intimate to us that in him is the principle, the cause, the virtue, the absolute idea of *truth, life, light,* and *resurrection.* And in what other being can we conceive of any thing like this, except the most high God himself? In like manner do we find it expressly said of the Son in the Epistle (1 John v. 20), that he is *the true God and eternal life;* in which declaration the title *eternal life,* which is nowhere given to the Father, but often given to the Son, most clearly intimates, that that also of the *true God* must in this place be understood of the *Son* as well as the Father.

Again, we find exclusively in this fourth Gospel, yet another appellation of the Lord Jesus; that of *only begotten Son,* or simply the *Only begotten.* We have already seen[1] how, among the synoptical Evangelists, St Luke fixes our thoughts particularly on the *only children of men,* who became the special objects of the compassion of Jesus, but *here* we have in Jesus himself *the only Son of God* (i. 14–18; iii. 16–18; 1 John iv. 9)—a name and relationship by no means to be confounded with the title of the First-born (Chief and King) *over all creatures,* by which Jesus is extolled by St Paul in the Epistle to the Colossians (i. 15). The *only begotten Son* is Christ in his eternal pre-existence. It is of him that our Gospel testifies further on, that he was *in the bosom of the Father,* that is to say, in the most intimate conceivable communion of life and existence with the Father.

The name *Son of God,* and still more of *Son,* used absolutely and without any further addition, occurs nowhere so often as in this Gospel, or with so copious an

[1] See p. 192.

explanation of the depth of meaning involved in it (compare xix. 7, with v. 18). As, moreover, Jesus is here called *God's only begotten Son* (by St Paul,[1] *God's own Son,* in contradistinction to all sonship in a general sense, whether by adoption or by creation); so, on the other hand, God is said in this our fourth Gospel to be Jesus's *own Father* in an equally exclusive sense.

In connexion with this community of existence between the Father and the Son, we find the word *glory* (Gr. *δόξα*), which, in St John's Gospel, is applied in a very special manner to the Son equally with the Father: *we beheld his glory, as of the only begotten of the Father* (i. 14); and when, afterwards, the miracle performed at the marriage feast at Cana is described, the Evangelist adds (ii. 11): *This beginning of miracles did Jesus in Cana of Galilee, and manifested forth his glory.* This *glory* he had with the Father *before the world was* (xvii. 5, 24); this *glory* is one with that of the Father (xi. 4): *The sickness of Lazarus was not unto death, but for* THE GLORY OF GOD, *that the* SON OF GOD MIGHT BE GLORIFIED THEREBY; and when the dead is just about to be called forth from the tomb, Jesus saith to Martha, *Said I not unto thee, that, if thou wouldest believe, thou shouldest see the glory of God?* Here, accordingly, the glory of God is the same with that of Jesus, as appears also in a most striking manner from the remarkable quotation made in this Gospel from the prophet Isaiah (xii. 37–41). The reciprocal glorification of the Son by the Father, and of the Father by the Son, forms also one of the chief peculiarities of this Gospel book (xiii. 31, 32): *Now is the Son of Man glorified, and God is glorified in him;* and (xiv. 13): *And whatsoever ye shall ask in my name, that will I do, that the*

[1] Romans viii. 32.

Father may be glorified in the Son And in the intercessory prayer (xvii. 1): *Father, the hour is come; glorify thy Son, that thy Son also may glorify thee.* Believers, mere men, are said *to glorify God,* and also *to be glorified with Christ;* but it is the prerogative of the Son alone to be directly *glorified by the Father.*

Yet another word, very simple and of everyday occurrence in the languages, but of the highest signification in things divine, is that of *to be* or *to exist,* which quite in a peculiar manner indicates the Godhead, and that too of the Son. By Moses, the God of the patriarchs made himself known as the Being who, in an absolute and altogether unique sense, could call himself, I AM.[1] The same God testifies of himself in Isaiah (xliii. 13): *Before the day was,* I AM. Could it then be without the utmost significance that Jesus, in our fourth Gospel, expresses himself in a similar way: *Before Abraham was,* I AM? In which place (viii. 58) what we have particularly to remark is the antithesis between the verb BECOME, *begin to be,* employed for the creature, *before Abraham* CAME TO BE (Gr. γένεσθαι); and that of *exist* (εἶναι), which Jesus applies to himself: I EXIST (I AM) (ἐγὼ εἰμι). Of the same kind is the previous antithesis of these same words in the opening of this Gospel (v. 1–3): The Word *was* (ἦν)—all things *were made* (ἐγενετο).

This sublime and intimate oneness between the Father and the Son is of a piece, also, with the majestic simplicity with which the Christ in this Gospel speaks both of his appearance in the world, and of his future resurrection and ascension. With an expression found nowhere but here in this sense, he speaks of his procession (ἐξέρχεσθαι) *from* the Father, of his *return* or *hence-*

[1] Heb. אֶהְיֶה; Exodus iii. 14. It is the incommunicable name of JEHOVAH.

going (ὑπάγειν, πορεύεσθαι) *to* the Father. Thus (xiii. 3): *Jesus knowing that the Father had given all things into his hands, and that he was* COME FROM GOD, AND WENT TO GOD; and afterwards, viii. 42, xvi. 27, 28, 30, xvii. 8, xiv. 2, 3, 12, 28, xvi. 7, 28, &c.

With an allusion to the affecting prophecy in Isaiah (liii. 7), the Saviour is compared in the New Testament to a *lamb*. St Peter speaks of his *precious blood, as of a lamb without blemish and without spot* (1 Pet. i. 18, 19). St Paul had in view a sacrificial lamb, the Paschal lamb in particular, when he comprised the whole work of pardon and sanctification through Christ in these words (1 Cor. v. 7, 8): *For even Christ our passover is sacrificed for us: therefore let us keep the feast, not with old leaven, neither with the leaven of malice and wickedness; but with the unleavened bread of sincerity and truth.* But it is only in our fourth Gospel, and in the book of Revelation, that the lowly yet glorious name of *the Lamb* is given to Jesus directly, and by way of title. Even in the time of the preaching of St John the Baptist (i. 29, 36), we read, *Behold the Lamb of God, which taketh away the sin of the world.* And in the book of Revelation the Lord is proclaimed and addressed in prayer, in his heavenly and divinely royal glory, hardly by any other name. The beatified and glorified, represented under the image of the four living creatures and the four-and-twenty elders, fall down (v. 8, 9) before the Lamb, and sing the new song in his praise: *Thou art worthy to take the book, and to open the seals thereof: for thou wast slain, and hast redeemed us to God by thy blood out of every kindred, and tongue, and people, and nation.* And the angelic hosts (v. 12) say: WORTHY IS THE LAMB THAT WAS SLAIN *to receive power, and riches, and wisdom, and strength, and honour, and glory, and blessing.* And all creatures in heaven and on earth, and under the earth and in the sea (v. 13) say: *Blessing, and honour, and glory, and power, be unto him that sitteth upon the throne, and* UNTO THE LAMB *for ever and ever.* Anon, we find this most sublime and awe-inspiring prophecy speaks (vi. 16) of *the face of him that sitteth on the throne, and of the* WRATH OF THE LAMB, and (vii. 17) of *the* LAMB *which is in the midst of the throne, and shall lead his redeemed unto living fountains of waters.* And further, xiii. 8, xiv. 1, 4, 10, xvii. 14, xix. 7, 9, xxi. 22, 23, 27, xxii. 1, 3.

Another choice expression, occurring in St John's Gospel alone in *this* sense, is that of *lifting up* for the crucifixion of Jesus, when he himself foretells his expiatory death (ὑψοῦν, ὑψοῦσθαι), with an evident allusion to the *lifting up* of the brazen serpent in the wilderness, and to which every Israelite that had been bitten by the serpents in the wilderness, had only to look in order to his being completely cured. Jesus himself speaks thus to Nicodemus (iii. 14): *And as Moses* LIFTED UP *the serpent in the wilderness, even so must the Son of man be* LIFTED UP (ὑψωθῆναι). And (viii. 28): *When ye have* LIFTED UP *the Son of man, then shall ye know that I am he.* And that by this *lifting up* nothing but the crucifixion must be understood, again appears from the Evangelist's own declaration, on his communicating our Lord's words on another occasion (xii. 32): *And I* (says Jesus), *if I be* LIFTED UP *from the earth, will draw all men unto me. This he said* (the Evangelist adds), *signifying what death he should die.*

As all things in this Gospel are viewed and represented in their highest causes, in their deepest foundations; in like manner do we find in it the word and the idea of God's *gift and giving*, occurring with the same frequency. The first cause in all things is the *gift of God.* What the Father *hath given to* the Son, what anew the Son *gives* or *hath given* to men, to those who believe in him, is again and again pressed on our attention. The Father gives to the Son: *For as the Father hath life in himself, so hath he* GIVEN *to the Son to have life in himself* (v. 26); and (36) *The works which my Father hath* GIVEN *me to finish—bear witness of me. My sheep—shall never perish, neither shall any man pluck them out of my hand. My Father which* GAVE *them me, is greater than all*; and in the intercessory prayer (ch. xvii.) with reiteration, *I have manifested thy name to the men which thou* GAVEST *me out of the world* (v. 6); *for I have* GIVEN *unto them the words which thou* GAVEST *me* (v. 8); *I pray not for the world, but for them which thou hast* GIVEN ME (v. 9), &c. To this is intimately allied another expression which occurs in this Gospel, in a very striking manner: *No man can come to me, except the Father, which hath sent me,* DRAW *him* (vi. 44). But besides, both this Gospel and the book of Revelation abound in expressions intimating what God, and specially the Son, *gives* to those who believe in him: *But as many as received him, to them* GAVE *he power to become the sons of God* (i. 12): *He* GIVES *them living water* (iv. 10, 14, 15): *He* GIVES *them that meat which endureth unto everlasting life* (vi. 27): He GIVES *them* that *eternal life itself* (*and I* GIVE *unto them eternal life,* x. 28). He GIVES them his peace: *Peace I leave with you, my peace I* GIVE *unto you: not as the world* GIVETH GIVE *I unto you* (xiv. 27). He GIVES *them the glory which the Father hath* GIVEN *him: And the glory which thou* GAVEST *me I have* GIVEN *them* (xvii. 22). And in the Revelation of his glorious advent *he* WILL GIVE *a crown of life to the faithful, and to them that overcome* (ii. 10); *to him that overcometh* HE WILL GIVE *a white stone, and in the stone a new name written, which no man knoweth, saving he that receiveth it* (ii. 17); *to him that is athirst* WILL HE GIVE *of the water of life freely* (xxi. 6). We read further, in different places in that prophetical book, of *giving* in the sense of *permitting*, as (xiii. 5): *There was* GIVEN *unto him* (the Beast), *a mouth speaking great things and blasphemies*, &c.

The *world* (Gr. κόσμος) is again one of the words we find frequently recurring in this Gospel and in the Epistle, with some difference or modification in the meaning, being employed to express *sometimes* mankind collectively *before* God their creator, or as *opposed to* God their creator; *sometimes* the *great majority of the human race*, in contradistinction either to Israel or to believers; *sometimes* an indefinite multitude or extension. Employed in the first of these meanings, for example, in the account of the discourse held by our Lord with Nicodemus, it is said (iii. 16): *God so loved the* WORLD (men, of themselves his enemies through sin), *that he gave his only begotten Son, that whosoever believeth in him should not perish, but have everlasting life.* In the second meaning it occurs, among other instances, in the Samaritans' exclamation (iv. 42), *We know that this is indeed the Christ, the Saviour* (not only of Israel, but) *of the* WORLD; or of the human race which remains in unbelief, in opposition to the Church which believes (xvii. 9): *I pray not for the* WORLD, *but for them which thou hast given me.* Finally, in the third meaning (xii. 19), *The Pharisees therefore said among themselves, Perceive ye how ye prevail nothing? behold, the* WORLD *is gone after him;* or (xxi. 25), *If all the things which Jesus did, should be written every one, I suppose that even the* WORLD *itself could not contain the books that should be written.*

We have already pointed generally, among other characteristics of St John's Gospel, to the elucidations of various sorts which it presents, whether for the purpose of reconciling apparent contradictions, or for preventing objections. These elucidations, introduced chiefly in the way of parenthesis, bear more than once on local circumstances. There is a freshness and artlessness, combined with a strict and careful attention to accuracy, in such observations as the following: JOHN *also was baptizing in Ænon near to Salim,* BECAUSE THERE WAS MUCH WATER THERE (iii. 23); and at the multiplication of the loaves (vi. 10): *And Jesus said, Make the men sit down.* NOW THERE WAS MUCH GRASS IN THE PLACE. *So the men sat down, in number about five thousand.* And anon (v. 22–24), *The day following, when the people which stood on the other side of the sea, saw that there was none other boat there, save that whereinto his disciples were entered, and that Jesus went not with his disciples into the boat, but that his disciples were gone away alone; (howbeit* THERE CAME OTHER BOATS FROM TIBERIAS NIGH UNTO THE PLACE WHERE THEY DID EAT BREAD, AFTER THAT THE LORD HAD GIVEN THANKS): *When the people therefore saw that Jesus was not there, neither his disciples, they also took shipping, and came to Capernaum, seeking for Jesus.* See also viii. 1, 2, 15, 16, xix. 41, xx. 7, xxi. 8, &c.

But this Gospel is especially rich in precise statements of *hours* and *days,* as well as in the indication of *numbers* in general. It gives us exactly to know, for example, that on *the day after* the answer of John the Baptist to the Pharisees who had been sent to him, Jesus (after the temptation in the wilderness, of which we are informed in the other Gospels) returned anew to the waters of Jordan (i. 29). *Again the next day after,* John the Baptist (ver. 35) was there with two of his disciples, and when he pointed Jesus out to them as the Lamb of God, they followed him. These two disciples were Andrew, Peter's brother, and (as we shall see hereafter) the author himself of this Gospel, who records in set terms the hour, still fresh in his recollection, and indelibly impressed on his memory (i. 39): *it was about the tenth hour* (according to our reckoning, four in the afternoon). He subsequently records how, *further, on the day following,* the return to Galilee was undertaken, and Philip called to the Gospel (ver. 43), and (ii. v. 1) how, on *the third day after* the discourse with Nathanael, the marriage feast at Cana of Galilee was attended by Jesus and his disciples. There he mentions exactly the *number* of the water-pots of stone which, in compliance with the directions given by Jesus, were filled with the water which afterwards was made wine (v. 6); subsequently (v. 20) we are told the precise *number* of years which it took Herod to build the temple. The hour, too, is carefully recorded at which Jesus met the sinful Samaritan woman at Jacob's well (iv. 6)—*it was about the sixth hour* (that is, about *noon*); the *two days* likewise passed by Jesus in Samaria (v. 40), and shortly afterwards (v. 52), the hour at which Jesus had promised at Cana to the nobleman of Capernaum, that his son would be cured, and how, in point of fact, the fever left him *precisely at that hour.* He notes the *number* of the porches at Bethesda (v. 2), together with the years during which the paralytic who was cured by Jesus had been ill (v. 5). He records *the distance* at which the disciples were already at sea, when Jesus, during the night following the multiplication of the loaves, came to them walking on the waters (vi. 19). We find, subsequently, the number recorded in the exclamation of the Jews, called forth by the saying of Jesus, that *Abraham rejoiced to see his day* (viii. 57). *Thou art not yet* FIFTY *years old, and hast thou seen Abraham?* Then come the *four* days that elapsed betwixt the death and the resurrection of LAZARUS (xi. 6, and 39). Finally, at the burial of our Lord, he mentions the exact *quantity* of pounds of myrrh and aloes that was brought by Nicodemus for the purpose of embalming the body of Jesus (xix. 39). And again, at the close, in relating our Lord's appearing after his resurrection at the sea of Tiberias, we are told the precise *number* of the fishes caught at his command (*as many as an hundred and fifty and three*), as well as the precise distance at which the fishermen were from the land when this last miraculous draught of fishes took place (xxi. 7, 8).

We shall afterwards return to the consideration of the weight, in point of evidence, presented by the precision of these numerical details, as militating against all possibility of fiction or of *mythical* origin. This remark conducts us to the discovery of a very important peculiarity in our fourth Gospel: namely, its great utility in indicating the order of time in tracing the history of our Lord's life on earth, and of the work which he accomplished. It is true, that we have already seen St Luke mark the epochs of our Lord's birth, and of his entry on his ministry, in their connexion with the general history of the world at that period, and more than once enter into sundry chronological details.[1] But those details, though sufficient to establish the attention to order which distinguishes the third of the Gospels, are far from being extended to the apparently trifling minutiæ of *days*, nay, even of *hours*, as we have them in this *fourth* Gospel.

But what we have here most of all to remark is, that while it is quite impossible to make out, from the first three Gospels alone, the number of years occupied by our Lord's public labours upon earth, St John's Gospel conducts us, in a very simple manner, to a result which it is impossible to question; namely, by the special indication of the great feasts which Jesus, according to the custom of the law, went to the city of the Temple to celebrate on each occasion of their recurrence. Of those great feasts noted by St John, three are the feasts of the Passover, including the day on which our Lord was crucified; so that by means of this Gospel we can calculate, certainly, that our Lord's public ministry on this earth occupied a space of about three years.

The *chronological* character of our Gospel further manifests itself in the important statement, whereby we learn first of all from it (xii. 1), that it was *six days before the Passover*, while Jesus sat at Bethany, at the table with Lazarus, after his restoration to life, that Mary anointed his feet with costly ointment; and that the day following (v. 12), the multitude went before our Saviour with palm branches and hosannahs, and accompanied him from thence on his entrance into Jerusalem. To this chronological exactness of our Evangelist, we ought to add what we shall yet see to be a peculiarity of his, namely, the particular notice he takes of the Israelitic *festivals*.

[1] See p. 151.

And further, here the Apocalypse is anew distinguished by a character perfectly homogeneous with this Gospel. For, from the beginning to the end, is not that most sublime book a prophetical division of the ages to come into great periods, such as that of the *seven seals* (chap. vi.), that of the *seven trumpets* (chap. viii.), that of the *seven vials* (chap. xv. 7), &c.? To the same peculiarity in St John, we may likewise refer the *three and a half years,* or *twelve hundred and sixty days,* during which the Holy City was to be trodden under foot, and the two witnesses were to prophesy (chap. xi.); and, finally, the *thousand years* of the reign of the saints with their Lord and King. The Revelation is the book of the signs of the times, and sets before us, in a series of sacred representations, the things *that were to come,* and the advent of Jesus in his highest glory, in like manner as our fourth Gospel relates the things *already accomplished,* of his advent as a despised and suffering Saviour.

Slowly and majestically throughout, does the pen of our last Evangelist unfold the great events most prominently described by him, in their origin, their causes, and their development. No other, for example, conducts us so regularly through all the various preparatory incidents, down to the violent arrest and crucifixion of our Lord. Again and again he mentions how the Jews sought to slay him, to stone him (v. 16–18, vii. 1, 19, 20, 25, viii. 37, 40, x. 31–33, xii. 8–53); but they *could* not (as is clearly explained in this Gospel), BECAUSE HIS HOUR WAS NOT YET COME (vii. 30, viii. 20).

That hour *came* at last. The history of the passion commences with the remark, that Jesus knew that hour (xiii. 1); and the intercessory prayer of our great High Priest opens with the exclamation: *Father, the hour is come!* pronounced before his entering Gethsemané (xvii. 2).

Nor have we only, the regular development and connexion of events. St John loves in like manner to communicate the *first commencement*, the *earliest origin*, often likewise the *end* of things. His Gospel commences with that which *was* already at the beginning, when the world did not yet exist. The book of Revelation closes by pointing to the *consummation* of all things with the return and the reign of Jesus. The *beginning* of the miracles which Jesus did is noted by him alone (ii.); and, as a sort of counterpart to that, a miracle performed by our Lord during his sojourn upon earth *after his resurrection.* That some of the disciples of Jesus had *previously* been disciples of St John the Baptist, is a circumstance which in like manner we know only from St John the Evangelist (i. 35–43). The discourses of Jesus with the disciples (particularly Philip and Andrew), and the mention of *the lad who had five barley loaves,* precedes, in his Gospel alone, the multiplication of the loaves. It is he alone, in like manner, who records the explanations and discourses by which that same miracle was followed up at Capernaum (vi. 5–9, 25–58.).

Further, it is from St John alone that we know, that *before* supper at the Passover our Lord washed the feet of his disciples, and that we have detailed to us the conversation and discourses that took place *at the close* of that last supper (xiii. 2, and following, 31–38, xiv., xv., xvi). The apprehension of Jesus in Gethsemané is preceded here by the statement, that the soldiers and officers went backward and fell to the ground, on our Lord uttering these simple words, *I am he* (xviii. 3–6).

The thrust of the spear into the side of Jesus, which followed his death on the cross, is mentioned by St John alone (xix. 31, 34).—Is there not, moreover, in all this, more or less of a subtile harmony with the glorious title of God and Christ, found only in the book of Revelation : *The first and the last, the Alpha and the Omega, the beginning and the ending?* (i. 8, 11, 17).

In connexion with this chronological character of our fourth Gospel, and also with the whole tone, at once *solemn* and *joyful*, which pervades it, we find the frequent mention of *Israel's festivals.* While the other three Gospels speak of but one of these, the passover, and principally, if not solely, of *that* passover at which Jesus was crucified ; our fourth Gospel mentions many such festive occasions, and several different Paschal feasts. Thus St John speaks of *a feast of the Jews,* perhaps that of Pentecost, on the occasion of our Lord's curing an infirmity of thirty-eight years' standing, at the pool of Bethesda (v. 1);—of *the feast of tabernacles* (vii. 2); and, in particular, of *the midst of that feast* (v. 14), still called, at the celebration of that feast to this day among the Jews, the *middle days,*—and of the *last* and *great* day of the feast (verse 37) ; finally, of the feast of the *dedication of the temple,* which fell in winter. But of the feast of the passover he speaks again and again : thus (ii. 13), Jesus went up to Jerusalem when the Jews' Passover was at hand, and for the first time purified the temple ; and at that passover (verse 23) many believed in his name, when they saw the miracles which he did ; and again (vi. 4), on the approach of another passover, he multiplied the loaves in the wilderness of Galilee. The *third* paschal feast, which he mentions afterwards, was that, in fine, at which our Lord was apprehended and crucified.

Reckoning back each time from this feast, our fourth Evangelist notes down various particulars bearing on the approach and preparation of our Lord's passion. When *the Jews' passover was nigh at hand, and many went out of the country up to Jerusalem before the passover, to purify themselves* (xi. 55), he represents the multitude as occupied with conjectures as to whether or not Jesus would come to the feast; immediately after this (xii. 1), he mentions how Jesus, *six days* BEFORE *the passover,* came to Bethany, where he sat at the table with Lazarus; then (xiii. 1) what took place, BEFORE *the feast,* on the evening of the *passover;* later still (xviii. 28), how the Jews were afraid of defiling themselves in Pilate's judgment-hall, so as to prevent them from eating the passover, that is, the paschal meal; finally (xix. 14, 31), that the day on which Jesus was crucified, was the *preparation* for the *great,* that is, the *Paschal Sabbath.*

Again, in the book of the Revelation, we find that this same character of solemn festivity re-occurs. There the heaven opens before the beholder, and a high *holiday* is represented as being held in the glorious courts above; and, in the visions of our Lord's second coming, a celestial *paschal hymn* is employed as the song of praise sung by the redeemed, by the angels, and by the whole creation, in honour of the *Lamb that was slain* (v. 6–11). A divine *feast of tabernacles* is celebrated in white robes, and with palms in their hands (vii. 9), *by a great multitude, which no man could number, of all nations, and kindreds, and people.* It is a high *festival* of heavenly triumph and rejoicing that we read of in that sublime book, when, for example (xi. 15, 19), *the temple of God was opened in heaven,* and there *was seen in his temple the ark of his testament* against the time of judgment; or, after that (xv. 2–8), when the victory over the beast, and (xix. 2–5), the fall of Babylon, the great whore, are celebrated; or, finally (verses 11–21), when the Lord's return at the head of his saints is described, and, at the close of all (xxi. 1), *the new Jerusalem cometh from God out of heaven, prepared as a bride adorned for her husband.*

Intimately connected with these festivals, whether the national ones of Israel or those of the Jerusalem above, is *the marriage feast,* mentioned also in this Gospel as well as in the book of Revelation, not without the most striking emphasis. It was at the *marriage-feast table* that Jesus for the first time manifested his glory, by performing a mighty miracle, and this miracle and that marriage feast are nowhere spoken of but in this last Gospel (ii. 1–12). Soon afterwards, St John the Baptist calls himself THE FRIEND OF THE BRIDEGROOM, *which standeth and heareth him, and rejoiceth greatly because of the bridegroom's voice.* And turn we to the book of the Revelation, there too are re-echoed the many and various prophecies and declarations of psalmists and prophets, that God has *espoused* a peculiar people to himself—that the true Israel *has the Lord for her Maker and her Husband*—and there we find proclaimed the felicity of believers, in the exclamation (xix. 9), *Blessed are they which are called* UNTO THE MARRIAGE SUPPER OF THE LAMB!

We have seen how the Apostolic Gospel of St Matthew is remarkably distinguished by its close relation to the Old Testament. We found it marked by an eminently prophetical character. We saw that the two next in succession, always assuming the fulfilment of the ancient prophecies, and always building on that foundation, abound less in Scriptural quotations at full length, as compared with their predecessor, the Gospel of St Matthew. But our *fourth* Gospel rivals St Matthew's in the superabundance of passages adduced from Israel's prophets and psalms. Those passages are for the greater part entirely new, and, so to speak, fresh in St John, never having been cited any where before in the New Testament. The form or manner of the quotation, too, is somehow differently modified, and has a depth and subtlety not to be found in the other Gospels; as when, at the purification of the temple, after recording the words of our Lord (ii. 16): *Take these things hence; make not my Father's house an house of merchandise;* we find this followed by the quotation of one of the prophetical sayings in the book of Psalms (v. 17), *And his disciples remembered that it was written, The zeal of thine house hath eaten me up;* and in the discourse with the Jews in the synagogue at Capernaum (vi. 44, 45), *No man can come to me, except the Father which hath sent me draw him; and I will raise him up at the last day.* IT IS WRITTEN IN THE PROPHETS: AND THEY SHALL BE ALL TAUGHT OF GOD. *Every man therefore that hath heard, and hath learned of the Father, cometh unto me.* And on the last day of the feast of Tabernacles (vii. 37, 38), *Jesus stood and cried, saying, If any man thirst, let him come unto me, and drink. He that believeth on me,* AS THE SCRIPTURE HATH SAID, *out of his belly shall flow rivers of living water.* And when he reproved the Jews for their unbelief, and the hardness of their hearts (xii. 36–41): *These things spake Jesus, and departed, and did hide himself from them. But though he had done so many miracles before them, yet they believed not on him:* THAT

THE SAYING OF ESAIAS THE PROPHET MIGHT BE FULFILLED, WHICH HE SPAKE, *Lord, who hath believed our report? and to whom hath the arm of the Lord been revealed? Therefore they could not believe, because that Esaias said again, He hath blinded their eyes, and hardened their heart; that they should not see with their eyes, nor understand with their heart, and be converted, and I should heal them.* THESE THINGS SAID ESAIAS, WHEN HE SAW HIS GLORY, AND SPAKE OF HIM. And when the traitor Judas is pointed out at the supper, where St Matthew and St Mark merely make an allusion, here the quotation is direct and express (xiii. 18): *I speak not of you all: I know whom I have chosen: but that the Scripture may be fulfilled,* HE THAT EATETH BREAD WITH ME HATH LIFTED UP HIS HEEL AGAINST ME; and in the course of what fell from his lips at the Paschal table (xv. 25): *But this cometh to pass,* THAT THE WORD MIGHT BE FULFILLED THAT IS WRITTEN IN THE LAW, THEY HATED ME WITHOUT A CAUSE; and among the last words on the cross (xix. 28): *After this, Jesus knowing that all things were now accomplished,* THAT THE SCRIPTURE MIGHT BE FULFILLED, SAITH, I THIRST; and when the legs of the two malefactors were broken, and the body of Jesus remained untouched (xix. 36): *For these things were done, that the Scripture should be fulfilled,* A BONE OF HIM SHALL NOT BE BROKEN.

The prophetic character, moreover, that marks our fourth Evangelist, is not confined to his deeply significant allusions to the *ancient* oracles of God. It was his special vocation to point attention to what was prophetical in our *Lord's own* words, making these to crown, as it were, the golden series of testimonies given by the seers who spake before Him. Thus (ii. 22), after recording the words in which the Saviour compares his approaching crucifixion and resurrection to a destroying and building up again of the temple of God, he adds: *When therefore he was risen from the dead, his disciples remembered that he had said this unto them;* AND THEY BELIEVED THE SCRIPTURE, AND THE WORD WHICH JESUS HAD SAID. Thus, when he remarks how it behoved to come to pass, that Jesus was to be put to death not after the manner of the Jews, but after that of the Romans, that is, that he *was to be crucified*, he expresses himself as follows (xviii. 31, 32): *Then said Pilate unto them, Take ye him, and judge him according to your law. The Jews therefore said unto him, It is not lawful for us to put any man to death:* THAT THE SAYING OF JESUS MIGHT BE FULFILLED, *which he spake, signifying what death he should die.*

The prophetical element operates in yet another manner in this Gospel. Its author calls us several times to observe how enemies themselves, without being conscious of it, and without designing it, behoved to utter words with a prophetic sense. Thus it was with Caiaphas, when he recommends that measures should be taken against Jesus (xi. 49–51), because it was expedient THAT ONE MAN SHOULD DIE FOR THE PEOPLE, AND THAT THE WHOLE NATION PERISH NOT. *And this spake he not of himself: but being high priest that year, he* PROPHESIED THAT JESUS SHOULD DIE FOR THAT NATION, &c. Thus, afterwards, with Pilate, when he himself had caused the title for the cross to be drawn up in three languages, announcing *Jesus of Nazareth to be King of the Jews:* and when the Jews complained to him, saying, *Write not, The King of the Jews; but that he said, I am King of the Jews:* and the Roman governor answered, *What I have written I have written.*

In a somewhat different manner still, the enemies of Jesus are represented in the Gospel of St John as prophesying, or as testifying to the accomplishment of the prophecy, as, for example, where some of the people said (vii. 41, 42): *Shall Christ come out of Galilee? Hath not the Scripture said, that Christ cometh of* THE SEED OF DAVID, *and out of* THE TOWN OF BETHLEHEM, WHERE DAVID WAS? Or, subsequently (xii. 34): *We have heard out of the Law that Christ* ABIDETH FOR EVER: *and how sayest thou, The Son of man must be lifted up?*

In connexion with this prophetical character of this fourth Gospel, it is almost unnecessary to remind the reader of the book of *Revelation,* which from beginning to end not only consists of prophecies and visions bearing upon futurity and the last times, but borrows also its whole prophetical language from the Old Testament prophets; yea, gives us back, as it were, all the prophetical elements of the Old Testament, recast so as to form a new mass, somewhat like the Corinthian brass of ancient times, which was said to have been composed of various costly and selected metals, fused together into one new whole. With respect alone to the agreement betwixt the book of *Revelation* and the *fourth Gospel,* in regard to the prophetical character only, we would simply remark, that the former commences with the very same prophecy which closes the series of narratives comprised in the latter. The piercing of the Saviour's side, after he had expired on the cross, is explained to us in the Gospel (xix. 37) by the prophecy of Zechariah, *They shall look on him whom they* PIERCED; the Apocalypse, linking itself, so to speak, to the Gospel, commences (after the six introductory verses) thus: *Behold, he cometh with clouds; and every eye shall see him, and they also which* PIERCED *him: and all kindreds of the earth shall wail because of him.*

Our attention is further called, in our fourth Gospel, to the *symbolical,* as allied to the *prophetical* element. The synoptical Gospels have preserved for us many of the similitudes of our Lord. Now, in our fourth Gospel, some of our Lord's actions constitute a sort of parables, inasmuch as they possess a symbolical character. Such, among others, was the washing of the disciples' feet, with which the account of the last Supper commences in this Gospel. That incident is recorded thus (xiii. 2–7): *And supper being ended*[1] *(the devil having now put into the heart of Judas Iscariot, Simon's son, to betray him); Jesus knowing that the Father had given all things into his hands, and that he was come from God, and went to God; he riseth from supper, and laid aside his garments, and took a towel, and girded himself. After that he poureth water into a basin, and began to wash the disciples' feet, and to wipe them with the towel wherewith he was girded. Then cometh he to Simon Peter: and Peter saith unto him, Lord, dost thou wash my feet? Jesus answered and said unto him, What I do thou knowest not now; but thou shalt know hereafter.* The explanation follows immediately from our Lord's own mouth, and is twofold; first (8–11), *Peter saith unto him, Thou shalt never wash my feet. Jesus answered him, If I wash thee not, thou hast no part with me. Simon Peter saith unto him, Lord, not my feet only, but also my hands and my head. Jesus saith to him, He that is washed needeth not save to wash his feet, but is clean every whit: and ye are clean, but not all. For he*

[1] Or rather: *having commenced,* as we shall see hereafter.

knew who should betray him; therefore said he, Ye are not all clean. And again (12–14), *So after he had washed their feet, and had taken his garments, and was set down again, he said unto them, Know ye what I have done to you? Ye call me Master and Lord: and ye say well; for so I am. If I then, your Lord and Master, have washed your feet, ye also ought to wash one another's feet.* After this, in the garden of Gethsemané, Jesus surrenders himself to his enemies without any further stipulation than what was instantly granted (xviii. 8), *if therefore ye seek* ME, *let* THESE *go their way;* immediately whereupon we have the deep meaning involved in our Lord's acting thus: *that* (says the Evangelist, verse 9) *the saying might be fulfilled, which he spake, Of them which thou gavest me have I lost none.* Thus it appears, that the preservation of the disciples from the carnal hand of enemies was at the same time a *symbol*, an *emblem*, a *type*, of that everlasting and spiritual salvation effected by means of the sacrifice of the Son, in all its plenitude, in the room of those who cleave to him by faith, who are given unto him by the Father.—In all that we have above observed with respect to the festivals, including among these the marriage feast spoken of in this Gospel, there is involved in like manner, from the nature of the case, a similar character, at once *historical* and *symbolical.* Need we remind the reader, that this *symbolic* element is further one of the great peculiarities of the book of Revelation?

The Gospel with which we are now occupied is further distinguished by a high *mystic* character, equally affecting and sublime. After having had our Lord represented to us in the other three Gospels rather in his saving activity *among* men, and his all-powerful working *upon* men, here we find placed most in the foreground his intimate *communion with* men, his spiritual *dwelling in* his own. This we have already observed in the striking and multiplied use made by our Evangelist-Apostle of these small words *in* (Gr. ἐν) and *to be in.* To belong to the Saviour by faith; to be a sharer in his grace for time and for eternity; to have received, and from moment to moment to receive afresh from him that *new* life in which lies involved the germ of *everlasting* life, is expressed every where in St John as *a being in the Son,* and *an abiding in him* (xvi. 7). He is the *vine,* and they are the *branches,* and it is only *by abiding* IN *him* that they can bear fruit, and *without him* they can do nothing: *He comes unto them with the Father, and makes his abode with them* (xiv. 23). He does not *thus manifest himself unto the world* (verse 22).—In the Gospel, as in the first Epistle, all is comprehended in *love. God is* LOVE (1 John iv. 8). *The Father* LOVETH *the Son* (John v. 20). *The Son* LOVETH *his own; he* LOVETH *them to the end* (xiii. 1). *The Father, in like manner,* LOVETH *them, and hath* LOVED *them* (xvii. 23.) Jesus *loveth* them with a special personal love, each *by name.* He *loved* Lazarus, and Mary, and Martha, and the disciple who lay in his bosom at the Paschal table (xi. 5, xiii. 23).

But neither do the most affecting nor the most sublime views exclude, in the case of our fourth Evangelist, an attention to accuracy in regard to external, historical, material details. We have seen quite the contrary appear in our observations on the studious regard which he shews in all things for precision with respect to dates and numbers.[1] The same may be remarked in this Gospel with

[1] See p. 257.

respect to the *names* of men, of witnesses, of believers, of enemies. They are given here with a fulness and precision found nowhere else. St Peter we find often mentioned under his Jewish and Apostolic names combined: *Simon Peter* (i. 41; vi. 8; 68, &c., &c.)—The traitor among the twelve is here explicitly named: *Judas Iscariot* (*son of Simon*) (vi. 71; xii. 4; xiii. 2, 26); and, in contradistinction to him, *Judas* (*son of James*) is called, in a manner equally simple and significant, *Judas, not Iscariot* (xiv. 22). We are here informed of particular circumstances and sayings respecting *Andrew, Philip, Thomas,* and *Nathanael* (probably the *Bartholomew* of the other three Gospels), together with their names, as we nowhere find in those (i. 41, 42, 45–52, vi. 5, 8; xi. 16; xiv. 5, 8; xx. 24–31; xxi. 2.) Besides the two sisters, Martha and Mary, previously made known to us by St Luke, the name of their brother *Lazarus* starts up before us, as it were, in this Gospel (xi. xii.) In the narrative of the passion it is here only that we find mentioned, along with Caiaphas, *Annas,* who was also his father-in-law, and of the same sacerdotal family (xviii. 13, 24). Among the well-intentioned counsellors at Jerusalem, he mentions, as associated with Joseph of Arimathea, with whom we were already acquainted, his no less interesting colleague *Nicodemus* (xix. 39; vii. 50; iii. 1). We know only from this Gospel, that the name of the high priest's servant whose ear was cut off by one of the disciples, was *Malchus* (xviii. 10); and also what the other Gospels lead us only to suspect, at all events do not say, that the disciple who drew his sword on that occasion was none other than *Simon Peter.*

It is further remarkable in this Gospel, that it repeatedly

unites in itself a Hebrew and a Greek cast of thought, and exhibits, at one and the same moment, a Jewish, and, if we may so express it, a cosmopolitan[1] character. Greek philosophy, we have already seen, furnished our author with a sublime term for the expression of our Saviour's divine nature, the *Logos;* but, notwithstanding, no other Gospel intimates to us so often his real humanity by giving him the Jewish title *Rabbi*, *Rabboni*, that is to say, *Master* (i. 38, 50; iii. 2, &c.) Further, it is St John only who adds its Roman name when speaking of the sea of Galilee (vi. 1): *After these things* JESUS *went over the sea of Galilee*, WHICH IS THE SEA OF TIBERIAS (compare this with xxi. 1). Thus, too, he adds to the Jewish name of *Thomas* the Greek name of the same signification, *Didymus* (xi. 16; xx. 24; xxi. 2): *Thomas, called Didymus.* The expression: *Come and see*, transplanted from the soil of Judea to that of Greece, is to be found in this Gospel only.

We find the same thing reappearing in the book of Revelation, in the repetition of a Greek expression by adding a Hebrew translation, or *vice versa;* thus, to the Greek word ναὶ (*yea—even so*), is added the Hebrew word *Amen* (i. 7). After the Hebrew word *Hallelujah* (xix. 4), the same exclamation follows in Greek (verse 5): αἰνεῖτε τὸν Θεὸν ἡμῶν—*Praise our God.* The perverse doctrine of the Nicolaitanes, who were the Apostle's contemporaries, is coupled with that of Balaam in the days of Israel under Moses (ii. 14, 15). Coupled with the song of Moses the leader of *Israel*, we have the song of the Lamb who taketh away the sins of the *world* (xv. 2, 3). Besides the Hebrew name of the angel of the bottomless pit, *Abaddon*, we have the Greek translation of that

[1] In the original Dutch, *wereldburgerlyk*, i. e., citizen-of-the-world-like.

appellation, *Apollyon.* Coupled with the *manna* with which the history of Israel brings us acquainted, we have the *white stone* from that of the nations of Gentile antiquity (ii. 17). Coupled with the *twelve tribes of Israel,* mentioned by name, we have (vii. 4–8) *a great multitude, which no man can number, of* ALL *nations, and kindreds, and people, and tongues* (verse 9). Finally, coupled with that most sublime name of God in Isaiah, *the First and the Last,* we have one signifying the same thing, but formed from the Greek alphabet, *the A and the Ω* (xxi. 13).[1]

From all that we have hitherto observed, it may be sufficiently seen in what manner, and by what an abundance of details peculiar to itself, our fourth Gospel is distinguished from the other three, nay, among the evangelical testimonies holds a place altogether unique, and its own. Here, in fact, we have found, as it were, quite a new Gospel.

Quite a *new* Gospel! Nevertheless not, as many men of our day in Germany have sometimes fancied, from not having sufficiently studied those diversities, *quite another* Gospel. No doubt the fourth Gospel stands in a sense isolated among the four; yet it only presents a richer development, a deeper comprehension, a more heavenly mode of contemplating, a minuter elaboration of the same subject, the same truths, the same supernatural order of facts. Yes, it is ever the same subject, the same revela-

[1] This last name also may be considered as taken from the Jewish Theology, by whose doctors the infinite God is often also called א and ת, after the first and last letters of the Hebrew alphabet. Yet one feels how much more fitting and sublime the expression becomes when the Greek tongue is employed, in which the alphabet opens and closes with two letters of the same sort, by the two principal vowels A and Ω.

tion, the same truths; but in this, at once the most heart-affecting and the most sublime of the four Gospels, these are contemplated and represented from their greatest altitude to their lowest depths, from their inmost essence to their external aspects. Hence the Gospel of *the Word* forms in that beautiful quartette, if we may so express it, the *bass* of a full harmony; or, if you would rather have it, the highest copestone which terminates, completes, and crowns the well-founded and well-built fabric; or, further still, if one would rather borrow an image from the circle of the sacred Scriptures themselves, then our fourth Gospel stands out from among the other three pre-eminent, as the Sabbath or Feast-day in Israel among the days of the week,—as the office of the priesthood among the functions of the Levites,—or like the gleaning of the grapes of Ephraim, which was *better than the vintage of Abiezer.*[1]

And this will appear to us much more clearly still, when we notice the point on which anew the consentaneous testimony of the most remote ages of the Church is borne out by the internal structure of our evangelical quaternion; to wit, that our fourth Gospel was written long after the other three had been composed, and generally known and circulated among the churches; that, accordingly, our last Evangelist must have very certainly had in his hands, and must have availed himself of the results of the labours of his predecessors, and may and must have written on the assumption that their narratives were generally known. But if it once be admitted that our fourth Gospel was undertaken and composed *posterior to* an already written and extant threefold testimony to the life, death, and resurrection of our Saviour, then, surely, it lay in the very nature of the case that this fourth testi-

[1] Judges viii. 2.

mony should worthily, and in the manner required, *supply* what still remained wanting, and start from a manifestly special and different point of view. With an *historical* character which it is impossible to mistake, we find some further peculiarities combined in this composition of St John. Here we perceive the evangelical narratives of St Matthew, St Mark, and St Luke taken up and indissolubly incorporated in the sublime soul of their last fellow-Evangelist, with the doctrinal announcements of St Paul, of St Peter, of all his apostolical predecessors; so that, lo! we have a new composite work of all the greater value—a fourth Gospel, powerfully and gloriously distinguished in object, tone, and conception, from all the former—a Gospel at once practical and theological, purely historical, deeply prophetical, and eminently doctrinal.

It appears from the simplest and most obvious circumstances, that our fourth Gospel proceeds on the assumption that the three first were known; that it goes on enlarging on what had been already testified and established by them; that it ever and anon reverts to them, makes allusion to them, tacitly points to them, sometimes even by an apparent contradiction or discrepancy stamps them with the seal of the fullest confirmation. This we have to make clearer by examples, of which we here present a few.

Who is there that, in a Gospel of the life and doctrine of Jesus Christ, does not look for a nomenclature of his twelve Apostles? Accordingly, we find such an exact list of them given more than once in the synoptical Gospels (Matth. x., Mark iii., Luke vi., and Acts i.) Yet no such list occurs in the last Gospel. How are we to account for this? Shall we say, because it differs in respect to the number, or the names, or the behaviour of those chosen persons? Assuredly not. Again and again mention is made of *the Twelve* (vi. 70, xx. 24), and certain details, as we have seen, are given concerning the most of them, which we should not have been made acquainted with from any of the preceding Gospels. All this, as any one may see, has arisen from the author being able to assume, and, in point of fact, because he did assume, the list of the Twelve Apostles to be perfectly well known to his readers. Accordingly, we need not expect this list to re-appear once more in the Gospel of the beloved disciple; but, as if to compensate for this, in the last prophetic scenes of his Apocalypse, he speaks of the names of the Twelve Apostles as found on the twelve foundations of the New Jerusalem (xxi. 14). This last Gospel could dispense entirely with the mention of their number, the history of their general calling, and the details of their Apostolic office or mission; but all this being assumed as known, it remained for the last of the Evangelists, as it were in a separate picture, to preserve from oblivion, in connexion with the whole object of his composition, some characteristic discourses, interesting moments, and special incidents that had occurred in their intercourse with their heavenly Master.

In like manner our Gospel altogether omits our Lord's genealogy, birth at Bethlehem, and education at Nazareth, as facts sufficiently well known from the Gospels of his predecessors. Its special vocation is to shew in what a sublime and incomparable sense Jesus Christ is the Son of God. Nevertheless, the human birth of our Lord loses nothing of its evidence on that account in St John; for its most important particulars are recalled in his Gospel, sometimes by a passing word from the mouths alike of friends and of enemies. *We have found him* (said Philip to Nathanael (i. 45), among the very first conversations recorded in this Gospel), *We have found him of whom Moses* in *the law and the prophets did write, Jesus of Nazareth,* THE SON OF JOSEPH ; and here we see all the ignominy that rested among the Jews on that little town of Nazareth, concentrated, so to speak, in the exclamation of that sincere Israelite, Nathanael, when he replied, *Can there any good thing come out of Nazareth ?*

The same peculiarity of this Gospel—to wit, that of *concentrating* rather than *extending* the incidents and discourses already known to us from the preceding ones, enables us at the same time to meet the surprise that has sometimes been manifested with respect to the absence of the *similitudes* in St John. The statement itself that they are wanting, is true only in a very limited sense. True it is, that St John does not record any *parables,* in so far as we are to understand by that term similitudes *in the narrative form* in which they occur in the synoptical Gospels ; but, as respects the essence of the thing, our fourth Gospel most decidedly gives us, *under the form of metaphor,* the similitudes of its predecessors, according to the exquisite and profound method which is peculiar to it. Thus, for example, in the synoptical Gospels, we read that Jesus compares himself to a shepherd who seeks after and brings back his stray sheep. Now, it is true that we do not again meet with this comparison in our last Evangelist in the form of a parable, but we certainly do again find the fundamental idea in the form of a metaphorical sentence : *I am the good shepherd,* says Jesus of himself (x. 11) ; and, with a still more profound application of the image than in the other Gospels (v. 11), he says: *The good shepherd giveth his life for the sheep.* Again, in the book of Revelation, by an apparent contradiction, such as belongs to the peculiar character of that sublime composition, the LAMB *is represented as that* SHEPHERD *that shall feed his sheep, and shall lead them unto living fountains of waters* (vii. 17).

In like manner we do not read in St John, as in the synoptical Gospels, of the preaching of the kingdom of God being compared to a sower going forth to sow, the Word of God to a grain of seed, the repentant heart to the good ground, the consummation of all things and the day of judgment to the time of harvest (Matth. xiii. 1–9, Mark iv. 1–20, Luke viii. 1–15); but the fundamental idea is to be found in our fourth Gospel (iv. 35, 36), although in a wholly different form, and one quite peculiar to itself: *Say not ye, There are yet four months, and then cometh harvest? behold, I say unto you, Lift up your eyes, and look on the fields;* FOR THEY ARE WHITE ALREADY TO HARVEST; and then, in a still more profoundly significant use of the same idea, in which it is employed to throw light on the relation between the ministry of the prophets of the Old Testament, and that of the Apostles of the New (v. 37, 38), it is said: *And herein is that saying true, One soweth, and another reapeth. I sent you to reap that on which you bestowed no labour.*

Quite as little do we find here, as we find in the other three Gospels (Matth. xxi. 33–41, Mark xii. 1–9, Luke xx. 9–18), the kingdom of heaven directly compared to a vineyard, into which its owner sends husbandmen, or to a marriage feast, to which the master of the house invites guests. But the fundamental ideas do occur there quite in the same manner, only with a still more profoundly significant application. Here Jesus himself is the *vine,* and *his Father the husbandman* (xv. i.); and, as respects the idea of a marriage feast, we have seen already with what striking significancy that figure occurs both in the Gospel and in the Revelation of St John.[1]

Thus, then, the absence of parables in their historical or narrative form in this Gospel, we repeat, is not to be regarded as a discrepancy, but much rather as a harmony between the synoptical Gospels and that under consideration. In place of the detailed simile, we have the terse and concise metaphor,[2] the ideas remaining fundamentally the same.

Such, likewise, is the case with regard to another difficulty which has been alleged against the authenticity of our fourth Gospel—a difficulty meanwhile which, in an earlier period of neology, was in every way reckoned as redounding to its honour; namely this, that in manifest discordance with the statements made in the first three Gospels, there is nowhere any mention whatever made of the casting out of unclean spirits, as little as there is of the Saviour's being tempted of the devil in the wilderness. For here, too, our fourth Gospel, reposing with perfect confidence for the historical details on the testimony of its predecessors, gives us the same thing again, in short results, nice allusions, and invariably in its own ever most elevated style and manner. We do not, indeed, see there Jesus casting out devils, or maintaining a conflict with their prince in the wilderness; but we hear him give utterance to the final issue, the last concluding result effected by that *power of casting out devils* (xii. 31): *Now shall the prince of this world be cast out;* and

[1] P. 265.

[2] Instead of the παραβολή of the synoptical Gospels, we have here the παροιμία, translated in the English authorized version *proverbs*, and in the margin improperly *parables* (chap. xvi. 25).

(xiv. 30) *the prince of this world cometh, and hath nothing in me;* and (xvi. 11) *the prince of this world is judged.* And as a counterpart or antithesis to this, where do we find expressed more positively or more powerfully, Satan's taking possession of a wicked soul (xiii. 26, 27): *And when he (Jesus) had dipped the sop, he gave it to Judas Iscariot, the son of Simon. And after the sop* SATAN ENTERED INTO HIM? The last and decisive casting out and condemnation of the evil one by the might and majesty of Jesus, is found delineated anew in the most brilliant colours in the book of the Revelation (xix. 19–21, xx).

It has been objected also to this Gospel, that, contrariwise to the synoptical Gospels, it makes no mention either of the prophecy of the destruction, or of the expectations entertained of the final restoration, of Jerusalem. Yet the silence of St John's Gospel with respect to both, admits of a complete explanation, from the comparatively later period at which it was written, (more than probably) when Jerusalem was already destroyed; the prophecy of Jesus with respect to it, being fully recorded in the synoptical Gospels (Matth. xxiii., Mark xiii., Luke xxi.), did not therefore require to be repeated. And yet, even with respect to this most important circumstance, our fourth Gospel is not without a striking, but withal highly characteristic, allusion. True, the prediction of the fall of Jerusalem, as it came immediately from the mouth of our Saviour, is omitted here; but, in harmony with the whole plan of this altogether unique Gospel, it records a Balaam's prophecy of the approaching fall of city and temple, which fell from the mouths of the hostile high priests and Pharisees (xi. 47). While engaged in mutually exciting each other's apprehensions and resentment at the alarming progress of the doctrines and miracles of Jesus; the pretext of which they avail themselves to justify their determining to take violent measures against them is, that if they let him alone (v. 48), all men will believe on him, *and the Romans shall come and take away both our place and nation.*

Yet not only does our fourth Gospel either tacitly assume, or compress into brief sentences what we find recorded at large in the synoptical Gospels; but these, on the other hand, in more than one instance, receive a powerful elucidation from particular circumstances, first expressly mentioned by our last Evangelist, though undoubtedly known to all of them, and present to their minds when they wrote their Gospels. Thus, for example, the false testimony mentioned in St Matthew (xxvi. 61) and St Mark (xiv. 57, 58), receives an interesting, and, one might almost say, indispensable elucidation, from a saying of our Saviour's, first recorded by St John (ii. 19), Jesus answered and said unto them, *Destroy this temple, and in three days I will raise it up.* That saying, uttered prophetically by Jesus in reference to his own body, the false witnesses had interpreted as if it had had for its object the temple at Jerusalem (Mark xiv. 58), *We heard him say, I will destroy this temple that is made with hands, and within three days I will build another made without hands.* Nothing is more natural than that such an incident should have been known to the former Evangelists, and should have been present to their minds when recording the testimony of the false witnesses, but that the direct communication of the fact, and consequently the complete explanation of this remarkable incident, should have been reserved for being recorded by our concluding Gospel. In like manner, it is in this Gospel only that we are informed of the true cause of the flocking together of the people, and of their acclamations, on the day when Jesus repaired from Bethany to Jerusalem. That cause was the resurrection of Lazarus from the dead, a fact not recorded by any of the other Evangelists: *The people therefore* (so we read in St John's Gospel, xii. 17, 18) THAT WAS WITH HIM WHEN HE CALLED LAZARUS OUT OF HIS GRAVE, AND RAISED HIM FROM THE DEAD, *bare record,* that is, testified to his having done so. FOR THIS CAUSE THE PEOPLE ALSO MET HIM, FOR *that they heard that he had done this miracle.* But if we will now go back to the matter as related by the first three Evangelists, we shall clearly perceive that they could not have been ignorant, either of that event, or of the connexion of the rapturous exclamations of the multitude with that event, although they have mentioned neither. This may be seen in St Matthew (xxi. 10, 11), *And when he was come into Jerusalem, all the city was moved, saying, Who is this? And the multitude said, This is Jesus the prophet of Nazareth of Galilee;* and in a still higher strain in St Luke (xix. 37), *And when he was come nigh, even now at the descent of the mount of Olives, the whole multitude of the disciples began to rejoice and praise God with a loud voice* FOR ALL THE MIGHTY WORKS THAT THEY HAD SEEN.

Thus, then, the Gospel testimony of our fourth Evangelical author is quite at one with that of the synoptical Evangelists; thus, then, above all, is the Divine leading personage who appears on its pages, Jesus, *the Son of God,* no other than the Jesus Messiah of the synoptics.

And yet there is a difference—a difference which detracts nothing from this identity, but enhances it all the more—a difference between the first three Gospels and the last, necessarily resulting from the greater depth of comprehension peculiar in all things to St John. Even in the sphere of ordinary human life, a great man will present a very different picture under the pen of his different biographers, according to the different points of view in which they contemplate him, or according to the particular quality or characteristic that chiefly interests each. A Julius Cesar, a Charlemagne, a Charles the Fifth, will furnish materials for very different, though all true and faithful historical portraits, according as the subject is treated in its military, political, philosophical, literary, or Christian bearings;—a mere human teacher, such as Socrates, being more thoroughly comprehended by Plato, will on that account be differently described by him from what we find him described by Xenophon, without our having to infer from this diversity any thing to the prejudice either of the genuineness and authenticity of the two writings, or of the fidelity of the two portraits; and yet shall we be surprised, or allow ourselves to give way to scepticism, because that same Jesus (that Jesus *in whom are hid all the treasures of wisdom and knowledge*)[1] is comprehended and portrayed, by the last of his Gospel biographers, in a different manner from that of any of his fellow Apostles or Evangelists who preceded him? Shall we wonder if we find that there were reserved, for the purpose of being communicated by such a Gospel, particular incidents, traits of character, sayings, explanations, developments, all maintaining a necessary harmony with the writer's

[1] Colossians, ii. 3.

deeper insight into his subject, and the greater elevation of the point from which he contemplated it. Yet how, even here, diversity reposes on unity, how it just brings out in all the stronger relief the unity of the whole, may be demonstrated from those glorifications of the Master's divinity, in which our fourth Evangelist, while he keeps the same truths, the same subjects and incidents before his mind, nevertheless appears notably to differ from his predecessors in point of expression, connexion, and the use of terms. We may adduce of this the following examples :—

In St Matthew, and still more in St Luke, we have a detailed account of the supernatural conception of Israel's Messiah by a virgin, without man's intervention, through the power of the Holy Ghost. In our fourth Gospel, not a single circumstance is recorded in reference to that first of all the miracles of the New Testament revelation. But, on the other hand, what a striking summary of the whole matter do we not find in that one short sentence : *the Word was made flesh?* How can we possibly mistake the allusion here ? Again, what a mysterious yet sensible reference to the miraculous conception at the very commencement of our Gospel, in which all who by faith have received the Son (i. 12, 13), are called *sons of God : which are born, not of blood, nor of the will of the flesh, nor of the will of man, but of God!* Of this spiritual or second birth of sinful men, we find that invariably, according to the whole tenor of the New Testament doctrine, the miraculous birth of the sinless Saviour is represented as the foundation, the antitype, the impetrating and efficient cause. Thus, then, the miraculous conception and birth of Jesus Christ according to the flesh, are not, it is true, *directly* narrated in our fourth Gospel, but nevertheless assumed, pointed to, and glorified, in their bearing upon and connexion with the Christian second birth.

In the first three Gospels, the reality of our Lord's *human nature* comes out in all manner of ways. In these we behold him sharing, feeling, practically experiencing all human wants, exigencies, and sentiments, only without sin. Thus, when he went without food, at last he was *an hungered* (Matth. iv. 2, Luke iv. 2). Our fourth Gospel does not speak of the *hunger* felt by the Saviour; but, on the other hand, it, and it alone, and more than once, speaks of his *thirst.* It presents him to us (iv. 6, 7), oppressed by the noonday heat, athirst, and asking to drink; but at the same time discovering to the Samaritan woman, to whom his request was addressed, the need she had of *the living water*, which he alone could give. At a later period we find, in this Gospel only, our Saviour completing his sufferings of soul and body in that significant exclamation: *I thirst* (xix. 28).

In St Matthew and St Mark we hear the Saviour testify, that *he came not to be ministered unto, but to minister, and to give his life a ransom for many* (Matth. xx. 28, Mark x. 45). In our fourth Gospel, it is true, we do not find these very words, but we find the thing itself stated in a much more striking manner. There we find Jesus called *the Lamb of God, that taketh away the sins of the world.* It is recorded of him there, that leaving the Paschal table, *he took a towel, and girded himself, and began to wash the disciples' feet* (xiii. 3, 5).

In the synoptical Gospels, the Saviour is represented as exercising his power over nature; he stills the storm and the waves—he dries up a green fig-tree. Our fourth Evangelist passes over these miracles; but he shews us the power of Jesus over the creation, in that *beginning of miracles* which he did at Cana, and which was in fact a blessing bestowed on marriage, a symbol of all the blessings of the Gospel: common water was changed into the most costly wine.

In the synoptical Gospels, the Saviour declares, that in matters relating to the exercise of his ministry as a divine teacher, he knew neither mother nor brethren (Matth. xii. 47–49), *Then one said unto him, Behold, thy mother and thy brethren stand without, desiring to speak with thee. But he answered and said unto him that told him, Who is my mother? and who are my brethren? And he stretched forth his hand toward his disciples, and said, Behold my mother and my brethren! For whosoever shall do the will of my Father which is in heaven, the same is my brother, and sister, and mother.* Our fourth Gospel does not repeat these details; but on another and a more solemn occasion, when Jesus for the first time manifested forth his glory at Cana, it shews us the Saviour intimating the broad line of separation between all natural relationships and the discharge of his functions as the Messiah, in that most important answer to the remark addressed to him by his mother, (ii. 4) *Woman, what have I to do with thee? mine hour is not yet come.*

In the synoptical Gospels, we see Jesus in Gethsemané, straitened, and exceeding sorrowful even unto death, addressing a prayer to his Father that *this cup* (that of his sufferings) *might pass from him* (Matth. xxvi. 39, Mark xiv. 35, Luke xxii. 42). But quite the reverse was the case, at it would at first sight appear from our fourth Gospel. According to it Jesus had already, before passing the brook Cedron, in his solemn intercessory prayer, given full expression to the determination he had made, to devote himself to death. That prayer is a testament reposing on the certainty of his approaching propitiatory death. And yet, essentially, there is no difference between the synoptics and St John. Even in the synoptical Gospels we find it put beyond all question, that the Redeemer had come into the world for this very end, that he should drink of that cup of suffering. But it was *their* special office to place the struggle of the Saviour's *human* nature in the strongest and clearest light: it belonged to *them* to make it appear how the sufferings of Jesus were sufferings which he had freely taken upon him, from which, without sin, his manhood could, and necessarily did, at first recoil, only to merge itself absolutely afterwards, when the fearful struggle down to the bloody agony was past, absolutely and entirely in the higher will, in the Divine counsel. As a counterpart to this, we find placed in the foreground, in our fourth Gospel, the immutability of the Divine purpose, the Divine certainty of the sacrifice that was to be accomplished. Yet even in it the struggle of our Saviour's human soul is not concealed. In it we have, so to speak, the germ of the agony and the prayer of Gethsemané, in those words, uttered some days before at Jerusalem (xii. 27, 28): *Now is my soul troubled; and what shall I say? Father, save me from this hour: but for this cause came I unto this hour.* Here too, again, we find in our fourth Gospel the *higher* aspect of our Lord's personality put forward, while the (ever holy) *human* aspect appears most prominently in the other three; but neither of these aspects is wanting in any one of the four; in each and all Jesus is the same incarnate Lord, and suffering Redeemer in one person.

In the synoptical Gospels we read of heaven and earth giving testimony to the greatness of the crucified Saviour in the last moment of his sufferings. As he gave up the ghost, the sun was darkened, the earth did quake, and the rocks rent; the graves were opened, and the veil of the temple was rent in twain. Nothing of all this do we find in the fourth of our Gospels. But, on the other hand, it directs our regard to a sign that was made on the dead body of our Lord himself (xix. 34): *But one of the soldiers with a spear pierced his side, and forthwith came thereout blood and water.* Thus here, likewise, there is no substantial difference. In the three first Gospels the visible creation occupies the first place at that awful and critical moment; in the fourth, the flesh itself in which the Son of God appeared.

The synoptical Gospels take us up to the lofty mountain, where Jesus shews his glory to the three chosen disciples, thus giving them a foretaste, and view by anticipation, of his heavenly kingdom (Matth. xvi. 28; xvii. 1–8; Mark ix. 1–9; Luke ix. 27–36; 2 Pet. i. 16–18). The fourth Gospel does not give any account of the transfiguration on Mount Tabor; but as *a whole and throughout* it is a Gospel of the glorification of Jesus, alike in his life and in his sufferings.[1] Of this, too, the line is carried on and completed in the book of the *Revelation.* What else, indeed, is that book but a continuous display, under various figures, of that glory which John, and James, and Peter witnessed, at the transfiguration on the mount?

Here, accordingly, and in the synoptical Gospels, Jesus Christ is always the same; the same, but, like the sun in our visible sky, shining with a different kind of splendour, according as he rises, or sets, or appears in the full efful-

[1] See pages 230 and 251.

gence of his noontide radiance; the same, but such as, even according to the testimony of the synoptical Gospels, he appeared after his resurrection to his own, every time in a different aspect, and was recognised by them as the same Jesus only after some moments of amazement, and after having had *their eyes holden* for a time, that *they should not know him* (Mark xvi. 12, Luke xxiv. 16).

One very simple example will make it abundantly evident, that differences in point of form and expression in the Evangelists, may have been, and actually were the result, not of an original difference or uncertainty with respect to the expression actually employed by our Lord; but, on the contrary, of a particular manner, an important and highly remarkable operation in the mind and soul of his disciple and witness. The multiplied use of the Hebrew *Amen* (*verily*), *I tell you*, at the commencement of so many of the Saviour's declarations in these writings, is familiar to us all. No less obvious, with respect to this word also, is a remarkable and uniformly observed difference between the synoptical Gospels and the concluding one. In the latter this expression, indicative of solemn asseveration, is always, and without a single exception, *repeated*—AMEN, AMEN; no less uniformly, and without exception, do the three first Gospels keep to *a single* AMEN[1] or *Verily*. Now, whence this uniform and invariably observed difference?

To say, that Jesus must sometimes have uttered the *Amen* only once, and at others with a reduplication of the term, does not resolve the difficulty; all the less

[1] In the book of Revelation (iii. 14), Jesus calls himself the AMEN; and immediately afterwards, as if by way of explanation, *the faithful and true Witness*.

after it is observed, that sometimes the same sentences that in the synoptical Gospels are accompanied with a single *Verily*, appear with a double in that of St John. Thus, for example, in the passage in which the treason of Judas is foretold :—

MATTH. xxvi. 21.	MARK xiv. 18.	JOHN xiii. 21.
And as they did eat, he said, VERILY *I say unto you*, that one of you shall betray me.	And as they sat and did eat, Jesus said, VERILY *I say unto you*, one of you which eateth with me shall betray me.	When Jesus had thus said, he was troubled in spirit, and testified, and said, VERILY, VERILY, *I say unto you*, that one of you shall betray me.

And where St Peter's denial of his Master is foretold :—

MATTH. xxvi. 34.	MARK xiv. 30.	JOHN xiii. 38.
Jesus said unto him, VERILY *I say unto thee*, that this night, before the cock crow, thou shalt deny me thrice.	And Jesus saith unto him, VERILY *I say unto thee*, that this day, even in this night, before the cock crow twice, thou shalt deny me thrice.	Jesus answered him, Wilt thou lay down thy life for my sake? VERILY, VERILY, *I say unto thee*, the cock shall not crow, till thou hast denied me thrice.

Whence, then, this uniformly repeated *Verily* in our last Gospel? Why, from his own soul?[1] The *Amen*, or *Verily*, with which the Master confirms, and, as it were, pronounces with an oath, his divine utterances, calls forth a response from the bosom of his beloved disciple and witness. *Amen*, replies the Spirit in his inmost soul to the *Amen* of his Lord, with the same sort of echo wherewith, for example, at the close of the *Revelation*, to the

[1] Lightfoot, t. i., p. 401. "Neque quidem existimo, Christum hac vocis repetitione usum fuisse (nam permirum mihi videtur, ipsum ita fecisse in his sermonibus quorum mentionem facit Johannes, atque in illis, quos cæteri referunt, non ita fecisse, cum probabile sit eundem aliquando utrobique fuisse sermonem): verum ego suspicor vocem reiterasse Evangelistam."

words of Jesus, *I come,* there is answered, *Yea, come* (Rev. xxii. 20).

Now, what takes place with regard to the reduplication of the divine *Amen,* may serve at the same time as a key to many other places in the fourth Gospel, where a word or a sentence of Jesus is from time to time repeated or renewed, like a clap of thunder by the echo of the rocks, or like one and the same object reflected from mirrors placed over against each other, Is this not evidently the case (not to adduce other examples here) with the manifold varieties of expression wherewith, in the sixth chapter of St John's Gospel, the saying of Jesus, *I am the bread of life,* is over and over again repeated, elucidated, and developed? Much the same sort of merging together in one, of the words uttered by Jesus and those of the Evangelist who was to relate and to expound them, may be seen too in the divine Master's thanksgiving at the tomb of Lazarus (xi. 41, 42), *Father, I thank thee that thou hast heard me. And I knew that thou hearest me always;* (the Evangelist-Apostle's spiritual extension and authentic elucidation here evidently follow, and we have no longer the actual expressions of our Lord): *but because of the people that stand by I said it, that they may believe that thou hast sent me.* Is not our Lord's declaration to Nicodemus (iii. 14, 15) followed up, in like manner, with an almost imperceptible transition, by that explanatory statement of the Apostle himself (v. 16), *For God so loved the world, that he gave his only begotten Son, that whosoever believeth on him should not perish, but have everlasting life*—and the following verse?

Thus, then, are both the discourses recorded as delivered by Jesus, and the whole method and arrangement, narrative, and dramatic representation, in our fourth Evangelist, in strict and necessary unison with his particular individuality, with the special object at which he aimed, and with the peculiar conception which he had of his subject. That object, that conception, that individuality, we have seen retain their consistency throughout, in the most harmonious manner. In the writer of our fourth Gospel, we have seen throughout the man who, in the view which he has taken of the incarnate Saviour, had the power of combining the loftiest heights with the most profound depths—the nicest accuracy with the amplest freedom—the minutest precision in material details with the sublimest views in the philosophy of heaven—that is to say, in the knowledge of God and of Christ; the man who, in his soul, in his testimony, in his writings, unites, and as it were fuses together the first of things and the last—the Old and the New Testament—the Israelitic economy and the economy of the elect Heathen, in a way that no other Evangelist has done. We have seen in him the man who announced *the Word that was with God, and that was God,* recording for us the sayings of that *living Word,* along with the echoes which these called forth from his own heart; the witness who testified of the Son as he *is in the bosom of the Father, and declares the Father to us;* the herald of the glory of *the Lamb that was slain,* and who *taketh away the sins of the world.*

It is time now that we proceed to complete the harmonies which these various speculations have suggested in the way of mere remarks and comparison, by a final inquiry into the name and person of the writer. It is time that, in accordance with one of the main objects of these speculations, we should exhibit the evidence supplied by all the various particulars which we have indicated in this Gospel, in proof of its being really and truly the word of none other than the disciple whom Jesus loved, of that St John, the son of Zebedee, who was surnamed by his divine Master, *the son of thunder*.

Among the many names which we find expressly mentioned in this our fourth Gospel, we are struck with *nowhere* finding that of one of the Apostolic twelve who, from the very first, had a prominent place among them. We allude to that of the Apostle St John.[1] But while this is the case, the Gospel before us speaks again and again of a disciple who lived in the closest intimacy with Jesus, *without introducing his name*, but with indications that unequivocally point to that disciple, *both* as an eye-witness *and* as a select Apostle. Can it admit of a doubt, that of the two disciples who (i. 35, 40) left the Baptist, to follow Jesus the Lamb of God, as directed by him; and of whom one was Andrew, the brother of Peter (v. 41), the other must have been the author of this Gospel? That anonymous disciple who, according to the Gospel of St John, accompanied Andrew, is *certainly* no other than the disciple who afterwards, on the occasion of the Paschal supper, makes himself known to us as the one whom Jesus loved, and who, while at the table, leaned on Jesus' bosom (xiii. 23); the same who, later still, during the interrogatory of Jesus in the house of Caiaphas, speaks of himself as that *other disciple* who followed with Simon Peter, and who was known unto the high priest—who went in with Jesus into the palace of the high priest, and afterwards went out and brought in

[1] Wherever the name John occurs in this Gospel, it is the Baptist that is meant.

Peter (xviii. 15, 16). This *disciple whom Jesus loved* we again meet with, standing by the cross when the dying Saviour confides his mother to him (xix. 26, 27). In the narrative of the death of our Lord on the cross, he makes himself distinctly known more than any where else as an eyewitness and author of that Gospel. When he relates (v. 34), how one of the soldiers pierced the side of our Lord with a spear, whereupon there forthwith came thereout blood and water, these words immediately follow (v. 35): *And he that saw it bare record, and his record is true; and he knoweth that he saith true, that ye might believe.* We again meet with this *disciple whom Jesus loved,* in the account we have of our Lord's resurrection (xx. 2–4); and once more afterwards, when the risen Saviour, near the sea of Tiberias, shews himself to his own for the third time (xxi. 7): and, finally, immediately after the question, thrice addressed by our Lord to Peter, *Lovest thou me?* we find the same anonymous disciple mentioned, in a manner which not only necessarily leads to the presumption that that disciple held a distinguished place among the Apostles, but evidently supposes this to have been the case (xxi. 20–24).

Who else but the Apostle St John, the son of Zebedee, could this disciple be? Who but he could be the author of our fourth Gospel, as the unanimous testimony of the first Christian Churches proclaim him to have been?

Now, with respect to the former of these two intimately connected suppositions, all that is said in our fourth Gospel *of this disciple who is not named,* intimates to us the eyewitness, the man who enjoyed the greatest intimacy of his divine Master while he sojourned on earth. Certainly we should never think of looking for such a witness beyond the circle of the Twelve. But we have long since ascertained by looking at the synoptical Gospels, that of those Twelve, *three* in particular were called to be the most favoured witnesses at once of the passion and of the glory of their Lord. These were St Peter and the two sons of Zebedee. Now, of these three, St Peter, whose character so entirely differed from that imprinted as the style of our fourth Gospel, does not fall under our consideration here at all; as little does St James, who, so early as about the commencement of the Apostolical era (Acts xii.), fell under the sword of Herod Agrippa. Thus, of this small number who enjoyed the closest intimacy with the Saviour, there remains but *the Apostle John*, whose name and memory have been inseparably associated with this Gospel from the earliest ages of the Church.

And now the name of St John, of the disciple whom Jesus loved, placed at the head of our fourth Gospel, makes every thing harmonize with all that we have hitherto been able to gather, according to the method of observation we have pursued with respect to the peculiarities and the character of that portion of Scripture. Does not the Apostle and the eyewitness reveal himself to us in that exuberance of local details, that exactness in the statement of numbers, and of days and hours—that full expression given to names and surnames—those explanatory parentheses, so naturally suggested by his vivid recollections of what had passed before his eyes—those artless and off-hand accounts of what fell from the lips of all sort of interlocutors concerning the things of the kingdom of God, amid the ordinary intercourse of the people with our Lord, or with each other—that multiplicity of other particulars, all so full of life and reality, which crowd upon us in perusing this Gospel? To whom, for instance, but to an eyewitness, filled and penetrated with the recollection of the things which he himself had seen and heard, and in which he had taken *a personal part,* could it have occurred to incorporate with his narrative all those details of the tumultuous current of popular life, intermingling these with the exposition of the most sublime mysteries, and the most profound truths of the salvation now proclaimed to the world? Who but such an one, for example, in speaking of the miraculous change of water into wine at the marriage feast at Cana, could have thought of giving a place to that altogether material exclamation of the ruler of the feast to the bridegroom, in which, nevertheless, the testimony to the change that was effected is clearly implied? *Every man at the beginning doth set forth good wine; and when men have well drunk, then that which is worse: but thou hast kept the good wine until now* (ii. 10). Or, to take another instance, at the time of the cure of the man that was born blind, who else would have thought of recording with such a natural simplicity, all that passed in the way of remark and conversation among the persons interested in that miracle (ix. chap.)? or, once more, on the occasion of the last miraculous draught of fishes, who but he would have given the exact number of cubits at which the little ship was at the time distant from the land (xxi. 8)? To whom but to an author possessing the most complete moral certainty of his intimate connexion with Jesus, and with the history of his life and of his passion, would it ever have occurred never to mention himself, except by that denomination, at once so humble and so distinctive, of *the disciple whom Jesus loved?* Who but St John, surnamed *the son of thunder*, could have followed up with such energy of expression, what he says of the depth of the love of God, with his mention of the wrath of God (iii. 36)? *He that believeth on the Son hath everlasting life: and he that believeth not the Son shall not see life; but* THE WRATH OF GOD *abideth on him.* Or, again, who else would have followed up the most magnificent and touching promises to his chosen Apostles, with so severe a character of the traitor, speaking of him as *a devil,* and *as the son of perdition* (vi. 70, 71, xiii. 10, 11, 26, xvii. 12)? Who can fail in all this to recognise the work of an Apostle, elsewhere known to us as a pillar of the primitive Church (Gal. ii. 9)? Who can fail to recognise in the *disciple* who accompanied St Peter on proceeding to their Master's sepulchre (xx. 14), that St John, whom, at the commencement of the Apostolic ministry, after the descent of the Holy Ghost, we still continue to meet, accompanying St Peter in the preaching of the word, and in sharing the persecutions that ensued upon it (Acts iii., iv., v.)?

Is it matter of surprise that when, now twenty years ago, one of the learned men of Germany published certain scientific doubts reflecting on the authenticity of the Gospel of St John, the result of the investigations to which this attack gave rise in the theological world, proved so effectual a counteractive to such scepticism, that the difficulties that had been started were openly retracted by the very man who had first propounded them; and that the authenticity of the Gospel of St John, whether viewed intrinsically or extrinsically, was triumphantly established on surer evidence than ever?

And that evidence in support of the pure and perfect Apostolic authenticity of our fourth Gospel, becomes, if possible, clearer still, when we view it in connexion with the other writings from the same hand that have come down to us; that is to say, the Epistles and the Apocalypse. Our plan does not permit us to enter deeply here into an examination of these two compositions. All that is required is to set over against each other the Gospel of St John, and the first of the Epistles that bear his name, in order to become profoundly convinced that both must certainly and evidently be referred to the same sacred author. We have the same style, the same construction of sentences, the same favourite ideas and expressions, the same form of doctrine, the same testimony. The Epistle is manifestly, so to speak, a practical abridgment of the Gospel; it may possibly have been, as has lately been suggested by some one, that the Epistle was the accompanying letter transmitted along with the Gospel to the churches. As for what concerns the Apocalypse, without any thought in our mind of defending here the divine authenticity of that sublime book, we have more than once been led insensibly, in the course of these speculations, to call the reader's attention to the numerous points of agreement which, in several characteristic traits, it presents with our fourth Gospel. To these we shall only further add, that the objection started, on the ground of difference of style and language, against the identity of the authors of the book of Revelation and of our fourth Gospel, is sufficiently met by pointing to the difference of the subjects, and, above all, to the Hebrew and Old Testament element, which, from the nature of the case, distinguishes this divine prophetical book—the New Testament.

Here we might close our examination of the Gospel of St John, fully expecting that a comparison of the several accounts of our Lord's passion, presented to us in the four Gospels, will throw a still more satisfactory light on the essential oneness of the fourfold testimony that they comprise. The comparison of a very important narrative in the Gospel of St John, with the corresponding passages in those of his predecessors, will further serve as an introduction to the object we have proposed to ourselves, and we therefore introduce it here. The passage we have selected is that which records *the multiplying of the loaves,* and what happened immediately afterwards, particularly on the sea of Galilee.

The multiplication of the loaves is a miracle of so eminently important a nature, that all four Evangelists, one after another, have given it a place in their narratives, in the following manner, and with the following differences.

MATTH. xiv. 13, 14.

When Jesus heard of it, he departed thence by ship into a desert place apart: and when the people had heard thereof, they followed him on foot out of the cities. 14. And Jesus went forth, and saw a great multitude, and was moved with compassion toward them, and he healed their sick.

MARK vi. 32–34.

And they departed into a desert place by ship privately. 33. And the people saw them departing, and many knew him, and ran afoot thither out of all cities, and *outwent them*, and *came together unto him.* 34. And Jesus, when he came out, saw much people, and was moved with compassion toward them, because *they were as sheep not having a shepherd:* and he began to teach them many things.

LUKE ix. 10, 11.

And Jesus went aside privately into a desert place belonging to the city, called Bethsaida. 11. And the people, when they knew it, followed him: and he received them, and *spake unto them of the kingdom of God*, and healed them that had need of healing.

JOHN vi. 1–4.

After these things Jesus went over the sea of Galilee, *which is the sea of Tiberias.* 2. And a great multitude followed him, because they saw his miracles which he did on them that were diseased. 3. And Jesus went up *into a mountain*, and there he sat with his disciples. 4. *And the passover*, *a feast of the Jews*, *was nigh.*

This introduction assumes the same circumstances in

all the four Gospels : Jesus with his disciples passes over the sea of Galilee, and collects the multitudes around him in a desert place—the vast bushy wastes of Bethsaida. He is moved with compassion towards them, and teaches them the things concerning the kingdom of God. Here St Mark gives us anew his characteristic supplementing of St Matthew's narrative : the multitudes that hastened on foot out of all the cities, took care *to outrun the disciples,* and came thus about Jesus (v. 33). *Jesus was moved with compassion towards them, because they were as sheep not having a shepherd,* a comparison used on this occasion only in St Mark (v. 34). St Luke (v. 10) names the precise place where the incident occurred—*a desert place belonging to the city called Bethsaida,* and repeats what St Matthew (v. 13) says of *the healing of the sick,* whilst at the same time mention is made *of the kingdom of God* (v. 11). St John assumes the knowledge of all these particulars, but nevertheless notes them in passing : the crossing of the sea of Galilee, which he calls *the sea of Tiberias* also (v. 1),—*the great multitude* that followed Jesus, and the miracles, above all, the cures he wrought, and on account of which they followed him. The two words peculiar to him, *After these things* (Gr. μετὰ ταῦτα), by which he is wont to inclose, as if in a picture apart, the several portions of his Evangelical history, here open the narrative. St John alone speaks of *the passover, a feast of the Jews, being nigh,* and thus fixes the date.

MATTH. xiv. 15–21.

And when it was evening, his disciples came to him, saying, This is a desert place, and the time is now past; send the multitude away, that they may go *into the villages,* and buy themselves victuals. 16.

MARK vi. 35–44.

And when the day was now far spent, his disciples came unto him, and said, This is a desert place, and now the time is far passed: 36. Send them away, that they may go into the *country round about, and*

But Jesus said unto them, They need not depart; give ye them to eat. 17. And they say unto him, We have here but five loaves, and two fishes. 18. He said, Bring them hither to me.

19. And he commanded the multitude to sit down on the grass, and took the five loaves, and the two fishes, and, looking up to heaven, he blessed, and brake, and gave the loaves to his disciples, and the disciples to the multitude.

20. And they did all eat, and were filled: and they took up of the fragments that remained twelve baskets full. 21. And they that had eaten were about five thousand men, *besides women and children.*

St Luke ix. 12–17.

And when the day began to wear away, then came the twelve, and said unto him, Send the multitude away, that they may go *into the towns and country round about*, and lodge, and get victuals; for we are here in a desert place. 13. But he said untō them, Give ye them to eat. And they said, We have no more but five loaves and two fishes; except we should go and buy meat for all this people. For they were about five thousand men.

14. And he said to his disciples, Make them sit down *by fifties in a*

into the villages, and buy themselves bread: for they have nothing to eat. 37. He answered and said unto them, Give ye them to eat. And they say unto him, Shall we go and buy two hundred pennyworth of bread, and give them to eat? 38. He saith unto them, How many loaves have ye? go and see. And when they knew, they say, Five, and two fishes.

39. And he commanded them to make all sit down by companies upon the green grass. 40. And they sat down in ranks, by hundreds, and by fifties. 41. And when he had taken the five loaves and the two fishes, he looked up to heaven, and blessed, and brake the loaves, and gave them to his disciples to set before them; *and the two fishes divided he among them all.*

42. And they did all eat, and were filled. 43. And they took up twelve baskets full of the fragments, and of the fishes. 44. And they that did eat of the loaves were about five thousand men.

St John vi. 5–15.

When Jesus then *lifted up his eyes*, and saw a great company come unto him, *he saith unto Philip*, Whence shall we buy bread, that these may eat? 6. (*And this he said to prove him: for he himself knew what he would do*). 7. Philip answered him, Two hundred pennyworth of bread is not sufficient for them, that every one of them may take a little. 8. One of his disciples, Andrew, Simon Peter's brother, saith unto him, 9. There is *a lad* here, which hath five *barley* loaves, and two small fishes: but what are they among so many?

10. And Jesus said, Make the men sit down. *Now there was*

company. 15. And they did so, and made them all sit down. 16. Then he took the five loaves and the two fishes, and looking up to heaven, he blessed them, and brake, and gave to the disciples to set before the multitude.

17. And they did eat, and were all filled: and there was taken up of fragments that remained to them twelve baskets.

much grass in the place. So the men sat down, in number about five thousand. 11. And Jesus took the loaves: and when he had given thanks, he distributed to the disciples, and the disciples to them that were set down; and likewise of the fishes *as much as they would.*

12. When they were filled, he said unto his disciples, Gather up the fragments that remain, that nothing be lost. 13. Therefore they gathered them together, and filled twelve baskets with the fragments of the five barley loaves, which remained over and above unto them that had eaten. 14. *Then those men, when they had seen the miracle that Jesus did, said, This is of a truth that prophet that should come into the world.* 15. *When Jesus therefore perceived that they would come and take him by force, to make him a king, he departed again into a mountain himself alone.*

Here again we find the first three Gospels maintaining their consistency in the character of their here very slight mutual differences. St Matthew gives the first outline; St Mark fills up that outline with some important and picturesque details; St Luke in his own style faithfully follows St Mark. But St John's gleanings are here again highly important. We can perceive at a glance the personal recollections of the eyewitness and the apostle in the introduction of what passed between our Lord and the two Apostles—Philip (verses 5–7) and Andrew (verse 8)—previous to the miracle. Equally evident is it that the same fourth Evangelist, assuming as known through the first three Gospels the words addressed by the disciples to Jesus (St Matth. v. 15; St Mark v. 35, 36; Luke v. 12), proceeds to fill up and complete the narrative with the words which the Saviour expressly addressed to *Philip*, instead of what the first three Gospels (St Matth. v. 16; St Mark v. 37; St Luke v. 13) have recorded as spoken to the disciples in general. We there also find the explanatory parentheses which we have repeatedly remarked as peculiar to St John. The precise statement of the sum (*two hundred pence*), requisite for buying the quantity of bread that was necessary, is found among the synoptical Evangelists only in St Mark (v. 37); it is from him that St John takes it (v. 7). Further, our fourth Evangelist introduces his short and simple parenthesis: *Now there was much grass in the place.* But what strikes us as especially interesting is the mention, found only in his Gospel, of the *lad* (v. 9) who had five loaves and two fishes. Slight as we may think this additional detail, it enhances, nevertheless, both the unvarnished truthfulness of the narrative and the perfect consistency of the occurrence. Further, St John is the only one who tells us what kind of bread it was that was multiplied; they were not *wheaten* but *barley* loaves (v. 9, 13); whence we infer that it was the bread of the humbler classes. There is something touching, too, in our being told, when the fishes are mentioned, that of this additional food, there was granted (v. 11) *as much as they would;* as likewise the principle laid down only here with respect to the gathering up of the fragments that remained: *that nothing be lost.* The close of the narrative is not less important and characteristic. The multitudes that had witnessed this mighty miracle, proclaimed that Jesus was the great prophet that was looked for in Israel; nay, they would by force, were it necessary, and acting according to their carnal notions, make him *king.* Jesus is aware of their design. He disengages himself from that unlawful movement, and departs into the mountain alone. Thus, again, does our apostolic Evangelist give a reason, as it were, in passing, for what the Synoptics had already mentioned; namely, that the disciples, in compliance with their Lord's express order, had returned towards the sea *alone*, while he himself remained ashore, on the mountain, there to pray, and to observe them from a distance. What happened afterwards on the sea in the course of the night, we find recorded by St Matthew and St Mark alone of the three synoptical Evangelists, while by St John it is here, in his own peculiar manner, assumed as known, but elucidated, and further completed.

MATTH. xiv. 22.	MARK vi. 45.	JOHN vi. 16.
And straightway Jesus constrained his disciples to get into a ship, and to go before him unto the other side, while he sent the multitudes away. 23. And when he had sent the multitudes away, he went up into a mountain apart to pray: and when the evening was come, he was there alone. 24. But the ship was now in the midst of the sea, tossed with waves: for the wind was contrary. 25. And in the fourth watch of the night Jesus went unto them, walking on the sea. 26. And when the disciples saw him walking on the sea, they were troubled, saying, It is a spirit; and they cried out for fear. 27. But straightway Jesus	And straightway he constrained his disciples to get into the ship, and to go to the other side before unto Bethsaida, while he sent away the people. 46. And when he had sent them away, he departed into a mountain to pray. 47. And when even was come, the ship was in the midst of the sea, and he alone on the land. 48. And he saw them toiling in rowing; (for the wind was contrary unto them:) and about the fourth watch of the night he cometh unto them, walking upon the sea, and would have passed by them. 49. But when they saw him walking upon the sea, they supposed it had been a spirit, and cried out: 50. (For they all	And when even was now come, his disciples went down unto the sea, 17. And entered into a ship, and went over the sea toward Capernaum. And it was now dark, and Jesus was not come to them. 18. And the sea arose by reason of a great wind that blew. 19. So when they had rowed about five and twenty or thirty furlongs, they see Jesus walking on the sea, and drawing nigh unto the ship: and they were

spake unto them, saying, Be of good cheer; it is I; be not afraid.
28. And Peter answered him and said, Lord, if it be thou, bid me come unto thee on the water.
29. And he said, Come. And when Peter was come down out of the ship, he walked on the water, to go to Jesus.
30. But when he saw the wind boisterous, he was afraid; and beginning to sink, he cried, saying, Lord, save me.
31. And immediately Jesus stretched forth his hand, and caught him, and said unto him, O thou of little faith, wherefore didst thou doubt?

saw him, and were troubled:) and immediately he talked with them, and saith unto them, Be of good cheer; it is I; be not afraid.

afraid. 20. But he saith unto them, It is I; be not afraid.

32. And *when they were come into the ship, the wind ceased.* Then they that were in the ship came and worshipped him, saying, Of a truth thou art the Son of God.

51. *And he went up unto them into the ship; and the wind ceased:* and they were sore amazed in themselves beyond measure, and wondered.

21. *Then they willingly received him into the ship:*[1] *and immediately the ship was at the land whither they went.*

Here, again, all apparent contradiction is removed, by distinguishing correctly the several plans and objects of the writers. St Matthew and St Mark on the one hand, and St John on the other, *seem,* at first sight, on more

[1] Ἤθελον λαβεῖν αὐτὸν, *they willed to take him in,* here means not mere will and intention, but the willingness with which the thing was done, as the translation very well expresses it: *they willingly received him into the ship.* This use of the word ἐθέλειν, *to will,* is justified among other passages by a very decisive one in Xenophon *de Cyri disciplinâ,* lib. i. cap. i. § 3. Ἤθελον αὐτῷ ὑπακούειν, *they willed to obey him,* that is evidently, *they obeyed him willingly, with joy.*

than one point, to differ. In the *first* place, According to the two former Evangelists, it was Jesus himself that sent away the multitudes ; according to St John (at verse 15th, as we saw above,) Jesus withdrew, and repaired to the solitude of the mountain, *because he perceived that they would come and take him by force, and make him a king.* The contradiction disappears, provided we but read attentively the passage in St John, and carefully distinguish the successive moments of time. The *sending away* of the multitudes, mentioned by St Matthew and St Mark, must be understood to apply to the moment when the repast was over, although that particular, placed out of the chronological order, as is usual with those two writers, might appear, according to their representation, to have *followed after* the departure of the disciples (ver. 45, 46). Here we cannot have recourse to St Luke, as that Evangelist says nothing of the transactions of the night in question. So much the more important are the elucidation and amplification we receive from St John's Gospel. Now it is he that bids us remark that Jesus, knowing what passed in man's heart, and wishing to elude all attempts towards a movement intended for the purpose of making him a king, immediately (Matth. v. 22) obliged his disciples to embark without him, while he himself withdrew from the observation of all men, repairing to the mountain as the multitude were looking for him among the disciples. Further light is cast on these circumstances by the parenthesis contained in verses 22–25, which likewise presents a strong confirmation of the miracle of our Lord's walking on the sea of Galilee (v. 25). *Secondly,* According to the two synoptical Evangelists, the night was already far spent when Jesus came upon the waters of the sea to the vessel in which the disciples had embarked. St John alone mentions, according to his usual practice, *the precise distance* at which the disciples were from the land when they saw the Lord. Neither is there here the shadow of a contradiction ; but while the synoptical Evangelists call attention to the length of the time, St John informs us of the little progress they had made during all that time. No wonder : *the wind was contrary* (Matth. v. 24, Mark v. 48), and (John v. 18), *the sea arose by reason of a great wind that blew.* In the *third* place, St John here says nothing of the trepidation of the disciples, who thought that they saw a spirit, or even of what occurred and was said betwixt St Peter and our Lord ; all this he assumes as sufficiently known already, and confines himself to the person and the doings of his Master, simply setting his apostolical seal to the testimony of the synoptical narratives, by his brief mention of that great miracle, and by the addition, in precise terms, of a circumstance (*the five and twenty or thirty furlongs,* v. 19), to which none but an eyewitness, with a lively recollection of all that passed, would have thought of adverting here. And, *fourthly,* Whereas the synoptical Evangelists represent Jesus as entering the ship along with St Peter, and the other disciples as lost in amazement and adoration at what they had seen, St John further directs our attention to but one striking trait : those who but a moment before had cried out in terror and dismay at the sight of Jesus, supposing that they saw a spirit, *now received him willingly.* The subsidence of the boisterous sea, the cessation of the contrary wind, and their progress without further hindrance until they reached the other side—all this is expressed by St John in this very simple conclusion : *and immediately the ship was at the land whither they went* (v. 21). Here ends the narrative, which the synoptical Evangelists have in common with St John. The latter then follows it up, by giving the practical and spiritual application of the miracle of the loaves. He alone has preserved for us the discourses of Jesus at Capernaum (vi. 25–59) : *I am the bread of life. Whoso eateth my flesh and drinketh my blood, hath eternal life.*

VI. RESULT OF THE PRECEDING OBSERVATIONS.

We are now, in this section, to present, we would fain hope, in a more palpable manner, the results obtained from the collective observations put down in the preceding pages, in the course of our review of each of the four Gospels; and to exhibit these in their application to our Lord's passion, which, in all the four Gospels, crowns the entire work of their inspired narratives.

Before, however, proceeding to this last part of our design, we conceive that it will be useful to state these results in a few lines, and in their grand features, in order that we may attain to a definite determination of the principles required for a true and solid harmony of the Gospels.

To us who look for the true certainty and defence of the Scriptures in the Scriptures themselves, these results possess a double interest. They establish, in what to us appears a peremptory manner, upon a true and sure principle, the perfect accordance that exists among the Gospels; but they demonstrate, also, to the satisfaction of any sound and clear understanding, the authenticity and divine origin at once of the contents and structure of *each* severally, and of the general plan and collective character of the four Gospels *as one whole.*

We begin this view with the second point we have mentioned, to end it afterwards by glancing at the principal results and rules which may and ought to guide us in the establishment of a sound and true harmony of the Gospels.

We have examined the Gospels, successively and separately, in connexion with the *individuality* of the authors whose name they bear, and in connexion, too, with the truths to which they testify. And we have found in all of them alike, a character of authenticity that could never have been imitated, or even approached, by any writer of fiction, or even by any one who was not himself a Christian. We have seen at once, in the manner in which the Evangelists tell their story, especially when they point to themselves, or rather, as much as possible, withdraw from view, shun publicity, abase, and, so to speak, annihilate themselves—the grand fundamental principle of their Master's preaching—self-denial, humility. Those same men whom we have seen, according to what they themselves say, during their intercourse with their Master on earth, disputing with each other about precedence, with all the eagerness of men who are as averse to disgrace and suffering as they are bent on temporal greatness and glory—those same men, together with their fellows and followers, *now* present in their writings (always without any premeditation or ostentation), the most unequivocal proofs of the change of heart and mind that had taken place in them: *now* they have nothing so much at heart as to give glory to their Lord, to practise humility, to esteem every one his neighbour better than himself, and wholly to forget their own personality. That the writer of the first of the four Gospels was St Matthew, he who was called to the apostleship from the receipt of custom, was proved, just by the manner in which, *as respects himself*, he gives prominence to the general disrespect in which the publicans were held; and on the contrary, as respects his fellow Apostle, St Peter, to the latter's faith and priority of calling, along with his brother Andrew.[1] St Mark, on the contrary, who was the intimate and confidential friend of St Peter, shews the extent to which that Apostle influenced his narrations, precisely by the circumstance, that what he has recorded with respect to him, has a tendency rather to his humiliation than his exaltation.[2] St Luke, notwithstanding the important place he held in the history of the preaching of the Gospel, conceals both his name and person, under a modest and humble *we*.[3] Even St John, at a far advanced time of life, and when he might be said to be on the verge of eternity, makes himself known to us only by one anonymous denomination, and that so simple withal, *the disciple whom Jesus loved.* Assuredly this is not the manner in which men who seek to acquire influence and authority are accustomed to act with respect to themselves or to their designs; we may be satisfied that so just a conception, and so natural an expression

[1] See pp. 1 and 3. [2] See p. 48. [3] See p. 108.

of the spirit of Christianity, *of the mind of Christ*, never can be reconciled with any idea, either of premeditated invention, or of party spirit, or of selfish contrivance.

To the same result we are more and more conducted, by a more extensive and deeper view of the four Gospels. We found each of these, in its general structure, its style, its composition, nay more, even in the minutest of its individual details, giving an equally manifest and unpremeditated expression of the respective individuality of its author. We found, reversing the process, an individuality, consistent throughout with itself, so distinctly marking each of the Evangelists, that from the tenor and contents of the writing, the person and personal qualities of the writer discovered themselves to us with the most convincing certainty. Thus it was that we saw in each of the details peculiar to St Matthew, in the entire tendency of his narrative, in the point of view from which he delineates events, in his whole style and language, the manifest expression by himself of the publican received into favour, the apostolical eyewitness, the disciple sprung from Israel. In the Gospel of St Mark, the whole style and plan of the narrative revealed to us the Roman soldier converted to Christ, nay (in connexion with the proofs of his close intimacy with St Peter) that soldier who was of the household of Cornelius the centurion, who was deputed on the part of that household to go to the Apostle, and who conducted him to it. St Luke's Gospel betrayed to us in every particular the intimate friend and companion of St Paul, the physician by profession, the active, affectionate, and faithful servant of the Churches, a Gentile in point of origin, a friend of Israel, and the author of the Acts of the Apostles. St John's Gospel enabled us to see into the very soul of the disciple who, in the flower of early manhood, enjoyed the most endearing familiarity with his Master, and in a not less flourishing old age, brought to light, with the most sublime simplicity, the profoundest manifestations of the divine subsistence, atoning love, and glorious future advent of the Lord.

And, in addition to all this, every kind of exuberance, both of variety and of harmony, is found in most intimate union with what we have remarked. Here are four Gospels, all not in unison, but in harmony with each other, of which the First lays the foundations, taking these from the Prophecies of the Old Testament; the Second builds upon that foundation, and elucidates and confirms its predecessor with the help of details that are always more definite, more rich, and more picturesque: the Third sets itself beforehand to arrange matters historically, develops its subjects regularly, and explains them psychologically; the Fourth deduces the whole anew from its first beginnings, and traces it back to its remotest origin;—the First relates artlessly and fully; the Second describes with life and energy; the Third gives us an interesting and substantial narrative; the Fourth, a solemn and impressive testimony; —the First is the work of an Israelite, designed originally for Israelites; the Second, that of a Roman, designed for Roman Christians; the Third, that of a Greek, and designed for all nations; the Fourth again, that of an Israelite, and written for the Church of Israel and the Gentiles, without distinction;—the First preaches Jesus Christ as prophet and king; the Third, Jesus Christ as sovereign, priest, and king; the Second, Jesus Christ as

Son of man; the Fourth, Jesus Christ as the only Son of God.

By the same simple view and comparison of Scripture which we have instituted, we come clearly to see the order of time in which the Gospels followed each other. A question which, in the learned world, has given rise to so many divergent conjectures, again finds its simplest decision here in the contents and structure of those writings. The order in which the sacred four have been placed in the New Testament collection, from the earliest ages (*first,* St Matthew, *next,* St Mark, *after him,* St Luke, and, *finally,* St John), readily proves itself to be the only true order. We have only to consider that the Evangelist who was an Israelite and eyewitness from among the Twelve, and who, by an uninterrupted series of quotations, deduces all *from,* and attaches all *to* the Old Testament, and to Israel's expectation of a Christ—the Evangelist who relates facts without attending to their order, and in their first freshness, and in their first fulness, necessarily behoved to be the first Evangelist in the order of time. We find in the Gospel of St Matthew, neither more nor less than a true *mother-gospel.* When, by the side of this first Gospel, by the side of this mother-gospel, we place that of St Mark, we see it follow its predecessor almost point by point, in the adoption even of entire phrases, and in an almost uninterrupted agreement in the course of the narrative; and yet we see, at the same time, that it is substantially distinguished from its predecessor by the most characteristic insertions, suppressions, emphatizings, and inversions; while St Luke, following, as well as St Mark, the main thread of St Matthew's narrative, borrows details from St Mark in the most evident manner, augments his history with new facts and additions drawn from other sources, and arranges the whole not only according to the design he announces (i. 1–4) *in order*, but also with a depth of conception for which there had as yet been no room in the first two Gospels.[1] It was evidently to be inferred at once, from the nature of things, that St John had read the Gospels preceding his, had made use of them, and availed himself of them as the basis of his Evangelical book, which stands so entirely apart by itself, and possesses so peculiar a character; St John, who had so long outlived all the rest—St John, whom we have seen so repeatedly make tacit allusions and references, not only to the facts related by the synoptical Evangelists, but also to those recitals themselves.[2] This, surely, is after the manner of the men of God in the times of old. The Psalmist and Prophet found spiritual delight and nourishment in the writings of Moses; Daniel received divine revelations while exploring the writings of Jeremiah. Each of the sacred authors sought and found nourishment in what had been written by his predecessors, never merging his individuality in them, yet never independent of them.

Here, then, in God's revelation, as in his creation and government of the world, all is progress, growth, development. As the New Testament is a development from the bosom of the Old; as in the Old itself the Prophets are a development first from Moses and then from each other; as in the New the apostolic Epistles are a development from the historical writings; and as the Book of Revelation is a development from the whole preceding

[1] See p. 27. [2] See p. 232.

Scripture, quite as organically (we may use this expression, since the Word of God is a *living Word*) do the four Gospels develop themselves the one from the other. Oral tradition (by which we mean the original preaching of the Gospel) passes, in the first written memorials of the Apostle St Matthew, into the state of a simple recital; in that of St Mark it becomes a description; under the pen of St Luke it runs into a formal historical narrative; in the soul and in the testimony of St John it becomes a science, a God-devoted, God-glorifying Theology.

On all sides, as a consequence, we meet with harmony. And this is not only between each Evangelist and the character of his work and tenor of his testimony, but also among the four Evangelists, viewed as the four parts of one sublime whole; and all this, notwithstanding, without the possibility of attributing this last harmony, with the least appearance of truth, to premeditation on the part of the authors, or to any human plan whatever. Or can we ascribe it to a *human* plan, to a *human* premeditated purpose, that two Apostles should open and close the Evangelical quaternion, while the authors of the two intermediate Gospels should be proved by us to have been on terms of the closest intimacy with two other highly privileged disciples and apostles, St Peter and St Paul? Could it be the effect of *human* premeditation, that precisely *such personal qualities*, and precisely *such talents*, were successively, regularly, and step by step, as it were, employed in constructing the edifice of the four Gospels, as we have seen to have been the case with St Matthew, St Mark, St Luke, and St John? What we have here, consequently, is the plan of Supreme Wisdom.

After the clear and glorious manifestation we have had of it, how can we fail to recognise in the putting together of the four parts of the Evangelical testimony, that God who every where makes His finger to be seen in the works of the visible creation, at once in the combination and mutual dependence of parts, and in the analysis of each of them in particular? Now, such a work of God is the Scripture also, carried out to its close, and executed by the instrumentality of men, living, thinking, inquiring, industrious as men, yet at the same time, even in the smallest matters, led, overruled, and impelled by God. Scripture, as a whole, is the work of God's wisdom. It is in all its parts, too, a work of *divine* inspiration, but at the same time a work of *human* operation. It is *altogether* a work of men called to it by the Church's Lord, and by Him in various ways fitted and prepared for it; it is *equally altogether* the work of God, the inspiration in particular of the Holy Ghost.

What holds true of the Holy Scriptures, considered as a whole, in general, is equally true of the four Gospels, considered as a fourfold testimony, in particular. Each book, or part, has its own proper qualities, its own utility, its special object. Each book, or part, has its own *perfection*, and yet they stand in need of each other in order to their *completion*. It holds with respect to these holy books as with our human body. Each member is *perfect* in itself, but each member is not *complete* in itself. Each of the Gospels has received, under the guidance of the Holy Ghost, all that was required for its answering its special destination. Still, had we had but one, or two, or even three, only of the four Gospels, the testimony would have been incomplete.

Had we known only St Matthew's Gospel, for example, we should certainly have had a perfect acquaintance with the *grand outlines* of the Gospel history, but we should have been kept in ignorance of a great many of its *details*, and these at once interesting, instructive, and necessary; we should have become acquainted with *one* of the four sides of the edifice, but should have remained ignorant of the *other three*. We should even have been on several points *in error*, not because the Evangelist himself had erred, or had failed in expressing himself properly, but because what he had written in order to its enabling us to have a complete and perfectly just idea of events, stood still absolutely in need of the ulterior elucidations supplied by his three successors after him; and so, in like manner, with the rest. The Holy Spirit gives us the whole and entire truth in the four Gospels *combined*, but not in any one Gospel *standing apart* and taken by itself.

And now let us return again, for a few moments, to the principles which we have thought capable of reconciling, without violence, all our four Evangelists. It is in vain that an infidel, neological, or wavering theology, would undermine the veracity and the authenticity of these writings by an ostentatious array of all sorts of contradictions which, according to it, are irreconcilable. And just as vainly have attempts been made on the other side to do away with these contradictions, by wresting and twisting the several testimonies according to the model of *one single testimony;* when persons would, by means of an attempt equally narrow-minded and unfortunate, attribute one sole and the same plan to all those writers, and in their eagerness to account for their diversities, place them all at one and the same point of view, with the aid of all sorts of arbitrary and unfounded suppositions. Far from this, it is rather the most accurate observation of the differences that gives us the key that reconciles them. The more we examine our Gospels in detail, as with a microscope, the more diversities will multiply under our eyes; but the more also shall we find these diversities consistent, and so consistent that they constitute in each of the four Gospels a particular and distinctive character. And once that we have found this special character of each Gospel, we have also found the way to bring all these *real diversities* and *apparent contradictions* into one final and harmonious unity.

What we have in this respect observed and discovered in the course of our analysis of the four Gospels, we may now be permitted to condense and exhibit in a few rules, and these we leave, with all confidence, to be applied to the whole contents of these sacred writings, although it is of some portions only that we could treat in this Essay.

1. The four Evangelists, although the one who immediately precedes may have been known to, and used as a source of information by, the next in succession, nevertheless wrote with an equal *independence* with respect to each other, and with an equal *dependence* on the Holy Ghost.

2. The four Gospels do not *all* present us with a narration of the *same* facts, neither do they *all* relate the same discourses in the *same* words. Each Evangelist has made his own choice according to a certain fixed plan; to each had been assigned his own part, according to his particular character and calling.

3. The Evangelists often differ the one from the other with regard to the order in which they place the facts that had happened, as well as with regard to the words that had been pronounced.

4. St Matthew joins together, and accumulates *homogeneous* facts and discourses. St Luke places facts and words in their historical succession. St Mark makes the transition betwixt the first and the third Gospel. According as his plan seems to require, he either adheres to the order of St Matthew, or corrects it, proceeding at once to supply particulars that St Matthew had omitted in his narrative. St John seldom displaces, unless it be in the way of the insertion of some new detail, or to account for some particular circumstance.

5. St Matthew relates matters fully, and with an abundance of expressions, yet without any fulness of descriptive details. St Mark presents quite a richness of *details*, by which he elucidates and delineates the incident he relates, and places it as if fully before our eyes. The details given by St Luke touch more upon the interior of things. St John gives a variety of them, with much fulness, entirely new, and all in harmony with the depth and elevation of his sublime point of view, and his vocation as Apostle-Prophet.

6. The Evangelists often differ in the noting down of numbers and ciphers.

St Matthew loves the *plural*, which St Luke, and, for the most part, St Mark already before him, record in the effective *singular*. This *plural* of the mother-gospel may be traced to the point of view from which its author wrote, and which led him to look rather to the *species* than to the *individual*, to the *collective idea* more than to *isolated events.* The ciphers introduced by St John point to his being an eyewitness, and complete the perfect accuracy of the entire testimony.

7. The Evangelists have committed to writing the words of different speakers, and of the Lord Jesus himself, in different manners. All give a true expression of the *meaning*, being *authentic interpreters* as well as *truthful annotators.* St Matthew, by means of periphrastic expressions, elucidates the sentences which he records, or clothes with words mental ideas originally expressed not in words. St Mark repeatedly gives the precise literal and original word. St Luke is equally precise and simple in mentioning the words as in relating the facts. St John renders the words and discourses as he has preserved them, as they still sound in his ears, as they developed themselves in his own soul.

VII. THE NARRATIVES OF OUR LORD'S PASSION.

WHAT the Apostle Paul says, in writing to the men of Corinth, *I determined not to know anything among you, save Jesus Christ, and Him crucified,* we already find strikingly realized in the composition of the Gospels. Alike in describing the details of our Lord and Saviour's life, and in preaching the power of his name and the truth of his doctrine—his cross, the blood of his cross, that is to say, his propitiatory sufferings and death, is the point in which the whole Gospel, so to speak, is summed up and concentrated. The history of his last passion and of his death, of his burial and glorious resurrection, is properly the focus of the Gospel. To the description of that scene of sorrow, that death, and that resurrection, all the four Gospels have given the greatest extension, by fully recording the details therewith connected. Here, however, as well as everywhere else, they preserve their proper character, all severally presenting the same mutual bearings to each other as in the rest of their writings. In the narrative of the passion, as well as elsewhere, all the details are not recorded by all of them; in the narrative of the passion, as well as elsewhere, each of the four Evangelists sees, describes, relates, testifies in the manner peculiar to his own particular point of view. A glance at the history of *our Lord's passion,* as it makes an important part of the fourfold harmony of our Gospels, may supply us with a final means of proving the truth of the observations which we have offered in detail in the course of these pages.

The history of our Lord's passion may be regarded as having for its introduction the last celebration of the Passover, which was at the same time the institution of the Holy Supper. We have been accustomed to comprise in that history also the last supper at Bethany, on account of the close connexion between the two. We shall, for the like reason, include the supper at Bethany and the treachery of Judas, in giving that part of the Gospels which we are now about to review; and not only those facts, which occurred two days before the Passover, but, further, the entrance of the Lord Jesus into Jerusalem, on the foal of an ass, on the first day previous to that feast, because of the intimate connexion of that event with the whole history of the passion; especially, we may add, because these different parts, in their intimate connexion, will bring out the great importance of the Gospel of St John, in particular, in establishing the true sequence of events.

THE ENTRANCE INTO JERUSALEM.

MATTH. xxi. 1–11.	MARK xi. 1–10.
And when they drew nigh unto Jerusalem, and were come to Bethphage, unto the mount of Olives, then sent Jesus two disciples, 2. Saying unto them, Go into the village over against you, and straightway ye shall find an ass tied, and	And when they came nigh to Jerusalem, unto Bethphage and Bethany, at the mount of Olives, he sendeth forth two of his disciples, 2. And saith unto them, Go your way into the village over against you: and as soon as ye be

a colt with her: loose *them*, and bring
them unto me. 3. And if any man
say ought unto you, ye shall say,
The Lord hath need of them; and
straightway he will send them.

4. All this was done, that it might
be fulfilled which was spoken by
the prophet, saying, 5. Tell ye
the daughter of Zion, Behold, thy
King cometh unto thee, meek, and
sitting upon an ass.

6. And the disciples went, and
did as Jesus commanded them, 7.
And brought the ass, and the colt,
and put on *them* their clothes (Gr.
ἐπ' ἀυτῶν), and they set him thereon (Gr. ἐπ' αὐτῶν)—*lit.:* on *them.*

8. And a very great multitude
spread their garments in the way;
others cut down *branches* from the
trees, and strawed them in the way.
9. And *the multitudes that went before, and that followed*, cried, saying, Hosanna to the son of David:
Blessed is he that cometh in the
name of the Lord; Hosanna in the
highest.

10. And when he was come into
Jerusalem, all the city was moved,
saying, Who is this? 11. And the
multitude said, This is Jesus the
prophet of Nazareth of Galilee.

entered into it, ye shall find a colt
tied, whereon never man sat; loose
him, and bring *him*. 3. And if any
man say unto you, Why do ye this?
say ye that the Lord hath need of
him; and straightway he will send
him hither.

4. And they went their way, and
found the colt tied by the door
without, in a place where two
ways met; and they loose him.
5. And certain of them that stood
there said unto them, What do
ye, loosing the colt? 6. And they
said unto them even as Jesus had
commanded: and they let them go.
7. And they brought the colt to
Jesus, and cast their garments on
him (αὐτῷ); and he sat upon him
(ἐπ' αὐτῷ).

8. And many spread their garments in the way; and others cut
down branches off the trees, and
strawed them in the way. 9. And
they that went before, and they that
followed, cried, saying, Hosanna;
Blessed is he that cometh in the
name of the Lord: 10. Blessed
be the kingdom of our father David,
that cometh in the name of the
Lord: Hosanna in the highest.

LUKE xix. 29.

And it came to pass, when he
was come nigh to Bethphage and
Bethany, at the mount called the
mount of Olives, he sent two of his

JOHN xii. 12.

On the next day much people
that were come to the feast, when
they heard that Jesus was coming
to Jerusalem, 13. Took branches

disciples, 30. Saying, Go ye into
the village over against you; in the
which at your entering ye shall
find a colt tied, *whereon yet never*
man sat: loose *him*, and bring *him*
hither. 31. And if any man ask
you, Why do ye loose him? thus
shall ye say unto him, Because the
Lord hath need of him.

of palm-trees, and went forth to
meet him, and cried, Hosanna:
Blessed is the King of Israel that
cometh in the name of the Lord.

14. And Jesus, when he had
found a young ass, sat thereon; as
it is written, 15. Fear not, daughter
of Zion: behold, thy king cometh,
sitting on an ass's colt. 16. These
things understood not his disciples
at the first: but when Jesus was
glorified, then remembered they that
these things were written of him,
and that he had said this.

32. And they that were sent
went their way, and found even
as he had said unto them. 33.
And as they were loosing the colt,
the owners thereof said unto them,
Why loose ye the colt? 34. And
they said, The Lord hath need of
him. 35. And they brought him
to Jesus: and they cast their garments upon the colt, and they set
Jesus thereon.

36. And as he went, they spread
their clothes in the way. 37. And
when he was come nigh, even now
at the descent of the mount of
Olives, the whole multitude of the
disciples began to rejoice and praise
God with a loud voice for all the
mighty works that they had seen;
38. Saying, Blessed be the King
that cometh in the name of the
Lord: peace in heaven, and glory
in the highest.

17. The people therefore that
was with him bare record that he
had called Lazarus out of his grave,
and raised him from the dead. 18.
For this cause the people also met
him, for that they heard that he
had done this miracle.

39. And some of the Pharisees
from among the multitude said
unto him, Master, rebuke thy disciples. 40. And he answered and
said unto them, I tell you that, if
these should hold their peace, the

19. The Pharisees therefore said
among themselves, Perceive ye how
ye prevail nothing? behold, the
world is gone after him.

**stones would immediately cry out.
41. And when he was come near,
he beheld the city, and wept over
it, 42. Saying, If thou hadst known,
even thou, at least in this thy day,
the things which belong unto thy
peace! but now they are hid from
thine eyes. 43. For the days shall
come upon thee, that thine enemies
shall cast a trench about thee, and
compass thee round, and keep thee
in on every side, 44. And shall
lay thee even with the ground, and
thy children within thee; and they
shall not leave in thee one stone
upon another; because thou knewest
not the time of thy visitation.**

The three synoptical Gospels agree here, almost literally, at least at the commencement; *differences*, nevertheless, are not absolutely wanting. The place designated by St Matthew (verse 1) under the name of *Bethphage* only, is called by St Mark (verse 1), and by St Luke (verse 29), *Bethphage and Bethany.* By these three last words one must not understand (as we shall see hereafter) two different places, but the meeting-point at which Bethphage (a small place belonging to the territory of Jerusalem) adjoins Bethany, which is situated at some distance from the capital.

As to what follows with respect to the *animal* on which Jesus made his entrance into Jerusalem, it must be observed that St Matthew alone makes mention of the *colt, and of the she-ass of which it was the foal,* while St Mark and St Luke speak only of *the colt.* This particular is intimately connected with the prophecy of Zacharias, which, we may again observe, St Matthew alone (verses 4 and 5) quotes, and where both are expressly named. To the Prophet, as well as to the Apostle whose Gospel has the closest affinity with the Old Testament prophecies, the mention of the *she-ass* serves only to indicate that the *ass* was *a colt* whereon (as St Mark and St Luke afterwards express it) *never man sat.* The two last Evangelists had only to do with the fact as it actually happened in the fulfilment; on this account they nowhere speak of any thing but the *colt* on which the Saviour was placed by his disciples. St Matthew alone, after his peculiar manner, so identifies[1] in this passage the two objects in the words he employs, that in the seventh verse he each time uses a plural, which, literally taken, would produce a kind of *nonsense.* What he evidently *means* to say is nothing more than what St Mark (verse 7), and St Luke (verse 35), express in simple terms, namely, that Jesus was seated, not certainly on two beasts of burthen, but only on *the colt.* That, nevertheless, at the time of the entrance into Jerusalem, the ass should have accompanied the colt is not only a very possible circumstance, but one which it is all the more easy to conceive to have happened, from the colt having suffered itself to be detached and mounted without resistance.

St Mark (verse 4) indicates exactly and graphically the spot where the colt was found tied *by the door without, in a place where two ways met,* to wit: precisely on the confines of Bethany and Bethphage.

St Mark (verses 6 and 7), and St Luke (verses 33 and 34), give a fuller report also of the conversation betwixt the two disciples and the men of Bethphage than we find in St Matthew, who, with respect to that circumstance (verse 6), is very concise.

Again, we find our Lord's going to Jerusalem given in greater detail by St Mark (verses 5 and 6); but by St

[1] P. 61.

Luke (verses 36–38) the motives that influenced the people are more fully expressed than by St Matthew (verses 8, 9). To the cries of *Hosannah* which burst from the multitude, St Mark adds that important insertion: *Blessed be the kingdom of our father David, (the kingdom) that cometh in the name of the Lord!* instead of the *Hosannah to the Son of David,* which we find in St Matthew. Then St Luke fixes our attention rather on the *inward* emotions of the multitude of the disciples; the joy,[1] and the praises to God resulting from that joy,[2] and the cause that particularly gave birth to that feeling, to wit, *for all the mighty works that they had seen;* all which is more fully explained to us in St John (verse 17) by the resurrection there mentioned of Lazarus.

After this, St Matthew (verse 10) transports us into the midst of Jerusalem, where the whole people are in a state of excitement, there to fix our regards anew on the prophetic ministry of the Saviour (verse 11).

St Luke (verses 39–44), as we have remarked on a preceding occasion,[3] has preserved for us that touching address to Jerusalem, called forth by the bitter enmity expressed by some of the Pharisees, and pronounced by the meek and compassionate Saviour as he wept over the city (verse 41).

St John sums up all that happened in details, which are remarkable at once for their brevity and their freshness (verses 12–19). In relating these, he follows an order which is peculiar to himself; first, the *Hosannah;* after that, parenthetically, the placing of Jesus on the colt, and, in connexion with this, the calling to mind of the prophecy of Zacharias; then what called forth the shouts of joy from the multitude; and, finally, the desperate and deep-seated

[1] See p. 174, sqq. [2] See p. 175, sqq. [3] See p. 182.

animosity of the Pharisees. Then, further, he exactly determines the time (verse 12) : *on the next day,* and the occasion, *the feast;* immediately after that, the waving of the branches *of the palm-tree,* which, according to the Israelitic custom, accompanied the shouts of *Hosannah* (verse 13).[1] Here, too, only do we find the title of *King of Israel* (verse 13). In quoting the prophecy, he adds the manner in which the disciples for the first time, but not until the departure and glorification of Jesus, *remembered that those things were written of him* (verse 16). St Matthew (verse 5) gives the very words of Zacharias, with a supplementary quotation from Isaiah.[2] In St John we read those words in a very abridged form.

And now let us reply to the allegation of an apparent contradiction, the solution of which has been acknowledged by many interpreters to be a matter of great difficulty. It is twofold. 1*st,* According to the synoptical Gospels, the going from Bethany to Jerusalem seems to have taken place immediately, and as if it were a prolongation of the journey to Jericho and Jerusalem, without there being the slightest mention made of any delay, of any supper, or of any spending of the night at Bethany (as these are mentioned by St John). 2*d,* This sojourn of Jesus at Bethany does not seem to agree with what is positively recorded by the synoptical Evangelists; namely, that on his approaching BETHPHAGE *and Bethany* the two disciples were sent to seek the ass's colt, a circumstance totally *inexplicable* if Jesus really passed that night at Bethany.

Now, with respect to the *former* of these objections, the

[1] Gr. τὰ βάϊα τῶν φοινίκων.

[2] Zach. ix. 9, Isa. lxii. 11.

solemn entrance of Jesus into Jerusalem is no doubt immediately connected by the three first Evangelists with his coming from Jericho. But while *their* main object was to give a representation of the *public* life of Jesus, the object of St John is more particularly to give a picture of his intercourse *with his most intimate and fondly-loved friends.* Hence, also, it is that what took place in the town of Mary and her sister Martha behoved mainly to pertain to the plan of the fourth and last Gospel; namely, the resurrection of Lazarus, the supper, and the anointing in the house of Simon, the sleeping in the village, &c. Now all this, passed over in silence by the synoptical Evangelists, is inserted in the Gospel of St John; and here again, consequently, there is no contradiction, but only a filling up, an explanation, a development. Viewed in this light, the two accounts reciprocally throw light on each other. What, in fact, is more natural than that solemn entrance into Jerusalem, starting from Bethany in consequence of the ecstasy into which the multitude were thrown by their having witnessed the raising of Lazarus from the dead?

On the contrary, how very unlikely that Jesus, without any particular cause for it, on coming directly from Jericho with the twelve, should have met with so splendid a reception and convoy from the multitude! The simple state of matters is as follows:—The synoptical Evangelists give the history of our Lord's entrance as one of the scenes of his public life, and as one of the circumstances attending his last days on earth. St John goes back to the cause and origin of the popular excitement, and gives us a view of the event in all its completeness, by conducting us at the same time to the inner circle of intimate friends at Bethany.

The *second* objection finds its solution simply in a more accurate knowledge of the locality. Former commentators have already intimated, that *Bethphage and Bethany*, of which St Mark and St Luke speak, must not be understood as meaning each of those places *separately*. Were this the case, it would indeed be inexplicable how Jesus, after having, as St John tells us, slept at Bethany, could have sent forward his disciples to that same Bethany to untie the colt. But this *Bethphage* AND *Bethany* is in reality nothing else than the simple *Bethphage* of St Matthew, and signified (as a more ample description of the latter of those places) *Bethphage bordering on Bethany*. It is on this account also, that *Bethphage* is named *first*, although belonging to the territory itself of Jerusalem, since, without that, *Bethany* ought to have had the precedence in speaking of those places. To people travelling towards Jerusalem, Bethany lay naturally before Bethphage; if, then, we were here to understand the village that bore that name, the Evangelists behoved to have said: (*first*) Bethany and (*then*) Bethphage.[1] When Jesus, with his disciples, drew near to this *Bethphage* AND (that is to say, NEAR TO) *Bethany*, he had that last village behind him, and having travelled on foot from Bethany, where he had passed the night, as far as Bethphage, he sends, when he is at some distance, his two disciples to that same Bethphage. It was *from thence*

[1] LIGHTFOOT, Opera ii., p. 409, ad Marc. xi. 1. "In itineratione sua accessit Christus ad Bethaniam, ibique pernoctavit (John xii.) et ab oppido isto pervenerat jam per spatium fere milliaris antequam pertingeret ad Bethphagen. Et tamen ab iis dicitur isto ordine: *Ad Bethphagen et Bethaniam*, ut demonstraretur historiam esse intelligendam *de loco ubi se mutuo contingunt Bethania et Bethphage:* MATTHÆUS ergo *Bethphagen* nominat solam." Cff. p. 44, 148, 202, 569, et 570, 754. So likewise WETSTEIN: "Quidquid est in ambitu exteriore Hierosolymorum vocatur Bethphage." Cf. BENGEL ad Marc. xi. 1

that, shortly afterwards, the procession to Jerusalem commenced.

St John's narrative concerning the Saviour's sojourn at Bethany before the entrance into Jerusalem, throws much light also on what the Synoptics relate with respect to what occurred afterwards; to wit, how in those days Jesus repaired uniformly before night from Jerusalem to the mount of Olives, or to Bethany (Matth. xxi. 17, Mark xi. 11, 12, Luke xxi. 37).

THE SUPPER AT BETHANY, AND THE TREASON OF JUDAS.

MATTH. xxvi. 1–16.

And it came to pass, when Jesus had finished all these sayings, he said unto his disciples, Ye know that after two days is the feast of the passover, and the Son of man is betrayed to be crucified. 3. Then assembled together the chief priests, and the scribes, and the elders of the people, unto the palace of the high priest, who was called Caiaphas, 4. And consulted that they might take Jesus by subtilty, and kill him. 5. But they said, Not on the feast-day, lest there be an uproar among the people. 6. ¶ Now when Jesus was in Bethany, in the house of Simon the leper, 7. There came unto him a woman having an alabaster-box of very precious ointment, and poured it on his head, as he sat at meat. 8. But when his disciples saw it, they had indignation, saying, to what purpose is this waste? 9. For this ointment might have been sold for much, and given to the poor.

10. When Jesus understood it, he said unto them, Why trouble ye the woman? for she hath wrought

MARK xiv. 1–11.

After two days was the feast of the passover, and of unleavened bread: and the chief priests and the scribes sought how they might take him by craft, and put him to death. 2. But they said, Not on the feast-day, lest there be an uproar of the people. 3. ¶ And being in Bethany in the house of Simon the leper, as he sat at meat, there came a woman having an alabaster-box of ointment of spikenard very precious; and she brake the box, and poured it on his head. 4. And there were some that had indignation within themselves, and said, Why was this waste of the ointment made? 5. For it might have been sold for more than three hundred pence, and have been given to the poor. And they murmured against her.

6. And Jesus said, Let her alone; why trouble ye her? she hath wrought a good work on me.

a good work upon me. 11. For ye
have the poor always with you;
but me ye have not always. 12.
For in that she hath poured this
ointment on my body, she did it
for my burial. 13. Verily I say
unto you, Wheresoever this gospel
shall be preached in the whole
world, there shall also this, that
this woman hath done, be told for
a memorial of her.

7. For ye have the poor with you
always, and whensoever ye will ye
may do them good: but me ye
have not always. 8. She hath
done what she could: she is come
aforehand to anoint my body to
the burying. 9. Verily I say unto
you, Wheresoever this gospel shall
be preached throughout the whole
world, this also that she hath done
shall be spoken of for a memorial
of her.

14. ¶ Then one of the twelve,
called Judas Iscariot, went unto
the chief priests, 15. And said unto
them, What will ye give me, and
I will deliver him unto you? And
they covenanted with him for thirty
pieces of silver. 16. And from that
time he sought opportunity to betray him.

10. ¶ And Judas Iscariot, one of
the twelve, went unto the chief
priests, to betray him unto them.
11. And when they heard it, they
were glad, and promised to give
him money. And he sought how
he might conveniently betray him.

LUKE xxii. 1–6.

Now the feast of unleavened
bread drew nigh, which is called
the Passover. 2. And the chief
priests and scribes sought how they
might kill him; for they feared the
people.

JOHN xii. 1–11.

Then Jesus six days before the
passover came to Bethany, where
Lazarus was which had been dead,
whom he raised from the dead. 2.
There they made him a supper;
and Martha served: but Lazarus
was one of them that sat at the
table with him. 3. Then took
Mary a pound of ointment of spikenard, very costly, and anointed
the feet of Jesus, and wiped his
feet with her hair: and the house
was filled with the odour of the
ointment. 4. Then saith one of his
disciples, Judas Iscariot, Simon's
son, which should betray him. 5.
Why was not this ointment sold for
three hundred pence, and given to
the poor? 6. This he said, not
that he cared for the poor; but
because he was a thief, and had
the bag, and bare what was put
therein. 7. Then said Jesus, Let
her alone: against the day of my
burying hath she kept this. 8. For

the poor always ye have with you;
but me ye have not always. 9.
Much people of the Jews therefore
knew that he was there: and they
came not for Jesus' sake only, but
that they might see Lazarus also,
whom he had raised from the
dead. 10. ¶ But the chief priests
consulted that they might put Lazarus also to death; 11. Because
that by reason of him many of the
Jews went away, and believed on
Jesus.

3. ¶ Then entered Satan into Judas
surnamed Iscariot, being of the
number of the twelve. 4. And he
went his way, and communed with
the chief priests and captains, how
he might betray him unto them.
5. And they were glad, and covenanted to give him money. 6.
And he promised, and sought opportunity to betray him unto them
in the absence of the multitude.

Let us first observe some striking details in the different narratives, and then mark the light that is thrown on the order and general aspect of the facts that they relate, by a reciprocal comparison.

In St Matthew's Gospel (v. 1) the narrative commences with his ordinary mode of making a transition: *And it came to pass when Jesus had finished all these sayings,* &c. We do not find here, either in St Mark or in St Luke, any words addressed by Jesus to his disciples, but only the essential fact mentioned: *the feast of the Passover was nigh.* St Mark (xiv.) adds to this, by way of explanation, the words, *of unleavened bread,* being the name by which the feast was best known among strangers.

Anew we find abridged by St Mark and St Luke, the more circumstantial mention made in St Matthew of the assembling together of the chief priests and the scribes.

The dread expressed by our Lord's enemies *lest there be a tumult* (Matth. v. 5, Mark v. 2), is not to be found *at this point* in our third Evangelist; he recurs to it afterwards in passing, where he speaks of the betrayal of our Lord (v. 6).

Thus far we have the introduction, in which St John does not run parallel with the first three Evangelists; it is only afterwards (xii. 10) that he evidently alludes to their mention of the council held by the high priests, adding further this new particular: *they consulted that they might put Lazarus also to death.*

Here we lose altogether the thread of history as supplied by St Luke, who makes no mention of the supper at Bethany. What we miss in his Gospel we find more than replaced in the fourth, where the Apostle elucidates and extends, in the most marked manner, the narratives of St Matthew and St Mark.

After the naming by the two synoptical Evangelists of the master of the house at whose table Jesus had sat and been anointed, we find at the first glance, on looking into St John (v. 1), two particular circumstances of some importance, in order to our obtaining a complete view of all that occurred: he gives us, *first*, to know the fact which led to the touching circumstances that marked this same supper: *Lazarus was there also, whom Jesus had raised from the dead;* then, *secondly*, that the ever diligent and active Martha, his sister, served at the supper. Thus it is that St John, and he the first and alone of the four, puts that supper at Bethany in its clearest light, by enabling us to see the connexion in which it stands with the greatest miracle wrought by the Saviour—that is to say, the raising of Lazarus from the dead.

Now follows the anointing of Jesus by the grateful and

loving woman who, as is further to be observed, is not named by the synoptical Evangelists. We receive an agreeable surprise when, on looking into St John, we find in her the sister of the risen Lazarus, the Mary whom elsewhere we had come to know as seeking the one thing that is needful, and in the softness of her character, a meek and quiet spirit, sitting at Jesus' feet, and hearing his word.[1]

The sweet-smelling ointment spoken of in St Matthew (v. 7), in general terms, as *very precious*, is more fully described by St Mark (v. 2), as being of *spikenard*. Afterwards (v. 5), its price is mentioned: *it might have been sold for more than three hundred pence*, a reckoning adopted by St John from the second Gospel. In that Gospel too, what the woman did is expressed with animation: she *brake* the alabaster-box and poured it forthwith on the head of her Lord. Here we find anew in St John,[2] the exact statement of number and weight (v. 3): *a pound*. It is he who points out to us more specially the anointing of the feet of Jesus, which she afterwards wiped with her hair; it is he who gives us to know that interesting detail, which, moreover, is not without its spiritual meaning, that *the house was filled with the odour of the ointment*.

Thus do we perceive, in the transition from St Matthew to St Mark, and from the latter to St John, more and more light almost insensibly diffused on the bitter remark to which that anointing gave rise among the disciples. According to the first (v. 8), it appears as if the reprimand of Mary were attributed to all the disciples. But St Mark at once limits and explains the general terms of his predecessor by that of *some* (v. 4);

[1] Luke x. 39. [2] See p. 260.

and, finally, St John gives us more positive information by making it the exclamation of the traitor only (v. 4): *one of his disciples, Judas Iscariot, Simon's son,* &c. Others, possibly, might have been led away for a moment by the hypocritical exclamation of Judas, and (as St Mark expresses it) *had indignation within themselves* against the woman; but St John attributes the words that were pronounced, as well as the motive, *exclusively* to Judas. It is in like manner to St John that we are indebted for our first coming to know that it was avarice that on this occasion wrought in the traitor's heart; he tells us (v. 12), *This he said, not that he cared for the poor: but because he was a thief, and had the bag, and bare what was put therein.*

After this, the three Gospels entirely agree with regard to the declaration of Jesus concerning this woman's action. St Mark alone (v. 7) strengthens the sentence that relates to the poor by the marked amplification: *and whensoever ye will, ye may do them good;* and that relating to the woman, by those encouraging words: *she hath done what she could.* We do not find any recurrence in St John, of the expression of the two synoptical Evangelists (Matth. v. 10, and Mark v. 6): *good work;* this Apostle employs that expression *exclusively* in speaking of our Lord's miracles.[1]

Further, in St John we find fresh light thrown on the meaning of the expression *anointing for the burial,* used by St Matthew and St Mark. He explains it thus: AGAINST THE DAY *of my burying hath she kept this (ointment).*

The prediction, of the accomplishment of which we are this day witnesses, after the lapse of eighteen centuries, and which foretells that the woman and her action would be

[1] John x. 32, 33.

spoken of *wherever the Gospel shall be preached*, is not repeated by St John after being mentioned by the two synoptics; he had already done homage to that act of love by giving the name of the woman.

The details which follow, and are recorded only by him (v. 9–11) are important; as when he tells us that much people of the Jews came to Bethany, not for Jesus' sake only, but that they might see Lazarus; how the chief priests consulted not only to put Jesus to death, but Lazarus also; how, at the same time, many of the Jews believed on Jesus after that stupendous miracle.

Here the fourth Gospel leaves us, but in return St Luke proves himself anew the historian by way of eminence, in furnishing details which are no less interesting. He opens the narrative of the conspiracy of the traitor with the council (v. 3), with a strong expression. Immediately after (v. 4), he alone makes mention, with historical exactness, of the chief priests and the captains.[1] St Mark (v. 11), and St Luke after him, pointedly speak of the satisfaction that the proposal of Judas gave them. According to his usual custom, the latter, in speaking of the impious contract, employs the proper juridical terms (v. 5 and 17): they *covenanted* (Gr. συνέθεντο), and he *promised* (Gr. ἐξωμολόγησε).

It is St Matthew only that has recorded the amount of the price of blood (x. 15): *thirty pieces of silver;* this he has done in keeping with his prophetical point of view, *since* he places them afterwards in connexion (ch. xxvii. 3–10) with the prophecy of Jeremiah with respect to that sum, *the price for which the Lord was sold;* and *since* that whole part of the history of the passion (the

[1] Compare Luke xxii. 52. The *captains* were likewise *priests*, placed over the guards of the Temple.

treason committed by one of the twelve, predicted long before, and foreseen by Jesus himself), is a point of capital importance with this Evangelist. It suited him more than any of the other three (in conformity with the well-known character of his work), not to keep out of view, but to give prominence to all that redounded whether to the glory or the shame of the apostleship.[1]

Let us now mark further an apparent difference between the narratives of St Matthew and St Mark on the one hand, and that of St John on the other, in so far as respects the determining of the time when the supper at Bethany took place. According to St Matthew (v. 1 and 6), followed here too by St Mark (v. 1 and 3), the supper, and the anointing at Bethany, took place TWO DAYS *before the feast of the passover*. St John (xii. 1) seems to speak positively of SIX DAYS. The apparent difference disappears on our simply noticing, that in St John the second verse ought not to be considered as immediately following on verse first. On the contrary, the contents of verses 2–11 appear to us a parenthesis, in which our last Evangelist mentions, by way of anticipation, the supper at Bethany, which took place in reality only some days AFTER the entrance into Jerusalem, that is to say (as we know already from the two first synoptical Gospels), *two days before the passover*. St John, too, neither adds any thing, nor makes any change on that date; he merely gives us the details which we have just gone over. The words, *on the next day* (v. 12), ought then to be understood as referring to the day after the arrival of Jesus at Bethany, as mentioned at verse first.

Now, by putting together our now concluded observations on the entrance of our Lord into Jerusalem, and

[1] See pp. 14, 15.

the supper at Bethany, we arrive at the following results with respect to the chronological order of the incidents that are recorded in the four Gospels.

1. The arrival of Jesus at Bethany six days before the passover, that is to say, on the first day of the week (according to St John, xii. 1).

2. The entrance of Jesus into Jerusalem on the day following, that is to say, on *Monday* (according to the same Evangelist, xii. 12).

3. First entrance into the Temple that same day (Mark xi. 11).

4. The day following (*Tuesday*) the malediction of the fig-tree (Mark xi. 12).

5. The cleansing of the Temple that same day (Mark xi. 15, &c).

6. Supper at Bethany two days before the passover (according to Matth. xxvi. 2, and Mark xiv. 1).

7. Covenanting of Judas with the council of the Jews.

THE LAST SUPPER OF JESUS WITH HIS DISCIPLES.

Matth. xxvi. 17.	Mark xiv. 12.	Luke xxii. 7.
Now the first (day) of the (feast of) unleavened bread, the disciples came to Jesus, saying unto him, Where wilt thou that we prepare for thee to eat the passover?	And the first day of unleavened bread, when they killed the passover, his disciples said unto him, Where wilt thou that we go and prepare, that thou mayest eat the passover?	Then came the day of unleavened bread, when the passover must be killed.
18. And he said, go into the city to such a man, and say unto him,	13. And he sendeth forth two of his disciples, and saith unto them, Go ye into the city, and there shall meet you a man bearing a pitcher of water:	8. And he sent Peter and John, saying, Go and prepare us the passover, that we may eat. 9. And they said unto him, Where wilt thou that we prepare?

	follow him. 14. And wheresoever he shall go in, say ye to the goodman of the house,	10. And he said unto them, Behold, when ye are entered into the city, there shall a man meet you, bearing a pitcher of water; follow him into the house where he entereth in. 11. And ye shall say unto the goodman of the house,
The Master saith, My time is at hand; I will keep the passover at thy house with my disciples.	The Master saith, Where is the guest-chamber, where I shall eat the passover with my disciples? 15. And he will shew you a large upper room furnished and prepared: there make ready for us.	The Master saith unto thee, Where is the guest-chamber, where I shall eat the passover with my disciples? 12. And he shall shew you a large upper room furnished: there make ready.
19. And the disciples did as Jesus had appointed them; and they made ready the passover.	16. And his disciples went forth, and came into the city, and found as he had said unto them: and they made ready the passover.	13. And they went, and found as he had said unto them: and they made ready the passover.

The harmony of the synoptical Evangelists, as respects the preparation for the passion, requires no elucidation. In this short introduction, nevertheless, all of them display their several characters. St Matthew enters into no details. He gives the main outline in a few words, and then distinguishes himself solely by the properly Hebrew expression (v. 18), *such a man* (Gr. ὁ δεῖνα, in the Hebrew פְּלֹנִי); after that, (in the same 18th v.), by the very significative insertion, *My time is at hand.* St Mark and St Luke give a fuller explanation of the feast by this parenthesis: *when they killed the lamb of the passover* (St Mark, v. 12); and (St Luke, v. 7) *when the lamb of the passover* MUST BE *killed;* both wrote, in the first instance, for persons not Israelites by birth.

While St Matthew speaks in general of the *disciples*

(v. 17, 18), St Mark limits his designation to two from among them (v. 13) ; St Luke again (v. 8) names the two, Peter and John. What St Matthew and St Mark put at first into the mouths of the disciples, *Where wilt thou that we prepare for thee to eat the passover?* &c., appears, from the more regular narrative of St Luke, to have been said only in reply to the Lord's command, *Go* (v. 8), to which the subsequent indication, by our Lord in his reply, of the apartment in the city, corresponds.

With respect to that indication of the place, we again find St Matthew brief. By way of extension and elucidation, *first* in St Mark (v. 13), we have the detail of the man bearing a pitcher of water, and *then* in St Luke (v. 10), in nearly the same terms.

The large upper room furnished and prepared, is also indicated first by St Mark; after him also by St Luke (v. 12.)

MATTH. xxvi. 20–35.	MARK xiv. 17–31.
Now when the even was come, he sat down with the twelve.	And in the evening he cometh with the twelve.
21. And as they did eat, he said, Verily I say unto you, That one of you shall betray me.	18. And as they sat and did eat, Jesus said, Verily I say unto you, One of you which eateth with me shall betray me.
22. And they were exceeding sorrowful, and began every one of them to say unto him, Lord, is it I? 23. And he answered and said, He that dippeth his hand with me in the dish, the same shall betray me. 24. The Son of man goeth as it is written of him: but woe unto that man by whom the Son of man is betrayed! it had been good for that man if he had not been born.	19. And they began to be sorrowful, and to say unto him one by one, Is it I? and another said, Is it I? 20. And he answered and said unto them, It is one of the twelve, that dippeth with me in the dish. 21. The Son of man indeed goeth, as it is written of him: but woe to that man by whom the Son of man is betrayed! good were it for that man if he had never been born.
25. Then Judas, which betrayed him, answered and said, Master, is it I? He said unto him, Thou hast said.	
26. And as they were eating, Jesus took bread, and blessed it, and brake it, and gave it to the disciples, and said, Take, eat; this	22. And as they did eat, Jesus took bread, and blessed, and brake it, and gave to them, and said, Take, eat: this is my body. 23.

is my body. 27. And he took the
cup, and gave thanks, and gave it
to them, saying, Drink ye all of it:
28. For this is my blood, the (blood)
of the new testament, which is shed
for many for the remission of sins.

29. But I say unto you, I will
not drink henceforth of this fruit
of the vine, until that day when
I drink it new with you in my
Father's kingdom.

30. And when they had sung
an hymn, they went out into the
mount of Olives. 31. Then saith
Jesus unto them, All ye shall be
offended because of me this night:
for it is written, I will smite the
shepherd, and the sheep of the
flock shall be scattered abroad.
32. But after I am risen again, I
will go before you into Galilee.
33. Peter answered and said unto
him, Though all men shall be
offended because of thee, yet will I
never be offended. 34. Jesus said
unto him, Verily I say unto thee,
That this night, before the cock
crow, thou shalt deny me thrice.
35. Peter said unto him, Though I
should die with thee, yet will I not
deny thee. Likewise also said all
the disciples.

And he took the cup, and when he
had given thanks, he gave it to
them: and they all drank of it.
24. And he said unto them, This is
my blood (the blood) of the new
testament, which is shed for many.

25. Verily, I say unto you, I
will drink no more of the fruit of
the vine, until that day that I
drink it new in the kingdom of
God.

26. And when they had sung an
hymn, they went out into the mount
of Olives. 27. And Jesus saith
unto them, All ye shall be offended
because of me this night: for it is
written, I will smite the shepherd,
and the sheep shall be scattered.
28. But after that I am risen, I
will go before you into Galilee.
29. But Peter said unto him, Although all shall be offended, yet
will not I. 30. And Jesus saith
unto him, Verily I say unto thee,
That this day, even in this night,
before the cock crow twice, thou
shalt deny me thrice. 31. But he
spake the more vehemently (Gr.
μᾶλλον ἐκ περισσοῦ): If I should
die with thee, I will not deny thee
in any wise. Likewise also said
they all.

LUKE xxii. 14–39.

And when the hour was come,
he sat down, and the twelve apostles with him. 15. And he said
unto them, With desire I have desired to eat this passover with you
before I suffer: 16. For I say unto
you, I will not any more eat thereof, until it be fulfilled in the king-

JOHN xiii. 1–38.

Now, before the feast of the passover, when Jesus knew that his
hour was come that he should depart out of this world unto the
Father, having loved his own
which were in the world, he loved
them unto the end. 2. And supper being *begun*,[1] (the devil having

[1] Gr. τοῦ δείπνου γενομένου, which in our translation is wrongly rendered, *supper being ended.* It was in the nature of things, as well as according to the known custom of the Jews, that such washings did not *follow*, but *precede* the taking of food. Bengel has remarked on this passage: "Γενομένου, *cum fieret.* Pedilavium sub initium cœnæ." Compare v. 4 and 12.

dom of God. 17. And he took
the cup, and gave thanks, and said,
Take this, and divide it among
yourselves: 18. For I say unto
you, I will not drink of the fruit of
the vine, until the kingdom of God
shall come.

now put into the heart of Judas
Iscariot, Simon's son, to betray
him,) 3. Jesus knowing that the
Father had given all things into
his hands, and that he was come
from God, and went to God; 4.
He riseth from supper, and laid
aside his garments; and took a
towel, and girded himself. 5.
After that he poureth water into a
bason, and began to wash the disciples' feet, and to wipe them with
the towel wherewith he was girded.
6. Then cometh he to Simon Peter:
and Peter said unto him, Lord,
dost thou wash my feet? 7. Jesus
answered and said unto him, What
I do thou knowest not now; but
thou shalt know hereafter. 8.
Peter saith unto him, Thou shalt
never wash my feet. Jesus answered
him, If I wash thee not, thou hast
no part with me. 9. Simon Peter
saith unto him, Lord, not my feet
only, but also my hands and my
head. 10. Jesus saith to him, He
that is washed needeth not, save
to wash his feet, but is clean every
whit: and ye are clean, but not
all. 11. For he knew who should
betray him; therefore said he, Ye
are not all clean.

12. So, after he had washed
their feet, and had taken his garments, and was set down again, he
said unto them, Know ye what I
have done to you? 13. Ye call
me Master and Lord: and ye say
well; for so I am. 14. If I then,
your Lord and Master, have washed
your feet, ye also ought to wash
one another's feet. 15. For I have
given you an example, that ye
should do as I have done to you.
16. Verily, verily, I say unto you,
The servant is not greater than his
lord; neither he that is sent greater
than he that sent him. 17. If ye

know these things, happy are ye
if ye do them. 18. I speak not of
you all; I know whom I have
chosen: but that the scripture
may be fulfilled, He that eateth
bread with me hath lifted up his
heel against me. 19. Now I tell
you before it come, that, when it is
come to pass, ye may believe that
I am (he). 20. Verily, verily, I
say unto you, He that receiveth
whomsoever I send, receiveth me;
and he that receiveth me, receiveth
him that sent me.

19. And he took bread, and
gave thanks, and brake it, and
gave unto them, saying, This is my
body which is given for you: this
do in remembrance of me.

20. Likewise also the cup after
supper, saying, This cup is the
new testament in my blood, which
is shed for you. 21. But, behold,
the hand of him that betrayeth me
is with me on the table. 22. And
truly the Son of man goeth, as it
was determined: but woe unto that
man by whom he is betrayed! 23.
And they began to inquire among
themselves, which of them it was
that should do this thing.

21. When Jesus had thus said,
he was troubled in spirit, and testified, and said, Verily, verily, I
say unto you, That one of you shall
betray me.

22. Then the disciples looked
one on another, doubting of whom
he spake. 23. Now there was
leaning on Jesus' bosom one of his
disciples, whom Jesus loved. 24.
Simon Peter therefore beckoned to
him, that he should ask who it
should be of whom he spake. 25.
He then, lying on Jesus' breast,
saith unto him, Lord, who is it?

24. And there was also a strife
among them, which of them should be
accounted the greatest. 25. And he
said unto them, The kings of the Gentiles exercise lordship over them;
and they that exercise authority
upon them are called benefactors.
26. But ye shall not be so: but he
that is greatest among you, let him
be as the younger; and he that is
chief, as he that doth serve. 27.
For whether is greater, he that sitteth at meat, or he that serveth?
Is not he that sitteth at meat? but
I am among you as he that serveth.
28. Ye are they that have con-

26. Jesus answered, He it is to
whom I shall give a sop, when I
have dipped it. And when he had
dipped the sop, he gave it to Judas
Iscariot, the son of Simon. 27.
And after the sop Satan entered
into him. Then said Jesus unto
him, That thou doest, do quickly.
28. Now no man at the table knew
for what intent he spake this unto
him. 29. For some of them thought,
because Judas had the bag, that
Jesus had said unto him, Buy those
things that we have need of against
the feast; or, that he should give
something to the poor. 30. He

tinued with me in my temptations.
29. And I appoint unto you a
kingdom, as my Father hath appointed unto me; 30. That ye
may eat and drink at my table in
my kingdom, and sit on thrones,
judging the twelve tribes of Israel.
31. And the Lord said, Simon,
Simon, behold, Satan hath desired
to have you, that he may sift you
as wheat: 32. But I have prayed
for thee, that thy faith fail not:
and when thou art converted,
strengthen thy brethren. 33. And
he said unto him, Lord, I am ready
to go with thee, both into prison,
and to death. 34. And he said, I
tell thee, Peter, the cock shall not
crow this day, before that thou
shalt thrice deny that thou knowest
me. 35. And he said unto them,
When I sent you without purse,
and scrip, and shoes, lacked ye
any thing? And they said, Nothing. 36. Then said he unto
them, But now, he that hath a
purse, let him take it, and likewise
his scrip: and he that hath no
sword, let him sell his garment,
and buy one. 37. For I say unto
you, That this that is written must
yet be accomplished in me, And he
was reckoned among the transgressors: for the things concerning me
have an end. 38. And they said,
Lord, behold, here are two swords.
And he said unto them, It is
enough. 39. And he came out,
and went, as he was wont, to the
mount of Olives; and his disciples
also followed him.

then, having received the sop, went
immediately out; and it was night.
31. Therefore, when he was gone
out, Jesus said, Now is the Son of
man glorified, and God is glorified
in him. 32. If God be glorified
in him, God shall also glorify him
in himself, and shall straightway
glorify him. 33. Little children,
yet a little while I am with you.
Ye shall seek me: and as I said
unto the Jews, Whither I go, ye
cannot come; so now I say to you.
34. A new commandment I give
unto you, That ye love one another; as I have loved you, that
ye also love one another. 35. By
this shall all men know that ye are
my disciples, if ye have love one
to another. 36. Simon Peter said
unto him, Lord, whither goest
thou? Jesus answered him, Whither
I go, thou canst not follow me now;
but thou shalt follow me afterwards. 37. Peter said unto him,
Lord, why cannot I follow thee
now? I will lay down my life for
thy sake. 38. Jesus answered
him, Wilt thou lay down thy life
for my sake? Verily, verily, I say
unto thee, The cock shall not crow,
till thou hast denied me thrice.

The connexion and succession of the various things that were done, and discourses and sayings that were uttered, all as they occurred at the last Paschal supper of the Lord with his disciples, could not be traced with any clearness from our Evangelists when placed in parallel columns, were it not that the plan of St Luke supplies us with the clue that enables us to do so. Following him with our eye constantly directed to the succession of the main events, we find placed before us one consistent whole, which afterwards receives all needful completeness from the addition of new details by St John, as well as from the grand leading facts mentioned by St Matthew and St Mark. Consequently let us not leave out of sight, especially at *this* part of the Gospel history, the line traced by St Luke.

I. All the three synoptical Gospels (Matth. v. 20, Mark v. 17 and 18, Luke v. 14) are quite at one in their statement of the precise time when our Lord first sat down with the twelve; while St John (v. 1), after determining that time with relation to the feast, directs our regards to higher particulars: our Lord's *knowledge* of all that was then about to happen—his leaving this world to go to the Father—his love for his own—his loving them to the end.

II. After this we find in St Luke, given in the most evident manner, the solemn opening of the feast with these words, preserved by him alone, pronounced immediately after the guests had seated themselves at the table (v. 15 and 16): *With desire I have desired to eat this passover with you before I suffer: for I say unto you, I will not any more eat thereof, until it be fulfilled in the kingdom of God.* After this he takes up a cup and passes it round among the guests (17), adding a declaration to the like effect (v. 18). This *first* cup is that with which the Jews to this very day bless the opening of the Sabbath and of festivals (*kidousch*). It must be carefully distinguished from the cup *after* the supper, of which particular mention is made in the exact narrative of St Luke (v. 20); while St Matthew, and along with him St Mark, in conformity with their less developed manner of exhibiting things, make no positive distinction between these two cups, and on that account (Matth. 29, Mark 25) make no mention of the words pronounced by our Lord on passing round the first cup, until after the institution of the Lord's Supper.

III. It is in St John alone that we find what immediately followed this solemn commencement of the repast. The supper having thus commenced (for this, as we have seen, ought to be the rendering in his Gospel of the words *τοῦ δείπνου γενομένου*), the Master, before breaking bread, rises from his place at the table, and performs that action, so sublime in its humility and its love, which we find described here in all its details. These details, as well as the main fact itself (v. 1–19), were pre-eminently in their proper place in this fourth Gospel. We find in it that depth of feeling, that emblematic language, that sacred mysteriousness, which particularly strike us among the characteristics of the Apostle St John.[1] In accordance also with this, we find the expressive remark that Jesus, when he girded himself to wash his disciples' feet, *knew that the Father had given all things into his hands, and that he was come from God and went to God* (v. 3). Here too, accordingly, it is in the full consciousness of his divine greatness that Jesus stoops to perform the humblest and most self-abasing human service. Immediately afterwards, the warmth and vivacity of Peter's character come strongly out in the few words that pass between him and his Master (v. 6–9). At the same time (v. 7), we have in a short but very significant sentence those

[1] Page 233, &c.

words, which may be applied by the believer with so much comfort to himself in a great variety of circumstances: *What I do thou knowest not now; but thou shalt know hereafter;*—further on in the proceedings (v. 19), we have the true and entire purification of the inner man powerfully pointed out to us under the external emblem of the washing of the feet. None of the three synoptical Gospels had previously mentioned this solemn and most significant action; but it serves in the most glorious manner to explain what St Luke records afterwards (v. 24–27) on the occasion of the dispute among the disciples about which should be accounted the greatest. The words, *I am among you as he that serveth,* in our third Evangelist (v. 27), find a striking explanation in the action which was to be recorded for the first time at a subsequent period by St John, while in *his* Gospel the practical application of the divine example *immediately* follows (v. 12–17).

IV. St Matthew (v. 21), and St Mark (v. 18), make the supper commence immediately with this exclamation of Jesus: *Verily I say unto you, One of you shall betray me.* In this it is manifest that they have quite reversed the historical order which is afterwards observed by St Luke, with whom this prediction does not occur until after the institution of the New Covenant. It is, accordingly, in consequence of that transposition of the historical order, that St Mark and St Matthew repeat (Matth. 21, 26), no less than twice, the words, *As they did eat,* while in St Luke all follows its simple and regular course. He makes the institution of the supper of the New Covenant follow immediately after the commencement of the Paschal supper: *This is my body.* Here, again, it is the Israelitic custom which our Lord observes, while he at the same time sanctifies and elevates it as the seal of the covenant of a new economy. Therefore, also, it is, that St Luke is the only one who remarks that the institution of the cup, closely as it was connected with the broken bread, did not take place (always according to the manner of the Israelites, who concluded their repast with a cup of thanksgiving) till after the lapse of such an interval as the nature of things required (v. 20): *Likewise, also, the cup* AFTER SUPPER, *saying, This cup is the new testament in my blood,* &c.

We have already shewn the agreement between the institution of the Holy Supper, as we find it recorded in St Luke's Gospel, and St Paul's apostolical explanation on that point.[1] The difference, on the other hand, between the terms employed by the third and the first two Gospel writers is evident. St Matthew (v. 26) adds from recollection, as an Apostle, the words *Take, eat;* in which he is followed by St Mark (v. 22). That most important injunction, delivered on our Lord's handing the cup to the disciples, DRINK YE ALL OF IT, occurs in St Matthew alone (v. 27). In St Mark (v. 23) we find only the compliance with that injunction: AND THEY ALL DRANK OF IT. That which St Luke and St Paul record directly and concisely: *This cup is the new testament in my blood,* St Matthew, (v. 28) and St Mark (v. 24), give with a sort of explanatory repetition: *This is my blood (the blood) of the new testament.* After this, the only thing that St Luke has in common with his predecessors here, in writing the Gospel history, and not in common with St Paul (v. 12), is the insertion: *which is shed* FOR YOU (in St Matthew and in St Mark in an explanatory and general manner: FOR MANY). Finally, St Matthew further follows this up with

[1] See page 169.

these important words as an apostolical explanation : *for the remission of sins.* It is only in St Luke and St Paul that we find anew that other very important expression : *do this in remembrance of me* (Gr. *in order to* CALL *me to remembrance*, εἰς τὴν ἐμὴν ἀνάμνησιν).[1]

In St John the institution of the Holy Supper finds no record. He evidently assumes its being sufficiently known by means of the three other Evangelists, the epistle of St Paul to the Corinthians, and the long established usage of the Churches. Nevertheless, he has given us elsewhere in his Gospel, in a very detailed manner, the essential features of the ordinance in its simple and sublime emblematic signification. The whole of that discourse delivered by Jesus, in which he declares that he himself is *the bread of life* (ch. vi. 48–53), and that *whoso eateth his flesh and drinketh his blood, hath eternal life* (v. 54), is it not *in oral words* what the Lord's Supper represents to us, and gives to us, *in visible action?*

Now follows anew, in the order restored by St Luke, the announcement from the Lord's own mouth of the impending treason to be perpetrated by one of the twelve. All four Gospels are on this point remarkably full and varied. But let us first account for the transposition of this circumstance in the narratives of the first two Evangelists. The reason for it must be sought in the peculiar character which we have already remarked in St Matthew, who, both in virtue of his apostolic character, and owing to his close adherence to Old Testament prophecies, attaches particular importance to that treason by one belonging to the very circle of the Apostles, and to the foretelling of it in the psalm of the Prophet. Here St

[1] Ἀνάμνησις has the *active* meaning implied in it, and is carefully to be distinguished μνημόσυνον, which we find in Matth. ch. xxvi. 13.

Mark closely follows his predecessor. St Luke is the first who ceases to adopt an arrangement flowing from St Matthew's individual point of view, and gives us that which is purely historical in its stead.

In the details of this part of the narrative, St Mark (v. 18) gives an expressive extension of the words *one of you,* employed by St Matthew; making them, *One of you* WHICH EATETH WITH ME, *shall betray me.* St Luke, in immediate connexion with the blessing of the cup, expresses the same thing in different terms (v. 21): *The hand of him that betrayeth me is with me on the table.* This he follows up (v. 15) with what occupies an *anterior* place in the Gospels of his two predecessors, *And truly the Son of Man goeth as it was* DETERMINED;[1] in St Matthew (v. 24) and in St Mark (v. 21), *as it is* WRITTEN *of him,* (presenting a further powerful testimony to the Divine certainty and infallible truth of Scripture). What St Matthew and St Mark afterwards intend by that fearful expression: *It had been good for that man that he had not been born,* St Luke expresses in more concise terms: *Woe unto that man!* The horror of the disciples on our Lord's announcing that there was treason in the midst of them, is recorded in the liveliest manner by St Mark, by repeating the question in St Matthew (v. 22): *Is it I?* The latter distinguishes himself by expressly recording that question as put by Judas himself, and the answer also given to him by our Lord (v. 25). Here St Luke is very concise, and relates the matter in a summary manner (v. 23).

Then, again, we find St John inserting entirely fresh details of deep interest, and highly characteristic. In his Gospel alone do we read of an interchange of signs and

[1] Gr. κατὰ τὸ ὡρισμένον.

talk (v. 22–26) between St Peter and the beloved disciple; between the latter and his Lord, who, in giving the sop to Judas, intimates confidentially to St John *who* the traitor was. St Matthew (v. 23), and St Mark (v. 20), had given a more general expression to what was said by our Lord in these terms, *He that* DIPPETH *with me in the dish.* The prophecy, *He that* EATETH BREAD *with me, hath lifted up his heel against me* (xiii. 18), now becomes all the more salient in St John. After that there come some further details, equally important and altogether new (v. 27–35): the significant words of the Lord to Judas; the misapprehension of his meaning into which his disciples so naturally fell; the departure of the traitor, with the impressive remark, *and it was night* (v. 30); the Saviour's exclamation after his departure; his recalling what he had once said *to the Jews* about his own going to the Father; his exhortation to his disciples that they should love one another.

St Luke, in the meanwhile, conducts us to another most interesting incident at our Lord's table (v. 24–30). The disciples, now as ever, forgetful hearers and witnesses of their Master's most recent instructions by word and deed, could not, even at this solemn scene, relinquish their old strife about precedency. This gives our Lord occasion to refer to his washing of the disciples' feet at the commencement of the meal; a reference which St John (v. 12–17) records, as it were, in one breath with the fact itself of the foot-washing. But St Luke further follows this reprimand with what serves at the same time to cheer and encourage the Apostles (v. 28–30): *Ye are they who have continued with me in my temptations: and I appoint unto you a kingdom,* &c.

VII. At the table of the last supper Jesus not only

predicts the treachery of the avaricious Judas, but also the denial of him by the loyal St Peter. St Matthew, and along with him St Mark, have anew placed this part out of the historical order, to which it is forthwith restored, as before, by St Luke and St John. This transposition in the first two Gospels naturally arises from the connexion of ideas which St Matthew involuntarily causes to proceed onwards from the cup of the Israelitic thanksgivings (v. 29), to the no less Israelitic singing of a hymn at the close of the Paschal supper (v. 30). He then, as it were, retraces his steps, agreeably with the greater latitude he takes in his narrative, and goes back to an important detail—the prediction of the denial (v. 31–35). St Mark, who here, as elsewhere, is at no pains to re-establish the historical order, follows his predecessor on this occasion almost step for step. Only he enriches his statement with the striking detail (v. 30), that the cock shall crow TWICE.[1] And by the energetic expression he employs: *the more vehemently*, he puts in strong relief the infatuation of St Peter, from whose mouth he must have had this detail, at that critical moment of his life. The detail that follows alike in St Matthew (v. 35), and in St Mark (v. 31), is further remarkable here: *Likewise also said all the disciples.*

St Luke (v. 31–39) records the prediction at its true historical place, that is to say, *before* the departure to the mount of Olives; and, consequently, while they were still at the Paschal supper. But he also gives the prediction itself with details, in which Jesus especially reveals himself in his love, in his faithfulness, in his intercession (v. 31, 32): *First*, we have the words: *Simon, Simon*, reiterated; and in this the seriousness of the warning is

[1] Compare afterwards, Mark xiv. 68–72.

mingled with the blessed assurance of the never-failing love of God.[1] After this we have the declaration of Jesus: *I have prayed for thee that thy faith fail not;* thus, we perceive, the ardent Peter still *believed,* and his fall was the result of weakness, not of unbelief in the sense of falling from the faith; finally, we have the exhortation: *Therefore, when thou art converted* (properly, *shalt have returned*—Gr. ἐπιστρέψας—from thy fall) *strengthen thy brethren.*

VIII. Immediately after this, St Luke, and he alone, further gives us the Lord's powerful exhortation to enter on the spiritual conflict with the abnegation of all things (v. 35, 36)—the reminiscence of the prophecy of Isaiah: *He was numbered with the transgressors*—and, in general, of the prophecies of the New Testament concerning the Christ (v. 37); finally (v. 38), the misconception formed by the disciples of our Lord's object, when he exhorted them to buy *a sword.* This last particular explains to us how it happened that shortly thereafter St Peter could attack with a sword the servant of the high priest in the garden. (Luke xxii. 49, 50.)

IX. Finally, there follows upon this in the three synoptical Evangelists, the departure from the Paschal feast to the mount of Olives, after what St Matthew (v. 30) and St Mark (v. 20) had previously mentioned of the singing of the *Hallel,* or hymn composed of several psalms, and still practised to this day among the Jews.

St John dwells longer on the narrative of the Paschal supper. In accordance with the character of his whole

[1] The repetition of the name in the Lord's address always indicates a peculiar love to the person addressed, whether in the Old or in the New Testament: *Abraham, Abraham!* (Gen. xxii. 11); *Moses, Moses!* (Exodus iii. 4); *Samuel, Samuel!* (1 Samuel iii. 10); *Martha, Martha!* (Luke x. 41); *Saul, Saul!* (Acts of the Apostles, ix. 4).

Gospel, here again he gives us in great fulness the discourses held by the Lord with his disciples. Much of importance that was spoken by these we find recorded here; such as what was said by Thomas, by Philip, and by Judas *not Iscariot* (chap. xiv.) With a single word (xiv. 31) he shews us the Saviour rising from the table; and gives us thereafter (xv. xvi.) the discourses held on the way to the mount of Olives. Finally, at the close of these discourses we find the prayer addressed by Jesus to his Father (xvii.), to which we shall shortly return. The connexion (xviii. 1) seems to indicate that that prayer was uttered during some moments of repose *before crossing the brook Cedron.* The passing of that brook is, in some sort, the decisive point *at which our Lord's passion commences.*

Thus, then, while we distinguish instead of confounding the different lines followed by the four Evangelists, and their different objects, the succession of words and of actions at the last Paschal supper of the Lord becomes clear to us: 1. The moment of sitting down at the table (noted by the four Evangelists); 2. The opening with the blessing of the cup (by St Luke alone); 3. The washing of the feet of the Apostles (by St John alone); 4. The breaking of the bread and the blessing of the cup, or that act of the Saviour's Divine authority which transferred the feast of the Jewish Passover for all the ages that were to come, into the Holy Supper of the New Testament (by all the synoptical Evangelists); 5. The prediction of treachery, the agitation of, the questioning by, the disciples, with our Lord's replies which were the consequence thereof (by the four Evangelists); 6. The dispute among the Apostles about precedency, and the appeal made by Jesus to the example that he himself had given in the washing of their feet (by St Luke alone); 7. The discourses that followed between Jesus and the twelve (by St John); 8. The prediction of the denial of Jesus by St Peter (by all the Evangelists); 9. The announcement of the approaching spiritual conflict, and the accomplishment of the prophecies (by St Luke); 10. The singing of the hymn (by St Matthew and St Mark); 11. The discourse by the way; together with, 12. The Lord's intercessory prayer (by St John); 13. The passing over of the brook Cedron (also by St John).

THE AGONY IN GETHSEMANE.

MATTH. xxvi. 36–46.

Then cometh Jesus with them
unto a place called Gethsemane,
and saith unto the disciples, Sit ye
here, while I go and pray yonder. 37. And he took with him
Peter and the two sons of Zebedee,
and began to be sorrowful and
very heavy. 38. Then saith he
unto them, My soul is exceeding
sorrowful, even unto death: tarry
ye here, and watch with me.

39. And he went a little farther,
and fell on his face, and prayed, saying, O my Father, if it be possible,
let this cup pass from me: nevertheless not as I will, but as thou wilt.
40. And he cometh unto the disciples, and findeth them asleep, and
saith unto Peter, What! could ye
not watch with me one hour? 41.
Watch and pray, that ye enter not
into temptation: the spirit indeed
is willing, but the flesh is weak.
42. He went away again the second
time, and prayed, saying, O my
Father, if this cup may not pass
away from me, except I drink it,
thy will be done. 43. And he
came and found them asleep again:

MARK xiv. 32–42.

And they came to a place which
was named Gethsemane: and he
saith to his disciples, Sit ye here,
while I shall pray. 33. And he
taketh with him Peter, and James,
and John, and began to be sore
amazed, and to be very heavy;
34. And saith unto them, My soul
is exceeding sorrowful unto death:
tarry ye here, and watch.

35. And he went forward a little, and fell on the ground, and
prayed that, if it were possible, the
hour might pass from him. 36.
And he said, Abba, Father, all
things are possible unto thee; take
away this cup from me: nevertheless not what I will, but what thou
wilt. 37. And he cometh, and
findeth them sleeping, and saith
unto Peter, Simon, sleepest thou?
couldest not thou watch one hour?
38. Watch ye and pray, lest ye
enter into temptation: the spirit
truly is ready, but the flesh is weak.
39. And again he went away, and
prayed, and spake the same words.
40. And when he returned, he found

for their eyes were heavy. 44. And he left them, and went away again, and prayed the third time, saying the same words.

45. Then cometh he to his disciples, and saith unto them, Sleep on now, and take your rest: behold, the hour is at hand, and the Son of man is betrayed into the hands of sinners. 46. Rise, let us be going: behold, he is at hand that doth betray me.

them asleep again; (for their eyes were heavy;) neither wist they what to answer him.

41. And he cometh the third time, and saith unto them, Sleep on now, and take your rest: it is enough, the hour is come; behold, the Son of man is betrayed into the hands of sinners. 42. Rise up, let us go; lo, he that betrayeth me is at hand.

LUKE xxii. 40–45.

And when he was at the place, he said unto them, Pray that ye enter not into temptation. 41. And he was withdrawn from them about a stone's cast, and kneeled down, and prayed, 42. Saying, Father, if thou be willing, remove this cup from me: nevertheless, not my will, but thine, be done. 43. And there appeared an angel unto him from heaven, strengthening him. 44. And being in an agony (Gr. γενόμενος ἐν ἀγωνίᾳ), he prayed more earnestly (Gr. ἐκτενέστερον): and his sweat was as it were great drops of blood falling down to the ground. 45. And when he rose up from prayer, and was come to his disciples, he found them sleeping for sorrow, 46. And said unto them, Why sleep ye? rise and pray, lest ye enter into temptation.

JOHN xviii. 1–2.

When Jesus had spoken these words, he went forth with his disciples over the brook Cedron, where was a garden, into which he entered, and his disciples.

2. And Judas also, which betrayed him, knew the place; for Jesus oft-times resorted thither with his disciples.

The synoptical Gospels alone record the anguish of soul endured by our Lord in Gethsemane. St Matthew (v. 36) and St Mark (v. 32) agree, with the exception of a slight modification in the style. St Luke is here in general more concise ; at the very commencement (v. 40) he gives a succinct summary of the words of his two predecessors. It is remarkable, however, that he makes mention, not so much of the Saviour's expressed intention of engaging in secret prayer, as, on the other hand, of that exhortation *to the disciples* which his predecessors have not recorded until further on in the course of the narrative (Matth. v. 41 ; Mark v. 32) : *Pray that ye enter not into temptation.*

St Luke, moreover, describes the anguish of the Saviour's soul at a later point of time (v. 44). St Matthew and St Mark do it immediately (Matth. 37, 38 ; Mark 33, 34), almost in the same terms; those of the latter again, according to custom, being more forcible ; instead of, *to be saddened* (λυπεῖσθαι), as in his predecessor, he has it, *to be sore amazed,* properly, *seized with terror* (ἐκθαμβεῖσθαι).

Each of the three Evangelists expresses, after his own manner, how Jesus prostrated himself in prayer ; St Matthew has, according to oriental usage (v. 35), *Fell* ON HIS FACE *and prayed;* St Mark (v. 35), *Fell on the ground;* St Luke has simply, *Knelt down.* But he alone, with the exactness of an historian, makes mention of the Lord's being quite alone during his prayer, and the distance (*a stone's cast*) at which he departed from his disciples for that purpose.

In relating our Lord's thrice-repeated prayer, St Matthew, and after him St Mark, enter most into detail. In accordance with a peculiarity which we have already remarked in the latter,[1] previous to giving the very words of the prayer (v. 36), he gives the gist of its purport, (v. 35) : *He prayed* THAT *if it were possible the hour might*

[1] See page 101.

pass from him. And he said, &c. In the prayer itself he puts first the Aramæan *Abba,*[1] of which the exclamation, *Father!* is the translation (Ἀββᾶ ὁ πατὴρ). In St Matthew (v. 39), the prayer is given more in the form of a wish, *That this cup pass from me* (παρελθέτω); in St Mark (v. 36) and St Luke (v. 42) we find it in the form of a direct address to the Father, TAKE *away this cup from me; if thou be willing,* REMOVE *the cup from me.* The exhortation to watchfulness is addressed to all the disciples in all the three synoptical Evangelists, but in St Matthew (v. 40) more particularly to St Peter,—in St Mark (v. 37), with the introduction, too, of his name in that familiar and tender address of our Lord: *Simon, sleepest thou? Couldest thou not watch with me one hour?*

To the sleep of the disciples, as mentioned by St Matthew, St Mark again adds a touching detail: *Neither wist they what to answer him.* St Luke, the physician, explains this sleep more fully (v. 45): *He found them sleeping* FOR SORROW.[2]

But the Evangelist, who unites the historian and physician in his person, interests us most of all where he touches on two most striking and significant circumstances in the agony of Jesus on this occasion (v. 43), *the angel that appeared to him when wrestling in prayer, and strengthened him,* and that increase of strength only inducing a more violent agony, so that *his sweat was as it were great drops of blood.*

In the words of Jesus to the disciples after this internal preparatory struggle was over, *Sleep on now and take your rest: behold, the hour is at hand* (Matth. v. 45), the addition of the simple *it is enough* (Gr. ἀπέχει) in St

[1] See page 89. [2] See page 147.

Mark (v. 41) has a peculiar force in it; as also the mere transposition of the words of St Matthew (v. 46), *He is at hand that doth betray me,* in Mark (v. 42) *He that betrayeth me is at hand.*[1]

Let now us proceed to St John. He has given us only the moment of our Lord's entrance into Gethsemane (v. 1); anon (v. 2) he explains how Judas knew with so much certainty the place where the Master could be seized. But of the agony of our Lord's soul he says not a word. He must have supposed the details on that point sufficiently known by means of his three predecessors. Afterwards, however, we have evidently a reminiscence of their narrative in his Gospel (xviii. 11), where the Saviour says, *The cup which my Father hath given me, shall I not drink it?*

One word more, retrospectively, on the intercessory prayer, as given in the seventeenth chapter of St John. How are we to account for the fact that there (that is, before the passing of the brook Cedron) the Saviour's offering up of himself as a sacrifice, is represented not only as a *settled purpose*, but even as to be viewed as a *fully accomplished act*, while in the synoptical Evangelists, the Saviour wrestles even to blood in praying that the cup of suffering might be taken from him? It is to be referred to one of St John's peculiarities—a peculiarity which he has in common with the prophets of the Old Testament—that of speaking of the *future*, as it has been predetermined in the counsel of God and in the Scripture, as something *that has already happened.* Such, precisely, is the spirit and the meaning of the prayer which we find recorded and paraphrased by him, as offered up at the

[1] See page 99.

pause that took place before passing the brook Cedron. In that prayer Jesus looks upon himself as *having already accomplished all things,* because from a divine certainty he knew that he *was about to accomplish all things.* Hence those expressions : *And now* I AM *no more in the world* (xviii. 11);—*While* I WAS *with them in the world* (v. 12);—I HAVE *finished the work which thou gavest me to do* (v. 4). Is it not as if here we were listening already to the great High Priest of our profession, in his abiding character of intercessor for his people in heaven, *after* the accomplishment of his sacrifice on earth? Well, then, there is nowise any contradiction between this sublime point of view peculiar to the last apostolic and prophetical Evangelist, from which he shews us the Lord *before* his passion as already triumphing in the spirit, in virtue of his perfect knowledge of the future, and what the synoptic Gospels describe to us of the agony in Gethsemane. In the intercessory prayer recorded by St John, we have the Lord placed before us in his *divine* omniscience ; in the synoptical Gospels we see his holy *humanity* displaying a legitimate aversion to death as the wages of sin which he had not committed,—an aversion which soon gives place to the most perfect submission, on the part of the Lamb without spot and blemish, to the will of the Father and his own predetermined counsel to accept the expiatory passion.

THE APPREHENSION OF JESUS.

MATTH. xxvi. 47–56.

And while he yet spake, lo, Judas, one of the twelve, came, and with him a great multitude with swords and staves, from the chief priests and elders of the people.

48. Now he that betrayed him

MARK xiv. 43.

And immediately, while he yet spake, cometh Judas, one of the twelve, and with him a great multitude, with swords and staves, from the chief priests, and the scribes, and the elders.

44. And he that betrayed him

gave them a sign (σημεῖον), saying, Whomsoever I shall kiss, that same is he; hold him fast.	had given them a token (σύσσημον), saying, Whomsoever I shall kiss, that same is he; take him, and lead him away safely (ἀσφαλῶς, well secured).
49. And forthwith he came to Jesus, and said, Hail, Master (Rabbi); and kissed him.	45. And as soon as he was come, he goeth straightway to him, and saith, Master, Master (Rabbi, Rabbi); and kissed him.
50. And Jesus said unto him, Friend, wherefore art thou come? Then came they, and laid hands on Jesus, and took him.	46. And they laid their hands on him, and took him.
51. And, behold, one of them that were with Jesus stretched out his hand, and drew his sword, and struck a servant of the high priest, and smote off his ear.	47. And one of them that stood by drew a sword, and smote a servant of the high priest, and cut off his ear.
52. Then said Jesus unto him, Put up again thy sword into his place: for all they that take the sword shall perish with the sword. 53. Thinkest thou that I cannot now pray to my Father, and he shall presently give me more than twelve legions of angels? 54. But how then shall the scriptures be fulfilled, that thus it must be?	
55. In that same hour said Jesus to the multitudes, Are ye come out, as against a thief, with swords and staves for to take me? I sat daily with you teaching in the temple, and ye laid no hold on me. 56. But all this was done, that the scriptures of the prophets might be fulfilled. Then all the disciples forsook him, and fled.	48. And Jesus answered and said unto them, Are ye come out, as against a thief, with swords and with staves to take me? 49. I was daily with you in the temple teaching, and ye took me not: but the scriptures must be fulfilled. 50. And they all forsook him, and fled.
	51. And there followed him a certain young man, having a linen cloth cast about his naked body; and the young men laid hold on him: 52. And he left the linen cloth, and fled from them naked.
LUKE xxii. 47–52.	JOHN xviii. 3–12.
And while he yet spake, behold a multitude, and he that was called	Judas, then, having received a band of men and officers from the

Judas, one of the twelve, went
before them, and drew near unto
Jesus to kiss him.

48. But Jesus said unto him,
Judas, betrayest thou the Son of
man with a kiss?

49. When they which were about
him saw what would follow, they
said unto him, Lord, shall we smite
with the sword? 50. And one of
them smote a servant of the high
priest, and cut off his right ear.

51. And Jesus answered and
said, Suffer ye thus far. And he
touched his ear, and healed him.

52. Then Jesus said unto the
chief priests, and captains of the
temple, and the elders, which were
come to him, Be ye come out, as
against a thief, with swords and
staves? 53. When I was daily
with you in the temple, ye stretched
forth no hands against me: but
this is your hour, and the power of
darkness.

chief priests and Pharisees, cometh
thither with lanterns and torches
and weapons.

4. Jesus therefore, knowing all
things that should come upon him,
went forth, and said unto them,
Whom seek ye? 5. They answered
him, Jesus of Nazareth. Jesus
saith unto them, I am he. And
Judas also, which betrayed him,
stood with them. 6. As soon
then as he had said unto them,
I am he, they went backward, and
fell to the ground. 7. Then asked
he them again, Whom seek ye?
And they said, Jesus of Nazareth.
8. Jesus answered, I have told you
that I am he: If therefore ye seek
me, let these go their way: 9.
That the saying might be fulfilled,
which he spake, Of them which
thou gavest me have I lost none.

10. Then Simon Peter having a
sword, drew it, and smote the
high priest's servant, and cut off
his right ear. The servant's name
was Malchus.

11. Then said Jesus unto Peter,
Put up thy sword into the sheath:
The cup which my Father hath
given me, shall I not drink it?

12. Then the band and the captain, and officers of the Jews, took
Jesus, and bound him.

Throughout the whole of this narrative, St Matthew again lays the foundation on which the Evangelists that follow proceed to build. It is he alone who commences here (v. 47) with that *lo!* so natural to an eyewitness, and of such frequent recurrence in the narratives of the Bible. In like manner, he alone records those words which might so well have caused Judas to pause in his horrid purpose: FRIEND, *wherefore art thou come?* (p. 50); but evidently without observing the order of the succession of facts, since they were certainly uttered not *after* the traitor's kiss, but upon his approach. St Luke, on the other hand, has preserved for us (v. 48) those still more severe words pronounced by Jesus *after* the kiss: JUDAS, *betrayest thou the Son of Man with a kiss?* It is St Matthew alone who has recorded, or transferred to this particular moment, the words which we read here, entirely in the spirit of the Old Testament and of the Sermon on the Mount (v. 52), *For all they that take the sword shall perish with the sword.*—The *twelve legions of angels*, in the same Evangelist (v. 53), evidently bear anew the Israelitic character.—The *fulfilling of the Scriptures* is introduced with a sort of prolixity here (v. 54), and afterwards (v. 56), seeing that we find it but once in St Mark (v. 49), while St Luke and St John omit the direct mention of it. Here, anew, we find in St Mark his characteristic additions and accentuations. Among the enemies of Jesus he expressly names the *Scribes.* We not only recognise the language of the soldier in the use of the word, *watchword* (σύσσημον), instead of the more ordinary word, *sign* (σημεῖον), employed by St Matthew;[1] but also in his periphrasis of the traitor's perfidious expression: *Take him and* LEAD HIM AWAY SAFELY. There is a terrible truth afterwards in that repetition of the word

[1] Page 112.

Master, with which Judas addresses our Lord (v. 45): *Rabbi, Rabbi!* Here, again, St Mark has his well-known and characteristic *straightway* (εὐθέως). But he very particularly distinguishes himself at this point (v. 51, 52), by the introduction of that striking incident of the young man who with difficulty escaped from the hands of the soldiers. Various conjectures have been started who this young man was, and about the cause of his being there. That he was one of the disciples has, at all events, more probability than that the person whom St Mark meant to designate was *himself*. The question further does not come within our plan at this place. But here, again, St Mark's characteristic peculiarity lies in the graphic power with which he places the whole scene before us, and the striking idea which that scene suggests to us of the condition to which the friends of Jesus were reduced at that moment. There is something particularly striking in that flight of the young man in a state of *nakedness*. Here, really, the disciple of the Lord escaped *scarcely* (that is, with difficulty), as St Peter elsewhere expresses it, where he speaks of the salvation of the righteous (1 Peter iv. 18).

Again, we find in St Luke what is evidently the historical sequence of events. The seizure of Jesus, mentioned by the first two Evangelists *before* the wounding of the servant, occurs (as was to be expected from the nature of the thing) *after* that incident in St Luke's narrative (v. 54). He alone has recorded the question put by the disciple (v. 54), *Lord, shall we smite with the sword?* whereupon (quite according to the nature of human passion), he proceeds to strike without waiting for the reply. Then it is St Luke who is the first to intimate that it was the *right ear* that was cut off by the inconsiderate disciple (v. 50). Finally, that exclamation, *but this is your hour and the power of darkness* we find only in St Luke, in connexion, we believe, with the history of the temptation of our Lord in the wilderness, where it closes with the remark (iv. 13), *that the devil departed from Jesus for a season.* Now, in Gethsemane it was again *his hour.*

St John again carries us further back, and conducts us into details of yet deeper interest. First of all, the seizure of Jesus is preceded in his Gospel by a dread revelation of his greatness and his majesty (v. 3–9), which puts in strong relief the grand fact, that the self-sacrifice of the Saviour in his passion was not only voluntary, but also vicarious. To that last of the Gospels it was reserved to inform us how, upon Jesus pronouncing these simple words, *I am he,* the band of soldiers that came to seize him went backward, and fell to the ground; and how it was on our Lord's pronouncing these words: *If therefore ye seek me, let these go their way,* that he surrendered himself, but upon a condition, the emblematic meaning of which is elucidated by the Evangelist's remark (v. 9), *That the saying might be fulfilled which he spake: Of them which thou gavest me have I lost none* (chap. xvii. 12).

With respect to the place given to this insertion by St John, it is evident that what he mentions (v. 4–9) happened immediately *after* the kiss, by which Judas pointed out his Master to the band. St John's remark (v. 5, 6): *And Judas also, which betrayed him, stood with them,* in connexion with that particular, is of great weight, seeing that it shews that Judas placed himself manifestly after the kiss among the Saviour's enemies, thus excluding himself from the number of those *who had been given unto Jesus, that he might lose none of them* (chap. xvii. 12).

Assuming, as he ordinarily does, all to be known that is recorded by the synoptical Evangelists with respect to the perfidious kiss, St John gives us, on the other hand, the details which we have indicated concerning the person of the Saviour himself, and afterwards re-connects his narrative with that of the synoptical Gospels (v. 10). It is there that he is the first to inform us of the *name* of the impatient disciple who made such an imprudent use of the sword :—it was none other than *Peter*. He at the same time reports for us, with that minute attention to *names* which we have already remarked in St John, that the *servant of the high priest*, whose ear was cut off, was called *Malchus*. Whereas, in fine, the synoptical Evangelists speak of Jesus as being only *laid hold of and taken away*, St John alone here remarks that they also *bound* that patient Lamb of God. To this particular he afterwards returns in a remarkable connexion with other important details.

JESUS BEFORE THE HIGH PRIEST AND THE JEWISH COUNCIL.

MATTH. xxvi. 57–75.	MARK, xiv. 53–72.
And they that had laid hold on Jesus led him away to Caiaphas the high priest, where the scribes and the elders were assembled. 58. But Peter followed him afar off unto the high priest's palace, and went in, and sat with the servants, to see the end.	And they led Jesus away to the high priest: and with him were assembled all the chief priests, and the elders, and the scribes. 54. And Peter followed him afar off, even into the palace of the high priest: and he sat with the servants, and warmed himself at the fire.
59. Now the chief priests, and elders, and all the council, sought false witness against Jesus, to put him to death; 60. But found none: yea, though many false witnesses came, yet found they none. At the last came two false witnesses, 61. And said, This fellow said, I am able to destroy the temple of God, and to build it in three days. 62. And the high priest arose, and	55. And the chief priests and all the council sought for witness against Jesus to put him to death; and found none: 56. For many bare false witness against him; but their witness agreed not together. 57. And there arose certain, and bare false witness against him, saying, 58. We heard him say, I will destroy this temple that is made with hands, and within three days

said unto him, Answerest thou nothing? what is it which these witness against thee? 63. But Jesus
held his peace. And the high
priest answered and said unto him,
I adjure thee by the living God,
that thou tell us whether thou be
the Christ, the Son of God. 64.
Jesus saith unto him, Thou hast
said: nevertheless I say unto you,
Hereafter shall ye see the Son of
man sitting on the right hand of
power, and coming in the clouds
of heaven. 65. Then the high
priest rent his clothes (ἱματία),
saying, He hath spoken blasphemy;
what further need have we of witnesses? behold, now ye have heard
his blasphemy. 66. What think
ye? They answered and said, He
is guilty of death. 67. Then did
they spit in his face, and buffeted
him; and others smote him with
the palms of their hands, 68. Saying, Prophesy unto us, thou Christ,
Who is he that smote thee? 69.
Now Peter sat without in the palace: and a damsel came unto him,
saying, Thou also wast with Jesus
of Galilee. 70. But he denied before them all, saying, I know not
what thou sayest. 71. And when
he was gone out into the porch,
another maid saw him, and said
unto them that were there, This
fellow was also with Jesus of Nazareth. 72. And again he denied
with an oath, I do not know the
man. 73. And after a while came
unto him they that stood by, and
said to Peter, Surely thou also art
one one of them; for thy speech
bewrayeth thee. 74. Then began
he to curse and to swear, saying,
I know not the man. And immediately the cock crew. 75. And
Peter remembered the word of Je-

I will build another made without
hands. 59. But neither so did
their witness agree together. 60.
And the high priest stood up in
the midst, and asked Jesus, saying,
Answerest thou nothing? what is
it which these witness against
thee? 61. But he held his peace,
and answered nothing. Again
the high priest asked him, and
said unto him, Art thou the Christ,
the Son of the Blessed? 62.
And Jesus said, I am: and ye
shall see the Son of man sitting
on the right hand of power, and
coming in (Gr. μετὰ) the clouds
of heaven. 63. Then the high priest
rent his clothes (χιτῶνας), and saith,
What need we any further witnesses? 64. Ye have heard the
blasphemy: what think ye? And
they all condemned him to be guilty
of death. 65. And some began to
spit on him, and to cover his face,
and to buffet him, and to say unto
him, Prophesy: and the servants
(ὑπηρέται) did strike him with the
palms of their hands. 66. And as
Peter was beneath in the palace,
their cometh one of the maids of
the high priest: 67. And when she
saw Peter warming himself, she
looked upon him, and said, And
thou also wast with Jesus of Nazareth. 68. But he denied, saying,
I know not, neither understand I
what thou sayest. And he went
out into the porch (Gr. προαύλιον);
and the cock crew. 69. And a
maid saw him again, and began to
say to them that stood by, This is
one of them. 70. And he denied
it again. And a little after, they
that stood by said again to Peter,
Surely thou art one of them: for
thou art a Galilean, and thy speech
agreeth thereto. 71. But he began

sus, which said unto him, Before the cock crow, thou shalt deny me thrice. And he went out, and wept bitterly.

to curse and to swear, saying, I know not this man of whom ye speak. 72. And the second time the cock crew. And Peter called to mind the word that Jesus said unto him, Before the cock crow twice, thou shalt deny me thrice. And when he thought thereon,[1] he wept.

LUKE xxii. 54–71.

Then took they him, and led him, and brought him into the high priest's house. And Peter followed afar off. 55. And when they had kindled a fire in the midst of the hall, and were set down together, Peter sat down among them.

56. But a certain maid beheld him as he sat by the fire, and earnestly looked upon him, and said, This man was also with him. 57. And he denied him, saying, Woman, I know him not. 58. And, after a little while, another saw him, and said, Thou art also of them. And Peter said, Man, I am not. 59. And about the space of one hour after, another confidently affirmed, saying, Of a truth this fellow also was with him; for he is a Galilean. 60.

JOHN xviii. 13–27.

And led him away to Annas first; (for he was father-in-law to Caiaphas, which was the high priest that same year.) 14. Now Caiaphas was he which gave counsel to the Jews, that it was expedient that one man should die for the people. 15. And Simon Peter followed Jesus, and so did another disciple. That disciple was known unto the high priest, and went in with Jesus into the palace of the high priest. 16. But Peter stood at the door without. Then went out that other disciple, which was known unto the high priest, and spake unto her that kept the door, and brought in Peter.

17. Then saith the damsel that kept the door unto Peter, Art not thou also one of this man's disciples? He saith, I am not. 18. And the servants and officers stood there, who had made a fire of coals; (for it was cold:) and they warmed themselves: and Peter stood with them, and warmed himself. 19. The high priest then asked Jesus of his disciples, and of his doctrine. 20. Jesus answered him, I spake openly to the world; I ever taught in the synagogue, and in the temple,

[1] Or, *having returned to himself;* Gr. ἐπιβαλὼν, in the English translation: *when he thought thereon;* less accurately in the Dutch: *zich van daar makende.* Ἐπιβάλλειν (to wit, τὸν νοῦν), is the Latin *animum advertere.* Compare WETSTEIN on this passage.

And Peter said, Man, I know not
what thou sayest. And immediately, while he yet spake, the
cock crew. 61. And the Lord
turned, and looked upon Peter:
and Peter remembered the word of
the Lord, how he had said unto
him, Before the cock crow, thou
shalt deny me thrice. 62. And
Peter went out, and wept bitterly.
63. And the men that held Jesus
mocked him, and smote him. 64.
And when they had blindfolded
him, they struck him on the face,
and asked him, saying, Prophesy,
who is it that smote thee? 65. And
many other things blasphemously
spake they against him. 66. And
as soon as it was day, the elders
of the people, and the chief priests,
and the scribes, came together, and
led him into their council,

whither the Jews always resort;
and in secret have I said nothing.
21. Why askest thou me? ask
them which heard me, what I have
said unto them: behold, they know
what I said. 22. And when he
had thus spoken, one of the officers
which stood by struck Jesus with
the palm of his hand, saying, Answerest thou the high priest so?
23. Jesus answered him, If I have
spoken evil, bear witness of the
evil; but if well, why smitest thou
me? 24. (*Now* Annas had sent
him bound unto Caiaphas the high
priest.)

67. Saying, Art thou the Christ?
tell us. And he said unto them, If I
tell you, ye will not believe: 68.
And if I also ask you, ye will not
answer me, nor let me go. 69.
Hereafter shall the Son of man sit
on the right hand of the power of
God. 70. Then said they all, Art
thou then the Son of God? And he
said unto them, Ye say that I am.
71. And they said, What need we any
further witness? for we ourselves
have heard of his own mouth.

25. And Simon Peter stood and
warmed himself, [compare verse
18.] They said therefore unto him,
Art not thou also one of his disciples? He denied it, and said, I am
not. 26. One of the servants of
the high priest (being his kinsman
whose ear Peter cut off) saith, Did
not I see thee in the garden with
him? 27. Peter then denied again;
and immediately the cock crew.

Here we have but to follow the thread supplied by St Luke, and the historical sequence of events again becomes easily discernible amid the numerous details that reciprocally cross one another. The facts recorded by that Evangelist are then again elucidated and completed by the highly important details supplied by St John. But nothing can be more simple than the order of events in St Luke's narrative. We behold there the Saviour led away to the high priest, denied by Peter, maltreated by the officers, and on confessing that he was the Christ, the Son of God, declared by the council to be guilty of blasphemy.

All three synoptical Gospels mention how Jesus was led away from Gethsemane to Caiaphas, the high priest, and placed before the council which had met at his house. St John makes us acquainted with a new particular: to wit, that Jesus was first taken to Annas, the father-in-law of Caiaphas (v. 13), and in so doing, recalls the involuntary prediction of that chief of the priesthood, as previously recorded in this same Gospel (xi. 51). Anon (v. 24), he calls attention to the fact, that Jesus was sent *bound* by Annas to the house of Caiaphas.

Immediately thereafter, St Luke (v. 54–62) gives us a continuous narrative of St Peter's triple denial of his Master; St Matthew, St Mark, and St John, place the interrogatories put to our Lord before the high priest and the Jewish council, as well as his maltreatment by the servants, between the Apostle's seating himself in the lower hall, and his three denials of Jesus.

Throughout the whole of this combined narrative, we again find that the two first Gospels correspond with each other. St Mark, with the reservation of his characteristic abridgments and additions, keeps to the order adopted by St Matthew, an order which we ere long discover, from St Luke and St John, to have been by no means the historical one, but suggested by the personal impression made on our first Evangelist.

As respects the manner in which the particular incidents in the narrative are described; first of all, St Matthew here exhibits his most characteristic peculiarities. Observe his remarking (v. 58), that St Peter *wished to see how matters would end* in the hall of the high priest; anon, in his account of the meeting of the Jewish council (v. 61), we have a precise statement of the number of the false witnesses: *two,* with an evident reference to the number required by the law of Moses (Deut. xvii. 6): *At the mouth of* TWO *witnesses, or* THREE *witnesses, shall he that is worthy* of death *be put to death.*[1] After this, the truly Jewish *adjuration* of the high priest at the interrogatory (v. 63): the exclamation (v. 65): *he hath spoken blasphemy;* the express insertion of the title of *Christ* (v. 68), that it might be perceived that the mockery cast upon our Lord had for its object his royal as well as his prophetical dignity; finally, an oath uttered by St Peter at his *very first* denial of the Saviour (v. 72).

St Mark is here distinguished in the following manner. He brings the scene of St Peter's denial more vividly before us, by expressly stating, that St Peter *followed* INTO *the palace* where St Matthew (v. 58) has said more generally UNTO. He shews us (v. 54) the Apostle not merely *sitting with the servants,* but also WARMING HIMSELF AT THE FIRE, a detail to which St John recurs (v. 18, 25), while St Luke mentions it less directly (v. 55). He alone, when our Lord stands before the council, remarks, and that twice (v. 56 and 59), that the testimony of the witnesses did not agree. He records, at once fully and impressively, the false testimony itself: *We* HEARD *him say, I will destroy* THIS *temple* THAT IS MADE WITH HANDS, *and within three days I will build* ANOTHER, MADE WITHOUT HANDS. The circumstance of the high priest's standing up, mentioned by St Matthew (v. 62), he brings out more

[1] Meanwhile, it is remarkable that the *minimum* only of the requisite number could be brought to give evidence; and even then, as we are told by St Mark, *their witness did not agree together.*

fully by adding (v. 60) *in the midst.* Our Lord's silence he emphatizes by a repetition of the statement: *But he* HELD HIS PEACE *and* ANSWERED NOTHING (v. 61). Instead of *the Son of* GOD he has (v. 61) the literal expression employed by the Jews: *the Son of* THE BLESSED. In the words of Jesus, taken from the prophet Daniel (v. 24), he restores the much livelier expression actually used by the prophet: WITH (Gr. μετὰ) *the clouds of heaven,* where St Matthew has merely given the sense: ON (ἐπὶ) *the clouds of heaven.* It is St Mark who first tells us (v. 65), and after him St Luke (v. 64), that some of the mockers of Jesus *covered his face,* in contempt of his prophetic dignity. It is he, further, who is the first to remark (v. 65), that it was *the servants* who struck him with the palms of their hands. St John explains more fully and more exactly how this took place during the interrogatory before the high priest (v. 22).

It is St Mark who, passing with his predecessor from this part of the narrative to that which follows the denial, anew describes the place with most precision (v. 66). St Peter *was* BENEATH[1] *in the palace.* It was there that he was seen by one of the maids, whom St Matthew designates simply by that word, but whom St Mark distinguishes as *one of the maids of the high priest* (v. 66), and whom St John makes known to us as *the damsel that kept the door.* St Mark (v. 67), and St Luke (v. 56), depict the look cast upon the Apostle by this maid, and which instantly confounded him. The expression of the first denial is again redoubled here (v. 68): *I know not, neither understand I what thou sayest.* St Matthew (v. 70), records the latter of these expressions only, and St Luke the former (v. 57). But it is chiefly with respect to what

[1] Gr. κάτω, instead of the ἔξω (*without*) of St Matthew (v. 69).

took place *after* that first denial, that St Mark's narrative (v. 68) is of the utmost importance: namely, the *first* cock-crowing, after the Apostle had *gone down into the court.*[1] It is thus that we learn exclusively from St Mark, that Simon Peter *might* have even then withdrawn himself from the danger of a second and third denial—but ere long we find him returning into the hall below (v. 69). St Mark (v. 69) has further, at this place, what manifestly elucidates, and more precisely determines what had previously been stated by St Matthew; the maid designated by the latter (v. 71) as *another*, appears from the former to have been *the same* that confounded Peter on the first occasion. (St Matthew, in his more general and less developed narrative, designates her as *another*, by a very natural and very characteristic confusion of the persons who, in the bustle of the moment, took part in the attack against Peter. It is another example of the same principle to which the characteristic *plural* of the first Evangelist may be traced). St Luke also (v. 58) speaks of *another* of *those who were present*, and not of *another maid.* Thus, all may be resolved in the simplest manner, by a good or true combination of the three synoptical Gospels. To return to that of St Mark, we there find the suspicion created by St Peter's provincial accent more fully brought out (v. 70): *Thou art* A GALILEAN, *and thy speech agreeth thereto.* Anon, we have (v. 72) a *second* cock-crowing mentioned. On the other hand, nothing is said of the *bitterness* of Peter's repentance by his bosom-friend St

[1] The Greek word προαύλιον signifies the *fore-court*—the *vestibule;* that is to say, the large space before the gate (τὸ ἔμπροσθεν τῆς αὐλῆς), according to SUIDAS. In this narrative we must carefully distinguish, 1*st*, The *fore-court;* 2*d*, The *fore*, or *lower hall*, where the servants sat round the fire; and, 3*d*, The *upper hall*, or the highest part of the hall, where the high priest subjected our Lord to a *preliminary* interrogatory. (John, v. 19-24.)

Mark. St Matthew and St Luke alone have that striking expression: *he wept* BITTERLY;—St Mark has simply: *he wept.* The important word ἐπιβαλὼν (*having bethought himself—having returned to himself*), which, again, we read in St Mark alone, is afterwards explained and developed to us in a striking manner by St Luke (v. 61).

St Luke, likewise, has several characteristic details in this part of our Lord's passion. He shews us Peter's highly dangerous position, *in the midst* of the hall, in *the midst* of the servants around the fire, warming himself (v. 55). He notes the time that elapsed betwixt the different denials: *after a little while* (v. 58), and (v. 59) *about the space of one hour after*, (that is to say, counting from the *first*, not from the *second* denial). He is particularly affecting and striking in the account which he gives of the repentance of the Apostle, and describes it in immediate connexion with *the look of Jesus*, who, turning for a moment amid the sufferings he was enduring himself, to the fallen disciple, recalls to his remembrance what he had foretold of him, and touches his heart unto repentance. We evidently find a recurrence here of that mercy, that compassion, and at the same time that healing power in the Saviour, which St Luke puts so prominently forward in his Gospel. After this there follow (simultaneously with what passed with St Peter in the lower court) the mockery and insults offered to Jesus by the men who held him (v. 63–65); then (v. 60) the leading away of Jesus from the hall of the high priest to the apartment where the Jewish council had met (v. 67, 68); the protest delivered by Jesus before replying to the question: *Art thou the Christ?* Further, it is St Luke alone who distinguishes that question exactly from the one concerning his quality as the *Son of God* (Luke v. 70, compared with Matth. v. 63, and St Mark, v. 61). Here St Luke renders *literally* the declaration of Jesus concerning his approaching exaltation: *Hereafter shall the Son of Man* SIT ON THE RIGHT HAND OF THE POWER OF GOD, where St Matthew (v. 64) continuing the prophecy, speaks of *his coming in the clouds of heaven;* and in this is followed by St Mark (v. 67). It is not to be doubted that Jesus spoke as St Luke has recorded the words; while St Matthew and St Mark render these expressions by way of an *authentic* commentary.

But it is chiefly, as we have already intimated, by the re-establishment of the proper historical order, that St Luke is found of the utmost importance as respects the evangelical harmony at this place. We have already remarked how, while he abandons the order followed by St Matthew and St Mark, he makes the denials of Peter *precede* the appearance of Jesus before the Sanhedrim, and then (v. 63–65) represents the insults offered to the Lord by the servants, as occurring at the same time with the denials of him by Peter; that is to say, equally before our Saviour's being led away to the meeting of the council. That this was the real order, clearly appears from the circumstances themselves leaving no doubt as to the times at which they successively occurred. The denials by Peter took place contemporaneously *with the crowing of the cock;* the assembling of the elders and the high priests, and the interrogatory of our Lord before their council, according to St Luke (v. 66), *when it was day.*

St John confirms this view of the order of events, and further elucidates their mutual bearings with those details of his which are invariably so profoundly significant and touching. Let us trace these from the very commencement of this whole passage of Scripture. Starting from the apprehension of our Lord in Gethsemane, he represents Jesus as *first led away to Annas* (v. 12 and 13). Immediately afterwards (v. 13, compared with the 24th), he observes, that Jesus was taken from thence to *Caiaphas, which was the high priest that same year.* After this, he introduces a circumstance (v. 15, 16), omitted by all three synoptical Evangelists, but from which the original cause of St Peter's being present in the lower hall, becomes no less simple than it is fitted to throw light on all besides. St John, being already known in the high priest's house, is the first to enter with Jesus into the hall, while St Peter remained without: it was through the intervention of St John, that the woman that kept the door at length allowed the former also to come in. We then find anew in St John, a circumstance of great importance, which also takes place previous to the examination of our Lord by the whole council; to wit, a *private* interrogatory addressed to him by Caiaphas, in which the high priest questions the Saviour touching his disciples and his doctrine (v. 19). The reply follows (v. 20 and 21), and immediately thereupon we have another highly interesting circumstance connected with our Lord's passion (v. 22): one of the officers of the high priest strikes Jesus in the face, and Jesus, in conformity with his own command,[1] understood not in its fruitless material meaning but according to its spiritual import, offers to him the *other cheek* also, in these memorable words (v. 23): *If I have spoken evil, bear witness of the evil, but if well, why smitest thou me?* whilst (v. 24) it will be seen, that during the whole of this unworthy treatment *Jesus was bound*, for it was thus that *Annas had sent him*

[1] Matth. v. 39.

to Caiaphas.[1] This first smiting on the face, mentioned by St John alone, plainly enough appears to have been the occasion and the example of all the others that were given to Jesus by the servants, not, as one might suppose, from the order followed by St Matthew and St Mark *after* the trial, but, as appears from the historical connexion supplied by St Luke (v. 62–66), *previous to* our Lord's being led into the council hall; or properly, and according to St John, during the time that elapsed betwixt the private interrogatory before the high priest and that before the council. St Matthew's and St Mark's placing those insults at a later stage, can be accounted for by observing, that *after* the condemnation of Jesus, some members of the council may have insulted or mocked him; but this does not militate against the attacks and insults *of the servants* necessarily taking place sooner, and at a moment such as that which we have indicated, at which Jesus was solely and exclusively under the guard of these men.

But the comparison of St Luke with St John in the places referred to, throws new light also on this important circumstance,—that, after Peter's third denial, and during the second cock-crowing, the Lord looked upon him, and made him return to himself by a piercing glance of Divine love and omniscience. In what manner, and under what circumstances, may we represent to ourselves that striking moment? According to all we have hitherto observed, very simply thus: The denials were made in the *lower* hall, whilst *above*, in the same place,

[1] *Unus alterque οὖν supplet*, (according to our translators *now*, v. 24), *vel δὲ vel τέ. Nil opus est.* Jesum *ab Annâ ad Caiapham fuisse ductum indicârat Joannes*, v. 15, *in verbo συνεισῆλθε et ipsâ toties repetita pontificis appellatione: nunc vero id ipsum re-assumit, et expressius memorat cum mentione vinculorum, in quibus alapam indignissimam accepit Salvator.* BENGEL, ad h. l.

Jesus was first interrogated by the high priest; and afterwards, on the departure of the latter, abandoned to the insolence of the servants. All this occupies nearly an hour (Luke v. 59). But Jesus is now led away out of the public hall into another apartment in the house of the high priest, where the council was met. In order to reach that other apartment, he had to pass through the very place where Peter, surrounded with a menacing crowd of people, denies his Master. At that same instant, then, Jesus passes, turns as he is led along, and looks upon the disciple, who by that look is recalled to himself, and bursts into tears. But at the same instant the threatening danger is *turned off from St Peter*. For the attention of the crowd, as it presses upon him, is withdrawn from the disciple by the passage of the Lord himself; and thus the former has but to take advantage of the general confusion to effect his escape. Here, again, the Lord diverts evil from one of his *own* by attracting it towards *himself*.

Does there possibly remain some further difficulty with respect to an *entire* accordance among the four Evangelists concerning all the details of Peter's denials of our Lord, related as these are with so much fulness? Let us see, then, the apparent contradictions on which objections are founded, and then seek their solution by the application of the simplest principles. The apparent contradictions are summed up as follows:—1*st*, Jesus had foretold, *Thou shalt deny me* THRICE; and yet a greater number than *three* arises from putting together the different accounts given by the four Evangelists of the words uttered by the Apostle. 2*d*, The Evangelists differ with respect to the persons who attack St Peter and interrogate him. St Matthew at the second denial speaks of *two* maids; St Luke (v. 58), of *some one* of those who were present; St John (v. 25), of *several persons.* At the third denial, St Matthew (v. 73) and St Mark (v. 70) speak of the *spectators* in the plural; St Luke anew (v. 59) speaks of *one only;* St John (v. 26) speaks of a servant of the high priest, kinsman of Malchus, who was wounded by Peter in Gethsemane. 3*d*, In the synoptical Gospels, Peter is spoken of as *seated*—in St John, as *standing* at the fire.

There is no difficulty in reconciling these apparent discrepancies, provided we but attend to a proper distinction. 1*st*, With respect to the difficulty arising from the number of the denials by Peter, we must not take up this number *three*, in the accounts we have of what took place, in too strict and limited a manner: in such sense Peter disowned his Lord more than three times; but the *threefold* denial refers to the *attacks* directed against the Apostle, and reiterated *three times* from different sides, on each of which occasions he endeavoured to defend himself against *more than one* of the assailants or bystanders by that fearful falsehood: *I know him not.*—With respect to the *persons* indicated in the four Gospels in different manners, we must bear in mind that in the account of the first denial all four Evangelists attribute the attack equally to *a maid.* It is only at the *second* denial that there begins to be an *apparent* difference. In St Matthew (v. 71), this second denial commences after the mention of *another servant;* in St Mark (v. 69), after that of *the same* servant. We have already explained this slight difference.[1] St Luke's not speaking here (v. 58) of *a maid*, but of *a bystander*, and St John of *several bystanders*, may be easily explained by the

[1] See p. 377.

nature of the circumstance. Nothing more natural than that, after what had been said by the maid, the attention first of *one*, and then of *several* of the bystanders (such as the servants belonging to the house and others), should be drawn to Peter, and that thus they should all have joined in the attack commenced against him by the maid. Nothing more natural, also, than that the Apostle, in addressing *one*, should have used *certain words*, and to *another* have addressed *other words*, with no other object but that of getting out of the dispute.—At the third denial the difficulty becomes yet less. St Matthew and St Mark speak there of *bystanders* in the plural; St Luke positively of *one* of the multitude; St John, in accordance with the nature of his plan, gives us to know *one* by *saying* WHO *he was:* to wit, a kinsman of that Malchus whose right ear had been cut off by Peter in the garden. In fine, 3d, As for what concerns the difference among the Gospels with respect to St Peter, as to his being *seated* near the fire, or *standing* near it, the synoptical Gospels represent to us the Apostle *at the commencement* as *seated* near the fire; but St John does not contradict this statement when (v. 18–25) he says that Peter *stood*.[1] This description of the Apostle as *standing* applies to a *subsequent* moment, whilst nothing is more easily conceivable than that the agitation of mind into which he was thrown must have prevented him from keeping his seat, must have compelled him to get up and go away, to return again, and to remain standing. By simply attending to these observations, which at the same time discover to us afresh in each of the four

[1] It is evident that the words (v. 25, 26) are no more than a simple repetition of the 18th verse, to prevent ambiguity on resuming the thread of the narrative, after the intermediate statement comprised in v. 19-24.

Evangelists, and particularly in that of St John, the characteristics which we formerly described, all difficulty vanishes, and the harmony becomes evident.

The succession, therefore, of important incidents, from the apprehension of Jesus in Gethsemane to his condemnation by the Sanhedrim, is equally certain and regular on being viewed in the following manner:—1. Jesus is led bound before Annas (according to St John); 2. From thence, still remaining bound, he is taken away to the house of the high priest for that year, Caiaphas (according to all four Evangelists); 3. Guarded by servants, he is kept waiting there for some time in the upper hall (according to all four Evangelists); 4. St Peter, meanwhile, following the example of St John, is admitted by the porteress (according to St John); and, 5. Takes his place among a number of the servants near the fire in the lower hall (according to all the Evangelists); 6. The high priest subjects Jesus to an interrogatory (according to St John); 7. Jesus replies, and is struck upon the face by one of the officers (according to St John); 8. The high priest having again retired, and having left Jesus alone with the officers, the rest of these men seize this opportunity for striking and insulting our Lord (according to St Luke, compared with St Matthew and St Mark); 9. While the upper hall is the scene of all these things, Peter's denials of his Master take place in the lower hall. He denies him for the first time (according to all the Evangelists),—first cock-crowing (according to St Mark); 10. He goes out by the front door into the fore-court of the house (according to St Mark); but, 11. Returns and disowns his Master the second and the third time,—second cock-crowing (according to St Mark); 12. Shortly before that very moment an order comes for Jesus to be conducted before the council, which had met in another hall of the high priest's house; 13. Our Lord passes the place where Peter finds himself pressed and threatened by the multitude. He turns round and looks upon Peter (according to St Luke); 14, St Peter returns to himself, and weeps bitterly (according to the three synoptical Gospels); 15. Day dawns—the council is met—the false witnesses are heard (according to St Matthew and St Mark); 16. The high priest adjures Jesus to say whether he is the Christ (according to St Luke, compared with St Matthew and with St Mark); 17. He replies separately to that question and to that other, whether he is the Son of God (according to St Luke, compared with St Matthew and St Mark); 18. After these words the council condemns him on account of blasphemy, and declares him guilty of death (according to the three synoptical Evangelists).

JESUS BEFORE PILATE AND HEROD.

MATTH. xxvii. 1–31.

When the morning was come, all the chief priests and elders of the people took counsel against Jesus to put him to death.

2. And when they had bound him, they led him away, and delivered him to Pontius Pilate the governor. 3. Then Judas, which had betrayed him, when he saw that he was condemned, repented himself, and brought again the thirty pieces of silver to the chief priests and elders, 4. Saying, I have sinned in that I have have betrayed the innocent blood. And they said, What is that to us? see thou to that. 5. And he cast down the pieces of silver in the temple, and departed,

MARK xv. 1–20.

And straightway in the morning the chief priests held a consultation with the elders and scribes, and the whole council,

And bound Jesus, and carried him away, and delivered him to Pilate.

and went and hanged himself. 6.
And the chief priests took the silver
pieces, and said, It is not lawful for
to put them into the treasury, because it is the price of blood. 7.
And they took counsel, and bought
with them the potter's field, to bury
strangers in. 8. Wherefore that
field was called, The field of blood,
unto this day. 9. (Then was fulfilled that which was spoken by
Jeremy the prophet, saying, And
they took the thirty pieces of silver, the price of him that was va-
lued, whom they of the children of
Israel did value; 10. And gave
them for the potter's field, as the
Lord appointed me.)

11. And Jesus stood before the
governor: and the governor asked
him, saying, Art thou the King of
the Jews? And Jesus said unto
him, Thou sayest.

2. And Pilate asked him, Art
thou the King of the Jews? And
he answering, said unto him, Thou
sayest it.

12. And when he was accused of
the chief priests and elders, he answered nothing. 13. Then saith
Pilate unto him, Hearest thou not
how many things they witness
against thee? 14. And he answered
him to never a word; insomuch
that the governor marvelled greatly. (John xix. 9–10.)

3. And the chief priests accused
him of many things; but he answered nothing. 4. And Pilate
asked him again, saying, Answerest
thou nothing? behold how many
things they witness against thee.
5. But Jesus yet answered nothing; so that Pilate marvelled.

15. Now at that feast the governor was wont to release unto
the people a prisoner, whom they
would. 16. And they had then a
notable prisoner, called Barabbas.
17. Therefore, when they were gathered together, Pilate said unto
them, Whom will ye that I release
unto you? Barabbas, or Jesus
which is called Christ? 18. For he
knew that for envy they had deli-
livered him. 19. When he was
set down on the judgment-seat, his
wife sent unto him, saying, Have
thou nothing to do with that just

6. Now at that feast he released
unto them one prisoner, whomsoever they desired. 7. And there
was one named Barabbas, which
lay bound with them that had made
insurrection with him, who had
committed murder in the insurrection. 8. And the multitude, crying aloud, began to desire him to
do as he had ever done unto them.
9. But Pilate answered them, saying, Will ye that I release unto you
the King of the Jews? 10. (For
he knew that the chief priests had
delivered him for envy.)

man: for I have suffered many things this day in a dream because of him.	
20. But the chief priests and elders persuaded the multitude that they should ask Barabbas, and destroy Jesus. 21. The governor answered and said unto them, Whether of the twain will ye that I release unto you? They said, Barabbas.	11. But the chief priests moved the people, that he should rather release Barabbas unto them.
22. Pilate saith unto them, What shall I do then with Jesus which is called Christ? They all say unto him, Let him be crucified. 23. And the governor said, Why, what evil hath he done? But they cried out the more, saying, Let him be crucified. 24. When Pilate saw that he could prevail nothing, but that rather a tumult was made, he took water, and washed his hands before the multitude, saying, I am innocent of the blood of this just person; see ye to it. 25. Then answered all the people, and said, His blood be on us, and on our children.	12. And Pilate answered and said again unto them, What will ye then that I shall do unto him whom ye call the King of the Jews? 13. And they cried out again, Crucify him. 14. Then Pilate said unto them, Why, what evil hath he done? And they cried out the more exceedingly, Crucify him.
26. Then released he Barabbas unto them: and when he had scourged Jesus, he delivered him to be crucified.	15. And so Pilate, willing to content the people, released Barabbas unto them, and delivered Jesus, when he had scourged him, to be crucified.
27. Then the soldiers of the governor took Jesus into the common hall, and gathered unto him the whole band of soldiers. 28. And they stripped him, and put on him a scarlet robe. 29. And when they had platted a crown of thorns, they put it upon his head, and a reed in his right hand: and they bowed the knee before him, and mocked him, saying, Hail, King of the Jews! 30. And they spit upon him, and took the reed, and smote him on the head.	16. And the soldiers led him away into the hall (Gr. αὐλή) called Pretorium; and they call together the whole band. 17. And they clothed him with purple, and platted a crown of thorns, and put it about his head, 18. And began to salute him, Hail, King of the Jews! 19. And they smote him on the head with a reed, and did spit upon him, and, bowing their knees, worshipped him.
31. And after that they had	20. And when they had mocked

mocked him, they took the robe
off from him, and put his own
raiment on him, and led him away
to crucify him.

him, they took off the purple from
him, and put his own clothes on
him, and led him out to crucify
him.

LUKE xxiii. 1–26.

And the whole multitude of them
arose, and led him unto Pilate.

2. And they began to accuse
him, saying, We found this fellow
perverting the nation, and forbidding to give tribute to Cæsar, saying that he himself is Christ a
King.

3. And Pilate asked him, saying, Art thou the King of the Jews?
And he answered and said, Thou
sayest it.

4. Then said Pilate to the chief
priests and to the people, I find no
fault in this man. 5. And they
were the more fierce, saying, He
stirreth up the people, teaching
throughout all Jewry, beginning
from Galilee to this place. 6.
When Pilate heard of Galilee, he
asked whether the man were a Galilean? 7. And as soon as he knew
that he belonged unto Herod's ju-
risdiction, he sent him to Herod,
who himself also was at Jerusalem
at that time. 8. And when Herod
saw Jesus, he was exceeding glad:

JOHN xviii. 28–40.—xix. 1–16.

Then led they Jesus from Caiaphas unto the hall of judgment:
and it was early; and they themselves went not into the judgment hall, lest they should be defiled, but that they might eat the
passover.

29. Pilate then went out unto
them, and said, What accusation
bring ye against this man? 30.
They answered and said unto him,
If he were not a malefactor, we
would not have delivered him up
unto thee. 31. Then said Pilate
unto them, Take ye him, and judge
him according to your law. The
Jews therefore said unto him, It is
not lawful for us to put any man
to death: 32. That the saying of
Jesus might be fulfilled, which he
spake, signifying what death he
should die.

33. Then Pilate entered into the
judgment-hall again, and called
Jesus, and said unto him, Art thou
the King of the Jews? 34. Jesus
answered him, Sayest thou this
thing of thyself, or did others tell
it thee of me? 35. Pilate answered, Am I a Jew? Thine own
nation and the chief priests have
delivered thee unto me: What
hast thou done? 36. Jesus answered,
My kingdom is not of this world.
If my kingdom were of this world,
then would my servants fight, that
I should not be delivered to the
Jews: but now is my kingdom not
from hence. 37. Pilate therefore
said unto him, Art thou a king
then? Jesus answered, Thou sayest

for he was desirous to see him of a
long season, because he had heard
many things of him; and he hoped
to have seen some miracle done by
him. 9. Then he questioned with
him in many words; but he answered him nothing. 10. And the
chief priests and scribes stood and
vehemently accused him. 11. And
Herod with his men of war set
him at nought, and mocked him,
and arrayed him in a gorgeous
robe, and sent him again to Pilate.
12. And the same day Pilate and
Herod were made friends together;
for before they were at enmity between themselves. 13. And Pilate,
when he had called together the
chief priests, and the rulers, and
the people, 14. Said unto them,
Ye have brought this man unto me,
as one that perverteth the people;
and, behold, I, having examined
him before you, have found no fault
in this man touching those things
whereof ye accuse him: 15. No,
nor yet Herod: for I sent you to
him; and, lo, nothing worthy of
death is done unto him. 16. I will
therefore chastise him, and release
him.

that I am a king. To this end was
I born, and for this cause came I
into the world, that I should bear
witness unto the truth. Every one
that is of the truth heareth my
voice. 38. Pilate saith unto him,
What is truth? And when he had
said this, he went out again unto
the Jews, and saith unto them, I
find in him no fault at all.

17. (For of necessity he must
release one unto them at the feast.)

39. But ye have a custom, that
I should release unto you one at
the passover: will ye therefore
that I release unto you the King
of the Jews?

18. And they cried out all at
once, saying, Away with this man,
and release unto us Barabbas:
19. (Who for a certain sedition
made in the city, and for murder,
was cast into prison.) (Mark, v. 7).

20. Pilate therefore, willing to
release Jesus, spake again to them.
21. But they cried, saying, Crucify
him, crucify him. 22. And he said
unto them the third time, Why,

40. Then cried they all again,
saying, Not this man, but Barabbas. Now Barabbas was a robber.

what evil hath he done? I have found no cause of death in him: I will therefore chastise him, and let him go (v. 16 above). 23. And they were instant with loud voices, requiring that he might be crucified: and the voices of them and of the chief priests prevailed.

24. And Pilate gave sentence that it should be as they required. 25. And he released unto them him that for sedition and murder was cast into prison, whom they had desired; but he delivered Jesus to their will.

26. And as they led him away, they laid hold upon one Simon, a Cyrenian, coming out of the country, and on him they laid the cross, that he might bear it after Jesus.

xix. 1–16. Then Pilate therefore took Jesus, and scourged him.

2. And the soldiers platted a crown of thorns, and put it on his head, and they put on him a purple robe, 3. And said, Hail, King of the Jews! and they smote him with their hands. 4. Pilate therefore went forth again, and saith unto them, Behold, I bring him forth to you, that ye may know that I find no fault in him. 5. Then came Jesus forth, wearing the crown of thorns, and the purple robe. And Pilate saith unto them, Behold the man! 6. When the chief priests therefore and officers saw him, they cried out, saying, Crucify him, crucify him. Pilate saith unto them, Take ye him, and crucify him: for I find no fault in him. 7. The Jews answered him, We have a law, and by our law he ought to die, because he made himself the Son of God. 8. When Pilate therefore heard that saying, he was the more afraid; 9. And went again into the judgment-hall, and saith unto Jesus, Whence art thou? But Jesus gave him no answer. 10. Then saith Pilate unto him, Speakest thou not unto me? knowest thou not that I have power to crucify thee, and have power to release thee? 11. Jesus answered, Thou couldest have no power at all against me, except it were given thee from above: therefore he that delivered me unto thee hath the

greater sin. 12. And from thenceforth Pilate sought to release him:
but the Jews cried out, saying, If
thou let this man go, thou art not
Cæsar's friend: whosoever maketh
himself a king, speaketh against
Cæsar. 13. When Pilate therefore heard that saying, he brought
Jesus forth, and sat down in the
judgment-seat in a place that is
called the Pavement, but in the
Hebrew, Gabbatha. 14. And it
was the preparation of the passover, and about the sixth hour:
and he saith unto the Jews, Behold
your King! 15. But they cried out,
Away with him, away with him,
crucify him. Pilate saith unto
them, Shall I crucify your King?
The chief priests answered, We
have no king but Cæsar.

16. Then delivered he him therefore unto them to be crucified. And
they took Jesus, and led him away.

Some expositors have most unjustifiably concluded from certain of St Matthew's expressions (v. 1), adopted by St Mark (v. 1), that Jesus underwent a *second* trial before the Jewish council. The case stands simply thus: St Matthew and St Mark (who follows his predecessor step by step) had already recorded the interrogatory before the council, and the sentence to which it had led, as we have seen in the preceding section. But as they introduce Peter's denials of our Lord *between* these proceedings before the council and his being led away to Pilate, they here resume the thread of their narrative with a short abstract. This mention by St Matthew and St Mark, of the meeting of the council, and of the resolution to have Jesus put to death, is nothing more, therefore, than a recalling to mind, and a summary of what had been previously related at greater length, and on that account is not to be found either in the Gospel of St Luke (who makes the delivery of Jesus to Pilate follow immediately upon the judgment passed by the council) or in that of St John. Thus, we have another instance here of one of those repetitions of St Matthew's, which naturally arise from the greater freedom, and less strictness of attention to order, in the mode of writing by which he is distinguished; while St Mark, by a slight modification of what he has taken from St Matthew, points already to the true explanation: according to him, the decision of the council of the elders and the scribes, had evidently for its object not the condemnation of Jesus, for that was already settled, but his being delivered to Pilate (Mark xv. 1).

Next follows, in St Matthew, a passage again quite peculiar to himself, and every way in accordance with the plan and character of his Gospel. The horrific end of the traitor Judas, could be fitly recorded by no one so well as by a fellow Apostle; and how could we expect this to be done by St Matthew, without a reference to the word of prophecy? It is St Matthew who relates the catastrophe, and therefore we do not find it recorded in the regular order of time (for it is not likely that the suicide of Judas took place at so early an hour in the morning, but rather at a time when the condemnation of the Just one had been already pronounced by Pilate); but in one breath, so to speak, with the account of what took place at the meeting of the Sanhedrim. Moreover, the details which he gives us, are in harmony with the Israelitic and prophetic character of his whole Gospel. *First*, we have the repeated mention of the prophesied pieces of silver; *in the second place*, the admission of the innocence of Jesus by the very disciple who betrayed him; *thirdly*, the purpose to which that money was applied by the high priests, as well as their revulsion from the price of blood; *fourthly*, the quotation of the striking words of the prophet; *fifthly*, and finally (v. 5), the death of the culprit by self-strangulation, after confession of his offence (v. 4), but without any penitent recourse to the grace of God. All these details were *eminently* important as respects the impression they were likely to make on an *Israelite* reader.

In what he further records, St Matthew again supplies the groundwork for the narratives of his fellow Evangelists, but always with numerous details which do not cease to be peculiarly his own, and fully express both the point of view from which he contemplated the scenes he describes, and his personal calling and individuality, such as we have all along observed them.

The description given of Jesus (v. 11) STANDING BEFORE *the governor*, is found only in St Matthew. Did it not recall to his thoughts the words of the prophet: *as a sheep* BEFORE *her shearers?* Then the *silence* maintained by our Lord before Pilate, which St John places at a subsequent moment (v. 9, 10), and, as it would appear, at the proper historical place, is recorded by St Matthew (v. 12 and 14), followed here also by St Mark (v. 3 and 5), at the first interrogatory before the governor. St Luke mentions a like sublime silence only before Herod (v. 9).

Subsequently, when the question arises about the releasing of a prisoner, none of the Evangelists records in so striking a manner as St Matthew, the parallel between Jesus and Barabbas, and the accomplishment at that very moment of the prophecy: *He was numbered with the transgressors.* In his Gospel alone do we find the words addressed by Pilate to the people so distinctly given

(v. 17): *Whom will ye that I release unto you? Barabbas,* OR *Jesus which is called Christ?* And, again (v. 20): *The chief priests and elders persuaded the multitude that they should ask for Barabbas, and destroy Jesus;* and afterwards (v. 21), in the second question put by Pilate: WHETHER OF THE TWAIN *will ye that I release unto you?* St Mark already shews much more conciseness in this part of his Gospel; St Luke gives a summary statement of that intermediate event (v. 17 and 18); St John records it likewise in a few words, which terminate in the short and impressive observation: *Now, Barabbas was a robber* (v. 39, 40).

Further, it is in our first Gospel alone that we find the dream of Pilate's wife,[1] and in consequence of that dream, the warning sent to her husband: *Have thou nothing to do with that just man.* Revelations communicated by means of *dreams,* are intimately associated with the peculiar relation maintained by St Matthew with the Old Testament (Matth. i. 20, ii. 12, 13, 19). As a homage on the part of the *Gentiles* to the King of the *Jews,* this particular incident, too, found its most fitting place in St Matthew (comp. ii. 1, 2).

Meanwhile, it is by this *intervening* incident that St Matthew clearly explains to us what the precise moment was of which the high priests availed themselves to persuade the people to ask for the release of Barabbas and not of Jesus (v. 17–20).

When, afterwards, Pilate had no longer the courage to resist the tumult, but continues, nevertheless, to protest

[1] That at the time these events took place, Roman governors were allowed to take their wives to the provinces along with them, is in our days placed beyond a doubt. The reader may consult TACITUS, Ann. l. i. cap. 40; ii. cap. 55; iii. cap. 33.

in favour of the innocence of Jesus, and imagines that he in such a way could remain guiltless of shedding innocent blood, it is only in St Matthew that we find this protestation accompanied with a symbolical action, well known to the Jews from the writings of Moses, and to which other nations also were nowise strangers: *He took water, and washed his hands,*[1] *before the multitude* (v. 24).

Immediately afterwards (v. 25) St Matthew, and here again *none but him,* records, in conformity with the prophetic tendency which is peculiar to him, that frightful saying of the Jews, of which the accomplishment is still, after the lapse of eighteen centuries, before our eyes: *His blood be on us, and on our children.*

Here (v. 26), and afterwards in St Mark (v. 15), the scourging of Jesus is recorded without the addition of any accompanying circumstances; in a single word, as if by the way. It is only in St John that we find that part of the outrages inflicted on Jesus in its proper place and in its full connexion; while St Luke (as we shall see hereafter) fully informs us of the true nature of that scourging.

Then the outrages committed by the insolent soldiery in the Prætorium are recorded by St Matthew, and after him by St Mark, without their observing the precise order of events. It is only St John who throws sufficient light on that part of the Saviour's passion, to enable us to perceive that it did not *follow,* but *precede* the final acquiescence of the governor in the will of the people.

The mocking of Pilate's soldiers presents us with two

[1] Deut. xxi. 1–9. As respects the heathen *Ἔθος ἦν τοῖς παλαιοῖς* (says the Scholiast on the Ajax of Sophocles, v. 664), *ὅταν ἢ φόνον ἀνθρώπου ἢ ἄλλας σφαγὰς ἐποίουν, ὕδατι ἀπονίπτειν τὰς χεῖρας εἰς κάθαρσιν τοῦ μιάσματος.*

remarkable particulars as recorded by St Matthew: *first*, the reed placed instead of a sceptre in the hand of the suffering King; *then* the bowing of the knee in derision. For this St Mark employs the proper Roman word, *to salute*.[1] No doubt, in writing this description, the soul of St Matthew was impressed with the recollection of these words of the psalm: *I shall give thee the heathen for thine inheritance, and the uttermost parts of the earth for thy possession*.[2] In the very derision of the wicked there was, on the Lord's part, while permitting it, a hidden prophetic meaning.

St Mark, as we have seen, here follows closely the footsteps of St Matthew, only abridging here and there the narrative of his predecessor. His amplifications and modifications of expression are equally of the same nature, as we before observed. Thus (v. 4) he gives Pilate's impatient question in the expressive words: *Answerest thou nothing?* Thus he is the first who gives the striking elucidation (adopted afterwards by St Luke) concerning Barabbas, that *he lay bound with them that had made insurrection with him, who had committed murder in the insurrection* (St Luke here further adds only that this sedition had been *in the city*, v. 19). But what, above all, makes St Mark's Gospel interesting at this part, is the circumstance preserved by him alone, that the asking for the release of a prisoner at the feast, according to the usual custom, *came from the midst of the multitude* (v. 8); so that Pilate, in conformity with his whole mode of procedure in this affair (never acting *directly*, but always in the way of exercising his influence), even *takes advantage*

[1] Gr. ἀσπάζεσθαι. Lat. *aliquem regem vel imperatorem* SALUTARE.

[2] Ps. ii. 8. Comp. Rev. iii. 26, 27.

of this demand, in order, if possible, to save Jesus. The proposal is expressed in rather general terms by St John as well as by St Matthew ; and but for St Mark's observation, Pilate might appear (contrary to what we should expect from the pride of a Roman) to have been the first to suggest the release.—What we find further added in this second Gospel is not without meaning (v. 15): *And so Pilate,* WILLING TO CONTENT THE PEOPLE, *released Barabbas unto them.* Finally (v. 20), St Mark here again lays an emphasis on an important circumstance already recorded by St Matthew (v. 31): *After they had mocked Jesus, they took the robe off from him, and put his* OWN *raiment* (τὰ ἴδια,) *on him.* It would appear, then, from a comparison of this with St John's account (v. 13–16), that Jesus was delivered by Pilate to be put to death as *King of the Jews,* while he yet wore the royal garments put in mockery upon him.

St Luke pursues his historical course in placing facts in a new order, by means of some remarkable additions and modifications.

The charge of having wished to set up a worldly kingdom in the face of the imperial authority is fully brought out only by him (v. 2): *We found this fellow perverting the nation, and forbidding to give tribute to Cæsar, saying that he himself is Christ, the*[1] *King*—(and yet only a few days before, he had said, *Render unto Cæsar the things that are Cæsar's,* with a direct reference to the payment of tribute !) St Luke (xx. 26) observes on that occasion, that the Pharisees *could not take hold of his words before* THE PEOPLE. Now they wrest the

[1] Thus in the author's rendering, instead of "*a* king," as in our authorized Bible.—TR.

words of Jesus, and slander him falsely before THE GOVERNOR.

Here the question and answer respecting the Saviour's kingship (v. 3) are given with great conciseness. We shall find St John far more ample in his details. But St Luke, on the other hand, is the only one that records the sending of Jesus to Herod—a circumstance of the very highest importance (v. 4–17). Pilate, seizing the opportunity presented to him by the cry raised by the chief priests and the people (v. 5), inquires of them whether Jesus be a Galilean (v. 6); and, on their answering in the affirmative, imagines that he has found the means of ridding himself of the embarrassment which the affair was causing him, by sending the accusers to Herod,—not that he might have Jesus condemned by him, but in order to have the validity of the accusation preferred against Jesus on the ground of a disturbance in Galilee (v. 5, 14, 15), decided by the testimony of a Galilean prince. Here, consequently, we find in our historical Evangelist,—1*st*, The mention of a Herod, which we have already spoken of as characteristic in St Luke;[1] 2*d*, That most important particular (v. 8 and 9) of the silence observed by the Saviour in the presence of a man who wanted merely to gratify an idle curiosity by seeing him perform a miracle; as well as, 3*d*, The derision (v. 11) that followed that holy silence; finally, 4*th*, The observation how Pilate and Herod, formerly enemies, on this occasion became friends (v. 12)—a circumstance to which we further find a striking allusion made in a prayer of the Apostles (Acts iv. 27, 28).

But our Evangelist is of the greatest importance here in elucidating that leading circumstance in our Lord's pas-

[1] P. 153.

sion before Pilate, to wit, the *scourging.* In as much as St Matthew and St Mark make mention of this outrage immediately before Jesus was delivered over to be crucified, one might imagine for a moment, that what we have to contemplate here is that species of *flagellation* which used often to precede crucifixion as an aggravation of the punishment, much in the same way as, in the penal code of France, the right hand of the parricide, it is ordained, shall be cut off previous to his being beheaded. And such is the view that many have taken of the scourging of Jesus; others (with still less appearance of probability) have supposed it a kind of torture. St Luke enables us to see the matter in its true light. In his Gospel (v. 16), Pilate declares to the Jews, after his finding that the sending of the accused to Herod had produced nothing to his prejudice, that he should be *scourged* and *then set at liberty.* And now, when, previous to that projected *punishment,* the attempt still to save Jesus, by taking advantage of the privilege enjoyed by the people at the feast, had failed, the governor makes a second attempt to cause the accused to be *scourged* and then to be *released,* a measure by which he seeks to appease both the Jews and his own conscience (v. 22). This *chastisement,* then, was, according to the invariable accuracy that characterises St Luke's expressions, nothing more than the judicial expression for *scourging,*[1] which, in point of fact, is nowhere mentioned by St Luke but under that name. By this punishment the governor, in the exercise of his cruel benevolence, seems to have had in view some sensible *correction* or *punishment,* whereby a person who had not

[1] L. 7. Dig. *de pœnis.* "*Fustium* admonitio, *flagellorum* CASTIGATIO." In like manner the Evangelists and the Acts carefully distinguish betwixt the *beating* with rods, and the *flagellation* (scourging) with the whip.

been found guilty of any delinquency worthy of death, might, *after due warning*, be set at liberty.[1] For the purpose of engaging the feelings of the people by this means in his favour, he presents the victim thus cruelly insulted in his state of humiliation, held up in mockery as a king, as we shall see afterwards given in more detail by St John. But this half measure proved equally ineffectual for serving the governor's purpose.

As for the rest (v. 22, compared with v. 4, 14 and 15), St Luke here again attaches himself particularly to that declaration of the Saviour's innocence, repeated three several times by the governor.[2] The antithesis between the *Prince of life* and the *murderer*, stands out in strong relief in this gospel (v. 25).[3] He passes over the mocking by the soldiers in the Prætorium; but, as if to compensate for that omission, it is he alone who records for us, as we have seen, the mocking of Jesus by Herod and his satellites (v. 11); as respects which, also, the gorgeous, that is, the white robe,[4] has also its meaning, as an involuntary tribute to the innocence, as well as to the royal dignity of our Lord.

Here we again find the Gospel of St John of the utmost importance on account of his insertions, his explanations, and his fully recorded conversations, particularly those between Jesus and the governor; whilst he omits the sending of our Lord to Herod, and is very concise with respect to what passed regarding Barabbas.

[1] As in the Roman law an outrage committed against the *patronus*, for example, was punished according to L. 1. *D. de jure patronatûs:* "*Tantummodo* CASTIGARI *eum sub comminatione aliquâ severitatis non defuturæ, si rursus causam querelæ præbuerit, et* DEMITTI *oportet.*" See this *castigari et demitti* (the very words of Pilate in St Luke) also in L. 7. D. *de extraord. crimin.* Among such misdeeds punishable by magistrates with a discretionary penalty, GROTIUS reckons the introduction of foreign modes and objects of worship.

[2] Comp. p. 176. [3] Comp. Acts iii. 14, 15. [4] Vulg. *veste albâ.*

It is he alone who throws the clearest light on the insults done to Jesus in the Prætorium, in connexion with the objects which Pilate had in view. Let us look at the details :—

First of all, he directs our notice (v. 28) to the hypocrisy of the chief priests and scribes, who refrain from entering the pagan governor's Prætorium lest they defile themselves—while they at the same time call on him to put the innocent to death, thus truly *straining at a gnat, and swallowing a camel.*[1] At the same time, both here and afterwards (xix. 14), he fixes our attention on precise periods. Further, it is only in his Gospel that we find this circumstance—that Pilate complied with the scruples of the Jews, and from time to time came out of the Prætorium to address them (v. 29, 33, xix. 9). It is through St John alone that we see how the *good confession* of his kingship[2] was made by the Saviour in the governor's Prætorium, representing the Roman monarchy (v. 33 and following verses). It is only here that we have the first words that were exchanged betwixt the chief priests and the governor; and on the occasion of those words being spoken, the recalling of what had been said prophetically by Jesus himself, to wit, that he should be put to death, not after the manner of the Jews, but upon the *cross*, which was used for punishment by the Romans (v. 29–32)—and which death he had on several occasions in this same Gospel called his being *lifted up.* Not less remarkable here are the more ample explanations which the Saviour, with a Divine wisdom, asks and gives, before he comes to the direct confession : THAT HE IS KING. Then, from the simple words of Jesus (v. 36), it becomes very clear, with what full conviction Pilate

[1] Matth. xxiii. 24. [2] 1 Tim. vi. 13.

might consider the kingship of this accused person as something that never could prejudice the Roman authority. All that he sees now (as he oscillates between his fears and his raillery) in this title of King of the Jews, is a means of humbling the Jewish people whom he hates. By this same spirit are his soldiers also actuated afterwards, in the insults and mockery with which they indulge themselves in the Prætorium. It is only in St John that Pilate here, on each occasion of his having to address himself to the Jews, calls the Divine sufferer by the name of YOUR KING (xix. 14, 15). It is thus that he finally leads on the Jews to purchase, so to speak, the condemnation of their Messiah, by disowning that very royalty of Israel *itself*, and by an involuntary acknowledgment of the rights and of the authority of the Roman emperor. (v. 15): *Pilate saith unto them, Shall I crucify* YOUR KING? *The chief priests answered, We have* NO KING BUT CÆSAR. Nor does he relinquish his purpose of crucifying Jesus, only under his title of *King of the Jews*, to the great scandal of the chief priests, who, though eager to see him crucified for sedition and blasphemy, by no means desired that it should be with the title of *their king*. On the contrary, he persists in it, and proceeds to prescribe a superscription to that effect, which was to be written over the cross (xix. 19), and to which we shall ere long return.

We further find noted only by St John, certain other declarations of great importance which were made by Jesus before Pilate (v. 37); for instance, his declaration concerning *the truth*, on which occasion (v. 38) Pilate makes his characteristic answer, *What is truth?*

The declaration of the Jews also (v. 7), *We have a law, and* BY OUR LAW HE OUGHT TO DIE, *because he made himself the Son of God,* is of importance at this place for the understanding of what is implied in the expression *Son of God.* Be it observed that, for pretending to the Messiahship, the law of the Jews did not ordain any kind of capital punishment. Here, too, accordingly, they understood the expression—the *Son of God* (in the sense in which Jesus had declared himself to be such), as tantamount to what they themselves had said in other parts of this Gospel, to wit (v. 18), *that he had said also that God was his Father, making* HIMSELF EQUAL WITH GOD, nay (x. 33), MADE HIMSELF GOD.

It is chiefly, however, as we have said, with respect to the scourging and other outrages done to Jesus in the Prætorium, that the Gospel of St John throws the greatest light on the subject. The scourging mentioned cursorily by St Matthew and St Mark, elucidated in St Luke by a single word concerning its nature and the governor's object in inflicting it, becomes still more clearly intelligible in St John, by means of that connexion which it had with the last of the parleys betwixt Pilate and the Jews, and of which the fourth Gospel alone informs us.

We have already had sufficient intimations of Pilate's inclination and purpose. He wished to rid himself of the matter altogether—to avoid embittering the Jews against him, and nevertheless to humble them so far as he could—to save Jesus if possible—that Jesus of whose innocence he was convinced, and for whose person he felt at once the contempt of pagan infidelity and pride, and an involuntary respect: such was his object throughout the whole proceeding, and such the motives at the same time that led him to employ, instead of the simple and upright method of *absolving* and *dismissing* our Lord, every sort of artifice, and means that were partly cruel, partly ignoble. Such also were the motives which made him desirous from the very first (John, ver. 31) to abandon the matter entirely to the Jews; but, seeing that it involved a criminal charge, mixed up with the question whether a capital sentence should or should not follow, and that at that time, under the Roman domination, the Jews were not allowed to pronounce sentence of death, he had no choice, but was compelled to take cognisance of the case. When, however, his simply declaring that he had found no fault in the accused had availed him nothing, he seized the opportunity suggested to him by a word which had escaped from one of the accusers, to send him to Herod, for the purpose of collecting information and the evidence of witnesses. He then makes use of the scoffing yet favourable evidence thus obtained, in proposing a middle course—that of first *subjecting the accused to corporal punishment*, and then *setting him at liberty*. Nevertheless, previous to such proceeding, the shouts of the people demanding the release of a prisoner suggest another idea to him—that of offering to release Jesus on the feast. But this subterfuge likewise serves him not; the chief priests urge on the people to demand Barabbas. Meanwhile the governor returns to his former plan (Luke v. 22). Jesus consequently is scourged in the Prætorium. Now, St John makes us see still more clearly how this scourging made no part of the capital punishment, but, on the contrary, had for its object the avoidance of the crucifixion. *Pilate therefore took Jesus and scourged him* (xix. 1)—that is, *ordered* Jesus to be seized, and *ordered* him to be scourged by his soldiers. In strict connexion with this outrage are those mockings of the soldiers which St Matthew and St Mark had already mentioned very fully, and to which St John adds nothing but the act of *smiting him with their hands* (v. 3).

But what, in particular, as we said, is made clear to us by St John, is the use which the governor makes of that outrage, in order to propitiate the people in favour of Jesus, and to save him from undergoing the punishment of the cross. He knew that the chief priests had delivered him for envy.[1] He therefore addresses himself to the people, presents Jesus to them under the deepest humiliation, cruelly outraged, with the crown of thorns upon his head, and arrayed in the purple robe; all the while, nevertheless, repeating his protestation: *I find no fault in him*, and adding those striking words: BEHOLD THE MAN (v. 4, 5). But the chief priests, with the officers, proceed to undo this impression by dint of violent outcries. The governor, on his side, persists in declaring the innocence of Jesus (v. 6). But, behold, a few words uttered by the *Jews* (that is to say, as St John always has it, by *the chiefs of the Jews*) suggest to Pilate a new ground of alarm (v. 7, 8): *he made himself* THE SON OF GOD. This leads to a new question being put to Jesus (v. 9): *Whence* (from what origin, of what nature) *art thou?* with what follows (v. 10 and 11). And now he has almost made up his mind to release him (v. 12); but the Jews again inspire him with fresh apprehensions by saying (v. 12): *If thou let this man go, thou art not Cæsar's friend.* Pilate places himself on the judgment-seat[2] (v. 13), there to pronounce the final sentence. Once more he addresses

[1] St Matthew (v. 18) had already informed us of this. But what he says in general, *for envy they had delivered him*, St Mark (v. 10) explains by expressly saying that the envy was that of the *chief priests.*

[2] The *Lithostrotos*, in Hebrew *Gabbatha*, was a kind of mosaic flooring (*pavimentum tessellatum*) on which the Roman magistrates, in the conquered provinces, took their seat on solemn occasions.

the Jews in these words (v. 14): *Behold your King!* to which, when uttered by him, no meaning can be attached but this: If I deliver him to be crucified, it shall only be under the title and in the quality of *King of the Jews;* the reply to which, on the part of the chief priests, involves an absolute disavowal of all expectation of a Messiah: *We have no king but Cæsar* (v. 15). Afterwards, when Pilate actually places this title on the superscription over the cross (v. 19–22), he tortures these same chief priests by his answer to their complaint: *What I have written, I have written.* And now Pilate delivers him to be crucified! The precise moment when the solemn sentence to that effect went forth from Gabbatha, is recorded by St John alone (v. 14). *It was the preparation of the passover, and about the sixth hour;* to wit, as we shall see ere long, six hours *before the commencement of* that Sabbath's preparation; that is, *about nine o'clock in the morning.*

After this St John attaches himself anew to the synoptical Gospels. Like them he records for us how Jesus was led away (v. 16), and it is then that the details of our Lord's sufferings on the cross commence.

But before entering upon these, let us once more give a cursory glance at the section of which we have been treating, and the details of which succeed each other as follows:—1. The chief priests lead Jesus away to Pilate (according to all the Evangelists). It was early in the morning (according to St John). 2. Pilate presents himself to the Jews, and desires (in vain) to leave the trial in their hands (according to St John). 3. The chief priests begin to accuse Jesus of sedition (according to St Luke). 4. On Pilate's questioning him, Jesus declares himself to be a king (according to all the Evangelists);

nevertheless, not without having previously, 5, given a very precise meaning to the *kingship* which he claimed (according to St John). 6. Pilate declares that he finds no fault in him (according to St Luke and St John). 7. The chief priests insist. The governor, in consequence of some words that escape from them, sends him to Herod (according to St Luke). 8. Herod, too, finds him equally guiltless, but sends him back to Pilate, deriding him, and after having put upon him a white robe, (according to St Luke). 9. Pilate would fain release him after having chastised him (ibid). 10. The multitude begin to insist that, according to custom at the feast, Pilate should release a prisoner unto them (according to St Mark). 11. Pilate proposes that Jesus should be the person (according to all the Evangelists). 12. Meanwhile Pilate is called aside and warned by his wife (according to St Matthew). The chief priests avail themselves of this pause, in order to stimulate the multitude, 13, to call for the release of Barabbas (according to all the Evangelists). 14. The governor falls back on his former proposal (according to St Luke). 15. He causes Jesus to be scourged in the Prætorium (according to St Matthew, St Mark, and St John). To this the soldiers add all manner of cruel mockings (according to the same Evangelists). 16. Pilate causes Jesus to come out with a crown of thorns, and the robe put upon him in derision (according to St John). 17. The chief priests call anew for the crucifixion of Jesus (according to all the Evangelists). 18. They throw the governor into fresh embarrassment by pronouncing the name: *Son of God* (according to St John). 19. Fresh interchange of words between the governor and Jesus (according to St John); and after that, 20. between the governor and the Jews (ibid). 21. It is about nine o'clock in the morning. Pilate places himself on the seat of judgment (ibid). 22. He calls Jesus *the King of the Jews* (ibid). 23. The Jews declare that they have no king but Cæsar (ibid). 24. Pilate washes his hands before the multitude, and declares that he is innocent of the blood of *this just person* (according to St Matthew). 25. The people exclaim: *His blood be on us and on our children* (ibid). 26. Pilate delivers Jesus to be crucified (according to all the Evangelists). 27. That same day Judas also testifies that he had betrayed innocent blood, and hangs himself (according to St Matthew).

THE CRUCIFIXION.

MATTH. xxvii. 32–56.	MARK xv. 21–41.
32. And as they came out, they found a man of Cyrene, Simon by name: him they compelled to bear his cross.	21. And they compel one Simon a Cyrenian, who passed by, coming out of the country, the father of Alexander and Rufus, to bear his cross.
33. And when they were come unto a place called Golgotha, that is to say, A place of a skull, 34. They gave him vinegar to drink mingled with gall: and when he had tasted thereof, he would not drink.	22. And they bring him unto the place Golgotha, which is, being interpreted, The place of a skull. 23. And they gave him to drink wine mingled with myrrh: but he received it not.
35. And they crucified him, and parted his garments, casting lots: that it might be fulfilled which was spoken by the prophet, They parted my garments among them, and upon my vesture did they cast lots.	24. And when they had crucified him, they parted his garments, casting lots upon them, what every man should take. 25. And it was the third hour; and they crucified him.
36. And, sitting down, they watched him there; 37. And set up over his head his accusation written, THIS IS JESUS THE KING OF THE JEWS.	26. And the superscription of his accusation was written over, THE KING OF THE JEWS.
38. Then were there two thieves crucified with him; one on the right hand, and another on the left.	27. And with him they crucify two thieves; the one on his right hand, and the other on his left. 28. And the scripture was fulfilled, which saith, And he was numbered with the transgressors.

39. And they that passed by
reviled him, wagging their heads,
40. And saying, Thou that destroyest the temple, and buildest it
in three days, save thyself. If thou
be the Son of God, come down from
the cross. 41. Likewise also the
chief priests, mocking him, with
the scribes and elders, said, 42.
He saved others; himself he cannot save. If he be the King of
Israel, let him now come down
from the cross, and we will believe
him. 43. He trusted in God; let
him deliver him now, if he will
have him: for he said, I am the
Son of God.

29. And they that passed by
railed on him, wagging their heads,
and saying, Ah, thou that destroyest
the temple, and buildest it in three
days, 30. Save thyself, and come
down from the cross. 31. Likewise also the chief priests, mocking, said among themselves, with
the scribes, He saved others; himself he cannot save. 32. Let
Christ the King of Israel descend
now from the cross, that we may
see and believe.

44. The thieves also, which were
crucified with him, cast the same in
his teeth.

And they that were crucified
with him reviled him.

45. Now from the sixth hour
there was darkness over all the
land unto the ninth hour.

33. And when the sixth hour
was come, there was darkness over
the whole land until the ninth hour.

46. And about the ninth hour
Jesus cried with a loud voice, saying, Eli, Eli, lama sabachthani? that
is to say, My God, my God, why
hast thou forsaken me? 47. Some
of them that stood there, when they
heard that, said, This man calleth
for Elias. 48. And straightway one
of them ran, and took a spunge,
and filled it with vinegar, and put
it on a reed, and gave him to
drink. 49. The rest said, Let be,
let us see whether Elias will come
to save him.

34. And at the ninth hour Jesus
cried with a loud voice, saying,
Eloi, Eloi, lama sabachthani? which
is, being interpreted, My God, my
God, why hast thou forsaken me?
35. And some of them that stood
by, when they heard it, said, Behold, he calleth Elias. 36. And
one ran and filled a spunge full
of vinegar, and put it on a reed,
and gave him to drink, saying, Let
alone; let us see whether Elias
will come to take him down.

50. Jesus, when he had cried
again with a loud voice, yielded up
the ghost. 51. And, behold, the
vail of the temple was rent in
twain from the top to the bottom;
and the earth did quake, and the
rocks rent; 52. And the graves
were opened; and many bodies of
the saints which slept arose, 53.
And came out of the graves after

37. And Jesus cried with a loud
voice, and gave up the ghost. 38.
And the vail of the temple was
rent in twain from the top to the
bottom.

his resurrection, and went into the
holy city, and appeared unto many.
54. Now, when the centurion,
and they that were with him
watching Jesus, saw the earthquake, and those things that were
done, they feared greatly, saying,
Truly this was the Son of God.
55. And many women were there
beholding afar off, which followed
Jesus from Galilee, ministering unto
him; 56. Among which was Mary
Magdalene, and Mary the mother
of James and Joses, and the mother
of Zebedee's children.

39. And when the centurion,
which stood over against him, saw
that he so cried out, and gave up
the ghost, he said, Truly this man
was the son of God.
40. There were also women looking on afar off: among whom was
Mary Magdalene, and Mary the
mother of James the less and of
Joses, and Salome; 41. (Who also,
when he was in Galilee, followed
him, and ministered unto him;)
and many other women which came
up with him unto Jerusalem.

LUKE, xxiii. 26–49.

26. And as they led him away,
they laid hold upon one Simon, a
Cyrenian, coming out of the country,
and on him they laid the cross, that
he might bear it after Jesus. 27.
And there followed him a great
company of people, and of women,
which also bewailed and lamented
him. 28. But Jesus, turning unto
them, said, Daughters of Jerusalem, weep not for me, but weep for
yourselves, and for your children.
29. For, behold, the days are coming,
in the which they shall say, Blessed
are the barren, and the wombs that
never bare, and the paps which never
gave suck. 30. Then shall they
begin to say to the mountains, Fall
on us; and to the hills, Cover us.
31. For if they do these things in
a green tree, what shall be done in
a dry?
32. And there were also two
others, malefactors, led with him to
be put to death.
33. And when they were come
to the place which is called Cal-
vary, there they crucified him, and

JOHN, xix. 17–35.

17. And he, bearing his cross,
went forth into a place called the
place of a skull, which is called in
the Hebrew, Golgotha; 18. Where
they crucified him, and two other
with him, on either side one, and
Jesus in the midst.

the malefactors; one on the right hand, and the other on the left.

34. Then said Jesus, Father, forgive them; for they know not what they do. And they parted his raiment, and cast lots. 35. And the people stood beholding: and the rulers also with them derided him, saying, He saved others; let him save himself, if he be Christ, the chosen of God. 36. And the soldiers also mocked him, coming to him, and offering him vinegar, 37. And saying, If thou be the King of the Jews, save thyself.

38. And a superscription also was written over him in letters of Greek, and Latin, and Hebrew, THIS IS THE KING OF THE JEWS.

39. And one of the malefactors which were hanged railed on him, saying, If thou be Christ, save thyself and us. 40. But the other answering, rebuked him, saying, Dost not thou fear God, seeing thou art in the same condemnation? 41. And we indeed justly; for we receive the due reward of our deeds: but this man hath done nothing amiss. 42. And he said unto Jesus, Lord, remember me when thou comest into thy kingdom. 43. And Jesus said unto him, Verily I say unto thee, To-day shalt thou be with me in paradise.

19. And Pilate wrote a title, and put it on the cross. And the writing was, JESUS OF NAZARETH, THE KING OF THE JEWS. 20. This title then read many of the Jews: for the place where Jesus was crucified was nigh unto the city: and it was written in Hebrew, and Greek, and Latin. 21. Then said the chief priests of the Jews to Pilate, Write not, The King of the Jews; but that he said, I am the King of the Jews. 22. Pilate answered, What I have written I have written. 23. Then the soldiers, when they had crucified Jesus, took his garments, and made four parts, to every soldier a part; and also his coat: now the coat was without seam, woven from the top throughout. 24. They said therefore among themselves, Let us not rend it, but cast lots for it, whose it shall be: that the scripture might be fulfilled, which saith, They parted my raiment among them, and for my vesture they did cast lots. These things therefore the soldiers did.

25. Now there stood by the cross of Jesus his mother, and his mo-

44. And it was about the sixth hour, and there was darkness over all the earth until the ninth hour.

45. And the sun was darkened, and the vail of the temple was rent in the midst. 46. And when Jesus had cried with a loud voice, he said, Father, into thy hands I commend my spirit: and having said thus, he gave up the ghost.

47. Now when the centurion saw what was done, he glorified God, saying, Certainly this was a righteous man. 48. And all the people that came together to that sight, beholding the things which were done, smote their breasts, and returned. 49. And all his acquaintance, and the women that followed him from Galilee, stood afar off, beholding these things.

ther's sister, Mary the wife of Cleophas, and Mary Magdalene. 26. When Jesus therefore saw his mother, and the disciple standing by whom he loved, he saith unto his mother, Woman, behold thy son! 27. Then saith he to the disciple, Behold thy mother! And from that hour that disciple took her unto his own home.

28. After this, Jesus knowing that all things were now accomplished, that the scripture might be fulfilled, saith, I thirst. 29. Now there was set a vessel full of vinegar: and they filled a spunge with vinegar, and put it upon hyssop, and put it to his mouth. 30. When Jesus therefore had received the vinegar, he said, It is finished:

And he bowed his head, and gave up the ghost.

31. The Jews therefore, because it was the preparation, that the bodies should not remain upon the cross on the sabbath-day, (for that sabbath-day was an high day,) besought Pilate that their legs might be broken, and that they might be taken away. 32. Then came the soldiers, and brake the legs of the

first, and of the other which was crucified with him. 33. But when they came to Jesus, and saw that he was dead already, they brake not his legs: 34. But one of the soldiers with a spear pierced his side, and forthwith came thereout blood and water. 35. And he that saw it bare record, and his record is true; and he knoweth that he saith true, that ye might believe. 36. For these things were done, that the scripture should be fulfilled, A bone of him shall not be broken. 37. And again another scripture saith, They shall look on him whom they pierced.

I. Jesus is led towards Golgotha. St Matthew gives the outline only (v. 32): *They found a man of Cyrene, Simon by name: him they* COMPELLED[1] *to bear his cross.* St Mark (v. 21) adds to this a word which seems to put the living scene before your eyes: *a man* (Gr. παράγοντα) *who was passing by* (*that very place*); and then, a particular circumstance which St Luke (v. 20) adopts from him: *coming out of the country;* finally, another also, which is mentioned by none but St Mark, and bears upon the person of this Cyrenian: he was *the father of* ALEXANDER *and* RUFUS, men in Mark's time well known in the Church, and particularly in that of Rome.[2]

We are not, however, so to understand the matter, as if the cross were taken off our Lord's shoulders and transferred to those of this Simon; much less, as we see it sometimes represented in Bible prints and pictures—as if the men who were leading away Jesus, on seeing him sink under the weight, had therefore thought of laying it

[1] The Greek word ἀγγαρεύειν means literally *to press into the service.*

[2] Rom. xvi. 13.

on Simon as he was passing by. The improbability of this will be perceived at once, by attending to the circumstance, that among the Romans the cross was ordinarily fastened to the shoulders of the condemned person, and could not, accordingly, have been first unloosed by the soldiers, as this supposition requires. No! the Saviour's cross was taken off his shoulders by no one. But the soldiers must in irony have compelled Simon, who, in passing, had expressed his compassion for the adorable sufferer, to *lift*[1] the cross, and (as St Luke expresses it) to *bear it after him* (v. 26). Thus, Simon presents us here with an image of the true disciple of our Lord, sharing in his cross and in his ignominy; or, as St Paul expresses it, *filling up that which is behind of the afflictions of Christ.*[2]

In perfect accordance with this we find the expressive statement of St John (v. 17): Jesus, *bearing with pain* (βαστάζων) *his cross, went forth*, &c.

II. Jesus addresses the multitude, and in particular the women, on going to the place called Golgotha. This passage has been preserved for us by St Luke alone (v. 27–31), and is a further characteristic of that Gospel, which makes particular mention of the participation of *women* in the Evangelical history.[3] That particularity harmonizes again with the character of our third Gospel, in so much as it is a prediction of the approaching fate of *Jerusalem*,[4] and an utterance of *compassion* on the part of that Saviour who is faithful unto the end.[5]

[1] Gr. Αἴρειν, which we must be careful to distinguish here from βαστάζειν, *painfully to carry*, in St John, v. 17.

[2] Τὰ ὑστερήματα τῶν θλιψέων Χριστοῦ. Col. i. 24.

[3] See p. 189. [4] See p. 182. [5] See p. 185, and following pages.

III. The crucifixion is preceded in St Matthew (v. 34), and in St Mark (v. 23), with the offer of the *mingled wine*, with which it was customary to deaden the sense of pain in those who underwent capital punishment. It is precisely on that account that Jesus refused the stupifying drink; yet he tastes it, and thus there is accomplished in him the words of the psalm (lxix. 21), according to which he was to have given to him *gall* and *vinegar* for his *meat* and *drink*. St Matthew, with his eye fixed on the prophecy, mentions *wine made bitter with myrrh*, VINEGAR WITH GALL, according to the taste. St Mark gives the proper name, which indicates the true composition.[1]

IV. St Luke and St John do not repeat this circumstance; on the other hand, they expressly mention the very *act* of the crucifixion of our Lord simultaneously with that of the two malefactors, the one on the right hand, and the other on the left (Luke, v. 33), which St John records simply, but in still more striking terms (v. 18) thus: *on either side one, and* JESUS IN THE MIDST.

We have immediately following this, in St Luke, the first saying uttered on the cross; the Saviour's charitable intercession for his enemies and murderers (v. 34): *Father, forgive them, for they know not what they do.* St Matthew (v. 35), and St Mark (v. 24), give the moment of the crucifixion of Jesus only in passing, and mention afterwards (Matth. v. 38, and Mark, v. 27) the

[1] One may observe, moreover, with GROTIUS, that among the ancients VINEGAR (ὄξος) was sometimes called WINE (οἶνος). The difference between St Matthew and St Mark lies, therefore, solely in the manner in which they express *myrrh*, the one, like the prophecy, according to the *taste* of the drink, the other literally.

crucifixion of the malefactors with Jesus, subsequent to which, we have in St Mark (v. 28) a quotation from Isaiah.[1]

V. St Mark is the only one that records the precise hour of the crucifixion (v. 25): *the third hour*, that is to say, about nine o'clock in the morning. But how are we to make this agree with the passage in St John (xix. 14), where it is stated that it was *the preparation, and about the sixth hour*, which brings it to *about noon*, when Pilate placed himself on the judgment-seat? Many attempts have been made to do away with this difference, and among these we find even critical conjectures that have no authority whatever from the manuscripts. The matter may be fully cleared up without the smallest change in the text, according to the principles which we have already indicated with regard to the Gospel of St John, provided we but rightly apprehend what the last Evangelist means here by the *Preparation*. This word is generally understood to mean *the whole day, the whole of Friday* preceding the Sabbath. But St Mark's Gospel gives us quite a different explanation of the expression (Mark xv. 42): *it was the preparation, that is* (not as the authorized version renders the word: THE DAY *before the Sabbath*, but) *the fore-Sabbath* (προσάββατον). What we are to understand by this *before-the-Sabbath*, is very clear, from the nature of the language and of the thing itself: it was not *the whole* preceding day, but that part of the Friday which forms the transition from that day to the Sabbath, which is known to begin among the

[1] This verse, however, is not to be found in several of the best manuscripts, and has perhaps been transferred to this place from St Luke xxii. 37. Moreover, this manner of quoting Scripture: *And the Scripture was fulfilled*, is not properly St Mark's, but rather St John's.

Jews on Friday evening.[1] What we have, therefore, to determine is, when properly this *fore-Sabbath* or preparation (in other words, that *part* of Friday on which people *prepared themselves* for the day of repose among the Jews, by suspending the occupations of the week) commenced. And this, too, is rendered very clear to us by the testimony of antiquity. We find, for example, in Josephus, an ordinance of the Emperor Augustus, which exempts the Jews in the Roman empire from the necessity of appearing in law courts on receiving a summons to that effect, not only on the *Sabbath day*, but also during the time of the *preparation* BEFORE *that day, from the ninth hour*, that is, from three o'clock in the afternoon (of Friday).[2]

Now, then, if we have a just idea of that *preparation* spoken of by St John (xix. 14), but one more recollection becomes necessary in order to our arriving at a satisfactory agreement between that passage and what is said by St Mark. We have seen among the peculiar characteristics of the fourth of the Gospels, this further particularity, that St John is accustomed, when he comes to speak of the last days passed by Jesus on earth, to count *backwards* from the last feast of the passover.[3] Such, likewise, is his reckoning here. The words: *it* WAS *the preparation of the passover* (that is to say, the *Sabbath of the passover*, as appears here throughout, from the connexion of the whole),[4] *and about the sixth hour*, we must understand as simply implying: *it was about the sixth hour* BEFORE (the commencement) *of the prepara-*

[1] A celebrated Dutch interpreter remarks on Mark xv. 42: "It was the holy eve, or twilight which precedes the great Sabbath, between three and six o'clock in the afternoon."

[2] *Antiq. Jud.* Lib. xvi. c. 10. Ἐν σάββασιν καὶ τῇ πρὸ ταύτης παρασκευῇ, ἀπὸ ὥρας ἐννάτης, that is to say, of the preceding day.

[3] See p. 264.

[4] xix. 31, 42, &c.

tion, which corresponds exactly with our nine o'clock in the morning, precisely the time mentioned in set terms by St Mark. To wit, when Pilate took his place on the seat of judgment, it was *about* (say half an hour more or less BEFORE) nine o'clock in the morning, or six hours before the preparation, *which is the fore-Sabbath;* so that, supposing we take a full half hour for all that passed betwixt the condemnation of Jesus and his crucifixion, the reckoning will be in every way correct: *at nine o'clock in the morning* the crucifixion took place, equally according to St John, as according to the formal statement of St Mark.

VI. After the crucifixion comes the mention of the superscription placed above the cross, in conformity with the custom among the Romans, of intimating in that manner the crime or the accusation brought against the sufferer.[1] Yet the tenor of that superscription, recorded as it is by all the Evangelists, is not in any two of them the same; but these differences are clearly to be referred to the three different languages that were employed, the same superscription having been composed in these, with some slight variation of expression, and each of the Evangelists having given it according to the language and the form most accordant with his own plan or style. In St Luke, it is probably the Latin superscription which we have presented to us: *This is the King of the Jews;*[2] in St Mark it is the Hebrew: *The King of the Jews;*[3] St John gives it to us in the fullest form, which is the Greek: *Jesus of Nazareth, the King of the Jews.*[4] St

[1] St John gives the proper term: τιτλος (v. 19).

[2] HIC EST REX JUDÆORUM.

[3] המלך היהודים.

[4] Ἰησοῦς ὁ Ναζωραῖος ὁ βασιλεὺς τῶν Ἰουδαίων.

Matthew gives us a kind of combination: *This is Jesus, the King of the Jews.*

It is first St Luke, and afterwards St John, who makes express mention of the three languages, but in a different order. That followed by St Luke, we may perceive at once, from the nature of the thing, to be the historical. Over the cross, the Latin, as being the language of the dominant power, was naturally placed in the middle, the Greek above, and the Hebrew below. St John changes this order by naming the three tongues according to their antiquity and dignity: Hebrew, Greek, Latin (*ἑβραϊστὶ, ἑλληνιστὶ, ῥωμαϊστὶ*).

But here St John is distinguished by other particularities also. He remarks, that many of the Jews read what was written, inasmuch as the place where the crucifixion took place was *nigh to* the city (not *in* the city).[1] But it is chiefly in his Gospel that we again meet with the rankling and suppressed dislike entertained by the governor towards the Jews, to whom, as we have seen, he did not wish to deliver Jesus except under the designation of *King of the Jews.* Accordingly, it is in harmony likewise with this settled purpose, that he causes these words to be placed over the cross, with the view of at once humbling and disappointing the Jews, the Jewish royalty being set forth in them as *of itself* a crime. To this, consequently, the chief priests also are opposed. They insist that the crime of the condemned person is not *that he* WAS *the King of the Jews,* but that *he* HAD SAID *that he was the King of the Jews* (v. 21): little in consistency with themselves, seeing that in the bitterness of their hatred, they had quite disowned that royalty (the expectation of a Messiah)! And now, too, they complain

[1] Heb. xiii. 11-13.

in vain. In words at once highly significant, and at the same time one may say prophetical, the governor dismisses them (v. 22): *What I have written, I have written.*

VII. We next come to the parting of the Divine Sufferer's garments among the soldiers—a well-known custom among the Romans, and which was at the same time the fulfilment of the prophecy of the Psalm (xxii. 18). All four Evangelists mention the parting of his raiment, as well as the casting of lots; St Matthew and St John quote the very words of the Psalm: *They parted my garments among them, and upon my vesture did they* CAST LOTS; but St Matthew only in general terms (v. 35), whereas St John (v. 23 and 24), concerning the *casting of lots*, adds one of those equally deep and delicate and unlooked-for details with which his Gospel abounds: *Then the soldiers, when they had crucified Jesus, took his garments and made four parts, to every soldier a part; and also his coat: now the coat was without seam, woven from the top throughout. They said therefore among themselves, Let us not rend it, but cast lots for it, whose it shall be: That the Scripture might be fulfilled which saith, They parted my raiment among them, and on my vesture they did cast lots. These things therefore the soldiers did* (quite unconscious of what they were doing, and of what they were fulfilling).

VIII. The mockings. The synoptical Gospels, and especially St Matthew and St Mark, record with many details the mockings and the blasphemies of which the crucified Saviour was made the object on the part of various descriptions of men,—the populace—the chief priests and the Pharisees—the soldiers—and the malefactors who were crucified with Jesus. Here St Matthew is anew remarkable for copiousness of expression, but particularly for his characteristic reference to the foretelling of those insulting expressions in Ps. xxii. (v. 9), the very words of which he puts into the mouths of the calumniators of our Lord, not that these were literally the same that were used, but as a striking indication how their insulting language was precisely the accomplishment of a prophecy written so many ages before by the Psalmist. Here the appellation *Son of God* occurs more than once, while it is not to be found in St Mark (v. 32) or in St Luke (v. 35).

St Mark here again compresses and abridges the narrative. There is great force, on the other hand, in his addition of *Ah!* (v. 29)[1] as an exclamation of triumph on the part of the multitude, who, both in St Matthew and in St Mark, address themselves *directly* to the crucified Sufferer, and cast in his teeth the words that had been attributed to him with respect to the temple; while the chief priests and the Pharisees, as St Mark in set terms observes (v. 31), speaking *among themselves,* and without addressing the crucified Saviour personally, give utterance to their derision: *He saved others,* &c. There is force also in his Gospel in the intercalation of those words, expressive of incredulity: *Let us see* (v. 32): *Let him descend now from the cross that* WE MAY SEE, *and that we may believe.*

St Luke has expressed still more succinctly the mockings both of the populace and their chiefs (v. 35), and having mentioned these, follows them up immediately with the insolent language of the soldiers, in connexion

[1] Gr. Οὐὰ, Lat. *Vah!*

with which he introduces the presenting of vinegar to the Sufferer; while in the other three Gospels this seems as if done only at the last moment of the passion on the cross.

IX. But if St Luke is extremely concise with respect to the mockery of the soldiers and of the bystanders in general; as if to compensate for this, he alone has preserved for us the sublime incident of the converted malefactor, which we read of in v. 39–43. That particular circumstance evidently belongs to the peculiar field of this Evangelist, to whom the glorification of Jesus Christ, as a compassionate Saviour even for *the most deeply wretched*, was specially intrusted.[1] That, moreover, the converted malefactor is formally distinguished here from the criminal who was crucified along with him, and who, even in his dreadful position, could join in the insults offered to the Blessed One, is again, in conformity with the nature of this Gospel, a necessary elucidation of what is said in a general way by St Matthew (v. 44) and St Mark (v. 32): *The thieves also, they that were crucified with him* (in the plural) *reviled him.* Those who, in contradiction to the true spirit of the evangelical harmony, would fain explain St Luke in this passage by means of his two predecessors, and who therefore entertain the idea of blasphemies being uttered by *both* thieves, one of whom was suddenly converted and addressed himself to our Lord, do not consider that it is quite opposed to the nature of such a conversion, to imagine a penitent whose first act as a believer could have been sharply to reprimand a sinner like himself for doing what he himself had done only a few moments before! But now it is manifest, from the true principles of evan-

[1] See page 186 and following pages.

gelical harmony, that St Matthew's plural is here the general indication of the *sort* of men who insulted Jesus in his final extremity of suffering. St Mark, according to his usual practice in like cases, here follows St Matthew, though with some slight modifications. To St Luke it was reserved to state the striking difference between the two who were crucified with Jesus, and at the same time to preserve for us the *second* of the sayings uttered by Jesus on the cross; that addressed to the thief (v. 43): *Verily I say unto thee, To-day shalt thou be with me in paradise.* Before the evening had come on, and ere the Sabbath had commenced, Jesus *had* entered on his rest, and the converted thief was with him.

X. The Saviour's sufferings on the cross, which lasted six hours (from nine o'clock in the morning until three in the afternoon), are divided by all the Synoptics into two equal parts, very distinctly defined. The darkness that came on about the *sixth hour*—that is to say, at noon—forms the point of transition from the one to the other part. But it may easily be conceived that before the coming on of that terrible and most significant darkness, that most affecting incident must have occurred, which has been preserved to us by St John, and which likewise falls so completely within the scope and spirit of that Gospel of our Lord's deepest love. Jesus, *who loveth his own unto the end,* commits his mother to St John, and delivers his disciple to his mother as from thenceforth her son (v. 25–27); this being the third saying uttered on the cross: *Woman, behold thy son!* and to the disciple: *Behold thy mother!*

XI. With the darkening of the heavens at noon, there

opens a new part of our Lord's sufferings on the cross, and these now reach their last and direst extremity. For three hours forward from that awful moment, not a whisper of derision is heard all around the cross. All is hushed into absolute silence. Jesus is silent: the sufferings he endured at the hands of men now give place to more painful inward sufferings. The darkening of the heavens accompanies and expresses the dreadful darkness that prevails in the soul itself of the suffering Saviour, and is manifested by the exclamation: *My God, my God, why hast thou forsaken me?*[1]—the fourth of our Lord's sayings on the cross.

All the three Synoptics describe the darkening of the sun almost in the same terms. St Matthew and St Mark alone give the Saviour's complaint in the proper Hebrew terms of the Psalm (xxii. 2) in which it was expressed prophetically many ages before. Only St Mark has (instead of the Hebrew word *Eli*, employed by St Matthew) the Syriac word *Eloi*, as it was no doubt pronounced by Jesus himself.[2]

XII. Anew after the utterance of that exclamation, we have the mockings and the insults on the part of the soldiers who stood on guard around the cross. St Matthew (v. 47) and St Mark (v. 35) relate how the cry of *Eli*, or *Eloi*, suggested the shameful parody of the Saviour's agonizing exclamation, *This man calleth for Elias.* Thereafter both Evangelists mention how one of the soldiers, putting a spunge dipped in vinegar on the end of a reed (or bunch of hyssop), presented it to the Sufferer to

[1] *Forsake me no longer!*

[2] OLSHAUSEN, Bibl. Comment. ii. 472: "Mark, xv. 34, renders the Aramean ext more exactly. For the Heb. 'Ηλί=אֵלִי he has 'Ελωΐ=אֱלָהִי."

drink (Matth. ver. 48; Mark, ver. 36). But now there follows an apparent discrepancy betwixt them. According to St Matthew (v. 49) the rest (*οἱ λοιποὶ*), on this being done, exclaim, *Let be, let us see whether Elias will come to save him;* whereas, according to St Mark (v. 36), it is the man himself that presents the vinegar, who then utters these words in derision. This apparent contradiction admits of an easy explanation. St Matthew, by the use of his favourite plural, informs us of the complication of others in this insult, the common perpetration of insult and slander among these men. St Mark, relating what took place with a nicer attention to the exact reality of what happened, teaches us how even that taunting remark, *Let us see,* &c., was pronounced by the same soldier that brought the vinegar to Jesus, whether in this manner to conceal a feeling of sympathy under a gross jest, or that both deed and words proceeded from a mischievous spirit of mockery and insult; in either way, *the others* (according to St Matthew) may very well have repeated his words.

St Luke enters into no details with respect to that saying: *Let us see,* &c.; but evidently makes allusion to the circumstance when (v. 36) he speaks of the scoffs of the soldiers and of the *vinegar offered by them.*

It is St John, finally, who throws the fullest light on this presentation of the vinegar, a circumstance which had not previously been well explained by any of his predecessors, and this he does by inserting a particularity of the highest importance in the history of our Lord's passion, namely, the striking accomplishment anew of a prophecy (v. 28): *After this, Jesus, knowing that all things were now accomplished, that the Scripture might be fulfilled,*[1]

[1] Ps. xx. 16; lxix. 26; on the *thirst* of Jesus in this Gospel compare p. 241.

saith, I thirst (the fifth saying on the cross). It was in consequence of these words, therefore, that the soldiers, or rather one of them, offered the Divine Sufferer on the cross a drink from the vessel full of vinegar, which, according to the custom of the Romans, stood near the cross.

XIII. Jesus yields up the ghost, according to all four Evangelists, *with a loud cry*. St Luke (v. 46) gives the very words of that last exclamation: *Father, into thy hands I commit my spirit* (seventh saying on the cross). St John further intercalates in a very few words (v. 30) three very important particulars. He connects the offering of the vinegar with the words uttered immediately before, *I thirst*,—and with what immediately followed, *It is finished* (the sixth saying on the cross);—he remarks, in harmony with the whole tendency of his Gospel, which every where puts in strong relief all that was voluntary on the Saviour's part in his passion and death,[1] how Jesus FIRST *bowed his head* and then *gave up the ghost* (κλίνας τὴν κεφαλὴν παρέδωκε τὸ πνεῦμα).

One word more on the distribution of the seven utterances on the cross among the four Evangelists, before passing to the signs that indicated the moment of the Lord's death. Seven sentences were uttered by the Saviour on the cross. None of the Evangelists has recorded them *all;* each, on the contrary, has reported *one* or *more* according to their respective bearing on the entire tendency and whole plan of his writing. St Matthew gives the expression of the bitterest agonies of the passion, the anguish of our Lord's soul, the pang of being forsaken by God, in an exclamation which transports us at once into

[1] John x. 17, 18; xiii. 3, &c.

the territory of prophecy; namely, to the first words of that prophetic psalm of which one of the Fathers of the Church has justly said, that in that psalm is expressed *the essence of the Saviour's passion.* In St Mark we find nothing more than the simple repetition of that same saying, but with a literal exactness of dialect and pronunciation. St Luke has further still, besides the words of compassion and grace addressed to the penitent malefactor, the first and the last of the seven sayings, both commencing with the invocation, *Father!* (v. 34 and 46).[1] Finally, St John has recorded that one expression of the tenderest love (v. 26, 27)—that of the last accomplishment of the prophecies (v. 28)—that of triumph in so far as respects the completed work of sacrifice and salvation (v. 29, 30): Τετέλεσται—*It is finished!*

XIV. Now follow the signs and wonders that marked the death of the Prince of Life. All three synoptical Gospels record that *the veil of the temple was rent.* St Matthew (v. 51) and St Mark (v. 38) describe it more fully thus—*in twain, from the top to the bottom.* St Luke (v. 45) has *in the midst.* Just before, this last Evangelist (v. 45) once more mentions *the darkening of the sun* at the moment of the Saviour's death.

But at this rending of the veil (symbolizing the opening of the Holy of holies above through the blood of Jesus),[2] St Matthew alone adds further (v. 51), that *the earth*

[1] It is remarkable that the same writer has recorded in the Acts of the Apostles (vii. 59, 60) the last words of the first martyr of Jesus (Stephen), who likewise commits his spirit into the hands of God, and prays for the forgiveness of sinners. But let us mark the difference. The Saviour prays *first* for transgressors, *last* for himself; the martyr, *first* for himself, then for his murderers;—Jesus addresses his *Father*, Stephen calls upon the *Lord* (expressly JESUS).

[2] Heb. ix. 8; x. 19.

did quake and the rocks rent, besides that circumstance every way so full of prophetic meaning, *that the graves were opened, and many bodies of the saints arose, and came out of the graves after his resurrection, and went into the holy city, and appeared unto many.*[2]

After the testimony of the inanimate creation now follows, in the three synoptical Gospels, that of the hearts and consciences of men. The centurion who stood on guard near the cross, witnessed to the innocence and to the greatness of Jesus, according to St Luke, in these terms (v. 47) : *Certainly this was a righteous man!* an expression which, as given by St Matthew (v. 54) and by St Mark (v. 39), according to their own conception of the matter, runs thus : *Truly this was the Son of God!* We have here, then, anew in St Luke, the historian, the proper terms ; in St Matthew (whom St Mark exactly follows) the elucidation, explanation, or commentary of those same terms. St Matthew, further, attributes to the whole of the guard, words which, as St Mark and St Luke report the matter, could have been uttered only by the centurion. Both St Mark and St Luke bring back St Matthew's plural to the historical reality.

After this, St Luke describes the effect which the stupendous event of the crucifixion had upon the multitude (v. 48) : all the people, on their return from Golgotha, *smote their breasts*—a first preparatory movement for the great day of conversion which broke upon Jerusalem seven weeks afterwards on the day of Pentecost, as described by that same writer in the book of the Acts.

[2] We must understand these words, *after his resurrection* (v. 53), of the whole event; for the resurrection of those saints naturally took place not till after that of *the first of those that rose again*, who is Jesus himself. But St Matthew characteristically combines the rending rocks with the opening graves, and the coming forth from them of the dead.

St Matthew (v. 55, 56) and St Mark (v. 40, 41) speak again of the women who, as the disciples of Jesus, had followed him from Galilee, and mention who they were by name. St Luke, in an affecting manner, merges them all together in his record (v. 49) with *his acquaintance who stood afar off.* To these women, so full of faith, all three synoptical Evangelists return in the accounts they have given of the burial and resurrection of Jesus. St John, in mentioning (v. 25) the women who stood near the cross, gives us, when compared with Matthew (v. 56) and Mark (v. 40), a very important indication of the near consanguinity existing between the Lord Jesus and the beloved disciple. Salome, mentioned by St Mark under her own name, and by St Matthew as the *mother of the sons of Zebedee,* was more than probably that *sister of the mother of our Lord,* who, according to St John, stood with her by the cross of Jesus. Interpreters have recently suggested, on sufficient grounds, that the designation "his mother's sister" in St John (v. 25), is not to be understood of *Mary, the wife of Cleophas,* but that we have here *four* distinct persons mentioned in *two* different couples: 1. *The mother of our Lord;* and, 2. *Her sister* (to wit, Salome); 3. *Mary, the wife of Cleophas;* and, 4. *Mary Magdalene,*—St John having thus added a fourth person (the mother of the Lord herself) to the three already mentioned by the two first Evangelists.[1]

Finally, St John makes no mention of the signs made in nature, or of the emotions felt by the hearts and consciences of men on this great event. With him the account of the Saviour's death is accompanied with details

[1] The Syriac version and one Codex give expressly the conjunction *and* after the words: "his mother's sister." But the connexion and the sense are the same even without the conjunction.

of a very different kind, still more sublime and fraught with a deeper meaning. He confines himself exclusively to the *person* of our Lord. The signs which *he* mentions (v. 31–37) affected *the body itself of Jesus.* Thus he tells us (v. 31–33) how before the commencement of the paschal Sabbath the bones of the two malefactors were broken; while none of the bones of Jesus, who was in the midst, were broken, in conformity with the prophecy both of the Law and of the Psalms.[1] He tells us (v. 34–37) how one of the soldiers pierced the Saviour's side when he was already dead, so that there came forth *blood and water*, and how there thus was accomplished another prophecy.[2] *He testifies* (v. 35) to his having seen what he records, and to his knowing that he spoke the truth in order that we might believe. Here, then, we have in the Gospel of the beloved disciple a rich harmony of fulfilments of the Scriptures, of symbolical events, of harmonious dispositions of the Divine providence. Every thing had its special signification. Men are found accomplishing God's counsel, even without being aware of it, and without their intending it, the Lamb was slain, his blood was shed on the altar of the cross. Of the paschal lamb in Israel not a bone was to be broken: of Jesus, the Lamb of God, *our Passover*, not a bone was broken; but his side was pierced even after death. Thus it is *that he shall one day be seen in his glory even by those that have pierced him.* With these prophetic words of an ancient prophet, St John, the Apostle Evangelist-Prophet, *here* closes the narrative of the passion (v. 37), and *afterwards* opens the book of the Revelation (i. 7).

And here again we close this last division of our Evangelical history with a succinct view of the order in

[1] Numbers ix. 12; Ps. xxxiv. 21. [2] Zechariah xii. 10.

which the events took place. 1. Jesus is led to Golgotha (according to all the Evangelists); 2. Jesus bears his own cross (according to St John); 3. The soldiers compel Simon, the Cyrenian, to lift it up behind the Saviour, and to assist him in bearing it along (according to the synoptic Gospels); 4. Jesus addresses some words to the daughters of Jerusalem (according to St Luke); 5. The stupifying drink is tasted and refused by Jesus (according to St Matthew and St Mark); 6. Jesus prays for transgressors before the crucifixion (according to St Luke); 7. The crucifixion between two thieves (according to all the Evangelists); 8. At the third hour (according to St Mark and St John); 9. The superscription placed above the cross (according to all the Evangelists); 10. In three languages (named by St Luke and St John); 11. The discussions between Pilate and the Jews on the subject of this superscription (in St John); 12. The parting of the garments (according to all); together with, 13. The particular mention of the coat *that was without seam, and of the lot that was cast upon that coat* (in St John); 14. The mockings by four different sorts or classes of men (the synoptical Gospels); 15. The conversion and the promise of glory to the converted malefactor (in St Luke); 16. The recommending of Mary by Jesus to the disciple whom he loved (in St John); 17. The darkening of the sun (in the synoptical Gospels); 18. The heart-rending under the hidings of his Father's countenance (in St Matthew and St Mark); 19. The mockings of the soldiers (in the Synoptics); 20. The exclamation, *I thirst* (in St John); 21. The refreshment with vinegar (in all the Evangelists); 22. The exclamation, *It is finished* (in St John); 23. The giving up the ghost (by all the Evangelists); 24. The very words with which Jesus expired (according to St Luke); 25. The rending of the veil of the temple (in the Synoptics); 26. The earthquake, the cleaving of the rocks, the opening of the graves, the resurrection of the saints (in St Matthew); 27. The centurion's testimony (in the Synoptics); 28. The dismay of the multitude (in St Luke); 29. The presence at the sad scene of the women from Galilee (in the Synoptics); 30. The breaking of the bones of the two crucified malefactors, and the piercing of the Saviour's side, according to the prophecies (in St John).

NOTES AND ADDITIONS.

P. 27—" *Yet this Israelite and Hebrew character of our first Gospel does not necessitate,*" &c.

THE opinion that St Matthew's Gospel was originally written in Hebrew, has long been maintained by many learned men, after the example of the Fathers of the Church, and even in our own days it finds numerous defenders among distinguished divines.[1] It appears to us, however, that this opinion has been sufficiently refuted by the celebrated Professor Hug, in his *Introduction to the New Testament*, vol. ii. The conclusions he has drawn are mainly interesting as they bear upon the demonstration that the Greek tongue must have necessarily been that employed by St Matthew, *even when addressing Israelite readers*, from regard to the following considerations, which he sums up at the close of his demonstration in this manner :—

" 1. Asia, in consequence of the domination of the

[1] As, for instance, among English *literati*, Mr Samuel Prideaux Tregelles, whose *Dissertation on the Original Language of St Matthew's Gospel* (London, 1850) did not, however, convince the writer of these pages of the preponderance of his arguments over those of Hug and others on the subject.

Macedonians, was filled far and wide with Greek towns. These multiplied more and more under the dynasty of the Ptolemies and the Seleucidæ. Under this same influence, even such ancient cities as Tyre and Sidon changed their language. 2. The shores of Syria, Phœnicia, and Judea had in like manner towns which were entirely, or at least partly, Greek, scattered over them. The eastern parts of Palestine, from Arnon to Abilene, were towards the north Greek, and towards the south, in a great measure, in the possession of Greeks. In Judea and in Galilee there were towns entirely, or at least half, inhabited by Greeks. 3. Herod the Great had made unheard-of efforts to reform the Jews by transforming them into Greeks. 4. The domination of Rome was rather favourable than otherwise to this leaning toward Hellenism. 5. The religious authorities among the Jews, far from opposing obstacles in those times to the advance of Hellenism, were much rather disposed to do homage to the Greek tongue, down to the last moments of their political existence; they recognized it as a language in common use in their literary works, as, for instance, in the case of their historian Josephus, and even admitted it into their judicial proceedings. 6. This same language, thus received on all hands into favour, came to be diffused also by daily use among all classes, to such an extent, that the people (with but few exceptions) understood it, though naturally attached to their own tongue. 7. Even in the holy city there were whole congregations of Jews speaking Greek. It was of these and of Greek proselytes that the Christian Church at Jerusalem was partly composed." Thus, then (the consequence is evident), in order to his being understood by the great majority of the Jews, to whom in the first instance our first Evangelist addressed himself, he had no need to make use of either Hebrew or Araméan, but the Greek, on the contrary, suited him equally well, and in certain respects even better. It was particularly as it bore upon future times that the Greek could not but be preferable. Writing, as he did, in the closing period of his nation's political existence, penetrated with the predictions of his Divine Master, which announced the destruction of the Jewish polity as rapidly approaching, and already perceiving of himself the signs that harbingered it in the course of being accomplished, he naturally behoved to dismiss the use of that nation's language, seeing that soon it was to cease to be a nation, if at least he designed his work to outlast a few months or years, and if he desired that the remnant of the Jews, scattered and wandering in other lands, should have it in their power to make themselves acquainted with it. It is thus that, by a natural train of reasoning, we are at once led *a priori* to this result: that St Matthew's Gospel *must* have been written in Greek. There is nothing in the text itself of that Gospel opposed to such a supposition; on the contrary, more than one passage (as for example, chap. xxvii. 46) evidently supports it. And to such an extent does this hold true, that commentators, among others Olshausen[1] (who always preserved the tradition of a Hebrew Gospel of St Matthew), have been led to conclude that the Apostle must himself have written his Gospel *first* in Hebrew, *afterwards* in Greek, so that both must have been original Gospels. Others, like De Wette (*Kurze Erklärung*, S. 2, 3), have declared their inability to decide as to an original Hebrew *which no one has ever really seen.* Erasmus long ago combated the opinion that there must have been a St Matthew's Gospel in

[1] *Biblischer Commentar.* I, 11.

Hebrew, by pointing to the eminently Greek composition of that which we now possess.

P. 48—" *Get thee behind me, Satan!*"

The best critics are entirely agreed (on the authority of several eminent manuscripts, of the Vulgate, and several other ancient translations, as well as on that of the oldest and best Fathers of the Greek Church) that these words, *Get thee behind me, Satan!* here, are not in their place in St Luke's Gospel, but have been intercalated afterwards by copyists who had taken them from St Matthew (iv. 10). Bengel (in his *Apparatus*) says of them by way of elucidation : " Hæc verba : *Abi post me, Satana!* ascribere Domino non decuit Lucam, qui postea alium Satanæ memorat incursum. Ex Matthæo recentiores Græci huc traduxerunt." Compare also Griesbach and Tischendorf.

P. 107—" *The Roman characteristic remains,*" &c.

The Roman character further occurs, among other places, in a remarkable amplification by our Evangelist on the subject of divorce. At the declaration that the husband who leaves his wife and takes another commits adultery (Matth. xix. 9), St Mark judged it necessary to add in precise terms (x. 12) : *And if a woman shall put away her husband, and be married to another, she committeth adultery.* Wetstein in his commentary at this passage : " Ex eo autem quod Christus de viris uxores repudiantibus dixerat, Marcus infert multo scelestius esse, si mulier virum deserat: quod et Romanis quibus Marcus scripsit, licitum, et tum temporis, licentiâ supra modum grassante, familiare erat."

P. 109—"*The more we reflect on the expression, All the Jews,*" &c.

We are aware that in St John also, and sometimes even in St Matthew, there occurs that same expression: *The Jews,* notwithstanding that both those Gospel writers were themselves, unquestionably, of that nation. But what distinguishes the passage in St Mark is the conjunction AND: *the Pharisees* AND *all the Jews,* intimating that the writer himself belonged as little to the one as to the other of these. A still more evident indication, certainly, of the Gentile origin of our second Evangelist, may be seen in the remarkable insertion which he makes on the occasion of the purification of the Temple:

MATTH. xxi. 13.	MARK xi. 17.	LUKE xix. 46.
My house shall be called the house of prayer.	My house shall be called *of all nations* (Gr. πᾶσι τοῖς ἔθνεσι) the house of prayer.	My house is the house of prayer.

P. 111—"*In both we have the same emphatic repetitions,*" &c.

Thus, for instance, Cæsar's Commentaries abound with repetitions similar to those we have noted in St Mark's Gospel. Opening his *Gallic War,* we find at once, cap. vi. § 1, "Erant omnino *itinera* duo, quibus *itineribus* domo exire possent." § 4, "*Diem* dicunt quâ *die* ad ripam Rhodani omnes conveniant." Cap. xxiii. § 1, and passim "*postridie* ejus *diei.*" Cap. xxxi. § 1, "Uti sibi *secreto* in *occulto* de suâ omniumque salute cum eo agere liceret." Cap. xlix. § 1, "Ultra eum *locum* quo in *loco* Germani consederant;" and so in many other passages.

P. 111—"*The very word* straightway," &c.

The military character of this word *straightway* in St Mark's Gospel has been clearly perceived also by Lange (*Ueber die Authentic der Vier Evangelien* in the *Theologische Studien und Kritiken* of 1839): "Das Liebling's wort des Marcus is das frische *εὐθέως;* es kehret in seinem Erzählungen immer wieder.—Seine Losung war *εὐθέως* wie Blücher's Losung: Vorwärts!" Neither did the military character of many of our Evangelist's expressions escape the notice of Wetstein: "Habet plures voces Latinas aut *rem militarem* spectantes, ut *λεγέων, σπεκουλάτωρ, σύσσημον*" (*Introd. Comment. in Marc.*) It is surprising that, notwithstanding numerous notices of a military language in St Mark, no one appears to have been led to the idea that the person who wrote thus might himself have been a soldier. To the indications bearing upon that profession, we may add further expressions peculiar to St Mark as an individual—*δύο δύο, by two and two,* when the twelve were sent out (vi. 7); in like manner at the multiplication of the loaves (vi. 39, 40), his *συμπόσια συμπόσια, πρασιαὶ πρασιαὶ, ἀνὰ ἑκατὸν καὰ ἀνὰ πεντήκοντα*—a passage which, in its general aspect, quite suggests the idea of a military order: *And he commanded them to make all sit down by companies*—that is, round the turf which served on that occasion for tables —*upon the green grass. And they sat down in ranks by hundreds and by fifties.* In St Matthew we have only the *germ* of the picture presented by St Mark in the word ἀνακλιθῆναι (xiv. 19); St Luke and St John evidently follow, though in their own manner, the narrative of St Mark.

P. 116—"*Was no other than that same devout soldier,*" &c.

It is precisely on that account that it was not seemly, in accordance with the tenderness and delicacy of feeling that influenced our sacred writers, that the striking history of that other centurion, whose faith is so much praised in St Matthew and St Luke, should have been taken into his Gospel by St Mark. The eulogy of the Gentile, and especially of the Gentile soldier—of the Roman soldier—behoved to be omitted in a Gospel written by the *pious soldier* attached to the family of the *centurion* Cornelius. It is, accordingly, on that account that St Luke here fills the place of St Mark, by describing, with greater amplitude and detail, those facts of which St Matthew, in harmony with the character of his Gospel, has only given the general outline. (Matth. viii. 5–13, compared with St Luke vii. 2, 10.) Neither do we any where find taken into St Mark's Gospel that sentence uttered by our Lord which St Matthew gives in connexion with the great faith shewn by the centurion (viii. 11, 12), and which St Luke (xiii. 29) gives at its true historical place: *Many shall come from the east and from the west, and shall sit down with Abraham and Isaac and Jacob, in the kingdom of heaven:*

But the children of the kingdom shall be cast out into outer darkness.

P. 131—"*Neither the son,*" &c.

Bengel, upon the very passage in St Mark (xiii. 42): "Dices : Cur appellatur h. l. Filius, non sumptâ denominatione a naturâ humanâ? Resp. In enunciatis de Salvatore cum prædicato glorioso copulari solet subjectum demissum (Matth xvi. 28; John i. 12; iii. 13); cum prædicato demisso, subjectum gloriosum. (Matth. xxi. 3; 1 Cor. ii. 8.)

P. 142—"*There is yet another circumstance which we may infer,*" &c.

We willingly admit that the Gentile origin of St Luke would not be sufficiently proved by comparing v. 11 with v. 18 in the fourth chapter of the Epistle to the Colossians. It is only by combining this passage with the entire spirit of St Luke's writings that the proof which several interpreters have drawn with respect to this point from the passage in the Epistle to the Colossians, acquires its true force. There is another passage, however, in one of the writings of St Luke himself, which seems to us to prove directly his Gentile origin. It occurs in the Acts of the Apostles (chap. i. 19), where we read, when he is referring to the Jews, that the field *Aceldama* was thus called *in* THEIR *proper tongue.* It is clear that these words make no part of St Peter's discourse, he himself being an Israelite, but that they formed a parenthesis of the narrator St Luke.

P. 148—“ *Syria, in particular, was in those days highly reputed for the practice of medicine.*”

Strictly speaking, it was not until a later age that the medical reputation of Syria is proved with any historical certainty. But at all events, the practice of medicine was, so early as during the time of Augustus, in the hands of foreigners ; for the most part of Greek slaves or freedmen—in the case, for instance, of Antonius Musa, whom the Emperor raised to the rank of a Roman knight, and in whose honour afterwards a statue was set up in the temple of Esculapius.

P. 148—“ ——*while the termination of his name,*” &c.

Tholück, in his *Glaubwürdigkeit der Evangelischen Geschichte*, S. 148, at the second note : “ Die Endung ᾶς nämlich ist eine kontraction, welche ins besondere auch bei sklavennamen oft vorkommt.” Lobeck *de Substant. in* ᾶς *exeuntibus*, in *Wolff's Analecten* iii. § 49. At all events, *Lucas* is the contraction for the known name *Lucanus.* In some manuscripts of his Gospel we even read this name at full length.

P. 149—“ *The style of the ancient classical historian,*” &c.

The celebrated Valckenaer expresses himself in these terms, speaking of the style of St Luke : “ Stylus Lucæ in Evangelio talis est qualis historicum decet, simplex et purus, tamen a stylo reliquorum scriptorum N. T. longe diversus ; est enim stylus Lucæ magnam partem nitidus et Græcus, quum stylus reliquorum propius accedat ad vulgarem loquendi rationem, quæ inter Judæos Græce loquentes obtinebat locum, atque adeo formis ubique scateat quas Hebraismos vocant, quibus parcius utitur Lucas, suamque scribendi normam ad elegantiorum Græcorum regulas sæpenumero accommodavit."

P. 151—"*But he is no less accurate in giving epochs,*" &c.

To this further belongs the ulterior determination of the epoch of the Sabbath on which the disciples were reprehended by the Pharisees for having plucked the ears of corn on that day (Matth. xii. 1). St Luke gives to this Sabbath (vi. 1) a name which is found nowhere else: δευτερόπρωτον. That this *second-first* Sabbath is a properly Jewish denomination for some fixed and particular day of repose is not to be doubted, even although we should not be able exactly to say *what* day it was, or at what precise period of the year it occurred. Some are of opinion that the FIRST *Sabbath* means a GREAT *Sabbath*, a feast-day Sabbath (the first Sabbath after one of the great feasts), and go on to admit three such Sabbaths—namely, those immediately following the Feasts of the Passover, of Pentecost, and of Tabernacles, among which the Sabbath after Pentecost will then have been the δευτερόπρωτον, or *second great Sabbath.*

P. 156—"——*the language that is appropriate to the subject, purely and naturally employed.*"

We may take for an example of this exactness in St

Luke in Greek terminology, the description of the voyage into Italy, and of the shipwreck at Malta, in the 27th chapter of the Acts, where the following terms are worthy of remark, for characteristic Greek accuracy: ἀνάγεσθαι and κατάγεσθαι (v. 2 and 3), *to set sail,* and *to return* (*to port*); ὑποπλεῖν (v. 4 and 7), *to tack;* βραδυπλοεῖν (v. 7), *to sail slowly, to advance with difficulty;* ἀντοφθαλμεῖν τῷ ἀνέμῳ, *to go against, to* FACE *the wind;*[1] and ἐπιδόντες φέρεσθαι (v. 15), *to let the ship drive;* ὑποζωννύειν πλοῖον (v. 17), to *undergird the ship with ropes;* προςάγειν τινα αὐτοῖς χώραν (v. 27), *that they approached the land;* βολίζειν (v. 28), *to throw the lead;* χαλάζειν τὴν σκάφην (v. 30), *to let down the boat,* &c. &c.

The word ἐκπίπτειν should have been translated at v. 17, as well as at v. 32, by *to be carried along by the current.* The soldiers did not lower the boat into the sea, as (v. 30) had already been done by the sailors, but they cut the ropes, and thus made it useless by allowing it to float away, and this they did in order to prevent the sailors from succeeding in their project.

Compare, for a striking notice of the accuracy of St Luke as to sea terms and details of a sea voyage, "The Voyage and Shipwreck of St Paul." By James Smith, Esq. of Jordanhill, F.R.S., &c. London, 1848.

P. 158—"—— *in such sort, that many particulars, true at one time, if transposed,*" &c.

To the instances of this, which our observations on the Gospel of St Luke have supplied, a no less remarkable one, bearing on a passage in that of St Matthew, might

[1] If I mistake not, our seamen have the still more analogous expression to that in the Greek, of *digging into the wind's* EYE, when luffing up in a gale.—TR.

be added. St Matthew is the only Evangelist that makes mention of the *wife of Pilate* in the history of the Passion (xxvii. 19). Some passages of Suetonius (*in Augusto,* cap. 24) and others, from which we learn that down to the time of the emperor Augustus, governors were *not* at liberty to take their wives along with them into the provinces, might certainly have given infidel philosophers fine scope for disputing the entire historical truth of that particularity, *provided* we did not learn from passages, equally conclusive and well known, in Tacitus, that from the commencement of the reign of Tiberius, and even as early as towards the close of that of Augustus, that custom, or that abuse, had ceased to be opposed. Thus we read in the historian to whom we refer (Annal. iii. 33, 34), how Severus Cæcina moved in the senate *ne quem magistratum, cui provincia obvenisset, uxor comitaretur.* But it was to no effect. In consequence of various objections *Cæcinæ sententia elusa.*

P. 164—"*The signs that were to accompany the last times,*" &c.

There is, perhaps, no passage in the Gospels that has been the occasion of more pain to enemies, and that has more exposed their impotency, than the prediction of the destruction of Jerusalem, and of Israel's dispersion. The agreement between the prediction and the result could not be denied. The opposers have been driven, accordingly, to have recourse to the supposition that the prediction was inserted after the event! But the insufficiency of this subterfuge is exposed at once by the simple remark, that a prophecy made up after the event which it professed to predict, would necessarily be wanting in that character of simplicity and sobriety which so remarkably marks the prophetic passages in our Gospels that treat of this subject, and would, most unquestionably, not have failed to have entered into *much fuller details* of persons and of facts, such as we now know from history. Above all, in any such supposition, it is not possible to explain how the destruction of Jerusalem (which, in the case supposed, must have taken place when the prediction was written) should have been spoken of in such immediate connexion with the still future advent of the Saviour, and the final consummation of all things.

Nevertheless, a difficulty with respect to this double prediction of the fall of Jerusalem, and of the consummation of all things, here requires some further elucidation. But, first of all, let us once more contemplate the synoptical Gospels in juxtaposition, in the different accounts they have given of that prophecy, in order that we may place in its true light the connexion, as represented in the Gospels, between the judgment pronounced on Jerusalem and that pronounced on the world in our Lord's prophetical sayings.

MATTH. xxiv. 1.	MARK xiii. 1.	LUKE xxi. 5.
And Jesus went out, and *departed from the temple: and his disciples came to him*, for to shew him the buildings of the temple. 2. And Jesus said unto them, See ye not all these things? Verily I say unto you, There shall not be left here one stone upon another, that shall not be	And as he went out of the temple, *one of his disciples saith unto him, Master, see what manner of stones and what buildings are here!* 2. And Jesus answering, said unto him, Seest thou *these great buildings?* there shall not be left one stone upon another, that shall not be thrown	And as some spake of the temple, *how it was adorned with goodly stones and gifts*, he said, 6. As for these things which ye behold, the days will come, in the which there shall not be left one stone upon another, that shall not be thrown down. 7. And they asked him, saying, Master, but

thrown down. 3. And as he sat upon the mount of Olives, the disciples came unto him privately, saying, Tell us, when shall these things be? *and* *what shall be the sign* *of thy coming, and of* *the end of the world?*	down. 3. And as he sat upon the mount of Olives, over against the temple, Peter, and James, and John, and Andrew, asked him privately, 4. Tell us, when shall these things be? *and what shall be* *the sign when all these* *things shall be fulfilled?*	when shall these things be? and what sign will there be when these things come to pass?
4. And Jesus an- swered and said unto them, Take heed that no man deceive you. 5. For many shall come in my name, saying, I am *Christ;* and shall deceive many.	5. And Jesus an- swering them, began to say, Take heed lest any man deceive you: 6. For many shall come in my name, saying, I am (it);[1] and shall deceive many.	8. And he said, Take heed that ye be not deceived: for many shall come in my name, saying, I am (it);[2] *and* *the time draweth near:* *go ye not therefore after* *them.*
6. And ye shall hear of wars, and rumours of wars; see that ye be not troubled: for all these things must come to pass, but the end is not yet. 7. For nation shall rise against nation, and kingdom against kingdom: and there shall be famines, and *pestilences*, and earthquakes, in divers places. 8. All these are the beginning of sorrows.	7. And when ye shall hear of wars, and rumours of wars, be ye not troubled: for such things must needs be; but the end shall not be yet. 8. For nation shall rise against na- tion, and kingdom against kingdom; and there shall be earth- quakes in divers places, and there shall be famines and *troubles:* these are the be- ginnings of sorrows. 9. But take heed to yourselves: for	9. But when ye shall hear of wars and *com-* *motions*, be not terri- fied: for these things must first come to pass; but the end is not by and by. 10. Then said he unto them, Nation shall rise against na- tion, and kingdom against kingdom: 11. And great earthquakes shall be in divers places, and famines and *pestilences;* and fearful sights and great signs shall there be from heaven.
9. Then shall they deliver you up to be afflicted, and shall kill you:	they shall deliver you up to councils; and in the synagogues ye shall be beaten: and ye shall be brought before rulers and kings for my sake, for a tes-	12. But before all these, they shall lay their hands on you, and persecute you, de- livering you up to the synagogues, and into *prisons*, being brought

[1] Which our translation renders in Italics, *Christ.*—Tr.

[2] See preceding note.—Tr.

and ye shall be hated of all nations for my name's sake.

10. And then shall many be offended, and shall betray one another, and shall hate one another. 11. And many false prophets shall rise, and shall deceive many. 12. And because iniquity shall abound, the love of many shall wax cold. 13. *But he that shall endure unto the end, the same shall be saved.* 14. *And this gospel of the kingdom shall be preached in all the world for a witness unto all nations; and then shall the end come.*

timony against them.

10. *And the gospel must first be published among all nations.*

11. But when they shall lead you, and deliver you up, take no thought beforehand what ye shall speak, neither do ye premeditate; but whatsoever shall be given you in that hour, that speak ye: for it is not ye that speak, but the Holy Ghost. 12. Now the brother shall betray the brother to death, and the father the son; and children shall rise up against their parents, and shall *cause them to be put to death.* 13. And ye shall be hated of all men for my name's sake: but he that shall endure unto the end, the same shall be saved.

before kings and rulers for my name's sake. 13. And it shall turn to you for a testimony. 14. Settle it therefore in your hearts not to meditate before what ye shall answer: 15. For I will give you a mouth and wisdom, which all your adversaries shall not be able to gainsay nor resist. 16. And ye shall be betrayed both by parents, and brethren, and kinsfolks and friends; and *some of you* shall they cause to be put to death. 17. And ye shall be hated of all men for my name's sake. 18. *But there shall not an hair of your head perish.* 19. In your patience possess ye your souls.

15. When ye therefore shall see the abomination of desolation, spoken of by Daniel the prophet, stand in *the holy place*, (whoso readeth, let him understand,) 16. Then let them which be in Judea flee into the mountains: 17. Let him which is on the house-top not come down to take anything out of his house: 18. Neither let him which is in the field return back to take his clothes. 19. And woe unto them

14. But when ye shall see the abomination of desolation, spoken of by Daniel the prophet, standing *where it ought not*, (let him that readeth understand,) then let them that be in Judea flee to the mountains: 15. And let him that is on the house-top not go down into the house, neither enter therein, to take anything out of his house: 16. And let him that is in the field not turn back again for to take up

20. And when ye shall see Jerusalem compassed with armies, then know that the desolation thereof is nigh. 21. Then let them which are in Judea flee to the mountains; and let them which are in the midst of it depart out; and let not them that are in the countries enter thereinto. 22. *For these be the days of vengeance, that all things which are written may be fulfilled.* 23. But woe unto them

that are with child,
and to them that give
suck, in those days!
20. But pray ye that
your flight be not in
the winter, *neither on
the Sabbath-day:* 21.
For then shall be great
tribulation, such as
was not since the be-
ginning of the world to
this time, no, nor ever
shall be. 22. And
except those days
should be shortened,
there should no flesh
be saved: but for the
elect's sake, those days
shall be shortened.
23. Then if any man
shall say unto you, Lo,
here is Christ, or there;
believe it not. 24.
For there shall arise
false Christs, and false
prophets, and shall
shew great signs and
wonders; insomuch
that, if it were pos-
sible, they shall deceive
the very elect.

25. Behold, I have
told you before. 26.
Wherefore if they shall
say unto you, Behold,
he is in the desert; go
not forth: behold, he
is in the secret cham-
bers; believe it not.
27. For as the light-
ning cometh out of the
east, and shineth even
unto the west; so shall
also the coming of the
Son of man be. 28.
For wheresoever the
carcase is, there will

his garment. 17.
But woe to them that
are with child, and to
them that give suck, in
those days! 18. And
pray ye that your flight
be not in the winter.
19. For in those days
shall be affliction, such
as was not from the
beginning *of the cre-
ation which God cre-
ated* unto this time,
neither shall be. 20.
And except that the
Lord had shortened
those days, no flesh
should be saved: but
*for the elect's sake,
whom he hath chosen,*
he hath shortened the
days. 21. And then
if any man shall say
to you, Lo, here is
Christ; or, lo, he is
there; believe him not:
22. For false Christs
and false prophets shall
rise, and shall shew
signs and wonders, to
seduce, if it were pos-
sible, even the elect.

23. But take ye
heed: behold, I have
foretold you all things.

that are with child, and
to them that give suck,
in those days! for there
shall be great distress
in the land, and wrath
upon this people. 24.
*And they shall fall by
the edge of the sword,
and shall be led away
captive into all nations:
and Jerusalem shall be
trodden down of the
Gentiles,* UNTIL *the times
of the Gentiles be ful-
filled.*

the eagles be gathered together.

29. *Immediately* after the tribulation of those days, shall the sun be darkened, and the moon shall not give her light, and the stars shall fall from heaven, and the powers of the heavens shall be shaken: 30. And then shall appear the sign of the Son of man in heaven, and then shall all the tribes of the earth mourn, and they shall see the Son of man coming in the clouds of heaven with power and great glory.

24. But in those days, after that tribulation, the sun shall be darkened, and the moon shall not give her light, 25. And the stars of heaven shall fall, and the powers that are in heaven shall be shaken. 26. And then shall they see the Son of man coming in the clouds, with great power and glory.

25. And there shall be signs in the sun, and in the moon, and in the stars; *and upon the earth distress of nations, with perplexity; the sea and the waves roaring;* 26. *Men's hearts failing them for fear, and for looking after those things which are coming on the earth:* for the powers of heaven shall be shaken. 27. And then shall they see the Son of man coming in a cloud with power and great glory.

Here, again, one perceives easily that the points of difference and agreement are the same throughout as those which our previous comparison of the synoptical Gospels presented. We confine ourselves to the most important. All three have this in common, that they divide the Lord's prophecy into *three* distinct parts, namely, the prediction concerning the temple in particular, and the signs that were to harbinger the desolation; among which signs were the grievous oppression to be suffered by believers (Matth., v. 1–14; Mark, v. 1–13; Luke, v. 5–19);—the prediction of the siege and destruction of Jerusalem (Matth., v. 15–48; Mark, v. 14–23; Luke, v. 20–24);—and that of the last signs, and of the coming of the Son of man (Matth., v. 29, 30; Mark, v. 24–26; and Luke, v. 52–27.)

These three predictions, *in all three synoptical Gospels* most closely connected with each other, are, nevertheless, in St Luke, in conformity with his historical character, kept more distinctly apart from each other; in St Matthew, on the contrary, they run more, like objects drawn in distant perspective, into each other. St Mark, with the exception of the amplifications and inversions that are peculiar to him, generally follows his predecessor.—St Matthew, and he alone, comprises at once (v. 3), in the same question put by the disciples, the destruction of the temple and the end of the world. Anon (v. 9) he mentions the hatred of *all nations* to the Gospel on account of the name of Jesus, which we may regard as mainly referring to a later period; whereas St Mark (v. 13) and St Luke (v. 17) record only these words: *Ye shall be hated of all men* (that is to say, contemporaries), *for my name's sake.*

But St Matthew and St Mark distinguish themselves from St Luke more particularly in the second part of the prophecy. The two former do not even give the name of the city, but indicate it merely by the quotation from Daniel (ix. 2); whereas St Luke makes express and circumstantial mention of Jerusalem, that it would be invested with armies; and further, that the inhabitants of Judea would be put to death, and dispersed as captives and exiles; in fine, that Jerusalem would be trodden under foot, not for ever, but *until the times of the Gentiles be fulfilled.* St Matthew and St Mark here revert, in some details (one alone of which re-occurs in a different connexion in the historical narrative of St Luke, xvii. 23, 24), to the *false Christs* and *the false prophets that would appear* —a sign which, looking to the New Testament prophecies as a whole, may be considered as common to the final period of the Jewish polity, and the final period also of the world's present economy.

The transition to the prediction of the last events in the world's history, occurs, then, in St Matthew, in direct connexion with the judgment on Jerusalem, at the word *immediately* (v. 29), modified already by St Mark, or at least explained by him in the wider expression : *in those days*—a term which, in the Old Testament, does not always imply an identity of time, but only a relation of connexion in the *development* of times. In St Luke, the transition from the earlier to the last events in the Lord's discourse, is very evident. We perceive that verse 24 closes with a finished period, and the details of the 25th verse may, without any violence to the context, be readily referred to a remoter period of time.

It is, however, from this intimate connexion between the destruction of Jerusalem and the world's final judgment that people have been led to entertain the notion, that —not only in the personal expectation of the apostles and first believers, but according to the very predictions of Jesus, and the language of the writers of the New Testament—the end of all things and the coming of the Lord should have immediately followed the fall of the Jewish polity. To what this notion necessarily leads is very plain. But the error springs from ignorance of the manner in which the prophets viewed distant events, and of that peculiar mode of expression which was usual with them. Prophecy, alike in the Old and in the New Testament, does not always make known the difference of epochs and the space that keeps events at a distance. It rather heaps, as if upon one level or panel (unless where an express distinction of epochs and of years is essential to the matter in hand) events that are connected together by the same internal and remoter bond of relationship. Thus, for instance, Isaiah places before our view *simultaneously* the epochs of the sufferings and of the reign of the Messiah, without intimating to us the distance in point of time that was to lie between them in their fulfilment. Thus, in other passages, prophecy has identified the first and second destruction of the Holy City, and the different dispersions, as well as the different restorations, of Judah and of Israel. But in their accomplishment, the two events thus confounded in the prophecy stand apart, and attach themselves each to its own proper period. According to the same analogy, that blessed Head of all the prophets of the Old and New Testament has identified his prediction of Jerusalem's coming woes with the prophecy of the last days and of the final judgment, just as in a perspective before the eye of a traveller, a great many streams and fields disappear, as it were, between the heights of mountains at the two extremities. In the accomplishment, of course, the two different events distinguish themselves from each other, and take their respective places in history.

Let the same principle be applied to all the passages of the New Testament where the coming of the Lord is spoken of as nigh at hand, even when the apostles were living. Against all *narrow* conception of the strong expression, *at hand*, the apostle Paul himself has, in the Second Epistle to the Thessalonians (chap. ii.), given the requisite elucidation. Yes;—the return of Christ and the end of the present world are, and become more and more, *at hand* to us; but in that promise, nevertheless, there is manifestly comprehended the accomplishment of every thing that must previously take place as necessary for the ripening of all things for that all-decisive moment. And here the words of the Psalmist and

Apostle are peculiarly applicable, that *a thousand years in the Lord's sight are but as yesterday*, and that *one day is with the Lord as a thousand years, and a thousand years as one day* (Ps. xc. 4; 2 Pet. iii. 8.)

P. 168—"*In both alike we find the circumstance which bears so much on the history of the institution, that the cup was blessed and drunk* after supper."

By the *historical bearing* here adverted to, we mean chiefly the Israelitic origin of the New Testament supper. The breaking of bread, as it was done by the Master on the last night, as a sublime symbol of his approaching expiatory death, was then, and is to this day, in Israel, a common domestic solemnity, at the thanksgiving prayer *before the supper*. And in like manner, with the Israelites, at the Paschal table, four different cups are blessed, down to this day. Now, the passages adduced from St Paul and St Luke teach us that the *cup which was blessed* by the Lord, as a covenant token of the New Testament in his blood, was that which is drunk at the close of the repast (shortly before the hymn of praise). Thus did both the beginning and the end of the Israelitic Paschal supper become, by the word of the Lord, the expression of the beginning and the end of the whole of our Christian faith—the *Saviour's body broken*, and *his blood shed for our sins*.

P. 172—" *The narrative in St Luke as the searcher of men's hearts.*"

It is as such, that we find the apostles call upon Him at the time of the election of a twelfth in the place of Judas, in the book of the Acts, i. 24, *Thou, Lord,* WHICH KNOWEST THE HEARTS OF ALL MEN (*καρδιογνῶστα πάντων*), *shew whether of these two thou hast chosen.* From the whole connexion (especially from the second verse of this chapter), it is evident that the prayer then offered was addressed to Him who, in the Revelation of St John, witnesses of himself (ii. 23): *I am he which searcheth the reins and hearts.* How is it possible that such a title and such an attribute can ever have been conceived to belong to Christ as *less than,* as *differing from,* the eternal God —yea, Israel's Jehovah ? (Compare Jer. xi. 20; xvii. 10; Ps. vii. 9.)

P. 172—" *The narrative in St Luke might, so to speak, have for its title that saying of St Paul, that in Jesus Christ nothing is of any avail, but faith which worketh by love.*"—(Gal. v. 6.)

In this very saying of St Paul's, we find explained to us the twofold declaration of the Saviour (Luke vii. 47–50), namely, to the Pharisees: *Her sins, which are many, are forgiven; for she* LOVED MUCH ;—and to the woman herself: *Thy* FAITH *hath saved thee ; go in peace!* Between God and the sinner there is nothing but *faith* that saves. In the manifestation of the truth of that faith before men, *love* is the channel by which faith yields its fruits.

P. 175—"*A remarkable effect of this resemblance is found in the conjecture of Grotius, who attributes to St Luke the Epistle of Paul to the Hebrews.*"

See Grotius in the Introduction of his Commentary on that Epistle, where he recommends a comparison of Acts xxiii. 20, with Heb. v. 7; Luke xiii. 11, with Heb. vii. 3, 23; Acts vi. 3, and xvi. 2, with Heb. vii. 8, xi. 2, 5, 39; Luke ii. 26, and Acts x. 22, with Heb. viii. 5; Luke xxii. 26, with Heb. xiii. 7, 17; Acts iii. 15, v. 31, with Heb. ii. 10, and xii. 2.

P. 223—"*The expulsion of the son from the vineyard is given in details by all the three.*"

The *expulsion of the son* is an important element in the similitude, owing to its bringing out in strong relief one of the particulars in the passion, on which the Apostle lays much stress in the Epistle to the Hebrews; first, as respects the agreement with the type in the Old Testament (xiii. 11, 12): *For the bodies of those beasts whose blood is brought into the sanctuary by the high priest for sin, are burnt* WITHOUT THE CAMP; *wherefore Jesus also, that he might sanctify the people with his own blood, suffered* WITHOUT THE GATE; and afterwards, in his application of the parallelism to the Christian life of believers (v. 13, 14): *Let us go forth therefore unto him* WITHOUT THE CAMP, *bearing his reproach. For we have here no continuing city, but we seek one to come.*

P. 282—"*Yet the silence—destroyed.*"

That the Gospel of St John was written after the destruction of Jerusalem has been considered by us as highly probable. This apparent probability becomes a sufficient certainty, when we compare the passages where mention is made of Jerusalem as a city no longer in existence. *Near the city there* WAS *a garden* (xviii. 1; xix. 41): *Bethany* WAS *nigh unto Jerusalem* (xi. 18.) And there is no contradiction to this in its being stated (v. 2), *that there* IS *a pool at Jerusalem* (at the present time, ἐστι), for the pool remained after the city was destroyed. But in the whole prevailing tone likewise of this Gospel, when Jerusalem is spoken of, there is something (as Hug expresses it) *wie man von vergangenen Dingen spricht.*[1] That St Peter was no longer living in this world when the beloved disciple wrote his Gospel, appears not only from the prediction of his martyrdom recorded in its closing chapter (xxi. 18), but also (xviii. 10) from the mention of Peter's name when Malchus was wounded.

The three first Gospels bear with them and in them, manifest proof that they were written at a much earlier period; not only from St John's assuming their contents as known, supplementing them, and tacitly referring to them, but also from their very composition. No less distinctly can we recognise in the synoptical Gospels the colouring of a time at which the temple at Jerusalem was *still existing*, than we perceive in the Gospel of St John that of an epoch when city and temple *were no more.*

St Luke's writings admit, perhaps, of our fixing a little more definitely the time at which they were composed

[1] That is, intimating that the author is speaking of things gone by.

and published. The Acts of the Apostles (that is to say, the second book of his Gospel), closing with the residence and captivity of St Paul at Rome for two years, intimates by that conclusion, which comes upon us somewhat unexpectedly, or abruptly, that the author had brought his narrative down to the period at which his book was written. In fact, there is much reason to conjecture that St Luke, in the midst of his voyages and occupations of various kinds in the Churches, had taken advantage, for the composition of his books, of two periods of repose in his own career and that of St Paul,—namely, for the Gospel, the epoch of St Paul's imprisonment at Cæsarea (Acts xxi.–xxiv.), and for the book of the Acts, that of the two years' imprisonment of the Apostle at Rome (xxviii. 30.) Tholuck in his *Glaubwürdigkeit der Evangelischen Geschichte*, S. 141, thus expresses himself: "Wie nahe lag es nun für diesen, den ruhigen Aufenthalt in der Hauptstadt und die grössere Musze zur Abfassung seiner Apostelgeschichte zu benutzen, und wie sehr gewinnt noch diese Annahme an Wahrscheinlichkeit, wenn wir der gegebenen Ansicht beitreten, welche das Evangelium während der anderthalb Jahre abgefaszt seyn läszt, wo Lukas ebenfalls in der Nähe des zu Jerusalem gefangen genommenen Paulus, entweder in der Hauptstadt von Palästina oder in dem ganz nahen Cäsarea blieb. Dasz in diese Zeit die Abfassung des Evangelium's falle, hat gewisz viel für sich, denn wo hatte Lukas eher an die Ausführung dieses Unternehmens denken können, als in Palästina, wo schriftliche Berichte und Augenzeugen der Begebenheiten Jesu in so groszer Menge zur Hand waren? Hat er aber in dieser Gefangenschaft das Evangelium für seinen Theophilus abgefaszt, so gewinnt er nur desto gröszere Wahrscheinlichkeit, dasz die andere ebenso lange Gefangenschaft ihn zur Abfassung eines ähnlichen Werkes aufforderte, so dasz beide Annahmen sich wechselseitig unterstützen."[1]

The Gospels of St Matthew and St Mark bear less clearly in themselves any such recognisable mark of the precise epoch at which they were written. But according to the notices given by Clement of Alexandria, Eusebius, and Jerome, St Mark wrote his Gospel not only *from the information supplied by St Peter*, but during *that Apostle's life-time*, and certainly, as we have remarked on various occasions, the influence of the latter on the Gospel of *his son in the faith*, is not simply that of an already deceased predecessor, but of a living and present informant. The only one of the Fathers of the Church who seems to place the *publication* or *delivery to the Churches* of that Gospel *after* the death of St Peter, is Irenæus, where he writes thus: *Μετὰ δὲ τὴν τούτων (Πέτρου καὶ Παύλου) ἔξοδον, Μάρκος, ὁ μαθητὴς καὶ ἑρμηνευτὴς Πέτρου, τὰ ὑπὸ Πέτρου κηρυσσόμενα ἐγγράφως ἡμῖν παρέδωκε:* in which passage, however, by ἔξοδος it is not necessary to suppose that departure out of this life is meant, for *departure from the city or the country* may be all that is implied. The reader

[1] "How convenient was it for him to take advantage of his quiet stay in the capital, and the greater leisure he enjoyed, for the composition of his Apostolic history; and how much more likely does this supposition become, if we entertain the idea which some have suggested, that the Gospel was compiled during the year and a half when Luke remained in like manner in the neighbourhood of Paul when imprisoned at Jerusalem, either at the capital of Palestine, or at Cæsarea, which lay quite at hand. The idea that the Gospel was composed at that time has much to be said for it; for where could Luke have sooner thought of the execution of his design than in Palestine, where he must have had ready access to such a number both of written memorials and eyewitnesses? But if he really composed the Gospel for his friend Theophilus during that imprisonment, the probability is all the greater, that the other equally long imprisonment should have stimulated him to the composition of a similar work, so that the two suppositions mutually support each other."

may compare Grotius in his Introduction on St Mark. However this may be, the notice we have in Irenæus has nothing in it so very certain and explicit, as of itself to outweigh those supplied by other Fathers of the Church: all the less, too, as the most ancient testimony, that of Papias, from the mouth of John the Presbyter, contains nothing decisive on this accessary question.

The epoch at which St Matthew wrote his Gospel is fixed by some at *fifteen*, by others at *eight* years after the resurrection and ascension of the Lord; Irenæus places it later: but none of these external testimonies gainsays the conclusion we come to from the internal structure of the first two Gospels—that the Gospel of St Matthew was both known *to* St Mark and assumed *by* him as the basis of his own.

In treating of the epoch at which the Gospels were successively published, the question with respect to the *place* of publication has commonly been taken up, and is naturally associated with that of the *time*. It being generally admitted that St Matthew wrote his Gospel in Palestine, and specially at Jerusalem, we have strong grounds for regarding it as probable, that that Gospel which is *peculiarly* Israelitish should have first seen the light in the Jewish capital. With respect to that of St Mark, the balance lies between Rome and Alexandria, although the weight of evidence is evidently on the side of the former of those great cities. There also, as we have observed, St Luke's historical work was finished. As for the Gospel of St John, the no less widely renowned and wealthy city of Ephesus has been considered with sufficient unanimity as the place of its first publication. Hug's idea (in his *Einleitung*, 2ten Th. S. 67–69), that St John composed his Gospel in the island of Patmos, and that from thence he sent it, with a letter of introduction (his first Epistle), to his cherished Church at Ephesus, harmonizes fully with the general impression that has again and again been enunciated with respect to the epoch of its composition. Be that as it may, the four Gospels of our Lord were published in the three great capitals which we have mentioned, of the Israelitish, Greek, and Roman world. Verily, in this sense also, we may apply the Apostle's saying: *These things have not been done in a corner.* (Acts of the Apostles, xxvi. 26.)

P. 300—"*As for what concerns the Apocalypse—fourth Gospel.*"

There is not in all the Scriptures any book with regard to which *historical testimonies* give a more unanimous confirmation of its genuineness, than the *Revelation* of St John. The very impugners of that genuineness (particularly Dr Lücke) are constrained to acknowledge this. Whence, then, does there arise any doubt as to a genuineness which becomes so visible and palpable, on our perceiving the manifold and striking harmonies between the Gospel and the Revelation, some of which we have cursorily noticed? Why, in our apprehension, because, notwithstanding all the unity existing between the two writings, a very manifest *difference*, too, cannot be denied. But this very difference is just of that kind that serves to put in stronger relief the *identity* of the author, in the *difference* of his theme and his point of view. In the *Gospel*, St John is the witness testifying of things that have already taken place; in the *Revelation*, he is the prophet foretelling things yet to come. In the *Gospel*, the kingdom of Christ, the judgment of God, even at times the resurrection of believers, are with him, in contrast with the synoptical Evangelists, something profoundly inward, spiritual, and individual; in the *Revelation*, he delineates and announces to us those same things in the external, visible, and still future glory of the Lord and his elect.

It was in the very nature of things, too, that in his *historical Gospel*, St John should merely *indicate* who he was, and that in his *prophetical Revelation* he should expressly name himself (i. 9), *I John.* Thus, too, did the writers of the Old Testament. Not the *historians*, but the *prophets* in Israel put their names at the head of their writings.

The differences of language and of style which have often been appealed to, as invalidating an identity of origin in the two writings, bear upon the subject in an analogous manner. For, not to say that the examinations that have been made, both by Winer and even by Lücke, have led to these differences, being found far less considerable than had been formerly thought, they may fully be accounted for, by the fact of the latter of the two compositions adhering *to the language of Israel's prophets.* Hug, with his ever acute perception, long ago perceived something of this kind, and says in his *Einleitung* (Th. 2, S. 189): "Was aber weiter die Sprache des Buches betrifft, so ist sie weniger die Sprache des Johannes selbst als die der Propheten. Da, wo er aber selbst redet, muszte er sich nothwendig bemühen, ihrer Schreibart und Diction so sehr es möglich war, nahe zukommen, um die Gleichförmichkeit des Tönes zu erhalten. Diejenigen können also recht haben, welche behaupten, die Apocalypse habe den styl des Johannes nicht; nur müssen sie sich hüten, ihm darum das Buch abzusprechen, welches absichtlich aus fremden Bildern zusammengesetzt ist."[1]

Meanwhile, we have already seen, in our analysis of St John's *Gospel*, that same combination of Greek and Hebrew which in still ampler measure characterizes the *Revelation*. We have likewise seen, in our remarks on St John, how deeply even his *Gospel* is penetrated with the prophetic spirit which developes itself in all its fulness in the *Revelation*. Here let us but think again of the last part of the 21st chapter of the Gospel. On the other hand, we have uniformly found in St John the *Prophet*, the evident fundamental traits of the same St John the *Evangelist*.

Page 375—"*St Mark describes the locality more vividly*," &c.

St Matthew, on the other hand, is more precise here than St Mark; for he distinguishes (v. 58), more or less, two successive moments in St Peter's progress—first, his advancing *unto*—that is, *as far as*—the high priest's palace, *then* his going *into* the palace. These two steps in Peter's progress are afterwards explained with more detail by St John (xviii. 15, 16), where we read that Simon Peter followed Jesus with another disciple who went in with Jesus into the palace; whilst Peter still

[1] "As for what further relates to the diction of the book, it is certainly less the diction of John than that of the prophets. Even where he himself speaks, he he must have necessarily endeavoured to adopt their style and diction to the utmost, in order to preserve the uniformity of tone with theirs. Those, accordingly, may be in the right who maintain, that the Revelation has not the style of St John: only, they must guard against refusing to ascribe to him on that account a book which is designedly composed of foreign (Hebrew) images."

remained for some time outside, until that other disciple had spoken to the damsel that kept the door, and thus brought in Peter along with him.

REMARKS ON THE NARRATIVES OF OUR LORD'S BURIAL AND RESURRECTION.

In order to avoid unnecessarily adding to the bulk of this volume, we have confined ourselves in the 7th chapter *to the history of our Lord's passion*, without going into that of his burial and resurrection. In fact, the history of *the passion* was sufficient, in point of extent and minuteness, to attain *of itself* the end which we contemplated—that of closing the exposition of our theory of the distinctive characters and true harmony of the four Gospels, by selecting a portion of the Evangelical history ample enough for testing its applicability to the whole. One has now but to proceed according to the same method, in order to obtain the same results with respect to the entire contents of the writings of our *four inspired witnesses.* We willingly add, however, some *few* further observations, with the view of shewing how all that has been said in detail on the narratives of *the passion*, is susceptible of absolutely the same application to the several accounts that have been left us of *the burial* and *the resurrection* of Jesus.

Thus, for example, we see the special character of each of the four Evangelists manifested in the different manners in which they severally characterize *Joseph of Arimathea.* St Matthew, making an allusion to the prophecy of Isaiah (liii. 9), calls him *a rich man.* In St Mark he is designated by the use of a known Roman term, according to his dignified position, an *honourable* counsellor (Gr.

εὐσχήμων; Lat. *honestus*). St Luke, himself a good and a just man, calls him *good* and *just*, and specially remarks that *he had not consented to the counsel and deed of the Jews against Jesus.* Both St Mark and St Luke mention that he *waited for the kingdom of God,* while St Luke further adds an elucidation with respect to the place to which he belonged: *Arimathea, a city of the Jews.* Both St Matthew and St John call him a disciple of Jesus; but the latter of these Evangelists does not do so without adding that he had been so, till then, only *secretly, for fear of the Jews.*

In like manner, in the account of the Lord's burial, St Matthew gives an indication of his Israelitic point of view, among other things, by the mention, which we find only in him, of all that passed between the high priests and the Pharisees and Pilate with respect to the watch set over the sepulchre (Matth. 27–66). It is more than probable that these communings took place while it was yet but Friday *evening;* for otherwise a whole night must have passed without the sepulchre being watched, and the precautions of the Jews could have had no sufficient end. But St Matthew, ever in conformity with the Israelitic character of his Gospel, considers Friday evening as *the day itself following that of the preparation,*—that is, as the Sabbath itself.—St Mark, among other particulars pertaining to him, and sometimes indicated by a single word,[1] informs us of a very remarkable circumstance, with respect to the death of the Lord Jesus, by observing (xx. 44, 45) how Pilate marvelled if he were already dead, and how it was only after having had precise information on that point from the centurion, that he gave

[1] Compare the remark on Mark xv. 43 (*he went* BOLDLY in; Gr. τολμήσας), pp. 96, 97.

orders for the Lord's body being delivered to Joseph. It appears at the same time, from a comparison of this passage with that in St John (xix. 31), that Joseph of Arimathea's request to the governor that he might have the body of Jesus, was presented *between* the moment when the Jews besought that the bones of those that had been crucified might be broken, *and* the giving effect to that request.—St Luke distinguishes himself here particularly by the mention of the *rest observed by the women on the Sabbath day according to the commandment* (xxiii. 56) AFTER *having bought and prepared the spices and ointments;* so that it is with good reason that, in the translations, the aorist employed by St Mark (xvi. 1) has the *pluperfect* meaning given to it—(HAD BOUGHT). St John again here characterizes his narrative by the introduction, among others, of a new personage: to wit, Nicodemus, in company with his colleague, Joseph of Arimathea, and by the express mention of the *quantity of pounds of myrrh and aloes* brought by that excellent senator for the Lord's burial (xix. 39, 40).[1]

As respects the evangelical accounts of the Lord's *resurrection,* the application of our system of harmony leads to the perfect solution of a difficulty which has in all ages been strongly urged by the adversaries of the historical truth of the Gospels, and which, in so far as we can see, has not found an absolutely satisfactory reply on the part of the defenders of that truth. We allude to the apparent contradiction between what we are told by St Matthew (xxviii. 9) of the *women* on their return from the sepulchre being the first who met with the Lord after his resurrection, and St Mark's very positively affirming (xvi. 9) that the Lord appeared first to *Mary Magdalene.*

[1] Compare pp. 257, 259, and 273.

According to the theory which we have developed, nothing is more simple than the agreement between the two narratives. St Matthew, according to his usual custom, uses the *plural*, which St Mark, equally according to what was his usual practice, brings back to its true signification by NAMING *that one in particular among the women* to whose lot it fell first to behold the risen Lord. *The women* in St Matthew[1] expresses, in a general way, what St Mark and after him St John (xx. 11–18) apply with *the clearest and most minute preciseness* to Mary Magdalene, who had formed part of the company of the women that came into the sepulchre the very morning of the resurrection, but who, in consequence of the particular circumstances recorded by St John (xx. 1–10), had separated from the rest, in order to run to the disciples with the news of the sepulchre being found empty, and had afterwards returned with them and remained after them.

In the further application of the principles of harmony established in this work, to the series and the order of the different circumstances of which the account of the Lord's resurrection is composed, one will arrive without difficulty at the following result: 1. Two angels descend from heaven, before the earliest gleam of dawn, to remove the stone from the sepulchre from which He who had triumphed over sin and death was to come forth. 2. The keepers, terrified at this apparition, flee, and communicate what has happened to the chief priests, who bribe them with money to circulate a false report (according to St Matthew). 3. [The precise moment of the resurrection

[1] The words: "as they went to tell his disciples," ought to be considered here as only one of those forms of transition frequently occurring in St Matthew's Gospel.

is told us by none of the Evangelists. The fact (in virtue of a respectful sobriety which may be considered as the exclusive attribute of our sacred writings) is mentioned only in recording what took place subsequently to it, or in stating the consequences which necessarily resulted from it]. 4. A party of women, among whom was Mary Magdalene, had gone before daybreak to the sepulchre (according to all four Evangelists). 5. They find the stone taken away and the sepulchre open (according to St Mark, St Luke, and St John). 6. Mary Magdalene separates from the rest, and runs to Peter and John (according to St John). 7. The rest of the women go into the sepulchre, where the angels announce to them the Lord's resurrection. They return with this news to the disciples (according to the synoptical Gospels). 8. Mary Magdalene, during this interval, returns to the sepulchre, accompanied by Peter and John (according to St John). 9. The two disciples enter the sepulchre, and find the linen clothes laid by themselves (according to St Luke and St John). 10. Mary Magdalene remains near the sepulchre weeping, and, stooping down towards the inside, sees the angels, who address her (according to St John). 11. Jesus himself reveals himself to her, and she recognises him (according to St Mark and St John). 12. She announces to the disciples that she has seen the Lord (according to St Mark and St John); but, 13. Without finding credence from them in their sorrow. 14. Jesus shews himself that same day to two disciples on their way to Emmaus (according to St Luke, and St Mark xvi. 15). The two disciples, on their return in the evening, communicate to the eleven the interview which they had been privileged to enjoy. 16. They learn that the Lord had already appeared to Simon Peter (according to St

Luke). 17. The Lord's appearing to the eleven apostles in the absence of Thomas (according to the Synoptics compared with St John). 18. His appearing to the apostles, Thomas being present (according to St John). 19. His appearing to the Apostles and the disciples in Galilee (according to St John at the 21st chapter, where it would seem that the same appearance of the Lord is meant as that which St Matthew has in view at chap. xxviii., ver. 16 and 17; and St Paul, 1 Cor. xv. 6). 20. Last interview of the Lord with the apostles and disciples at Jerusalem and Bethany (according to the synoptical Gospels, Matth. xxviii. 20; Mark xv. 16–18; Luke xxiv. 46–49). 21. The ascension of Jesus to heaven forty days after his resurrection (Mark xvi. 19; Luke xxiv. 50, 51; Acts i. 1–9).

We think, that at the conclusion of a work on the harmony of the four Gospels, it may not be out of place to treat in a few lines of the important questions that have arisen with regard to the two different genealogies of our Lord, as given by St Matthew (i. 1-16), and by St Luke (iii. 23–38). To that end we offer here the following

REMARKS ON THE TWO GENEALOGIES OF THE SAVIOUR IN ST MATTHEW AND ST LUKE.

THE difference between the two genealogies in St Matthew and St Luke has been warmly assailed from the earliest ages by the enemies of the gospel. In our own days, especially since the appearance of Schleiermacher's *Essay on the Gospel of St Luke,* it belongs, according to the judgment of some learned men, to the *irreconcilable* variations between the two Gospels. But *untenable* and *irreconcilable* are, within the domain of the theological science of our days, terms about which it is not absolutely necessary that we should allow ourselves to be disquieted. With several of the truths that have been declared untenable by our modern critics, it is almost as with those generals of the enemy who, after being slain in the bulletins of Napoleon, were found all alive and well on his own territory.

From the first, the totally different genealogies in St Matthew (i. 1–16), and in St Luke (iii. 3-38), have been explained in two ways. According to some, we have in St Matthew the genealogy of Joseph only, while the genealogy in St Luke must be that of Mary. According to others, we have in St Luke, as well as in St Matthew, the ancestors of Joseph; but these, in the Gospel of St Luke, are given in the *natural* line, that is to say, so as that, by natural generation, Joseph actually traced his origin from David by Nathan; in St Matthew's Gospel, on the contrary, so as that, by the lineage of Solomon, he was descended from that same family-chief David, by a merely *legal* descent, or in other words, through the intervention of marriages *according to the law of the Levirate.* For ourselves, we hesitate not to declare in favour of the last of these views. But before proceeding to the proof, we would first demonstrate the incompleteness of the other attempt to solve the difficulty, by supposing that in St Luke we have the genealogy of Mary.

It is utterly impossible that the genealogy of the Gospel of St Luke can have any connexion with Mary. The terms used by that Evangelist (iii. 23), are clear, and admit of no other signification but this very simple and plain one: Jesus was (*as was supposed,* or rather, *as he was considered in the eye of the law,* Gr. ἐνομίζετο), the son of Joseph, the son of Heli (τοῦ Ἡλὶ).

To understand by this expression a relationship of *father-in-law* and *son-in-law* between Heli and Joseph, is irreconcilable with all usages alike Greek and Hebrew; but it would involve the further consequence, that the same relationship should subsist between all the other persons named in the genealogy, which would be absurd. As little can we admit another forced construction which has been attempted, in order to make out that Mary was *the daughter of Heli,* and which is this: Jesus *was supposed* to be the son of Joseph; but *he really* was a son, that is to say, a *grandson* of Heli, which Heli is then to be held the father of Mary. The whole genealogy in St Luke presents a succession from *father* to *son:* the idea neither of *son-in-law,* nor of *grandson,* can be expressed by the article τοῦ in the first step of the series, any more than in those that are beyond it. It is observed solely and exclusively with respect to the relationship between Jesus and Joseph, that it was not a *natural* relationship, but ὡς ἐνομίζετο.

But we have yet more to say. Nowhere in either of the two Gospels do we find it said, that the virgin Mary was *herself* descended from David.

In St Matthew, Joseph is most particularly put on the foreground by the side of Mary. This would make it less strange should no mention be made of the descent of Mary from David in this first Evangelist. But St Luke also, who, with respect to Mary, introduces so many details in the account he has given us of the Lord's conception, birth, and infancy—St Luke, too, nowhere attributes to Mary a descent from David. Quite the contrary! he evidently excludes her from that descent, in contra-distinction from her husband Joseph. One has only to read chap. i. 26, 27: *And in the sixth month the angel Gabriel was sent from God unto a city of Galilee, named Nazareth, to a virgin espoused to a man whose name was Joseph, of the house of David; and the virgin's name was Mary.* And, chap. ii. 4, 5: *And Joseph also went up from Galilee, out of the city of Nazareth, into Judea, unto the city of David, which is called Bethlehem; because* HE *was of the house and lineage of David* (Gr. διὰ τὸ εἶναι 'ΑΥΤΟΝ), *to be taxed with Mary, his espoused wife, she being great with child.* If ever the rule that *the inclusion of the one is the necessary exclusion of the other,* is admissible, it is certainly in such a connexion.

But what puts an end to all uncertainty in this question is, that in this same Gospel the true descent of the mother is clearly indicated to us. In the message of the angel, Mary is called in express terms *the cousin of Elisabeth* (i. 36). Now, this name of *cousin* (Gr. συγγενὴς) can have no other signification in the original but that of *descendant of the same family in the male line*, that is to say, in descent from the same male ancestor.[1] Here, then, in a more limited sense, but one quite the same in kind, Mary and Elisabeth are called *cousins*, because they were of the same tribe.

If, then, the tribe of Elisabeth be known to us, we know also that of Mary. But St Luke has told us in so many words what the descent of Elisabeth was (i. 5): *The wife of Zacharias (was) of the daughters of Aaron; and her name was Elisabeth.*

Christ, accordingly, was not of the race of David by his mother? No! and this, moreover, was not necessary in order to the fulfilment of the prophecy that the Messiah should be born of the house of David; for this very simple reason, that in Israel descent by the mother's side was not taken into consideration in making out the tribe to which a man belonged. The rule laid down by the Rabbins on this point, is the simple result of all that the Bible teaches and assumes with regard to it.[2]

What then? Shall we have no alternative but Strauss's dilemma? "If Jesus be of the tribe of David, then he can be so only through Joseph; but in that case, the fact

[1] AMMONIUS in Ἀγχιστεὺς. "Ευγγενεῖς οἱ ὄντες ἐκ τοῦ αὐτοῦ γένους, ΓΕΝΟΥΣ. It is in the same sense of extraction from the same masculine ancestors that St Paul calls all the Israelites his συγγενεῖς (Rom. ix. 3; comp. xvi. 7, 11, 21, and the note of Bengel on ver. 5, 7. *Erant Judæi.*")

[2] Bava Bathra, f. 110, 2, משפחת אב קרוית משפחה משפחת אם אינה קרוית משפחה: *The descent on the father's side only shall be called a man's descent; the descent by the mother is not called any descent.*

of his being conceived by the Holy Ghost must fall to the ground. If, on the contrary, he was conceived of the Holy Ghost, and not by Joseph, then his descent from David falls to the ground, seeing that that descent appears in the Gospels to have belonged to Joseph, but not to Mary."

For ever be such a conclusion far from us! Nay, both truths stand equally unshaken—that of the Saviour's descent from David, and that of his conception by the Holy Ghost. The solution of the apparent difficulty lies in our having a correct and a complete idea of what constituted *descent, according to the flesh,* in conformity with views truly Israelitic, and with the institutions and the will of God.

In the patriarchal world, and, after that, in the Israelite world, the woman who was given in marriage—(let the comparison be understood in a manner becoming the sacredness of the subject)—was viewed as a living possession, bearing fruit to the husband. Hence the expression we meet with every where: *She bore* HIM *sons and daughters.* The children belonged to the father—belonged to him just as the fruit of his field did; but they did not belong to him simply as an individual, but, through him, to his whole tribe and race. The fruit of a married woman's womb was a blessing in the house of her husband: it was a blessing by the propagation of his name and posterity in Israel. Hence, when a husband died without having left children, the obligation imposed by the law of Moses on the brother of the deceased to raise up a posterity by the widow, not for himself, but for his deceased brother; that is to say, to propagate that brother's posterity, and to possess *his* heritage. That same law was, by a legal extension, applied to relatives more remote, but always of the same tribe and family, as clearly appears by the history of Ruth and Boaz. Compare Michaelis, *Mosaïsch Recht*, ii. § 98.

Now, this first-born Son, whom Mary brought forth at a time when she was engaged by the marriage-bond to Joseph, belonged (so far as related to the Saviour's human origin and the law of Israel) to Joseph, and, through him to the race of David and the tribe of Judah.

But then, what are we to think with respect to his conception by the Holy Ghost? Why, that it alters not in one jot or tittle the *legal* relationship of the Son, borne by Mary to her husband Joseph. Mary was, and remained throughout, the field blessed by God, which bore its fruit to the house of David, to a son of David (in Matth. chap. i. 20, Joseph is so named by the angel with an evident emphasis). Being conceived, however, not according to the ordinary laws of nature, but by the power of the Holy Ghost, without human intervention; the fruit of Mary's womb was on that account not an ordinary man, or simply a *man*, but a *man-God*. Our Lord Jesus Christ accordingly had his incarnation by the Holy Ghost, his humanity by Mary his mother, his right and his name as a Son of David by Joseph, in conformity with the Israelitic laws and institutions. It is then in consequence of this *real* (that is to say, *legal*) relationship, and not merely from a *mistaken notion* among men, that Jesus is called again and again in Scripture *the Son of Joseph* (Luke ii. 41, and especially 48; John i. 46).

We find the same point very clearly decided, as it appears to us, by Wetstein, in the following manner (on Matth. i. 16): "When, however, from the statements immediately subjoined by St Matthew, it is evident that Jesus was not the son of Joseph according to the ordinary course of nature, it follows that we must understand him to have been so by *adoption*." And again: "When Joseph had received Mary his wife, and Jesus as a son and heir, given to him by God, it is manifest that Jesus entered into his family by *insertion*. Unless this be admitted, to what family can he be referred, seeing that females (among the Jews) were never entered on the genealogical rolls; and, assuredly, if a male child born to Joseph and Mary after consummated wedlock would most assuredly have been regarded as belonging to the pedigree of Joseph, so far must a miraculous intervention have been from deteriorating the condition of a child not so born, and of nullifying his claim to the family title, that the rather on this very account must he have been regarded with the strictest propriety as having preserved every natural right and claim full and unimpaired."[1]

Such, precisely, is what may be called a holy Levirate, acted upon by the Holy Ghost with respect to Joseph. It is clear, when we speak thus, that we mean only by an *analogy* (agreement in *principle*). That analogy is now manifest. The principle lies in the relation of each Israelite, and his offspring, to his tribe and his family. A husband in Israel leaves a wife without children. His brother, or his near relation, of the same tribe (*agnate*), is obliged to raise up children for the

[1] "Cum autem ex iis quæ mox a Matthæo subjiciuntur, constet Jesum non fuisse filium Josephi naturalem, consequens est ut intelligamus filium adoptivum. * * * Cum Josephus Mariam uxorem et Jesum filium et heredem A DEO DATUM accepisset, manifestum est Jesum in ipsius familiam INSERTUM fuisse. Quod nisi admittatur, ad quam familiam referetur, cum MATERNUM GENUS (apud Judæos) IN CENSUM NON VENIAT? Imo, cum puer, matrimonio inter Josephum et Mariam consummato natus, certissime ex genere Josephi fuisset, tantum aberat, ut per miraculum interveniens fieret deterioris conditionis et nullius familiæ, ut hoc ipso potius, omnia jura, quæ natura dedisset, salva atque integra servâsse merito sit existimandus."

heritage, and for the name of the deceased. Such was the human Levirate in Israel. But in the case before us, in a sense infinitely higher, and yet equally true, neither Joseph, nor any human being, is in a condition to raise up for the house of David Him who, in order to the accomplishment of the prophecy, could be called, and who WAS *Emmanuel*, that is to say, *God with* us. The Holy Ghost stretched his vivifying wings over the espoused wife of the descendant of David, his legitimate heir ; and the fruit thus conceived, when brought forth by Mary, belonged to the man to whom she had been given in marriage. That holy thing, divinely implanted in the field which belongs to Joseph, belongs no less (according to a genealogical relationship in Israel) to Joseph, and through him to David and Judah. It is true, then, and an actual fact, that *our Lord sprang out of Judah* (Heb. vii. 14), that He is *the Lion of the tribe of Judah, the Root and the Offspring of David* (Rev. v.), not by the flesh and blood which he held from his mother, but by Divine implantation, in the marriage of that virgin with the heir of David, according to the well-known rule of law : *He is the father, to whom marriage points.*[1]

And it is precisely on this account that in a gospel of the birth of Jesus Christ, we had no need to make out any genealogy but that of Joseph. We find, accordingly, such a genealogical list *both* in St Matthew *and* in St Luke. But wherefore, then, this double genealogy ? and wherefore does the one list differ from the other ? To this difficulty *also*, the ancient Israelitic Levirate supplies the key.

It is known from what different points of view, and in what different relationships, the different genealogical lists

[1] *Pater est quem nuptiæ demonstrant.*

were anciently written in Israel.[1] Nothing, at all events, is more natural than a double genealogy of the same person, if, in the history of the genealogy, a Leviratic marriage intervenes once, or more than once. And in that case, can we well imagine a less violent explanation of the two different genealogical registers of the same son of David, Joseph to wit, than that the Royal or Solomonic line should have been extinguished at different times by childless marriages, and re-established and kept up on each such occasion, by virtue of the law of the Levirate? And further, is it not perfectly in harmony with the whole plan of the two Gospels, that St Matthew (the Evangelist of the *royalty* of Jesus) should have given us the *legal* descent, or that by Solomon; St Luke, on the contrary (the *historical* Evangelist), that by Nathan, that is to say, the *natural* descent of Joseph?

But is not this genealogy in St Matthew so drawn up, that, *owing to the small number of generations* between David and Joseph, it remains, after all, historically irreconcilable with that in St Luke? Here, too, the peculiar character of Israelitic usage explains all. That people's genealogies have not always for their object to give a regular succession from generation to generation, from father to son, but only to furnish proofs of the descent of an individual, or of a family, from some family chief, or patriarch, from whom his descendants inherited an interest in some privilege or promise on the part of God. In the genealogy given by St Matthew, all bears on Christ's descent from *David*, from *Abraham* (Matth. i. 1). It need be no matter of surprise, then, that in an ulterior development several intermediate names should be found omitted.

[1] The reader may consult, among other authors on this subject, the Thesis of Surenhusius, *de modis explicandi genealogias*, in his Βίβλος· καταλλαγῆς.

The catalogue indicates clearly enough the points of main importance. And that once admitted, what difficulty can there be in supposing, that the genealogical list borrowed by St Matthew from the family of Joseph (whatever may have been the reason that some names have not been recorded in it), should be capable of being divided by St Matthew, reckoning from Abraham to Christ, into three sets of fourteen generations each?

We have then, as a final result, both in St Matthew and in St Luke, according to their own expressive terms, the genealogy of *Joseph;* but in St Matthew his *legal* descent from David by the Levirate in the royal or Solomonic line; in St Luke, the *natural* descent of Joseph from the same patriarch David in the Nathanic line; in St Matthew, so to speak, by way of extract, but at the same time with remarks intercalated by the Apostle (in naming the women, for example, who ordinarily are not noticed in the genealogy); in St Luke in a simple but continued line from JESUS, by Joseph, David, Abraham, and Adam, up to GOD (Luke iii. 23-38).

THE END.

BALLANTYNE, PRINTER, EDINBURGH.

www.ingramcontent.com/pod-product-compliance
Lightning Source LLC
LaVergne TN
LVHW020913110826
845150LV00004B/665

* 9 7 8 1 4 2 5 5 5 6 0 3 7 *